IN THE F
ENEMY

IN THE FACE OF THE
ENEMY

The complete history of the Victoria Cross
and New Zealand

Glyn Harper
Colin Richardson

HarperCollins*Publishers*

National Library of New Zealand Cataloguing-in-Publication Data

Harper, Glyn, 1958-
In the face of the enemy : the complete history of the Victoria
Cross and New Zealand / Glyn Harper and Colin Richardson.
Includes bibliographical references and index.
ISBN-13: 978-1-86950-650-6
ISBN-10: 1-86950-650-2
1. Victoria Cross—History. 2. Military decorations—New Zealand.
3. New Zealand—Armed Forces—Biography. 4. Great Britain—
Armed Forces—Biography. 5. New Zealand—History, Military—
20th century. 6. Great Britain—History, Military—20th century.
I. Richardson, Colin (Colin Patrick), 1959- II. Title.
355.13420993—dc 22

First published 2006
First published in this format 2007
HarperCollins*Publishers (NewZealand) Limited*
P.O. Box 1, Auckland

ISBN-13: 978 1 86950 650 6

ISBN-10: 1 86950 650 2

Cover design by Matt Stanton, HarperCollins Design Studio
Typesetting by Janine Brougham

Printed by Griffin Press, Australia, on 79 gsm Bulky Paperback

Cover image of the Victoria Cross © New Zealand Defence Force
Cover image DA1562, Vickers crew in action outside Derna, 1941
© Kippenberger Military Archive, Army Museum Waiouru

**To all New Zealand service personnel
who have ever been in the face of the enemy.**

Peace, not war, shall be our boast,
But, should foes assail our coast,
Make us then a mighty host,
God defend our free land.
Lord of battles in Thy might,
Put our enemies to flight,
Let our cause be just and right,
God defend New Zealand.

The seldom-sung third verse
of *God Defend New Zealand*.
Words by Thomas Bracken.

CONTENTS

Acknowledgements

Two of the hardest things in writing a book are finding the inspiration to do it in the first place and someone to publish the completed work. The authors must therefore start by acknowledging HarperCollins New Zealand for commissioning this book and providing us with an enjoyable project to work through, giving us the support we needed while simultaneously allowing us the freedom to shape it as we liked. In particular we would like to thank Lorain Day and Eva Chan at HarperCollins for their work in bringing this project to fruition.

A new study of New Zealand and the Victoria Cross has been long overdue. The New Zealanders whose deeds form the core subject matter of this work were real heroes, who placed their lives on the line on more than one occasion. We hope that we have done justice to their memories.

No project of this size can be undertaken in isolation and we have enjoyed the support of many old friends. The New Zealand Defence Force Historian John Crawford assisted us in access to the NZDF's files and Peni Reti always responded quickly at Base Records. Carolyn Carr and her staff at the NZDF Library were especially helpful in identifying new sources, getting in anything they could and purchasing them if necessary. Mary Slater virtually appointed herself a researcher and deserves special mention. Dolores Ho at the Kippenberger Military Archive and Research Library provided research and pictorial assistance, and the Wanganui District Library provided details on Henry D'Arcy. Dr Richard Taylor vetted the New Zealand Wars chapter and provided valuable additional points. Andrew Macdonald vetted earlier draft chapters and helped source some photographs, while the RNZAF Museum in Christchurch provided additional photographs. Many other colleagues, both at Massey University and HQ NZDF, have discussed the issues with us and helped shape our thinking.

Finally we would like to thank our respective families, who have helped sustain our enthusiasm as well as keeping us fed and watered throughout the research and drafting processes. Susan, Julie-Anne and Philippa have been good sounding boards and helpful critics of our respective writing styles, syntax, grammar and the content. Compiling the index was a combined group project.

To all of you we express our thanks and gratitude. Any errors of fact, of course, remain our own.

Colin Richardson
Glyn Harper

October 2005

FOREWORD

'Who would true valour see,
Let him come hither.'
— John Bunyan,
The Pilgrim's Progress

Courage binds the Commonwealth together throughout history and ensures we never forget the extraordinary military contribution Great Britain received from her friends and partners in this grand alliance of nations from across the world. Through two world wars and a myriad of lesser but nonetheless deadly conflicts, Britain has depended on her friends for support and has received it with ungrudging generosity. The commitment of New Zealand, despite the modest size of her population, has stood out amongst other nations and so, especially, has the courage of her servicepeople. I know for I have had the privilege of fighting alongside New Zealanders in many wars and conflicts from Korea to the Gulf War of 1991.

The inherent bravery, companionship, humour and loyalty of this redoubtable people have stood me in equal good stead, as it has my own country.

Of all the qualities I came to admire in my New Zealand comrades in arms, their daring and audacity stand out and always prevailed whenever the fighting was at its most intense. It surprises me not at all that New Zealand has won a greater number of Victoria Crosses, as a proportion of its population, than any other country in the world including Great Britain. Flying Officer Lloyd Trigg VC, DFC is the last ever member of the New Zealand armed forces who will win this unique award, which has now been replaced by the Victoria Cross of New Zealand. Appropriately at this moment in history as we celebrate the 150th anniversary of Queen Victoria's promulgation of the British Victoria Cross, this book records for history those gallant New Zealanders of past conflicts who were recipients of the world's most distinguished recognition of valour in the face of the enemy.

Sir Winston Churchill remarked, 'Courage is rightly esteemed the first of human qualities . . . because it is the quality which guarantees all other.' Each of us possesses a bank of courage. Some have a significant credit balance, others little or nothing; but in war we are all able to make the balance last longer if we have training, discipline, patriotism and faith. With these attributes we can manage our fear while always remembering that on the battlefield unfairness and luck are ever present arbiters. However, our credit balance depletes as we make demands of it and, as in the heat of battle, we take risks. When a person's balance drops into the red then he is on the borders of a breakdown and a wise commander will recognise this and see that he is rested before he becomes a casualty of fear and stress.

Courage is a quality we all admire and a goal to which we all aspire; it is an essential ingredient at all rank levels in war. Each person possesses it in some measure, but our personal bank varies between individuals and no man knows his credit limit until tested. War offers people opportunities to test themselves to their limits. The award of medals recognises a person's courage in battle, but gallantry is not restricted to those who are decorated, still less to holders of the Victoria Cross. Holders of this award are deeply conscious of this recognition, which leads, almost without exception, to them becoming the most modest of people; they are ordinary people who do not wish to stand out in society and they are the first to salute those many sailors, soldiers and airmen who never receive recognition but put their lives on the line or die and without whom no commander is able to fight his battle or win his war. Each one is a hero.

Charles Upham, a dedicated farmer from Christchurch, in peacetime put his animals and his land before himself. In the Second World War he became a fierce patriot whose loyalty determination and singleness of purpose personified New Zealanders in combat, and he is unique in the world of gallantry for being the only combatant in history to win two Victoria Crosses; yet he epitomises VC winners by his modesty. His favourite weapon was the grenade; he would carry them by the sackful and returned to the very forefront of the battle time and again and despite severe wounds and illness. He was the sort of man that any fighting soldier aspires to be but few indeed achieve his levels of bravery and leadership in battle.

In the Face of the Enemy is a tribute to the nation's courage; a nation it has been my proud privilege to serve alongside. One commentator remarked on the death of Charlie Upham, 'New Zealanders like to cut their heroes down a peg or two, but in Charles Upham we found a man with whom it was difficult to find fault.' I know Upham VC and Bar would be embarrassed by such selective judgement and I commend readers of these national heroes to reflect on the words of Randolph Churchill:

'Your glory is enshrined forever
on the imperishable plinth of your achievements.'

That's how I see them all.

Peter de la Billière
January 2006

INTRODUCTION: Some signal act of valour

The Victoria Cross (VC) is a very special award. It is the highest of all honours that the monarch of the British Commonwealth can bestow, and it takes precedence over all other honours, awards and decorations, including knighthoods. Edward, the Duke of Windsor, when Prince of Wales, recognised the paradoxical nature of the VC award. He proclaimed it to be 'the most democratic and at the same time the most exclusive of all orders of chivalry — the Most Enviable Order of the Victoria Cross'.[1] It is probably this democratic feature of the VC decoration more than anything else that has fired the public imagination in those countries where it has been awarded. For the first time the highest chivalric award was available to all ranks of the military of those countries included in the warrants. A private soldier or a field marshal could win the VC, so could a lowly sailor or an admiral of the fleet. As C.E. Lucas Phillips pointed out: 'There was only one standard, the human standard of valour in deadly peril.'[2]

The original Royal Warrant for the VC, signed by Queen Victoria on 29 January 1856, specified that the award was to be made 'to those officers and men who . . . in the presence of the enemy shall have performed some signal act of valour or devotion to their country'. By a consolidating warrant of 1920 the criteria for winning a VC was redefined to read 'for most conspicuous bravery or some daring or pre-eminent act of valour or self-sacrifice or extreme devotion to duty in the presence of the enemy'.

When this country instituted the Victoria Cross of New Zealand in 1999 the criteria remained similar to that of the British VC, but the wording changed. To win the VC of New Zealand a person recommended has to have demonstrated 'most conspicuous gallantry, or some daring or pre-eminent act of valour or self-sacrifice or extreme devotion to duty in the presence of the enemy or belligerents'.[3] There are two constants in these changes. First, the award is only given for a pre-eminent act of valour, for an act of outstanding bravery at great risk to one's life. Second, that act of valour needs to take place in the presence of the enemy. This was a stipulation in the original VC warrant and it remains in the warrant for the VC of New Zealand, although in the latter award the enemy could also be a belligerent. This subtle difference permits an award to be made on military operations where there has not been a formal declaration of war — what the USA military calls Operations Other Than War (OOTW). Peace-enforcement operations, for example, would be covered under this change of wording. While some awards prior to the 1920 warrant were made that did not involve being in the presence of the enemy, all of the VCs won by New Zealand service personnel and by those people with a New Zealand connection have fallen into that category. All were awarded for some signal act of gallantry in the very face of the British Empire's or Commonwealth's enemies, hence the significance of this book's title.

It is the exacting standards of the various VC warrants that have made the decoration so exclusive. While the VC is open to any member of the military forces, the awarding of a VC is an extremely rare occurrence. There are also other reasons for this exclusivity. First, while many young men heading off to war have dreamt of glory, including the winning of a VC, most of these dreams have been shattered upon contact with the enemy. When this happened the focus for most of these young men switched to that of simple survival. One such soldier who experienced this reality was the young New Zealand sergeant, E.G. Pilling, who had his dreams of glory shattered on the slopes of Gallipoli. He recorded in his diary on 21 July 1915:

> One's old ambitions and childish visions of winning a VC or some other distinction fade away . . . we put little value on decorations now, and will be satisfied if we do our work and get back home alive.[4]

Another reason for the exclusivity of the VC is the award process itself. It is a sad fact of life that all military honours and awards are an unfair lottery, and this particularly applies to the VC. When a person is recommended for a VC, several things need to happen in the right order for the recommendation to succeed. First, the VC-winning deed must be witnessed by others and then thoroughly investigated. For every act of valour witnessed by those who survived the action to talk about it, hundreds and probably thousands of brave deeds went unseen or unrecorded and were therefore unrecognised. In most of the previous warrants, at least one of the witnesses to the deed or the person conducting the investigation into the merit of the recommendation had to be a commissioned officer. The investigating officer then had to draft a detailed recommendation that should address the vital criteria of the award as specified in the current VC warrant, criteria which have been increasingly tightly interpreted. Several eyewitness statements should support the recommendation if it is to have any chance of success. The recommendation then needs to have the approval of several senior military officers from the unit's commanding officer through to the theatre level commander. All of these officers must sign their assent on the recommendation proforma. Any one of them has the power to downgrade the VC recommendation to a lesser award or to veto it entirely. If an officer chose to do this, no reason for his actions was required. This has been quite a common occurrence and explanations have very seldom been given, so historians can only guess why such a decision was made.

Once the high-level commanders have given their approval, the recommendation must then be endorsed by several military and civilian committees before it finally reaches the British sovereign for his or her approval. Only when the sovereign has given approval and an official citation has been published in the *London Gazette* can the VC finally be awarded. At any point along this long approval chain a deserving VC recommendation can be overturned, simply forgotten or even lost, as seems to have happened with at least one New Zealand recommendation. That this happened to several New Zealand service personnel is revealed in the pages that follow.

These cases, and others like them, reveal the unfortunate fact that the act of valour by itself is not enough to win the award.

New Zealanders have been intimately connected with the VC since shortly after its inception in 1856. Twenty-one members of the New Zealand armed forces have won the VC fighting in four wars over a period of 80 years. Six more VC winners were New Zealand born, but won the award whilst serving in either British or Australian military units. Several more VC winners had strong New Zealand family connections whilst 14 British servicemen won the VC for military service in this country during the New Zealand Wars.

Along the way New Zealand has set the record for a number of 'firsts' in relation to the history of the VC. New Zealand's original VC, won for an action in the New Zealand Wars in 1864, was the first VC awarded to a member of a colonial military unit, but it was only approved after considerable argument and pressure from New Zealand to do so. Its success established a precedent for other colonies to follow. The first man to win the VC in aerial warfare had strong New Zealand family connections, and the only combatant soldier to win the award twice was a New Zealand infantry officer. This bar to the VC was also the only one awarded during the Second World War. The only award of the VC made on evidence provided by an enemy was to a New Zealand pilot during the Second World War. It was made following the interrogation of the captain and crew of a sunken German U-boat, the very enemy who suffered as a result of the VC action. New Zealand also has the only VC awarded to an army signaller. These are significant events, not only to the history of the VC award, but to New Zealand's military heritage as well. They deserve to be more widely known than they currently are.

There have been several other publications on New Zealand Victoria Cross winners, although most have been simple compilations of their service records and VC citations together with some photographs. The most detailed and enduring of these publications is G. Bryant's *Where the Prize is Highest: the Stories of the New Zealanders who Won the Victoria Cross*, which was published in 1972.[5] Bryant's work has been helpful in pointing the way for this book, as has his research material, which he generously donated to the Alexander Turnbull Library in Wellington. However, because *Where the Prize is Highest* is now more than 30 years old and contains several errors and omissions, this publication also had its limitations. Clearly the time was right for a more up-to-date and complete history of New Zealand and the Victoria Cross.

This book has tried to be as inclusive as possible. The 21 New Zealand service personnel who so deservedly won the VC feature in detail. Where evidence exists of a declined VC recommendation, these cases have also been included. The reasons given for these recommendations being overturned, when they can be identified, may surprise and indeed anger some readers. VC winners who were born in New Zealand but did not serve with New Zealand forces have also been included, as have those winners with strong family connections to this country. The VCs won on military service in New Zealand in the nineteenth century are the subject of a separate chapter. A brief history of the VC award follows on from this introduction and details some important New Zealand connections. The brief chapter before the Conclusion looks at the New Zealand winners of the George Cross and Albert Medal — the non-combat equivalents of the VC that existed at the time.

We have attempted to place the act for which each VC was awarded within a broader context of the conflicts concerned. This has been done by first providing a brief history of each campaign before narrowing the focus to the specific act of valour. As 19 of New Zealand's 21 VC winners fought in either the First or Second World War it is inevitable that those two great conflicts of the last century dominate this book. Each of these world conflicts raised several important problems and issues in relation to the VC award. These problems and issues have been addressed in a separate chapter preceding those dealing with the actual VC campaigns.

Before the VC was instituted in 1856, the only award that existed for gallantry in action was the Distinguished Conduct Medal, which was not solely restricted to being awarded for acts of gallantry and was only available to men in the ranks. Since 1856, several other gallantry awards have been created, including the Distinguished Service Order, the Military Cross, the Distinguished Flying Cross, the Military Medal, and so on. The net effect of these new gallantry awards has been to significantly raise the standard required to win a VC. The VC criteria have become more exacting and more demanding, which accounts for the high percentage of posthumous awards amongst recent VC winners. Yet everyone who won the VC must have been acknowledged at the time as being the very bravest of the brave. They must have committed an act of conspicuous valour, at considerable personal risk, one that was seen by others and stood the test of detailed scrutiny. The rigorous approval process ensured this happened.

There is no doubt then that the person who was the subject of a successful VC recommendation deserved to win it. But many other deserving cases missed out because of a lack of witnesses, because there was inadequate written testimony, or because, as happened to New Zealand commissioned officers in the First World War, the sheer bloody-mindedness of some senior military officers blocked a deserving recommendation. Where the deserving recipient or the unlucky subject of an unsuccessful recommendation was a New Zealander or had some connections with this country, they are the subject matter of this publication.

This book aims to record in detail the history of New Zealand and the Victoria Cross. As will be revealed in the pages that follow, New Zealand has a long and distinguished association with this most prestigious of awards. What will also be revealed is that, at times, this association has been neither smooth nor harmonious. Nor can it be said that the approval processes have always been fair and reasonable.

CHAPTER 1 A history of the Victoria Cross

Prior to the Crimean War in 1856, acts of bravery in the British Army were recognised by promotion, a mention in the commander's despatches or, for senior officers, by appointment to the Order of the Bath.[1] For soldiers and junior officers this was very unfair, as a mention in despatches carried no visible symbol. Those few soldiers promoted to be officers for their gallantry were generally not accepted by their fellows in a system where commissioned rank was purchased and where social class prejudices pervaded. Furthermore, if a soldier or a junior officer did do something of note, it was more usual for their commanding officer to receive the Order of the Bath as recognition, because he effectively owned the regiment, having purchased the command. By comparison, other European nations had medals available to all ranks, such as the French Legion of Honour or the Prussian Iron Cross. These were awarded solely on the merit of the act, rather than the individual's rank or social status.

The Crimean War, which started in 1854, saw Britain and France allied with Turkey against Russia. The original dispute in 1853 had arisen over the Russian claim to the sole right to protect Orthodox Christians within the Ottoman Empire and jurisdiction over the holy places in Jerusalem. When the Ottomans rejected these claims, Russia occupied Turkish territories in Moldavia and Wallachia, precipitating a declaration of war. In November 1853 a Russian fleet attacked a Turkish flotilla in the Black Sea, which resulted in a combined French and English fleet moving to the area and directing the Russians to withdraw. When they failed to do so, France and Britain declared war. In September 1854 the allies landed an expeditionary force on the Crimean peninsula and advanced on the Russian port of Sevastopol. The campaign itself involved significant fighting at the battles of Alma, Balaklava (which included the charge of the Light Brigade) and Inkerman in conjunction with the prolonged siege of Sevastopol itself.

The whole campaign was characterised by command and logistic failings by the British and French leadership. The French commander, Marshal Saint-Arnaud, was ill with cholera before the campaign commenced, and Lord Raglan, aged 66, was already in failing health. Both would die within the first year of the campaign. More importantly, the allies had not expected the port to be so well prepared for defence and had not planned for a long siege over winter. The Russians had blocked the port, preventing direct naval assault, and then established a series of linked strong points for landward defence. Initial operations were mounted slowly and were severely disrupted when a storm destroyed many of the forces' transports and much of the British supplies. The lack of supply and appropriate equipment, combined with disease, made conditions miserable for the British, and the French did much to hold the lines through the winter. The plight of the sick and wounded was highlighted in the press, leading to the work of Florence Nightingale.

In 1855 significant siege operations commenced, with major bombardments of Sevastopol's defences in April and naval operations through May to clear other Russian bases. From June, operations were characterised by a series of assaults on the strong points around Sevastopol, notably the Malakoff and the Redan. Initially these assaults were uncoordinated and resulted in heavy losses, but finally in September the French mounted a successful attack on the Malakoff. Though the simultaneous British assault on the Redan had again failed, French fire from the captured Malakoff forced this position to be abandoned and Sevastopol's subsequent evacuation by the Russians. Following further naval operations peace was finally agreed at Vienna on 1 February 1856.

The Crimean War itself was a critical element in the mix of circumstances that led to the institution of the Victoria Cross. It was the first European war the British had been involved in since the defeat of Napoleon at Waterloo, 40 years previously. The Duke of Wellington, victor of that battle and subsequently sometime commander in chief and then prime minister of Great Britain, had dominated the British Army until his death in 1852. Wellington had seen no reason to change the system of honours and awards that had worked for him. However, in that time technology had also advanced. The British public was comparatively much better informed about events in the Crimea than it had been regarding any of Wellington's campaigns thanks to the telegraph, steamships, the ready availability of newspapers and higher literacy rates in the general public. It was consequently apparent to many that the British commanders in the field were not solely responsible for any successes, if at all, and yet they were the only ones being mentioned and officially recognised. In a campaign marked by a general mishandling of forces and logistic inadequacy, such triumphs as were reported were most often the work of the junior officers, non-commissioned officers, or the soldiers and sailors involved in the actual fighting.

THE IDEA

The Times correspondent, William Howard Russell, was at the forefront of this reporting, which created a public outrage and led to the fall of Lord Aberdeen's government. It highlighted the point that the battles were soldiers' fights and yet the vast majority of promotions were given to officers in staff appointments. The Commander in Chief, Lord Raglan, wanted to give all his senior officers the Order of the Bath so as not to create 'invidious distinctions'.[2] Russell's solution was to commence publishing a column of soldiers' stories in *The Times* to make the public aware of the efforts of those not adequately covered or recognised in the drier, official despatches. The desire to create a mechanism that officially recognised personal gallantry had started to gain traction, however, and on 19 December 1854, Captain G.T. Scobell, MP moved in the House of Commons that the Queen:

> . . . institute an 'Order of Merit' to be bestowed upon persons serving in the Army or Navy for distinguished and prominent personal gallantry during the present war and to which every

grade and individual, from the highest to the lowest, in the United Services, may be admissible.[3]

Scobell, who had served in the navy during the Napoleonic Wars, was a Liberal member of Parliament between 1851 and 1857 and took an active interest in service matters.

The secretary of state for war at this time was the Duke of Newcastle, who had also expressed concerns about the systems for recognition and honours. He followed up several general letters and conversations, that had originally concerned extending the Order of the Bath, by writing direct to the Queen's husband, Prince Albert. In his letter dated 20 January 1855 Newcastle suggested that a new decoration be used to recognise gallantry; one that was 'to be confined to the Army and Navy, but open to all ranks of either service'.[4]

Prince Albert replied almost immediately on 22 January, enclosing a memorandum of his ideas. This discussion culminated with six points:

- That a small cross of merit for personal deeds of valour be established.
- That it be open to all ranks.
- That it be unlimited in number.
- That an annuity (say £5) be attached to each cross.
- That it might be claimable by an individual on establishing before a jury of his peers, subject to confirmation at home, his right to the distinction.
- That in cases of general actions it be given in certain quantities to particular regiments.[5]

Many of Prince Albert's basic ideas did, in fact, subsequently become part of the basis of the initial regulations, but were also taken by the Duke of Newcastle to indicate royal assent for the concept. Consequently, on 29 January 1855 in the House of Lords, he announced that:

. . . a separate and distinct Cross of Military Merit shall be given, which shall be open to all ranks of the army and which, I hope, will be an object of ambition to every individual in the service, from the General who commands to the private in the ranks.[6]

It is therefore fair to conclude that the thoughts of many came together, culminating in what we now know as the Victoria Cross. Russell had helped highlight the issue, but made no suggestion of official change. The Duke of Newcastle had been discussing the matter with Prince Albert, initially around the idea of extending the Order of the Bath and subsequently in recognition of the difficulty in doing this. However, he had not actually suggested any other alternatives. Both he and the prince were, however, in a frame of mind receptive to a good idea, and though the concept of the Victoria Cross now seems to be so obvious an answer, the man who actually suggested it was Captain Scobell. Once that suggestion was made, progress was rapid. Newcastle had already formulated and circulated a first draft warrant even before receiving Prince Albert's response.

THE CROSS

The day after the announcement in the House of Lords, however, the government fell. Nevertheless, much of Newcastle's memorandum, and the service comments on it, would effectively form the basis of the original warrant of 1856 a year later. The key elements were that the new distinction should bear the name of Queen Victoria, that there should be no different grades of it, that it should be a cross (possibly of bronze) and that it should be worn on the breast (with a blue ribbon for the navy and red for the army).[7] In effect, these four elements provide the broad physical parameters of the Victoria Cross as we know it today. The remaining points dealt with how it could only be earned for conspicuous bravery in the presence of the enemy, how it should be conferred and registered, and that its award should attract a small pension. The memo also established that cases outside the strict rules could be considered so long as conspicuous bravery was established. Numbers of recipients were to be unlimited and further acts of bravery would attract a bar to the decoration. There was only one negative element — misconduct would possibly cause forfeiture of the distinction.

Lord Panmure succeeded Newcastle as secretary for war. He directed that the regulations of similar awards in other countries should be examined. Over the next nine months, work continued on initial drafts of the warrant and the basic design of the medal. The draft warrant was finally submitted to the Queen in December 1855 and Prince Albert replied on 28 December, having made pencil amendments and recommending that the armed services be consulted. These changes were critical as it was here that the name 'Victoria Cross' was first inserted and different mottoes in English — 'The Reward for Valour', 'The Reward for Bravery', and 'For Bravery' — were suggested. Prince Albert also emphasised that the award should be a medal and not the symbol of membership of an order.[8] By 29 January 1856 the warrant was signed by the Queen at Buckingham Palace, and eligibility made retrospectively available to the start of the Crimean War.

At the same time the Queen was considering proposed designs for the medal. On 5 January she returned the designs marking the one she liked, but changing the motto to 'For Valour', to avoid any inference that those not awarded a cross were not also brave. Some have attributed the actual design to Prince Albert, but the consideration of drawings does not support this idea. Conversely it is not clear who did in fact produce the designs, though some other secondary sources gave credit to Hancocks, the manufacturing goldsmiths who produced the prototypes and all Victoria Crosses issued to date.[9]

From this point Queen Victoria herself became increasingly involved, with a proof example being sent on 4 February 1856. This is retained in the Queen's collection of medals at Windsor and has a plain back and bar, with round links. The Queen did not like the plain back and directed that bronze, with a greenish varnish and raised parts burnished, should be used. Such an example was completed within two weeks. At the same time a late suggestion by the Queen that the top link of the suspender should be a V was also incorporated. The original VC made to these specifications, together with some variations, was submitted for the Queen's final approval on 3 March 1856. The selected medal was then returned to the manufacturer to become the pattern. This medal was subsequently held by the Hancock family until 1922 and is now in the museum of the Royal Fusiliers.[10]

The Victoria Cross design is a cross paty, where each arm of the cross has straight sides and is wider at its end than at the point it leaves the centre, and is called a Maltese Cross in the warrant. The cross is 1.4 inches square and made only of bronze, which is slightly burnished on the highpoints. It is attached to its 1.5 inch wide ribbon by a bronze bar, with a laurel sprig motif on the front and a V link. The ribbon was to be blue for naval personnel and red for the army. On the obverse (front) of the medal is a lion surmounting a Royal Crown, with a scroll underneath containing the motto 'For Valour'. Each arm of the cross has a border composed of a raised double line. On the back of the bronze suspender bar is engraved the rank, name and unit of the recipient. The reverse of the medal itself has the same double-line border on each arm of the cross, with a double-bordered circle in the middle. At the centre of the circle, the date of the act for which the cross has been awarded is engraved.

Hancocks were directed to produce 106 specimens. During this process it was confirmed that the crosses had to be cast — that is, pouring molten metal into a mould — rather than struck, which is beating the metal into a die, a more traditional method of medal-making. This was because the bronze gunmetal was so tough that it shattered dies if the latter method was used. The medal therefore had very little intrinsic value, as casting is a cheaper method of production.

The metal employed to cast the medals was also free, as it came from the cascabels of captured cannons.[11] The widely accepted version is that these had been cut from Russian guns captured at Sevastopol. More recently there have been stories that for brief periods, cited either as during the First World War or in the 1920s and '30s, metal from Chinese guns was used.[12] Now some Internet sources assert that in fact the metal always came from these Chinese guns, and that this has been proven through testing the metal ingots used to cast the medals against the guns remaining in the ordnance collection.[13] It is of course possible that the interpretation arose simply because at the time when it was stated that the metal was to come from captured guns, it was assumed this meant the Russians because they were the enemy most recently defeated. The one agreed point remains, however, that the weapons providing the bronze were captured ones and thus there was no monetary cost in its provision.

Another issue was the status of the medal, which took several years to be settled. From the outset the Queen wanted those awarded the VC to be designated by a post-nominal, such as DVC for 'decorated with', or BVC for 'bearer of' the Victoria Cross. In the end practice got ahead of policy and they were simply annotated as VC alongside any other decorations or orders. The next issue was the order of precedence of the VC, both in regard to where it was recorded in relation to other orders and awards and where it should be worn. Rules dictated that the proper sequence should be: orders, decorations and then medals. However, there was also a feeling that the VC was meant to take precedence. Consequently, records and practice varied for some time. Many recipients simply wore the VC next to any campaign medal associated with the act for which it was granted. Others felt that as a medal it necessarily fell in order of precedence behind all orders, even after the creation of such decorations as the Distinguished Service Order, that were subordinate. The order of wear was finally resolved in 1904 when it was determined that the VC should be placed first, to the right of all other orders, decorations or medals. The issue of how the VC should be recorded lingered and was only finally resolved in 1912, following King George V's direction that 'there can be no doubt that the Victoria Cross should go first of all orders and decorations. It is quite apart from any order of Chivalry.'[14]

From 1916 it was decided that when ribbons alone were worn (as is the normal case in uniform), a miniature of the cross (two in the case of a bar) should be worn on the ribbon. This was specifically so that any holder of a bar to the decoration could have a mechanism to indicate this was the case, without wearing two ribbons. This reflected the rosettes produced at the same time for those awarded bars to the Distinguished Service Order, Distinguished Conduct Medal, Military Cross, and so on. Then from 1918 all VCs were issued only with red ribbons and both these developments were in the VC warrant of 1920. One other convention is that a holder of the VC is entitled to be saluted first by all military personnel, regardless of rank.

SELECTION

By the time the first crosses were ready to be presented, the Crimean War was over. Though some earlier retrospective claims were made, it was specified that the award commenced with the hostilities associated with the Crimean War and that eligibility only applied to members of the Royal Navy or British Army, of all ranks. Individuals had to be recommended by their commanders, or in certain instances a unit or ship might be directed to ballot members to receive the decoration in recognition of a collective act. It was also specified that individuals could make their own cases to receive the award, which would then be investigated by a board of officers and appropriate recommendations made.

The Crimean VCs were distributed relatively freely, as the intent and value of the decoration were not really understood by everyone. Some regiments held ballots while others recommended no one. The collation of these recommendations took time and it was not until 24 February 1857 that the first names of recipients were published in the *London Gazette*. This also was a matter of correspondence between the secretary of war and the Queen. Lord Panmure wished to lay the list before Parliament before it was published, but the Queen asserted it was a matter for the Crown. Once recommended by the appropriate military authorities and receiving royal assent, the awards and their respective citations were therefore to be published in the *London Gazette* without Parliament having any say. This practice persists to this day.

The first presentation of the Victoria Cross took place on

26 June 1857 at Hyde Park, where 62 recipients (of the 87 awards announced) were assembled, 15 from the navy and 47 from the army. The first man actually to be presented a VC on this occasion, and therefore the first ever, was Commander Henry Raby of the Royal Navy, because he was the senior officer recipient present from the senior service. However, Mate Charles Lucas of HMS *Hecla* undertook the first act of gallantry to result in the award of a VC.[15] On 21 June 1854 a British Squadron had been bombarding Bomarsund, a fort on the Aland Islands in the Baltic. A live shell fired from the fort landed on the *Hecla*'s upper deck, with a hissing fuse. Lucas ran forward and hurled the shell towards the sea, where it exploded harmlessly before it hit the water, thus avoiding any death or serious injury aboard. The first acts by army personnel that were recognised by the award of VCs were to six soldiers, for fighting at the Battle of Alma on 20 September 1854.[16]

The scope of eligibility for the award of the VC was gradually extended as events developed. Before the Hyde Park presentation had taken place, the first event of the Indian Mutiny occurred at Meerut on 10 May 1857. During the two years of the mutiny 182 VCs were awarded, including four to civilians who bore arms as volunteers against the mutineers. This was made possible by the extension of the warrant to cover the troops of the East India Company in 1857 and civilian personnel attached to them or British units.[17]

Another extension was granted in 1858, to allow the award of the VC in cases of conspicuous courage or bravery displayed under circumstances of danger, but not before the enemy.[18] This short-lived provision was only used twice and its circumstances preceded the establishment of the Albert Medal and Conspicuous Gallantry Medal of the Order of the British Empire, which were later superseded by the George Cross. The reason for the initial change was that the troopship *Sarah Sands*, carrying reinforcements and a considerable amount of gunpowder to the Indian Mutiny, caught fire and was abandoned by her crew. The troops of the 54th Regiment stayed aboard and successfully fought the fire and were recommended by both their officer commanding and the Commander in Chief,

General Sir Colin Campbell, for some form of formal recognition. All agreed that the circumstances did not fall within the warrant for the VC, but they all equally felt that a case could be made and this was therefore laid before the Queen. The Queen agreed to the extension of the warrant, but no actual nominations were forwarded until 1860, by which time the government had changed and the officials administering the process appear to have prevented any further action. However, in 1866 Private O'Hea was recommended for and received a VC for putting out a fire in an ammunition carriage at Danville station in Canada. O'Hea was later to serve in the New Zealand Armed Constabulary in 1872–73. The other incident happened in 1867, when Dr Douglas and four members of the 24th Regiment received the VC for bringing boats through dangerous surf on Little Andaman Island in the Bay of Bengal to rescue another party who were stranded there and believed to be at risk of attack by hostile natives.

The New Zealand Wars were the catalyst for the next extension to the warrant. Until the case of Major Heaphy was raised, there had been no recommendations for personnel from 'locally raised forces'. Heaphy's case will be discussed in detail in the next chapter, but in essence his nomination and subsequent lobbying resulted in an extending warrant, signed on 1 January 1867, approving the award of the VC to colonial troops.[19]

Fourteen years later, in 1881, a further short warrant finally reiterated the original 1856 intent that bravery or conduct in 'the presence of the enemy' should be an integral element for qualification, thus nullifying the 1858 warrant. At the same time eligibility was extended to British Auxiliary and Reserve forces. Two further extending warrants were developed, later in 1881 to include members of the Indian Ecclesiastical Service and in 1911 finally to include members of the Indian Army.

The Victoria Cross Warrant was completely consolidated and rewritten in 1920, to accommodate all the changes that had occurred. It included the changes necessary following the establishment of the Royal Air Force and provided eligibility for the merchant marine and women serving as nurses or otherwise under orders in the forces. It also specified that the VC could be awarded posthumously, although this had effectively been in practice since 1907. The 1920s' regulations also codified two important dress matters. Henceforth only the red ribbon was to be used, though this was already practice, and the wearing of a miniature cross on the ribbon was also included.

In 1931 substantial changes were made in regard to deleting the offences which would result in forfeiture, changing some departmental names and minor medallic matters. This new warrant was then extended to cover additional groups, the Burmese forces (1938), Warrant Officers Class Three (1939) and members of the Indian Air Force (1941).

An entirely new warrant was issued in 1942 to account for the plethora of forces still outside the warrant, such as some Indian and all Sudanese forces, Home Guards and Women's Auxiliary forces. This time provision was also made for the governments of dominions to be consulted where appropriate, though it appears neither New Zealand nor Australia ever exercised these rights under this warrant. However, by 1961 the status of the British Commonwealth was such that substantial changes were again required, so that the now sovereign governments of these countries could effectively make their own awards. New Zealand made no such use of these provisions, but Australia awarded VCs to four soldiers during the Vietnam War.[20] From this time the respective governments also assumed responsibility for any pensions associated with future awards.

POSTHUMOUS AWARDS

The most important element of the 1920 warrant was that it codified and regularised the situation pertaining to posthumous awards of the VC, which had been a vexed issue for some 40 years. The very nature of extreme acts of bravery in the presence of the enemy had always meant that death was a very real possibility. However, early interpretation by officials was that the VC was 'an order for the living',[21] though this application was evidently initially developed to deal with claims being made by relatives of deceased servicemen. Lord Panmure had made an early ruling that only the living could establish a claim to the decoration, though if they should survive the act, but die before the award, then they would be entered on the roll. In essence, therefore, the regulations required that the perpetrator survived. If the brave man did not survive — even if the act was noticed by a superior or someone capable of making a recommendation — then only a mention in despatches was possible.

Subsequently a system was developed which simply involved a memorandum being published in the *London Gazette*, stating that the individual would have been recommended to the Queen for the VC had they survived. The first case of this being employed was with regard to Lieutenants Teignmouth Melvill and Nevill Coghill of the 24th Foot during the Zulu War in 1879. They had managed to escape from the massacre at Isandhlwana in order to rescue their regimental colours from capture, but were run down by pursuing Zulus. Subsequent cases in Rhodesia and the Boer War led to growing pressure for medals in these cases actually to be awarded, including support from the theatre commander, Lord Roberts, VC.[22]

In late 1900 William St John Brodrick became secretary of state for war and Lord Roberts returned to England, from South Africa, as commander in chief in early 1901. Both men had previously supported the concept of posthumous awards and they continued to do so, but met some resistance from senior military personnel. Eventually an examination of cases revealed only six outstanding instances from the Boer War which the new King, Edward VI, approved.

However, this highlighted the six other instances from earlier campaigns where the memoranda had been utilised, but the King firmly declined these. This led some to believe that South Africa was to be a stand-alone case, setting no binding future precedent, though they recognised the logical incongruity of the position. At this stage Mrs Melvill, the wife of Lieutenant Teignmouth Melvill, petitioned the King directly and successfully. The decision was announced in the *London Gazette* of 15 January 1907 and from that time the VC has been one of the few awards that can be conferred posthumously. As time has progressed and additional subordinate decorations for gallantry have become available, the nature of the acts required to win a VC have become such that posthumous awards have made up almost half of those awarded since 1939 and were also a significant proportion of those awarded in the First World War.

That crucial, precedent-changing case was also to have an interesting New Zealand connection. Lieutenant Melvill had two sons, both of whom subsequently joined the army themselves. The younger, Charles William, was only one year old when his father was killed, and after service in India, aged 30, he moved to Otago in 1907 to take up farming. However, in 1911 he joined the New Zealand Staff Corps as a regular soldier and at the outbreak of war was studying at the Staff College, Camberley — only the second member of the New Zealand forces to do so. Initially Charles Melvill was mobilised and served with British units, with the agreement of the New Zealand government, but joined the New Zealand Expeditionary Force in November 1915. He was given command of a battalion in the Rifle Brigade before taking over 2 Brigade after the Somme battles. He temporarily commanded the New Zealand Division during the war and had won the DSO, CMG and CB by its end. He succeeded Major General Chaytor as chief of general staff in 1924, but died suddenly a year later.[23] Major General Sir Charles William Melvill is buried in the Karori Soldiers' Cemetery, Wellington, and his portrait is on display in Army General Staff.

FORFEITURE

As previously mentioned, provisions for the forfeiture of the Victoria Cross had been included in the warrants from the outset. This reflected the ambivalent status of the award. It was neither an order nor a medal, so the rules for it developed in accordance with existing practice, with some elements reflecting the behavioural standards associated with the orders of chivalry. The crimes specifically mentioned that could result in forfeiture were treason, cowardice, felony or infamous crime, or for the miscreant to be accused of such crimes and not to surrender for trial. In the event, eight men forfeited their VCs under this fifteenth clause.

No New Zealand winner of the VC forfeited his award, but the only officer to do so spent the last years of his short life here. Edward St John Daniel won his VC as a 17-year-old midshipman in the Crimean War. A Naval Brigade had been formed, commanded by Captain William Peel, RN,[24] and Midshipman Daniel (along with Midshipman Evelyn Wood, who won a VC in the army during the Indian Mutiny and subsequently became a Field Marshal) was acting as his aide. At the Battle of Inkerman, he was noted for carrying powder forward under heavy fire. During the unsuccessful assault on the Redan on 18 June 1855 he stayed with the wounded Captain Peel and assisted him to safety. He was awarded the VC in the first list of 24 February 1857.

Following this he stayed with Captain Peel and again accompanied him ashore at the siege of Cawnpore during the Indian Mutiny. Daniel, however, already had a significant drinking problem and, though Peel trusted him, others were less happy to serve with him. Unfortunately Peel died of smallpox in 1858, depriving Daniel of his mentor.

Daniel was commissioned lieutenant in September 1859 and was introduced to the Queen in April 1860. She was said to be impressed with him. However, his performance and career were plummeting. He was twice reported absent without leave in May 1860 and then in June reported as missing a watch because he was drunk. Daniel pleaded guilty, citing in extenuation his campaign experiences and showing his eight medals. He was sentenced to be dismissed from his ship and placed at the bottom of his rank for two years. Once he found another berth, however, things got worse. He was again drinking and was then placed under arrest 'for taking indecent liberties with four of the subordinate officers'.[25] On 27 June he was reported missing from the ship and marked as a deserter on 28 June.

Because it was obvious that he had failed to surrender himself for trial to avoid conviction, Daniel was removed from the registry of the VC on 4 September 1861. This seemed to escape public notice, much to the Admiralty's relief.

Somehow Daniel got to Melbourne, where in 1863 he enrolled for three years' service in the Taranaki Military Settlers, giving his correct name and age (27). He arrived at New Plymouth on 15 February 1864 and took part in several operations. He was also disciplined several times for drunkenness. After being discharged in May 1867, he took up farming but did not enjoy it, and soon sold his land grant. On 26 November 1867 Daniel enlisted for the last time as a constable in the Armed Constabulary Field Force. In March 1868 his unit was sent to Hokitika to help deal with Fenian disturbances in that region. Daniel was not well, however, and on 16 May was admitted to hospital, where he died on 20 May of 'delirium tremens'. He was given a funeral with full military honours and buried in the Hokitika Municipal Cemetery.

King George V held strong views that forfeiture should not occur. His private secretary wrote in July 1920 that:

> The King feels so strongly that, no matter what the crime committed by anyone on whom the VC has been conferred, the decoration should not be forfeited. Even were a VC to be sentenced to be hanged for murder, he should be allowed to wear the VC on the scaffold.[26]

From 1921 recipients convicted of crimes were not recommended for forfeiture, and from the 1931 warrant onwards only very broad provisions were made for that possibility and then only in extreme cases.

EXCEPTIONAL CASES

New Zealanders have been involved in a number of exceptions to the norm regarding the award and issue of VCs. Some of these stem from the remote location of New Zealand in relation to Britain, but others simply arise from unusual circumstances.

The first New Zealander to cause an issue was Major Heaphy, as previously mentioned. His case will be described fully later, but in order for him to be eligible to receive the VC, an amendment had to be made to the warrant to cover personnel in locally raised forces. Even then the fact that he was under the command of a senior British officer, who supported the award, was a crucial element in his success.

The first New Zealand-born soldier serving in a New Zealand unit to receive the VC was Farrier Sergeant Major William Hardham in the Boer War. Hardham's award was made in South Africa in July 1901, along with two others, by the Prince of Wales (later George V), who had taken some unnamed crosses with him for the express purpose of making some appropriate awards in a theatre of war. This was the only time unnamed crosses were ever presented.[27] Both the West Australian administrator and the general officer commanding South Africa ensured that the respective crosses were returned to London, to be properly engraved by Hancocks. Hardham's VC, however, was never returned — the only one of the 1350 awarded not to have been officially completed by Hancocks. The medal has been engraved correctly though, and it is thought possible that Hardham had it done by Hancocks himself while in England with the Coronation Contingent.

Engraving was also an issue with Captain Charles Upham's VC. Upham won his first VC on Crete in 1941, but remained on active service in Africa and was then captured. He did not actually receive his medal until May 1945, after his liberation from Colditz, when he and Sergeant Jack Hinton were invested by the King in London. By this time authorities were considering him for a second award for his actions at Ruweisat Ridge in 1942. This was subsequently approved, making him the only recipient of a bar to the VC in the Second World War and one of only three ever to take this honour.

To avoid further delay in making this presentation, a completely new medal, with the bar attached, was despatched to New Zealand. This was duly presented by the Governor-General in 1946, who had been directed that the original medal presented by the King in 1945 should be returned. King George VI, however, was not happy about this, as he felt that Upham should keep and use the original medal received from his own hands. Consequently, Hancocks were directed to prepare a bar for the returned medal, which was then to be formally swapped by the Governor-General in New Zealand for the one he had previously presented. Subsequently in 1957 the Military Secretary in England found an engraved VC and bar for Upham in his safe and queried why it was there. It eventuated that Upham had felt exactly the same as the King when presented with the second medal and had simply removed the bar and placed it on the VC he had received from the King, returning the duplicate medal. Once this was established the duplicate VC was returned to Hancocks to have the name removed and to be returned to stock; the duplicate bar was destroyed.[28]

Two New Zealanders in the Second World War were also awarded VCs after recommendations were received through unusual channels. From the award's inception it had been part of the process that the relevant chain of command should investigate each case and forward nominations for any individual deemed worthy. The recommendation for Sergeant Jack Hinton was therefore unorthodox, as it was received from a British medical officer, via the Red Cross, from a prisoner of war camp in Greece. In essence, ten officers, captured at the same time as Hinton, had approached the medical officer as the senior person in the camp, recommending Hinton. In England the unorthodox circumstances of this process were accepted, given that the prisoners had no other mechanism available to them. The second was even stranger, in that the recommendation was based entirely on the interrogation of enemy personnel. Flying Officer Lloyd Trigg, RNZAF, had been killed along with his entire crew in making their successful attack on a U-boat. It was the U-boat's captain and other survivors who bore witness to the act for which the VC was subsequently awarded.

ENDPOINT

To date, 1353[29] VCs have been awarded, of which 294 have been posthumous, including the penultimate two in the Falklands War of 1982. Three men earned two VCs, including Charles Upham. In addition, a VC was presented to the Unknown Warrior of the United States of America at Arlington Cemetery on 28 October 1921. The medal has been awarded to five civilians, and to six men for acts not in the face of the enemy, but as yet to no woman. Twenty-one members of the New Zealand armed forces, including one Maori, have won the VC. A further four New Zealanders living in Australia have won VCs while serving in Australian units,[30] and another four, either born in New Zealand or who had very strong connections to the country, won the award while serving with British forces.[31]

During the Queen's Birthday weekend in 1999 the New Zealand Prime Minister, Jenny Shipley, announced that a new range of national honours and awards would replace the British orders and honours. This came into effect from 20 September 1999, and included a set of bravery decorations for peacetime and gallantry awards for military operations. The New Zealand Cross (NZC) was resurrected as the premier national award for bravery, in nearly the same design as it was awarded during the New Zealand Wars, except that henceforth its ribbon would be blue, like that of the George Cross. However, the international status of the Victoria Cross remains such that this award was in effect nationalised as the Victoria Cross of New Zealand, remaining the premier award in this country for military gallantry in the presence of the enemy.

CHAPTER 2 The New Zealand Wars

Conflict was a feature of life in New Zealand before the arrival of the Europeans, with Maori engaging in endemic inter-tribal fighting. The Europeans were initially drawn into this way of life through their commercial activities. As they traded with Maori they necessarily took a side and were subsequently responsible for the provision of weapons, particularly guns. They were also subjected to hostile attack themselves. At the urging of missionaries, Britain eventually decided to extend its rule to New Zealand, as much to protect the Maori from the Europeans as vice versa. This also had the benefit of countering any potential French interest in the region.

Altruistic intent and self-interest aside, the formalisation of the relationship between New Zealand and the British Crown sowed the seeds for future conflict. First the British took onto themselves the role of regulating processes in the new colony, but did so according to their own perceptions and procedures. This included the concept of ownership of land, which the Treaty of Waitangi in 1840 effectively vested in those holding it at the time of the signing. However, this worked to the advantage of the more active tribes who had utilised the weapons they gained through trade to force an extension of their own territories, which were then effectively locked in. Second, the Maori adhered to a concept of group possession for land, which an individual might dominate or use so long as they were able, after which time it reverted to the group (much like a lease).[1] Conversely, the British believed in the concept of individual purchase and then perpetual title. Consequently, when Europeans proceeded to arrange the purchase of land from Maori, they did so with conflicting views of what purchase actually meant[2] and they often bought land from individual Maori or tribes whose right to give title was itself questionable.

The formalisation of New Zealand as a colony brought a governor, who from 1843 had British troops to enforce his authority, but it also brought greater numbers of colonists. From the outset there was conflict over land, sovereignty and influence. Aside from the Wairau incident, which Governor Robert Fitzroy felt was Captain Arthur Wakefield's own fault and therefore not requiring an official armed response, the first major incidents occurred in the Bay of Islands in 1844. Elements of the local Ngapuhi had taken early advantage of firearms and consequently dominated Northland. Initially they felt they gained much prestige from having the colonial administration centred in their territory, to the extent that one of their leading chiefs, Hone Heke, both spoke in support of the treaty and donated a flagpole to mark it. When the government centre and consequent trade moved south to Auckland, Hone Heke was affronted and in 1844 had the symbolic flagstaff cut down. Troops were sent, but the situation was diffused and Hone Heke replaced the flagstaff, only to cut it down again himself in January 1845. The troops returned to put up a third flagstaff for Hone Heke to fell. Tensions were now high and the site was garrisoned, with military blockhouses established.

On 11 March 1845, the blockhouses and Kororareka were attacked by elements of the Ngapuhi, resulting in 19 dead and evacuation of the colonists by sea. British troops then arrived from Sydney via Auckland and, in conjunction with pro-government Ngapuhi under Chief Tamati Waka Nene, commenced a campaign to deal with the various dissidents and their pa strongholds. At first the Maori gave up their fortified pa sites, until 8 May 1845, when a battle was fought at Puketutu pa on the shore of Lake Omapere. This cost the lives of 13 soldiers with no result, as the position was too strong and the attackers lacked any artillery. In this first real battle between British troops and Maori, indications of future trends emerged. The British attacked frontally, but could not penetrate the pa's defences. However, when a party of Maori attempted to attack the British in the open ground, they could not succeed against the volleys of gunfire from the disciplined troops.

The fighting then escalated, with the British bringing in more troops from Australia and the Ngapuhi feuding factions raising larger war parties. Hone Heke attacked Waka Nene's pa with 450 men, but was beaten when Waka Nene held his fire till the last moment, causing massive damage. Initiative passed to the British, who assembled a larger force of 600, with artillery, and then besieged Ohaeawai pa. The artillery, however, made little impression on the defence, so the British tried a direct assault on 1 July, at the cost of 40 lives, but again with no success. It was only because the defenders subsequently left the site that it was taken. The next objective then became Te Ruki Kawiti's pa, Ruapekapeka, for which an attacking force of 1600 was gathered, with heavy artillery, arriving at the site on 27 December 1845. By 10 January 1846 the artillery had created a breach, but the assault was delayed, at Waka Nene's suggestion, until 11 January when it was felt the site might be abandoned. When a reconnaissance was undertaken this appeared indeed to be the case, but in fact it was a Sunday and many of the Christian Ngapuhi were actually holding a service in the bush. The British got inside the pa and then used its defences against the tribesmen. The Ngapuhi defeat in the subsequent four hours effectively ended the rising.[3]

Also in 1846 there was some skirmishing around Wellington. Following the Wairau incident troops had been sent to guarantee the settlement's security, but as land pressure increased more troops were required. Eventually seven companies were assembled and some took up defensive positions in the northern Hutt Valley, at Boulcott's Farm, and at Porirua. At dawn on 16 May Boulcott's Farm was attacked, with the sentry being killed along with two others still in a tent. Drummer William Allen, a boy soldier, blew the alarm on his bugle to rouse the remaining troops. While doing so his right arm was cut off, but he continued to play using his left arm until he too was killed. The raiders withdrew on the arrival of a cavalry detachment and returned to the bush. The situation was largely brought under control after Governor Grey had Te Rauparaha, the Ngati Toa leader, captured and the remaining dissidents withdrew into the hinterland. Te Ati Awa, Ngati Rangitahi and most of Ngati Toa refused to join a rebellion, and resistance collapsed.

Next there were disturbances around Wanganui. Following the murder of Mrs Gilfillan and three of her children in May 1847, five offenders were captured by friendly Maori and handed over to the garrison. A war party assembled for their rescue, but the condemned men were hanged before it arrived and the attack was beaten off. This ended the war phase and resulted in a number of the troops returning to New South Wales.

Despite acts of bravery, such as Drummer Allen's, the soldiers concerned could receive no recognition. The few senior officers involved could become Companions of the Order of the Bath (CB), but the soldiers and junior officers could at best receive promotion or kind words. The pro-British Maori or militia elements involved were equally bereft of any mechanism for formal recognition of any acts of heroism, except in monetary terms or grants of land.

The Taranaki conflicts

In the period following the first war, some tribes began to organise themselves, both as a result of, and in resistance to, increased contact with and encroachment by the colonists. The King movement developed in the Waikato, as a mechanism for Maori to unite against and resist land appropriations. By 1860 pressures were again building, especially as settlers around New Plymouth attempted to move inland from the coast and establish farms in the Taranaki hinterland. The catalyst for open conflict came when troops advanced into the Waitara block in order to enforce its disputed acquisition, and on 17 March 1860 they attacked the Te Ati Awa pa at Te Kohia. Although they successfully maintained their defences during that day, the Maori withdrew by night. The key aspect of this conflict was, however, that instead of simply defending against, or preventing, hostile attack, the British troops were now being employed offensively to enforce land settlements.

The Taranaki Maori resisted this encroachment, and though they avoided direct confrontation with the British troops, they did attack isolated Europeans, forcing the settlers to evacuate to New

Plymouth. Then on 27 March they attacked the New Plymouth Militia from their positions at Kaipopo pa. The militia were hard-pressed, but the alarm was raised by Captain Francis Mace and the next day reinforcements were landed from the ship HMS *Niger*, who then made straight for the Kaipopo pa itself. The *Niger*'s commanding officer, Captain Peter Cracroft, then offered a £10 bounty to the man who brought down the enemy flags being flown in the pa. Leading Seaman William Odgers was the first man to gain entrance to the pa under heavy fire, and following heavy hand-to-hand fighting he was credited with 'assisting in hauling down the enemy colours'.[4]

The effect of the attack relieved the pressure on the militia troops, but more significantly in this instance resulted in the award of the first Victoria Cross associated with New Zealand. Queen Victoria had signed the warrant for the medal, available to all ranks of the navy and army for acts of gallantry in the presence of the enemy, in 1856 and the first awards had been made in 1857. As well as being awarded his £10 bounty, and being subsequently promoted, Leading Seaman Odgers was recorded in the *London Gazette* of 3 August 1860 as receiving the award of the VC for conspicuous gallantry at the storming of a pa at Waireka, New Plymouth, during operations against the rebel natives in New Zealand. Captain Mace, however, received no recognition, because he was a member of the Taranaki Militia and, as a colonial volunteer, was therefore ineligible.

Both sides were then reinforced, with the Maori receiving warriors from the Waikato and more British troops arriving from Australia. The tribesmen, however, were local, while the reinforcements lacked familiarity with the conditions and did not always seem to have absorbed the lessons of past experience in fighting the Maori. Consequently, when a combined British Navy and Army force tried to advance from the Waitara block and struck the fortified ridge called Puketakauere, they attacked this frontally after a short and ineffective bombardment. The British were heavily mauled, and their attempts to flank the position were equally unsuccessful. Nothing was achieved at the cost of 30 dead, including some wounded who had been left behind and were killed by the defenders where they lay.

Major General Thomas Pratt then came to New Zealand from Australia with further reinforcements. He was a more careful commander and over the succeeding months he cleared a series of fortified pa by developing entrenchments (saps) right up to their edges, which resulted in the defenders abandoning the sites with minimal fighting. He then acted rapidly to prevent a major movement of Waikato warriors south, by attacking them as they assembled at the old pa at Mahoetahi.

The Kingites, under Wiremu Kingi, established a new defensive line at Matarikoriko in December, but abandoned it before the assault and another at Huirangi in January 1861, before falling back to the Te Arei pa on the Waitara River cliff edge. The British employed the same process of sapping up to the defences, while the defenders achieved some success in ambushing their line of supply. By 11 March the attackers' sap trenches were 200 metres from the pa, when the defenders launched a night attack. The British had placed skirmishers from the 40th Regiment ahead of their most advanced works. Several soldiers were killed or wounded in the early exchanges, including the officer in command, so that Colour Sergeant John Lucas took over. He arranged the evacuation of the wounded to the rear and maintained the position until reinforcements arrived, for which he received the second VC of the New Zealand campaign.[5]

On 19 March 1861 Kingi abandoned Te Arei pa and on 8 April articles of peace were signed, ending the first Taranaki war. Pratt returned to Australia, to be replaced in New Zealand by Major General Duncan Cameron. Cameron had an impressive reputation, having commanded the Highland Brigade in the Crimea. He was thus a very professional officer and also very aware of the purpose and distinction attached to the Victoria Cross. However, the next two years were relatively quiet, though pressure to open further land for settlement increased against continued Maori resistance. At this stage Sir George Grey returned to New Zealand for a second term as governor. Two years later, in 1863, he tried to negotiate access to the

Waikato and achieve some resolution to the Taranaki disputes, but with no success.

Consequently, in March 1863 conflict broke out once again in Taranaki, this time around the Tataraimaka block when efforts were made to reclaim land that the farmers had been forced off in 1860. Redoubts were established and garrisoned. The first hostile act of the local Maori was a successful ambush of a prisoner escort, but then they established the Katikara pa. The pa was quickly reduced, with Captain Mace again distinguishing himself during this action so that this date was specifically mentioned in his subsequent citation for the NZC, the earliest date included in any such recommendation. Overall, the Taranaki region remained far from passive, requiring continued garrisoning of the redoubts and constant patrolling. An indication of this is that two further VCs were won there at Poutoko on 2 October, when a party from the 57th Regiment was attacked near the bush edge. Ensign John Down and Drummer Dudley Stagpoole went forward to rescue a fallen comrade under heavy fire.[6] The next year the pa at Kaitake was stormed and for actions here and beforehand Trooper Antonio Rodrigues received the NZC. However, the real trouble was now centred further north.

WAIKATO WAR

Fighting developed on the outskirts of Auckland in mid-1863, where Maori harassed settlers and burnt homesteads in the Hunua region and around Pukekohe. This situation escalated quickly, with confrontations between Maori bands and militia units. The government had decided to act and advertised for militiamen, who would occupy territory taken by the army. Shortly afterwards, in August, they established the Forest Rangers to assist with offensive operations in patrolling. Cameron led the initial movement in crossing the Waikato at Tuakau on 12 July 1863, followed shortly afterwards by a brief battle as the British assaulted the Waikato position at Koheroa. Before major military operations could commence, in the period July to October the ground either side of the Great South Road, behind the advancing force, was cleared and redoubts built to make ambush more difficult. From October river steamers were used to help move men and supplies forward, as well as supporting actions with their guns where possible. However, because of both a lack of troops and the logistic difficulties, progress was slow.

Seven weeks after the initial crossing, a skirmish at Cameron Town resulted in two further VCs being won when on 7 September the Maori ambushed a company of the 65th Regiment. The officers in the party were shot early in the exchange and Colour Sergeant Edward McKenna then took command of the survivors, leading a charge that successfully fought its way through the ambushers.[7] At the same time Corporal John Ryan and two others retrieved the body of their commander, Captain Smith, and removed it from the field. The three men remained with the body through the night, even though the enemy surrounded them. McKenna received the VC, as did Ryan, and the two privates with Ryan received the Medal for Distinguished Conduct.[8]

In October 1863, as the British continued to build up in the Waikato, the Forest Rangers entered the fray. They fought a minor skirmish at Lower Mauku, and Ensigns Gustavus von Tempsky and Thomas McDonnell carried out a close reconnaissance of the Maori positions at Paparata. This was the first act included in the subsequent citation for the NZC that McDonnell was awarded several years later, von Tempsky by then having been killed. By the end of that month Cameron was ready to commence further operations but, after a brief initial bombardment, found the pa at Meremere had been abandoned. Using this as a staging point he then advanced south on Rangiriri.

Cameron had about 1300 troops, including artillery and engineers, as well as naval support available for the assault. Although the main force arrived early on 20 November, the landing of forces from the river was delayed and the bombardment was ineffective. Cameron was aware of Pratt's previous success with deliberate sapping operations, but could not see much of the Rangiriri pa from the river. Consequently, because he underestimated its strength, he planned a quick attack. The forward Maori defences were taken quickly, but then the attackers ran up against the previously unseen main redoubt. First the infantry, then the artillery and finally the naval party attempted to assail the parapet — each failing, with significant losses. During the attacks two men won VCs — Lieutenant Arthur Pickard of the artillery and Assistant Surgeon William Temple.[9] Both were recommended for carrying water to the wounded and caring for them under the guns of the Maori. By evening Cameron called a halt to the attack and prepared to conduct a deliberate siege. The conventional understanding of events is that the pa had been surrounded and during the night the defenders ran out of ammunition whilst shooting at the investing troops, with the consequence that they had to surrender the next day. Maori, however, assert that in fact the chiefs could not agree on what to do next, with the result that some factions slipped away during the night and that it was only a small proportion of the original defenders who surrendered the next morning.

Rangiriri was the last position the Waikato tribes established in the good defensive terrain in the north of their territory. Cameron's forces were subsequently able to advance rapidly across the Waikato plains and by January 1864 had come up to the new Maori positions at Pikopiko and Paterangi. During the build-up the fortifications were engaged by artillery while the defending Maori periodically ambushed isolated parties.

On 11 February, south of Paterangi, a party from the 40th Regiment were bathing in a pool in the Mangapiko River, when they came under heavy attack. Reinforcements from the 50th Regiment soon came forward, including a dozen or so men commanded by Captain Charles Heaphy of the Auckland Militia, to drive off the raiders. Heaphy first led his group to prevent the ambushing party being reinforced and consequently managed to fall upon the enemy reserve, guarding the route to Paterangi. Having beaten this party off, he regrouped his forces and moved on to the ambush site, joining the attack on the ambush party's right flank. The tribesmen here were also beaten back, even though they outnumbered their British attackers, and then tried to escape. At this point one soldier, Private Cussan, tried to follow them into the bush, where he was shot. Heaphy and the remaining three men with him went to Cussan's aid but were fired upon as they got there, although the only casualty this time was Heaphy's revolver strap. Another group then fired on them from only four metres and Heaphy was hit in the hip, arm and ribs as well as having his coat holed, while two more of his men fell, one killed. However, Heaphy still tried to assist Cussan and the now-wounded McDoull, but he and Private Cooney were driven back. The two men continued to cover the wounded soldiers, thus preventing them being axed. Unfortunately, when they were rescued, McDoull had died and Cussan did so while being carried away.[10]

Lieutenant Colonel Henry Havelock, Heaphy's commander, ordered Heaphy to go and get his wounds treated, but he refused to. He remained in the field, guiding stretcher parties and was assisting in a fight to relieve the group he had originally crossed the river to support, when the Forest Rangers under von Tempsky arrived and finally drove off the Maori. This commenced the saga by which the first soldier serving in a New Zealand military unit was to be awarded the Victoria Cross, though his would be the last one granted for the New Zealand Wars. The subsequent developments in this case will consequently be dealt with more fully later in this chapter.

Cameron then decided to avoid a direct assault on the pa and adopted a strategy of depriving them of their food supplies instead. Leaving a small force to screen the forts, he made a night march on 20 February to the village at Rangiaowhia, which was taken after a short fight. The defenders of Pikopiko and Paterangi then withdrew to a hastily dug position at Hairini Hill near the village, but Cameron immediately mounted a quick attack with artillery support that easily broke the defence.

Chief Rewi Maniapoto subsequently established a hastily constructed pa at Orakau, near Te Awamutu. The British attacked it on 30 March, again employing a direct frontal assault and again being severely repulsed. During that day Major John McNeill, one of Cameron's aides, and two companions sighted a body of Maori as they were proceeding to Te Awamutu. Having sent one of his escorts to inform the infantry McNeill continued to observe the enemy, when he was himself ambushed. His remaining escort was unhorsed, but McNeill managed to catch the animal and assist the man to remount, after which they only just managed to escape. For this act McNeill won the VC.[11] The next day both sides were reinforced, but the Maori had constructed the fort without a ready water supply. Despite this the offer of surrender was declined with the words 'Friend, we shall fight you for ever and ever!'[12] Without water, however, the defence could not continue so Rewi broke out. This action effectively ended the Waikato war, as no further major points of resistance developed.

While Rewi fought the British in the Waikato, sympathisers on the east coast wished to join him but were prevented from doing so by Arawa tribes loyal to the Crown. Supported by Arawa and Forest Rangers, the British now had to deal with unrest by these Ngaiterangi tribesmen around the Tauranga area. The British garrison had been directed to await reinforcement, but the Maori had suggested battle at their pa site. Believing the British did not attack because of the pa's distant location, they erected a new fort more convenient to the settlement, which is remembered as Gate Pa. Cameron then arrived from the Waikato with significant reinforcements and artillery. Gate Pa was small, containing only about 300 defenders to the 1700 British attackers, but it was well constructed. Following a day-long bombardment on 29 April, a breach was made and the British assault went forward. The officers leading the attack reached the breach first and suffered severe casualties there. In trying to rescue his commanding officer at this point, Coxswain Samuel Mitchell of HMS *Harrier* won the VC.[13] The defending Maori had attempted to withdraw ahead of the initial assault, but had been forced back into their defences by the fire of the cut-off groups, sent to prevent their escape. Surrounded, they returned to defend against the now leaderless British assault, which they repulsed in ferocious fighting, aided, apparently, by the continued fire of the British cut-off groups which caused casualties to their own side as well. Assistant Surgeon William Manley won his VC as he tended the wounded under this fire before having to fight his own way back out.[14] Overnight the defenders managed to escape in small groups, and for the first time it was formally noted that the wounded were not killed and in fact a significant effort had been made by some Maori to bring them water and some comfort.[15]

Cameron was then called away to help deal with the Hauhau in the Taranaki. However, another battle was to be fought after he left when the Ngaiterangi constructed a pa at Te Ranga. The position was carried by frontal assault on 21 June, with another pair of VCs awarded. Captain Frederick Smith won one for leading his company in the attack and entering the hand-to-hand combat despite having already been wounded. Sergeant John Murray won his for attacking eight enemy single-handed and dealing with them all before carrying on the advance.[16]

HAUHAU

The focus of conflict now returned south where Maori resistance to the settlers' encroachments was reinvigorated by the Pai Marire ('good and gentle') cult, more commonly known as Hauhau. The prophet Te Ua Haumene based his teaching on a mix of Maori custom and traditions, along with biblical lessons from the Old Testament. Soon radical elements became predominant, reintroducing old customs such as taking heads, as well as introducing new beliefs including rituals to make themselves invincible to bullets. The Hauhau commenced by ambushing Europeans and made a failed attack on the Sentry Hill redoubt near New Plymouth. One large war party set off to attack Wanganui, but was repulsed in a battle on Moutoa Island in the Whanganui River by pro-government Maori under Tamihana Te Awe.

Cameron and his troops deployed by sea straight to Wanganui and from there, in January 1865, commenced a march west along the coast. On 24 January he was camped at Nukumaru when his picquets were attacked from the nearby bush. Captain Hugh Shaw, commanding this group, ordered a withdrawal as soon as he started taking fire, but on reaching a stockade slightly rearward he found that one of his wounded men had been left behind. He then led four volunteers back and successfully retrieved the fallen man. This was the last act for which a VC was awarded during the New Zealand Wars.[17]

The next day the Hauhau actually attacked Cameron's force and there was significant fighting, before they withdrew to their pa. Cameron continued the advance, but it was increasingly apparent that he did not believe in the task which he now firmly felt to be aimed at dispossessing the Maori of their land. The British authorities had also suggested that the colonial government should pay £40 a year for each imperial soldier on duty in New Zealand, as well as their campaigning costs. Given these potential costs, the colonial government decided they would be better to employ locally raised forces, whose motivation they could trust. They therefore started to move towards a policy of self-reliance in internal defence matters. Cameron meanwhile continued his advance slowly, driving off small Hauhau resistance and reached Patea. He then left New Zealand for England, via Auckland, in order to become the commandant of the Royal Military Academy, Sandhurst.

The trend towards self-reliance moved ahead when Governor Grey took command in the field and by 21 July 1865 his forces were in a position to attack the Hauhau base at Weraroa pa. Once this was brought under fire, the few defenders within scattered. Other Hauhau were pursued to Pipiriki on the upper Whanganui River, which was cordoned with blockhouses that the Hauhau in turn surrounded. Reinforcements lifted this siege on 30 July and the Hauhau dispersed. It is possible that both these engagements were exaggerated by the authorities, in order to build the perception that the self-reliant policy was effective. There were further skirmishes in Taranaki for the remainder of the year, and the followers of the Hauhau movement began to gain some support in the Bay of Plenty.

On 2 March at Opotiki one of Te Ua's disciples, Kereopa, had conducted the ritualistic murder of the Reverend Julius Volkner and then eaten his eyes. Governor Grey sent forces by ship to hunt the culprits, some of whom were by then attempting to escape to the Waikato and sanctuary in the King Country, while others remained with the east coast tribes. Some Ngati Porou had also followed Kereopa, but these were dealt with internally by the future Major

Rapata Wahawaha, with some assistance from HMS *Eclipse*'s shore party.

In September the major Hauhau concentration at Opotiki was dealt with by a force which arrived by sea but had considerable difficulty effecting a landing. This was furthered in October, when a significant group of Hauhau eventually surrendered at their Te Teko pa on the Rangitaiki River after pro-government Maori, under Major William Mair, had dug saps up to their defences. After dealing with a dual pa site on the bank of the Waioeka River, which included a rare cavalry charge when the Wanganui Cavalry caught a party in the open, the core of Kereopa's Hauhau withdrew into the Urewera hinterland. He was eventually captured and hanged. In November a further group of 400 Hauhau surrendered at Waerenga-a-Hika near Gisborne and were subsequently imprisoned on the Chatham Islands. Most of these actions had been fought by the colonial troops, as the British regiments were progressively withdrawn and the colonial government took on responsibility for internal security.

CAPTAIN CHARLES HEAPHY, VC

This withdrawal of imperial troops also meant that no further Victoria Crosses were recommended. However, the case of Captain Charles Heaphy of the Auckland Militia was still outstanding. Heaphy was actually an Englishman, born in London in 1822. He had trained at the Royal Academy as an artist before securing an appointment with the New Zealand Company as a draughtsman and surveyor. He arrived in New Zealand in 1839 aboard the *Tory* and subsequently made considerable explorations in the upper South Island[18] and Wellington regions before moving to Auckland in 1859. Heaphy had originally joined the militia in Nelson and enlisted as a private in the Auckland Militia when he moved there. He was commissioned in 1863 and became captain of the Parnell Company in August that year. As a militia officer and the local surveyor, Heaphy was employed by Cameron as a military surveyor and guide for the Waikato expedition. Initially his duties involved surveying the military road and the

Waikato River channels, but eventually he was attached to the staff of Lieutenant Colonel Henry Havelock VC as a guide, which is how he came to be at the Mangapiko.

Although he was under Havelock's command, it was Governor Grey who wrote to the Colonial Secretary, Lord Cardwell,[19] on 22 December 1864 conveying Major General Galloway's recommendations of Heaphy and Sergeant Kenrick for the Victoria Cross.[20] In his correspondence Grey noted that he was aware that Heaphy and Kenrick were not in the British Army and therefore potentially not eligible for the VC. However, the actions he cited occurred when both were under the direct authority and command of British officers. He noted that, if local forces were in fact generally eligible for the VC, he would have nominated three others, including one native soldier.[21] The authorities in London, however, took a strict view of the eligibility criteria. Civilians attached to British forces were now covered, but not locally raised militia, and therefore both nominations were declined. The bureaucrats concerned felt that unlike the British regular forces, the colonial government was in a position to reward its own troops through land grants and promotion.

Heaphy, however, was not happy to let matters reside there and pursued his own case by direct petition to Whitehall, where he had some family connections, supported by Grey, Cameron and Havelock. The contention that greater rewards were available to militia officers was refuted, and Lord Cardwell added his support to Heaphy's case. Official opinion began to swing, and though the process was delayed by a change of government, the concept of extending the VC warrant was approved, but included a provision that such recommendations should come through the regular British officer in command.[22] Heaphy already had such backing from Havelock and Cameron and it had earlier been highlighted that he was exercising command of regular British troops at the time of his act. However, nothing further was heard of Sergeant Kenrick's nomination, which had only ever been raised by Grey. The result was that Heaphy's case was reconsidered and Queen Victoria granted an instrument on 1 January 1867 to allow the Victoria Cross to be conferred on personnel of the local forces of New Zealand, this being notified in the *London Gazette* of 8 January 1867. Heaphy's award had, however, already been published in the *London Gazette* of 1 January, a week earlier, on the very day it was approved by the Queen.

Heaphy's nomination still remains a singular instance, with the result that no other New Zealanders have been awarded the VC for service in New Zealand. The fact that he personally pursued the decoration may seem odd today, but it was entirely in keeping with some of the original thinking surrounding the VC. Prince Albert had originally proposed that individuals might make a case to receive the award,[23] which would then be investigated by superior authority and decided as appropriate, which is relatively close to what occurred in this instance. Although Heaphy was also promoted to major for his actions, he ceased active campaigning in March 1864 and became chief surveyor for New Zealand. He was formally awarded his VC on 11 May 1867. Subsequently he also became a commissioner under the New Zealand Native Reserves Act and a judge of the Native Land Court. In 1881 his health deteriorated and he decided to move to Queensland for the warmer climate there. The change had no effect, and his health continued to decline until he died in Brisbane on 3 August 1881.[24] Charles Heaphy is buried in Brisbane, but his Victoria Cross is on display at the Auckland War Memorial Museum.

THE NEW ZEALAND CROSS

Despite the extension of eligibility for the VC to colonial troops, the New Zealand government faced two issues. First, the award continued to be administered through British channels that were not entirely responsive to an increasingly assertive local administration. Second, the withdrawal of the imperial troops made it increasingly unlikely that a regular British officer would either be present or in command of the colonial troops, consequently making it unlikely that a successful recommendation could even be raised. The New Zealand government, however, recognised the need for an award for military gallantry and therefore decided to institute its own, to rank next to the VC, and this was eventually called the New Zealand Cross (NZC). On 10 March 1869 Governor Bowen signed an Order in Council instituting the award that was available to members of the militia, volunteers and the armed constabulary. Five crosses were promptly awarded, so that effectively the whole process was a *fait accompli* before London was informed. Bowen was admonished for exceeding his authority, but as matters had progressed so far the Queen ratified the order and gave royal assent.[25]

The NZC's relationship to the VC was emphasised by its similarity in appearance to that decoration. It is a silver and gold cross paty surmounted by a Royal Crown. In each arm of the cross is a star, representing the Southern Cross. Surrounding the centre is a circular laurel wreath, inside which are the words 'New Zealand'. The cross was suspended from a crimson ribbon by a bar with a V link, again very similar to that of the VC. Only 23 of these crosses were awarded for military service and it is consequently one of the rarest military gallantry decorations ever awarded.[26]

Three of the recipients of the NZC have been mentioned, the actions for which they were recognised having occurred during the Taranaki and Waikato conflicts already described. These were Lieutenant Colonel McDonnell, Captain Mace and Trooper Rodrigues. From 1866 onwards the size of operations became smaller, but they continued across the central North Island for another five years, during which time a further 20 men were to win the NZC. Until 1868 activity was predominantly concerned with the suppression of the Hauhau, followed until 1872 by the pursuit of Te Kooti. The general thrust of the actions, and the context within which the NZCs were won, now follows.

The year 1866 commenced with the new British commander, General Sir Trevor Chute, marching a force from Wanganui to New Plymouth, this time staying close to the base of Mount Taranaki in order to stop the dissidents finding refuge in the bush. After a month's hard march they reached their destination. During the march, on 6 January, Sergeant Samuel Austin of the Wanganui Native Contingent rescued a wounded officer under fire at Putahi pa for which he was awarded the NZC (in addition, Austin later saved a man from being tomahawked, an action that formed another element of his NZC citation).Then, on 14 January, a significant fight occurred at Otapawa pa, which was stormed by the British 14th and 57th Regiments, supported by a Maori contingent. For leading a group of Maori in storming one of the strongholds, Dr Isaac Featherston was later recommended for the NZC.

Following a minor engagement near Cape Egmont, an advanced party found and captured Te Ua near Opunake on 2 February. Chute left the region shortly after, and command on the west coast fell to McDonnell. By September, Hauhau parties were again raiding and ambushing in the region around Waihi (the present-day Normanby). Ensign Henry Northcroft of the Patea Rangers attracted some attention in September when he posed as a surveyor in order to bait the warriors into a trap. When McDonnell moved to attack the Ngati Ruahine at Pungarehu in October, Northcroft was recommended for the NZC for rescuing a wounded man. The award was not made, however, until June 1910 — the last time this decoration was conferred.[27]

Meanwhile, internal fighting erupted on the east coast within several tribes divided by the Hauhau cult. At Napier, Lieutenant Colonel George Whitmore, a retired imperial officer, took command and was greatly assisted by loyalist Ngati Porou under Rapata. They dealt with a Hauhau pa at Omarunui in October 1866. Then in early 1867 operations in the Tauranga bush against the Pirirakau were required and these were supported by the 12th Regiment — the last direct action by imperial troops in the New Zealand Wars. The Pirirakau were increasingly bottled between government forces in the southeast and friendly Arawa under the Mair brothers, William and Gilbert, from the northwest. The only NZC awarded for operations that year, however, went to Cornet Henry Wrigg of the Bay of Plenty Cavalry, for carrying despatches between Opotiki and Tauranga. This was a controversial award, as Wrigg effectively campaigned and engineered the award for himself, until it was finally conferred on 26 February 1898, some 30 years after the event.[28]

By the end of 1867 the British regiments had nearly all departed, but the fighting continued. By then Te Ua's place at the head of the Hauhau had been assumed by Titokowaru on the basis of his chiefly status. In an attempt to impose some order on the defence needs and provide reliable forces for offensive operations, the government enacted a bill to establish the Armed Constabulary. Von Tempsky, the McDonnells and the Mairs were all early members and assumed key leadership positions, while volunteers came from existing units of the militia along with an increasing number of Maori, particularly Rapata's faction of the Ngati Porou, as well as Wanganui and Arawa men. Fortunately this coincided with a brief lull in operational tempo, which lasted until July 1868. Then almost simultaneously Titokowaru attacked Turuturumokai in Taranaki and Te Kooti arrived in the Poverty Bay region, having escaped from the Chatham Islands with the Hauhau survivors imprisoned there.

Turuturumokai was successfully defended, at a cost, and McDonnell then set out to attack Titokowaru at Te Ngutu-o-te-manu on 21 August, with a newly recruited and barely trained constabulary force.[29] Little was actually achieved, but after reinforcement in September by a native contingent of Wanganui tribesmen under Te Keepa Te Rangihiwinui (later to be known as Major Kemp) he attempted to attack the enemy at Ruaruru, by taking a longer route through denser bush. This took much longer than expected and ended at Te Ngutu-o-te-manu, where Titokowaru had now placed his men in ambush. Von Tempsky's and Kemp's troops were heavily engaged and many of the new troops deserted. McDonnell decided to withdraw, with Kemp's natives as rearguard, but as this was being organised von Tempsky was killed and the Hauhau managed to cut off this unit. Inspector John Roberts, the one remaining officer in the unit, then organised the survivors to fight their way out, the first action cited in his nomination for the NZC.

With McDonnell now discredited, overall operational command was given to Whitmore and he faced an increasingly confident Titokowaru, buoyed by his success against the colonial forces. The Hauhau moved once more down the Whanganui River and established a major position at Moturoa, which Whitmore attacked on 7 November 1868. Titokowaru let the assault come close in to the defences before firing, breaking it up and causing heavy casualties. Then the defenders moved into the bush, in order to exploit the confusion and kill more colonials. Only Captain F.Y. Goring and Inspector John Roberts, by leapfrogging their commands rearwards through each other in a delaying rearguard action, prevented things from being worse. As well as Roberts, the other recipients of NZCs for action on this day were Major Keepa Te Rangihiwinui and Constable Henare Te Ahururu. Ahururu had managed to enter the enemy pa from a flank, but it was too late to make an impact and later, though badly wounded, withdrew with his fellows. Te Keepa's citation was for guarding the flanks of the rearguard and bringing out his command.[30] Following up his success, Titokowaru built a new pa at Tauranga-ika, and in December during a mounted reconnaissance, Trooper William Lingard of the Kai-Iwi Cavalry won the NZC. He rescued a comrade whose horse had been shot, by riding forward and taking a remount from the defending Maori's horselines and then assisting his friend to escape.

However, by then Te Kooti and his followers had become the key focus of the colonial forces. Te Kooti had first landed back in the Bay of Plenty in July 1868, but had been pursued quite vigorously. After a series of indecisive fights, in which he had been wounded, he and his followers had managed to escape into the Ureweras. From there they raided and on 9 November they attacked Matawhero, killing over 70 settlers and local Maori, thus forcing the shift in government attention. However, despite the success of his lightning raids, Te Kooti decided to concentrate his followers and built a pa at Ngatapa. It was a strong position and the attackers were too thinly spread to surround it properly. In consequence those sections of cliff and bush considered impassable in either direction were only thinly guarded by the British.

A deliberate siege was then laid in December 1868 and saps were driven up to the defences, while the position was bombarded by Coehorn mortars.[31] When the saps got close, the defenders attacked them. While successfully driving off one such attack in January, Constables Benjamin Biddle and Solomon Black won the

NZC. Major Rapata, leading his Ngati Porou, also won the award for actions both early in the siege and later during the culminating stages. Sub-Inspector George Preece received the award while acting as an interpreter for Rapata's contingent. Finding himself trapped, Te Kooti managed to escape down a cliff face and through one of those sections lightly guarded by the encircling force. Many of his followers were rapidly hunted down and killed in the bush by Rapata and his men, but Te Kooti himself evaded his pursuers.

Thus freed of one threat, the colonial forces returned to Wanganui and moved against Tauranga-ika. However, Titokowaru had lost the faith of the other rebel chiefs when it was discovered he was having a relationship with another man's wife.[32] Tauranga-ika was abandoned and the withdrawing rebels were pursued back into Taranaki, during which time Sergeant Christopher Maling won the NZC for discovering an ambush before it was sprung. Constantly pursued, Titokowaru was nearly caught at Otautu on 13 March 1869 when Sergeant Richard Shepherd, working under Major Kemp, discovered their position. The Hauhau again escaped after inflicting casualties, including Shepherd, some of whom were treated under fire by Assistant Surgeon Samuel Walker. Both men received the NZC. A bounty system was then instituted for rebels, which proved a significant incentive for Major Kemp's men and greatly weakened the rebels. With Titokowaru having lost his influence, the Hauhau movement in Taranaki petered out.

The time spent in dealing with Titokowaru had again provided enough respite for Te Kooti to recover from his wounds and reassert some influence on the east coast. He commenced raiding settlements and pro-government tribes in the Bay of Plenty, before sacking the settlement at Whakatane. He then drove into Hawke's Bay, massacring the settlers at Mohaka and the occupants of the pa at Te Huke. A second pa at Hiruharama just managed to hold off the rebels, until a relief force arrived. During fierce fighting on 10 April Constable George Hill managed to lead a small party to the pa and assist its defence, which then held until a larger relieving force arrived and forced Te Kooti to move away. Hill was awarded the NZC for his actions.

Whitmore then concentrated his forces again at Tauranga, including allied Maori under Rapata, as well as a big contingent of Arawa. Three columns then drove inland through the Ureweras to search out the rebels, with their objective being Ruatahuna. This was achieved, but there was little fighting, with only women and children captured, before the force had to withdraw in order to resupply. Private Thomas Adams of the Corps of Guides was awarded the NZC for his part in an ambush at Ahikereru on 7 May 1869, however.

The next operational plan was to make for Taupo, and to prepare for this Lieutenant Colonel St John took a small cavalry escort to reconnoitre the route through the Rangipo Desert. However, riders carrying despatches forward were ambushed and killed, resulting in a follow-up attack on the advance element at Opepe. Nine men were killed there and one of the escapers, a wounded Cornet Angus Smith, was subsequently captured and tied to a tree. Escaping four days later, Smith managed literally to crawl to Fort Galatea. His was the last NZC awarded in 1869. Efforts to make a route to Taupo also foundered and the whole force eventually withdrew to Tauranga.

The colonial forces then began building redoubts, in order to restrict Te Kooti's freedom of movement. A pa in the Tongariro foothills, at Te Porere, was destroyed by McDonnell in October, causing heavy casualties, and Te Kooti was again wounded. Having already decided not to support him, Rewi Maniapoto and the Kingite chiefs now undertook to deny Te Kooti access to the Waikato and King Country. He was therefore forced to move into the upper Whanganui, where his raiding for supplies simply ensured that Kemp and his forces had ample motivation once again to mobilise. Despite now being encircled, Te Kooti still managed to slip the government forces and disappear.

Trying to avoid his pursuers, Te Kooti manoeuvred around Lake Taupo and then moved back via Rotorua into the Ureweras. McDonnell's force caught him at Patatere but the action was indecisive. Continuing across country Te Kooti planned to attack Rotorua on 7 February 1870, but was thwarted when the settlement was warned. Captain Gilbert Mair bluffed him as to the real strength of the defenders, by having old men, women and children carry weapons. When Te Kooti bypassed the settlement, Mair took such men as he had in pursuit and harried their rearguard, inflicting significant loss. Despite gallant service by all of the brothers, Gilbert was thus the only Mair to win the NZC. At the same time Sergeant Arthur Carkeek undertook the last act for which the NZC was awarded, when he carried news of the fight from Mair at Ohinemutu, through enemy country, to McDonnell's column.

Already wearied by the constant fighting, Te Kooti found his followers either deserting or being killed by the pursuing columns over the next two years. These columns were now composed of either pro-government Maori or seasoned European bush veterans who were led by men such as Majors Kemp, Rapata and Preece as well as the Mair brothers. Consequently the bush no longer provided his followers a safe refuge or operational base. Te Kooti himself continued to evade capture. However, after his supporters were no longer a threat he was given sanctuary in the King Country, and was eventually pardoned by the government years later. In this way the New Zealand Wars ended, quietly, in 1872.

In the 16 years since the inception of the Victoria Cross in 1856, conflict in New Zealand had been a permanent feature. In all, 15 men, including Major Heaphy of the Auckland Militia, won the decoration for service in New Zealand. Twenty-three others won the NZC after the withdrawal of British forces. While Heaphy is the first New Zealander to win a VC, Sergeant Kenrick was the first to be recommended, but not to receive it. This only serves to emphasise the part that luck and circumstance play in such matters. Not only must a gallant act be undertaken, but it must be seen to be done and appreciated for what it is by the observing party. It is then essential that the observing party has sufficient influence, or be able to convince someone who does, that a recommendation for an award should be made. Heaphy's eventual award of the VC must therefore be balanced against Kenrick and the three unnamed individuals that Grey thought should be considered, and the countless others whose acts were altogether unknown or who died whilst undertaking them.

It is also noteworthy that of the 15 Victoria Cross winners, ten of the acts for which recipients were cited, including Heaphy, involved giving aid to, or rescuing, wounded comrades. Only five VC awards, including the first to Leading Seaman Odgers, involved acts of offensive or defensive heroism, physically directed against the enemy.[33] This reflected the assumption, often supported by actual events, that a wounded man left in proximity to the supposedly savage enemy would in fact be killed. It was therefore considered both brave and virtuous to risk one's own life, and take responsibility for the safety of another, where capture or wounding also meant near-certain death for the rescuer. This initial trend would be reflected in the remainder of the VCs to be awarded to New Zealanders in the nineteenth century, but after this all subsequent acts of gallantry in the presence of the enemy were to occur in battles and conflicts fought overseas. The NZC has never been awarded as a military decoration other than for the New Zealand Wars and consequently is one of the rarest of gallantry decorations.

New Zealand reinstituted the award in 1999 as the country's highest award for civilian or non-combat bravery.[34]

CHAPTER 3 In Africa

The British Empire in the latter part of the nineteenth century must be viewed as a collective whole. It was not a confederation of independent nations, like the Commonwealth is now. Most countries in it were ruled directly from England, and only Canada, New Zealand, the Australian colonies and the South African dominions were accorded a measure of independence. Within this empire, the white populations predominantly regarded themselves as British, rather than identifying with the country in which they might happen to be resident, even if they were born there. As a result of this attitude, there was a considerable amount of formal and informal mobility. The formal movements were caused by the postings of colonial administrators and service personnel. The informal mobility was the result of these British people moving across the empire in search of new opportunities, either through missionary zeal, to obtain land, or simply following the series of gold rushes that occurred in this period.

Wherever they went, the British immigrants created pressure, because they felt an innate sense of superiority and rightness. Put simply, they imposed themselves, their religion and their attitudes anywhere and on anyone they could. This resulted in a continued expansion of the empire, particularly in Africa, which had remained largely unexploited in a colonial sense up to this point. Conflict with other European colonial powers was carefully avoided, albeit narrowly on occasion, but there was considerable fighting with local populations somewhat less convinced of the benefits of British rule. Consequently the young men of the empire felt no compunction at all in taking up arms in any of Britain's disputes, wherever they occurred. If they were already in location, then it was already their fight; if asked to volunteer for service overseas, then this was viewed as a duty to a wider imperial entity and fraternity to which they already belonged, rather than from any specifically localised or national perspective.

When the British initially moved into the tip of southern Africa, they were not the first Europeans to do so. In the wave of Dutch exploration and colonisation in the previous century, Calvinist Huguenots had immigrated there from what we would now regard as northern France, Belgium and Holland, in order to escape the Catholic French and Spanish regimes that were persecuting them.[1] Having already escaped rule by foreign powers and established a strong sense of independence, these Afrikaners, or Boers, at first reacted to the British annexation of the Cape Colony by moving away.

In this movement, known as the Great Trek, they were lucky because a significant upheaval of the indigenous African tribes had already occurred, both during and following the establishment of the Zulu kingdom under the warrior king Shaka. This had resulted in a significantly smaller black African population and the removal of many tribes that might have previously contested their movement or settlement. When the Trek and the Zulu nation did collide, at the Battle of the Blood River on 12 December 1838, the Boers defended themselves and then moved inland away from the coast, subsequently settling the regions that became the Orange Free State and the Transvaal. The Zulus were left in effective control of the region in between Natal and Mozambique.

At first, given comparatively large spaces and small populations of British settlers, the three parties coexisted, albeit uncomfortably. The Cape Colony was the British focus because of its strategic location on the routes to India and the Pacific. Consequently the British allowed the Orange Free State (1854) and Transvaal (1856) to assert their independence. Over the 75 years until 1878 the Cape tribes, mostly the Xosa, conducted various insurrections which were dealt with by the garrison or local militias. The new Boer republics, however, were expansionist and this created conflict with the Zulus, who blocked any attempted move east towards the sea, and also with the tribesmen in Basutoland. There were also civil wars in the Transvaal and Zululand. The Transvaal civil war lasted two years and was resolved in 1864, when Pretorius and Kruger reasserted control. The one in Zululand in 1856 settled the succession, when Cetewayo killed his brother at the Battle of the Tugela River, so that he subsequently obtained the throne in 1872.

In 1867 the catalyst for further conflict occurred when diamonds were discovered along the Orange River. Prospectors, predominantly British, moved north to exploit the find, but soon complained that they were not being fairly treated by the Boers. In 1871 Britain re-annexed the Hopetown region of the Orange Free State and also Basutoland, in the latter case to prevent further Boer expansion. Various prominent British settlers, notably Cecil Rhodes, then commenced advocating a federation of all South Africa, which resulted in Britain re-annexing the Transvaal in 1877. The Boers were naturally incensed and started to contemplate rebellion. However, Cetawayo had been consolidating Zulu military strength since his accession and he was no more accommodating to British expansionism than he had been to that of the Boers. Before the Boers made any overt move against the British, the British gave Cetawayo an ultimatum in December 1878, demanding to establish a protectorate over the Zulu kingdom. Cetawayo ignored the demand and mobilised his warrior regiments, known as impis.

THE ZULU WAR AND HENRY D'ARCY

On 11 January 1879, General Lord Chelmsford advanced into Zululand to enforce the British ultimatum. With him went a force of 5000 British and 8200 native personnel. The British forces comprised a core of regular army units along with many local volunteer and militia units, either raised or mobilised for the campaign, and also contingents of native troops. One of the European volunteer mounted units was the Cape Frontier Light Horse, commanded by the British officer Major Redvers Buller and including Lieutenant Henry Cecil Dudgeon D'Arcy. Chelmsford advanced his force in three widely dispersed columns, in order to achieve speed and to give himself the maximum chance of catching the Zulus. He needn't have worried.

The Zulus could muster 40,000 warriors, in disciplined impis, hardened to rapid movement and merciless fighting and they were not trying to avoid the British.

Chelmsford travelled with the central column, based on the 24th Infantry Regiment and European cavalry units totalling 1800 men, along with 1000 native levies. Having established a staging and resupply post at Rourke's Drift, garrisoned by a company of the 24th, the column advanced a further 11 miles and camped beneath the tall hill at Isandlwhana. Chelmsford and the cavalry then left the remainder of the 24th along with the natives and went to intercept a small Zulu force. However, a more significant force, of around 10,000 Zulus, surprised the camp on the morning of 22 January.

Normally, a regiment of disciplined troops, fighting in the open, would have stood some chance against a tribal force. The Zulu had some firearms, but were predominantly equipped with a short stabbing spear (assegai) and a cowhide shield. At close quarters, the Zulus were practised and deadly. They were disciplined and had an established tactic, described as the head of the bull. While the enemy was engaged frontally by the head, the horns of the bull swept around the sides and engulfed their enemy's flanks. However, volley fire from an organised defender securing their own flanks in a square or like formation had beaten similar enemies before, and the British were now equipped with the Martini Henry breech-loading rifle. Although this weapon was single shot, it was significantly quicker to operate and had greater range than the muzzle-loading weapons which preceded it in British service, and for close fighting it was equipped with a socket bayonet. Unfortunately for the British, their downfall at Isandlwhana was to be caused by surprise and logistics.

In the first place, the defence was not properly organised. The first Zulus sighted were assumed to be the ones being pursued by Chelmsford, so a small force was sent to deal with them and little was done in the main encampment. Then, when the extent of the Zulu force and their intentions were appreciated, it was effectively too late to completely organise a cohesive defence that included the native troops. Many of the latter, not being properly led or organised, panicked and ran, creating further confusion. The remaining defenders kept up a heavy fire and might have managed to hold their position, but they could not get ammunition quickly enough. The Martini Henry rounds were packed in heavy wooden boxes with lids that were screwed down. Legend has it that only a few boxes were opened before the battle started, and once under way there were not enough screwdrivers to open more boxes and supply the demand for ammunition. Consequently the Zulu impis managed to get to close quarters, where the assegai was a more effective weapon than the bayonet.

Some 850 British and 700 native volunteers were killed at Isandlwhana, while only 55 Europeans escaped. The adjutant of the 24th, Lieutenant Teignmouth Melvill, along with Lieutenant Nevill Coghill did manage to get away from the massacre, in an effort to carry the regimental colours to safety. Both, however, were run down by pursuing warriors. For their bravery it was gazetted that they would have been awarded the Victoria Cross, had they survived.[2] In 1907, King Edward VII granted a petition from Melvill's wife and the VC was awarded to these two officers, from which point the award was effectively universally available posthumously. As mentioned previously, Melvill's second son, Charles, joined the New Zealand Army in 1911 and died in 1925 as a major general while holding the post of chief of general staff.

At the same time as the massacre at Isandlwhana was occurring, another impi had moved to Rourke's Drift. Here the garrison used the time they had available to establish sound all-round defences based on the buildings and supplies they had there. The native element here also deserted at the sight of the impending attack, but the remaining soldiers were predominantly disciplined regulars under the leadership of Lieutenants John Chard and Gonville Bromhead. In addition, the officer in charge of supply, Commissary James Dalton, was a pragmatic and experienced soldier who opened ample ammunition boxes and then personally ensured the men on the firing line were kept well resupplied throughout. Consequently the garrison managed to fight off six attacks, with similar odds to those at Isandlwhana, at a cost of only 17 killed. Eleven VCs were awarded to members of the garrison at Rourke's Drift, the highest number ever for a single action fought by the British Army.

Chelmsford's returning mounted elements were consequently able to fall back to Rourke's Drift after they had discovered the massacre at Isandlwhana. Gathering such reinforcements as he could, Chelmsford then had to move to the coast in order to relieve his right-flank column, which had been effectively besieged at Eshowe on 28 January. This relief was not achieved until 4 April.

The left-flank column was under the command of Colonel Sir Evelyn Wood, who had won a VC during the Indian Mutiny.[3] On 28 March Wood had organised a mounted reconnaissance force of some 700 men, including 400 Europeans with the Cape Frontier Light Horse. They were to move on some major Zulu villages near Hlobane Mountain. In the steep terrain at the base of the mountain, this group was ambushed by the Zulu and forced to conduct a confused fighting withdrawal. At one point the Frontier Light Horse was amongst the rearguard where several men were wounded and unhorsed. In all, six separate instances were subsequently brought to the attention of Chelmsford, where officers or men returned to rescue companions from the certain death that would have befallen them had they been caught by their Zulu pursuers. D'Arcy was one of these. Having lost his own horse he had been given a mount to replace it, but shortly afterwards he dismounted and gave this horse to one of his wounded men and attempted to continue his own getaway on foot. He was then rescued himself by Buller, who carried him for some distance. Buller needed to regain what control he could of his force so, when he had his breath back, D'Arcy again dismounted and returned to running from the enemy before finally being taken up and carried back to safety behind another officer.[4]

The six men mentioned to Chelmsford were all recommended for the VC, and five of these, including Buller, were awarded it. D'Arcy was the man who missed out, apparently on the grounds that, as he was not a member of the imperial forces, he was not eligible.[5] The decision that D'Arcy was not eligible must have been a local one, reflecting a lack of awareness of the actual regulations. The Heaphy case had set the precedent so that the warrant for the award of the

VC had been amended in 1867 to allow members of properly raised colonial troops, recommended and commanded by regular officers, to receive the award.[6] Therefore, had the recommendation for D'Arcy been sent to London, given that he was in fact eligible and that his gallantry stemmed from the same action and for similar acts for which other awards were made, then it is probable he would have been similarly recognised. In the event this perceived slight to the volunteers caused a considerable amount of negative comment in the local press,[7] although D'Arcy himself appears to have avoided becoming embroiled in the controversy and his feelings may have been slightly assuaged by his promotion to captain.

Following another battle at Kambula on 29 March, where Wood's column beat off a Zulu force and inflicted severe casualties, the British ceased their advance on this wing as well. Overall, the British campaign thus far was going very poorly and regular army reinforcements were hurried to South Africa. It was also decided that Lord Chelmsford should be replaced and Major General Sir Garnet Wolseley was sent from England to take command. Before he arrived, however, Chelmsford consolidated the forces available to him and launched a second drive into Zululand. This time the advance was more careful, but there was still danger from the watching Zulu warriors, who followed the invasion while avoiding direct confrontation. On 1 June 1879, the day after the advance commenced, a reconnaissance party of cavalry was ambushed and Lieutenant Bonaparte was killed. Louis Napoleon Bonaparte was the great-nephew of Napoleon and the son of Emperor Napoleon III of France, who had been deposed nine years earlier following the French defeat in the Franco-Prussian War. As well as this being significant international news at the time, it was ironic that the Bonaparte dynasty should end when this young man was killed in a British war, effectively fighting for the country that had done so much to bring about his great-uncle's downfall.

Two days later the British column of about 5200, including 1000 natives, was approaching the Zulu royal kraal at Ulundi. This was a Zulu centre of gravity, the core of Zulu political and economic power, and Cetawayo was now forced to confront the invaders rather than having the luxury of choosing his moment. On 3 July 1879 Buller led a strong contingent of mounted troops, including the Frontier Light Horse, on a final scouting patrol before the battle. They spotted a significant herd of goats being tended by young men and decided to bring these in. However, the herdsmen managed to move the quarry away rapidly, which required the cavalry to pursue them for some distance. It was not until almost too late that Buller realised this was in fact a trap. The herdsmen were warriors, not boys, and the horsemen were being drawn into broken ground where very high grass impeded their movement and concealed much. The horsemen had just stopped when it became apparent they had done so only 100 metres from where the ambush was to be sprung. An impi was hiding in the foliage and snares of knotted grass had been woven to bring down the horses.

The Zulus opened fire on the mounted men and several were unhorsed, including Trooper Raubenheim from one of the other contingents. As he had done at Hlobane, D'Arcy immediately went to rescue the trooper. Initially D'Arcy simply planned to have the man mount behind him, which he succeeded in doing, but the horse kicked them off, hurting both. Raubenheim was a large man and in such a state that he could not remount, even with D'Arcy's efforts to assist him. D'Arcy himself had hurt his back in the fall when he landed on his pistol and he aggravated the injury in his attempts to lift Raubenheim onto the barely controlled horse. Not until he was almost completely exhausted and barely able to get on himself did D'Arcy remount and leave the wounded man, only just in time to escape his immediate attackers and fight his way clear.[8] The Zulus tortured Trooper Raubenheim to death, with his cries heard throughout the night by his comrades, confirming the certainty of one's fate if captured.

Captain Lord Beresford of the 9th Lancers had similarly attempted to rescue a fallen sergeant, who was so disoriented he refused help. Sergeant Edmund O'Toole, a friend of D'Arcy from the Frontier Light Horse, then came forward to forcibly assist the man. Together Beresford and O'Toole were able to effect a successful rescue.

D'Arcy was so badly injured that he could not take part in the final battle the next day. When the British confronted the 10,000 warriors, this time they were only outnumbered two to one and they were in the open. The infantry formed into a single square, thus protecting themselves on all flanks, with the cavalry inside. The Zulu impis shattered themselves in useless attacks against disciplined volley fire from the redcoats. When at last the Zulus' own discipline broke, the cavalry rode out from the square and chased down the fleeing tribesmen, effectively ending major Zulu resistance and the war.

D'Arcy was again nominated for the VC and Beresford was also recommended. However, D'Arcy refused to be nominated unless O'Toole was also recognised, so only Beresford's name was forwarded, though this did not become apparent until later. Beresford's award was gazetted on 23 August 1879 and he received his decoration personally from the Queen at Windsor on his return to England. Evidently at that time he intimated personally to the Queen that he preferred not to be decorated unless the man who shared the danger, O'Toole, was also recognised. The *London Gazette* of 9 October 1879 announced the award of the VC to both D'Arcy and O'Toole, thus resolving a number of awkward issues.[9]

Henry Cecil Dudgeon D'Arcy was born at Wanganui in 1850 and consequently, when he received his award from Lord Wolseley in Pretoria on 10 December 1879, he became the first New Zealand-born man to have won a Victoria Cross. His father, then Major Oliver D'Arcy of the 65th Regiment, had been posted in Wanganui as part of the garrison, and Cecil, as he was known, was his fifth son and seventh child. Six years later, the family returned to England and then three years after that moved to South Africa, when Major D'Arcy took an appointment in the 18th Royal Irish Regiment. He subsequently transferred to the Cape Mounted Rifles in 1860 and permanently settled the family in the garrison station, King William's Town.

Though he was born in and grew up on the British Empire's frontiers, Cecil D'Arcy thought of himself as British, or in fact Anglo-Irish, and therefore probably gave his New Zealand connection little thought. His father could not afford to purchase commissions for all his sons and so Cecil initially joined the Cape Colony's public service. However, during the various native risings that preceded the Zulu War, he joined the Cape Frontier Light Horse in 1877, initially as a private, but rising to sergeant before being commissioned. Much like the settlers in New Zealand in their confrontations with the Maori tribesmen, he would have given little thought to, or been troubled by, any of the political or ethical issues concerning either the subjugation of the Boer republics or the Zulu kingdom. Like most of the young colonial men of his time, he simply accepted these developments as the necessary requirements of consolidating the empire, ensuring security and making a future for his family, while also providing the potential for action and adventure.

Unfortunately Cecil D'Arcy's life was short. He was promoted again, to commandant of the Frontier Light Horse, thus succeeding Buller as the commander of this unit. He remained in command of the unit for the pacification of the Zulu after the war, until its disbandment. He subsequently joined the Cape Mounted Rifles as a captain and served through 1880 during the Basuto rising. D'Arcy then resigned his commission 'for private reasons' in April 1881. His health was not good and there was some contention that there had been some internal politicking over the command of the unit at that time. He may also possibly have been considering an offer of a post on Wood's staff when that general returned to South Africa.[10]

The official version of his death is now relatively clear. He had been advised to go to the highlands for his health and was staying with the Reverend Taberer. For some reason he left Taberer's house unannounced during the night of 6–7 August 1881, possibly during a period of delirium. It is known he was run down by his time in the field and it has been speculated that he might also have been affected by malaria or even bilharzia.[11] His remains, identified by his watch and ring, were found sitting upright in a cave in the

Amatola Forest of Cape Province early the next year. He was buried with full military honours in King William's Town.

There are, however, unofficial stories which suggest that D'Arcy actually engineered his disappearance and 'death' and escaped into anonymity. The possible motivations given vary, including a desire to avoid a scandal of some sort, or simply to escape the notoriety of his heroism. Some have it that, after he got away, he moved to Kenya where he settled in the vicinity of Mount Kilimanjaro. Another story is that he was recognised from his photograph by a cricketer playing in Newcastle, Natal, in 1926. Once confronted, the man he believed was D'Arcy pleaded that he 'wanted to remain dead to the world'.[12] Such myths reflect the almost classic desire for heroes to meet an epic end, dying in battle, or at least either to achieve happiness or struggle on. D'Arcy's young death, lacking any point or witnesses, just didn't seem to measure up to what a man of such consistent heroism deserved.

D'Arcy's medal was originally held by his mother and then, after her death in 1886, by his sister, until his nephew and godson, Cecil Armstrong, took it from her. It stayed in the Armstrong family, apparently with the knowledge of the D'Arcys, until Colonel 'Johnny' Armstrong died around 1965. It resurfaced in 1992, when it was reported in the press that it was to be put up for sale at Sotheby's. The vendor turned out to be the Royal Army Pay Corps Regimental Association (RAPCRA), who had inherited the medal from Armstrong. Following negotiations with the D'Arcy family, the medal was not in fact sold and is now held in their possession under a mutual trust with RAPCRA.[13]

THE BOER WARS

The Zulu War only delayed the inevitable. The discovery of diamonds in South Africa had maintained the colony's value, at the same time that the Suez Canal ostensibly made it less strategically important. The first organised Boer resistance occurred in 1880, when the Transvaal Afrikaners, under Kruger, revolted. The British suffered a series of stinging defeats, including Laing's Nek and Majuba Hill, where the imperial regulars were defeated by the long-range rifle fire of the Boer farmers. In 1881, the Boer Republic, with Kruger as president, was granted independence under British sovereignty. This was followed by a period of internal unrest in Zululand, and then the establishment of a German colony in Southwest Africa (modern Namibia) in 1884.

The most crucial event, however, was the discovery of gold in the Witwatersrand in 1886, thus making control of the Transvaal very significant. Cecil Rhodes continued to scheme to bring this area under united control, contending that the Afrikaners were exploiting the large numbers of British prospectors. Eventually, he even went so far as to support a 'raid' by 500 men, led by his friend Dr Leander Jameson, who had entered the Transvaal in 1895 hoping to spark a unilateral uprising. The Boers defeated Jameson's force with relative ease, but this and nearly 20 years of complaint and political manoeuvring led to a complete breakdown in 1899. The British were already gathering a force in Natal when, on 9 October, Kruger presented them with an ultimatum to disband it within 48 hours. When the British refused, war was effectively declared and the Afrikaners of the Orange Free State immediately allied with the Boer Republic.

The war was fought in three phases. In the first phase the Boers had superior numbers, superior mobility and the initiative but lacked the strategic military planning ability to fully exploit their advantages and achieve an outright success. In the second phase the British force numbers matched and then exceeded the Boers, who they were then able to defeat in conventional set-piece battles followed by the rapid seizure of their urban centres. The final phase was where the imperial forces had to utilise their overwhelming numbers to isolate and chase down the remaining Boer commandos, using firm bases and similar mobile tactics to their quarry.[14]

The initial campaigns were thus a disaster for the British. The Boers were able to gather superior forces and besieged a small force at Mafeking within four days, while pushing back the remaining British into Natal. By November these latter troops were themselves caught in Ladysmith, while Free State commandos had pushed another British force into Kimberley. The British commander was the now General Sir Redvers Buller, VC. Having fought in the Zulu War he was familiar with the terrain, climate and people and he was personally very courageous. However, he lacked moral courage and had difficulty making decisions or assigning priorities. By trying to do everything, he kept the British reinforcements dispersed and was unable to wrest the initiative from the Boers or to raise any of the sieges. The British also failed to adapt to the Boer tactics, which involved fast-moving mounted units, called commandos, delaying any British deployments by hit-and-run attacks. When they did concentrate, the Boers occupied high ground in entrenched positions, which the British were forced to assault frontally. In this way the British army was defeated throughout November and December 1899 at the battles of the Modder River, Stormberg, Magersfontein and Colenso. Thus stalled, the British appointed Lord Frederick Roberts, from command in India, to take over from Buller, with Lord Horatio Kitchener as his chief of staff.[15]

Roberts and Kitchener had to deal with the Boers in the field, relieve the besieged garrisons and separate the commandos from their means of support. This would require considerable manpower and increased mobility. There was a reticence to employ Indian troops, or indeed any 'native' force, against the white Boers,[16] so manpower and mounts needed to be found from somewhere. The conflict itself was seen as a 'just war' by the British and coincided with an increasing interest in military matters and defence issues throughout the empire. Large numbers of Yeomanry cavalry units therefore volunteered for service from Britain itself, but the perceptions of imperial interest and solidarity spread further. It coincided with a desire for increased involvement by the dominion and colonial peoples of New Zealand, Canada and Australia, as well as being a way of emphasising the importance of wider imperial security.[17]

Before Roberts' reorganisation could have an impact the British were to suffer more reverses in January and February 1900. Buller was repulsed in further set-piece battles, as he tried to cross the Tugela River, at the battles of Spion Kop and Vall Kranz. Kitchener, temporarily in field command, also attempted a frontal assault on Piet Cronje's forces at Paardeburg and was severely beaten. The only bright spot was the relief of the siege of Kimberley by Brigadier John French's cavalry brigades. Roberts, who had been ill at the time of Paardeburg, then organised his own siege of Cronje's 4000 men, who were rapidly starved into surrender on 27 February. The next day, having finally forced the Tugela at his third attempt, Buller relieved the garrison at Ladysmith.

With these two Boer reverses, Roberts was able to make advances on all fronts, so that Natal was cleared of insurgents and the Orange Free State could be annexed by 24 May. After a siege of seven months, Robert Baden-Powell's force at Mafeking was finally relieved on 17 May. Amongst the subordinate commanders there was Major Alexander Godley, who would later command the New Zealand Expeditionary Force in the First World War. Roberts then employed his ever-growing forces for an invasion of the Transvaal, which was completed by the end of June 1900. On 4 July the two major wings, under Roberts and Buller, met at Vlakfontein. The Transvaal was formally annexed on 4 September 1900 and Roberts believed operations had been sufficiently successful that he returned to England, having served overseas for over 40 years, in order to take over as commander in chief.[18]

Kitchener now assumed command, but it soon became apparent that much remained to be done, as for the next 18 months the Boer commandos waged their highly effective guerilla war. They forced the British to employ vast resources of manpower to protect their own supply lines. Kitchener then attempted to suppress the Boers' own freedom of movement by establishing lines of blockhouses, in conjunction with major sweeps, to drive the commandos onto these fixed positions. However, the Boers mostly avoided being fixed and slipped through the lines. The most effective British means eventually proved to be removing the Boers' sources of resupply, whilst keeping the commandos under constant pressure. Commencing under Roberts, the British rounded up all non-combatant Boer civilians in the area of operations and placed them in concentration camps. Their stock was confiscated and their farms and crops were burned.

The second element was the utilisation of mounted columns and units that remained in the field for prolonged periods, employing the Boers' own tactics of mobility and ambush to maintain constant pressure on the remaining commandos in the field.

These policies were undoubtedly cruel and as many as 28,000 Boer civilians perished in the concentration camps.[19] However, without sources of shelter or resupply, justifiably concerned for the welfare of their families and harried by an increasingly effective force of mounted troops, the Boer resistance eventually collapsed. A peace treaty was signed on 31 May 1902 at Vereeniging.[20] The Boers accepted British sovereignty but received compensation for the destroyed farms and lost livestock. In military terms they had inflicted more casualties on the enemy than they had sustained and, with no more than 83,000 men considered of combat age, had forced the deployment of British and empire troops of up to half a million men.

THE NEW ZEALAND CONTINGENTS

Even before fighting commenced in South Africa, Premier Richard Seddon had sought parliamentary permission in September 1899 to offer a mounted New Zealand contingent to serve there. There was no shortage of volunteers and the First Contingent, comprising 215 men, was drawn from existing volunteer units who were selected, equipped and finally sailed only ten days after the initial British ultimatum was rejected. They arrived in South Africa on 23 November, ahead of any of the troops from the Australian colonies.[21] Following the British requirement for more troops, the Second Contingent was formed by the government in February 1900, while the Third Contingent, which sailed shortly afterwards, was provided through public subscription. The Fourth Contingent, also raised through public subscription and sailing in March 1900, together with the Third, was christened the 'Rough Riders', apparently on the grounds that most of the men did not come from existing volunteer units.[22]

The First New Zealand Contingent was rushed into service with Sir John French's cavalry division in the northern Cape Colony. They fought as mounted infantry, like the Boers. This meant that in action they dismounted, fighting on foot using their rifles.[23] Their horses were only to get them to the fight. A significant disadvantage was that one man in four had to act as horse holder, which cut down their overall firepower. The New Zealanders' first real action was at Jasfontein on 18 December 1899 and here Private George Bradford achieved one of his two unenviable firsts as a member of a New Zealand force at war overseas. He was severely wounded in the fighting and as a result was captured by the Boers, the first New Zealander ever to become a prisoner of war. When he died of wounds ten days later, he was then the first New Zealand battle fatality.[24]

The First, Second and Third Contingents were subsequently grouped together as a regiment under the New Zealander, Lieutenant Colonel Alfred Robin, who had been promoted for this reason. They took part in the advance on Johannesburg and excelled at scouting. However, after six months of operations the force had been reduced to 300 of the 700 who had deployed in June 1900. Nearly half of these men then transferred to the South African police or other higher paid jobs. In July the remaining troops were incorporated into a mobile column to relieve Rustenburg and from September operated in the advance northeast from Pretoria. Commencing in October, men from the First Contingent who wished to return to New Zealand started leaving South Africa and had done so by December. The Second and Third Contingent personnel returned in March 1901 having been replaced by the Sixth Contingent. Before they left, however, they were involved in a costly fight at Rhenoster Kop in the Transvaal on 29 November, with five being killed and 23 wounded. They also took part in a long pursuit of Jacobus de la Rey's column in December, followed by service in the Cape Colony to deal with an incursion by General Christian de Wet's commando in February.

The Fourth and Fifth Contingents were both considerably larger than the first three contingents, together numbering 982 personnel plus 71 reserves. They were landed in Portuguese East Africa in

April and May respectively and were subsequently employed under the Rhodesian Field Force, having been concentrated at Mafeking in August 1900. They saw light skirmishing before their first action at Ottoshoop on 16 August, where they took a hill in a quick bayonet charge and then held the position for two days. These men then spent the remainder of their time in South Africa involved in the guerilla war, chasing the dispersed commandos. The columns worked to clear Boer farms in southwestern Transvaal through November and December, followed by operations in pursuit of de Wet's force. In January 1901 they participated in the capture of de la Rey's wagons and guns and then on 18 January they managed to capture 22 prisoners after a dawn attack on a Boer camp. Ten days later a section from the Fourth Contingent were themselves caught in an ambush at Naauwpoort and it was here that Farrier Sergeant Major James Hardham won the Victoria Cross. Both contingents continued to patrol and trek before being withdrawn into the Cape Colony in May and departing South Africa on 12 June 1901.

The 600-strong Sixth Contingent, formed to replace the Second and Third, arrived in theatre on 13 March 1901. They were employed in the previously unsubdued areas of northern Transvaal, around Pietersburg. They operated under Brigadier General Herbert Plumer in a series of treks and reconnaissances. On 1 June at Paardeplats, a party of 15 men was ambushed, with one officer killed and the remainder captured, but simultaneously the rest of their squadron captured the Boer wagons the ambushers had been trying to protect. After refitting, Plumer's column operated around Paardeburg and by September was in the Orange Free State. On 27 September 1901 a party was escorting a courier to Bastard's Drift, but this turned out to be occupied by the Boers, who opened fire at point-blank range. Corporal Hemphill's horse was shot, leaving the detachment commander stranded, when Trooper Ivanhoe Baigent returned for him. Under heavy fire he took the man up behind on his own horse and rode to safety. Baigent was recommended for the VC but received the Distinguished Conduct Medal.[25] The contingent undertook further treks and had several quite significant fights before leaving South Africa in April 1902.

The Seventh Contingent replaced the Fourth and was also 600 strong. It went into action from May 1901 as part of a column trying to capture the Transvaal government. As such they met stiff resistance and suffered a number of initial reverses, with a couple of parties being forced to surrender. In July they moved to the Orange Free State to help pursue General Jan Smuts' commando, but though they rounded up considerable livestock the Boers eluded them. In August they failed in an attempt to capture a Boer camp, but by breaking off the pursuit also managed to avoid being drawn into a trap de la Rey had set for them. For the next several months they were employed pursuing commandos under General Louis Botha that were raiding into Natal and in February 1902 managed to capture his remaining artillery. They were then employed in the major 'drives' where a continuous line moved across the country to drive the Boers onto the blockhouse lines. This succeeded in boxing up a considerable force as well as the Orange Free State government. In desperation on 24 February, de la Rey mounted a sharp attack on the Hol Spruit, held by the New Zealanders. Twenty-four New Zealanders were killed with 41 wounded in this action, and because there were no reserves available to help them a significant group of Boers managed to escape through the gap this created.[26] However, they had fought hard and three days later the net closed on some 780 remaining Boers and considerable livestock. Subsequent drives, with larger forces, over the next few months were not so successful, but kept the Boers under pressure. The Seventh Contingent ended its service in May 1902.

The Eighth Contingent of 1100 men was to replace both the Sixth and Seventh and had a regiment each from the North and South Islands, with a considerable proportion of their officers having already seen service in the conflict. Arriving in March 1902, they were deployed in northern Natal for the drive into the Orange Free State. During a move by rail to the Transvaal in April, one of the South Islanders' troop trains was hit by a goods train at Machavie and 16 men were killed with another 11 seriously injured. A month later the contingent took part in one last major drive, before the peace concord was signed on 31 May 1902.

The Ninth and Tenth Contingents numbered over 1000 men each. Both arrived in theatre before the peace, but not in time to undertake any significant fighting or patrols. Some men of the Ninth did, however, have a last skirmish after the peace. They encountered a Boer party unaware of the treaty and during a brief fight one officer was killed and another wounded. Both contingents had returned to New Zealand by August 1902.

Though it is now largely overshadowed by Gallipoli, South Africa was in fact New Zealand's baptism by fire as a nation participating in a war overseas. In all, ten New Zealand contingents, totalling 6507 men, along with 8000 horses, had served in South Africa by the conclusion of hostilities. Seventy-one men were killed or died from combat-related injuries, and another 26 died from accidental causes. A larger number, 133, died of disease, such as enteric fever. Others were killed or died after they had transferred to other forces, but most returned to New Zealand, though only one horse was to do so. Many of the men who returned subsequently served in the First New Zealand Expeditionary Force, helping to provide a cadre of experience and example. Several officers, such as Edward Chaytor, Richard Davies and Arthur Bauchop, were to join the regular army and rise to high command in that next war. The two significant awards for bravery won by New Zealanders in the conflict also continued a trend. Like Heaphy and D'Arcy's medals, they were both for saving men's lives under fire.

HENRY DONALD COUTTS AND THE QUEEN'S SCARF

The first of these awards was made to Trooper Henry Donald Coutts, number 96 of the First Contingent. After Lord Roberts' occupation of Bloemfontein on 13 March 1900, the First Squadron of the First Contingent was detached from French's cavalry brigade and joined a column under Brigadier General Broadwood, sent to regain contact with Boer forces. However, this column itself became the pursued and was caught in a carefully executed, mobile ambush by three separate commandos under the coordination of General Christian de Wet. Finding that the Boer forces he had located actually outnumbered him, Broadwood fell back quickly to Sanna's Post. This was near the location of the Bloemfontein waterworks, 20 miles east of the city in a valley on the Modder River. The road back to town forded both the Modder and two miles later its tributary, the Korn Spruit.

Broadwood had some 1700 men, including 300 mounted troops and two batteries of horse artillery. There was also a small garrison at Sanna's Post. However, the column had collected a significant column of refugees in addition to their own supply wagons. They had arrived at the post late on 30 March and, assuming the local garrison had adequate security so close to Roberts' force, took no additional precautions and sent out no patrols. Early next morning they woke to find the Boers had brought artillery, which outranged their own, up onto the surrounding hills. Using his infantry to guard the rear, Broadwood decided to move his wagons and artillery west towards the city in order to avoid being caught on the wrong side of the fords. However, de Wet had anticipated this and manoeuvred another commando down to cover the Korn Spruit.[27]

The ambushers waited until the slow wagons and artillery were straggling on either side of the ford, individually capturing wagons as they got across until one man alerted the column with a shot. In the confusion that followed the British lost seven guns and had 200 men captured as well as receiving significant casualties. Four men from Q Battery, Royal Horse Artillery, won the VC by ballot for their actions in first fighting and then withdrawing their guns in the face of the enemy. In addition, Trooper Coutts of the New Zealand Mounted Rifles was mentioned in despatches. Having seen a member of the Burma Mounted Rifles wounded and fall from his horse, Coutts had gone to the man under fire and carried him to safety.

Instead of any medallic recognition for this act, however, Coutts was one of eight men to receive a singular mark of recognition from their sovereign. The following notice from Field Marshall Lord Roberts appeared in the *London Gazette* of 17 June 1902:

I desire to place on record that in April 1900, Her Late Majesty Queen Victoria was graciously pleased to send me four woolen scarves, worked by Herself, for distribution to the four most distinguished private soldiers in the colonial forces of Canada, Australia, New Zealand and South Africa, then serving under my command.

The selection of these gifts of honour was made by the officers commanding the contingents concerned, it being understood that gallant conduct in the field was to be considered the primary qualification.

Trooper Coutts had been presented his scarf already by General Pilcher at Pretoria in September 1900.

Henry Coutts was born at Kaiapoi on 14 November 1866 and was farming near Hawera when he enlisted in the First Contingent in October 1899, having previously served in the militia. He returned to New Zealand as a corporal in January 1901, but promptly volunteered for the Seventh Contingent two months later. This time, however, he was commissioned as captain and quartermaster and he retained that job when he prolonged his service with the Ninth Contingent. Coutts finally returned to New Zealand in May 1902, but continued serving in the volunteer militia until 1910. On 2 August 1916 Henry Coutts enlisted as a private in the Auckland Infantry Regiment, having falsified his age. He sailed with the 19th Reinforcements and though there is a record of him being promoted as far as acting sergeant, he did not see active service in France and was discharged on medical grounds in April 1918.[28] He died at Wellington on 30 April 1944.

Contemporary papers describe the scarves as being the equivalent of, or next to, the VC.[29] Some subsequent correspondence asserts that the condition of award was that the recipient had to have first been recommended for the VC,[30] but nothing official was ever published to that effect. Another stillborn idea was that the recipients would be recognised with the post-nominal QS.[31] Given that the conditions for presentation specified only private soldiers then under Lord Roberts' command, with one from each colonial contingent (in addition to four given to British servicemen), it could not be guaranteed that the acts were of a consistent standard to merit the VC. However, the scarves remain some of the rarest gallantry awards ever presented to Commonwealth forces and are of national significance.

Following the death of both his wife and son, Coutts donated his scarf to the government in 1913.[32] An indication of its importance is that it was displayed for years in the Parliamentary Library and is now in the Queen Elizabeth II Army Memorial Museum at Waiouru. The Canadian and Australian scarves are each similarly preserved in their national war, or army, museums.[33]

WILLIAM JAMES HARDHAM

More importantly — in terms of this study — was the award of the Victoria Cross to Farrier Sergeant Major William James Hardham of the Fourth Contingent. As mentioned earlier, it was on 28 January 1901 that a section of the New Zealanders from the Fourth were ambushed by 20 Boers near Naauwpoort. They received no casualties in the initial exchange and were managing to extricate themselves successfully until Trooper John McCrae's horse was killed and he was wounded. Seeing this, Hardham returned under heavy fire and dismounted to help McCrae. Hardham lifted McCrae onto his own horse and then ran alongside it to bring the wounded man to safety.

Lord Kitchener forwarded a recommendation for Hardham to receive the Victoria Cross, and this was eventually notified in the *London Gazette* on 4 October 1901. It appears that the field commander, General Sir Ian Hamilton, in fact felt Hardham's actions deserved the Distinguished Conduct Medal, but Kitchener upgraded the citation, along with a couple of others. Lord Roberts, now the commander in chief in London, was to decide the matter. He wrote:

I would give the VC as recommended by Lord Kitchener. He is not likely to do this unless he is satisfied that it was deserved.

Moreover it seems to me desirable to show the Colonials that we appreciate their gallantry and their coming forward to help us. We may require them to do so again perhaps ere long.[34]

William Hardham therefore became the first New Zealand serviceman, serving in a nationally raised New Zealand force in combat overseas, to win the Victoria Cross. Lord Roberts' comments were not the only interesting element in his award. Hardham's VC was presented to him on 1 July 1901 by the Prince of Wales, who was visiting South Africa. The presentation preceded its publication in the *London Gazette* and the medal he was given was not engraved. No record exists of his VC ever being processed through official channels to be engraved, but it has been done and an engraved duplicate that was sent to the governor in New Zealand was returned in October 1902.[35] It is probable that Hardham himself had the work completed by Hancocks while he was in London with the Coronation Contingent in 1902.

William James Hardham was a larger-than-life character in many ways. He was born in Wellington on 31 July 1876 and after attending Mount Cook School he trained as a blacksmith. As a young man he had two keen interests, one being the military and the other rugby. As a rugby player he was successful at club and provincial levels, representing Wellington 53 times between 1897 and 1910. Hardham joined the Petone Company of the Naval Artillery in 1894 and served with that unit, through various designation changes until the outbreak of the First World War, with the exception of his periods of permanent duty in South Africa and with the Coronation Contingent. He joined the Fourth Contingent (Rough Riders) on 24 March 1900 and on his discharge on 11 August 1901 reverted to leading gunner in his old unit. He then offered to join the Ninth Contingent and was recommended for and received a commission as a lieutenant on 20 February 1902. However, he did not see any service in South Africa on this occasion as it was from there that he joined the Coronation Contingent. He then returned to civilian life and to the artillery at Petone, where by 1910 he was a sergeant and had been awarded the Long and Efficient Service Medal for 16 years' service.

At the outbreak of the First World War, Hardham sought and received a captaincy as second in command of Queen Alexandra's Squadron, Wellington Mounted Rifles. He sailed with them to Egypt on 16 October 1914 and landed with them at Gallipoli. On the peninsula he was badly wounded in the chest and hand on 2 June 1915. His wounds were serious enough that he required significant treatment and he was returned to New Zealand in February 1916.

Considering his wounds and his age, let alone his proven gallantry, many men might have accepted they had done their bit. However, during his two years back in New Zealand, Hardham waged a continuous campaign to return to the front. Though it had been intended to discharge him altogether after his convalescence leave, in June 1916 he had been given temporary employment as commander of Queen Mary Hospital at Hanmer Springs. Lieutenant Colonel Loach, the doctor in charge, was not efficient and both the district commander and the minister of defence wanted a replacement. Hardham did such a good job that they offered him the permanent post and promoted him to temporary major. He had married his fiancée, Constance, in March 1916, but still wished to return to his unit. After 15 months commanding Queen Mary Hospital, he was finally given a medical board and declared fit. Therefore, nearly two years after his evacuation from Gallipoli, he rejoined his regiment in Palestine as a major. However, unlike in all his previous periods of active service, his health was not robust and he was often sick. No doubt he was affected by the severe climate, but his wounds were probably also more debilitating than he would admit.

In 1919, following his final return to New Zealand, Hardham applied for a permanent commission in the army, but he was rejected because of his health. He was formally discharged from the New Zealand Expeditionary Force in March 1920 and eventually was placed on the Retired List of Officers in June 1927, after 32 years' service. Unfortunately William Hardham never recovered his health and he died a year later of stomach cancer, on

14 April 1928. William Hardham was accorded a funeral with full military honours and is buried at the Karori Soldiers' Cemetery, Wellington.[36] His medals are on display at the Queen Elizabeth II Army Memorial Museum in Waiouru.

Lord Roberts' words of 1900 regarding the possible need for further military assistance from the imperial colonies were indeed prophetic, as the subsequent careers of both Coutts and Hardham were to show. The next conflict would see many more New Zealanders awarded the VC, not only in the New Zealand Expeditionary Force, but also with the Australian and British forces. Among those who were to be recognised within the British forces were a sailor, for fighting submarines, and also the first airman to receive the award. The interesting departure from the trend of the previous century was that the vast majority of these men were to win their awards for their aggressive combat action against the enemy, where their three predecessors who had won the VC, as well as Trooper Coutts, had all been recognised for attempting to save the lives of their fellow soldiers. This reflected the nature of total war in a mechanised age.

CHAPTER 4 The First World War: problems and issues

From a population of just over one million people, more than 100,000 New Zealand men embarked for overseas service during 1914–18. This is a staggering figure, one that provided the first real opportunity for a large number of New Zealanders to win the highest of military honours — the Victoria Cross. Unfortunately though, primarily for reasons of personality, it was an opportunity that was only partially fulfilled and New Zealand's record of granting the VC during this conflict reveals a pattern of stinginess, neglect and ignorance. As Chris Pugsley has written of the lack of awards made to New Zealand soldiers during this conflict: 'What stands out about New Zealand awards for gallantry in World War I is how few we got.'[1] The reasons for this paucity are explored later in this chapter.

Of all the VCs awarded to date, almost half of these, some 663, were for actions during the First World War, with 187 being posthumous awards. The total figures and those for Australia and New Zealand VCs appear in the table below:

VICTORIA CROSS NUMBERS IN THE FIRST WORLD WAR

Totals of all VC awards		
Country	Awarded to living recipient	Awarded posthumously	Total awarded
New Zealand	8	3	11
Australia	50	16	66
All countries	446	187	663

With only 11 VCs awarded to New Zealand soldiers from a total of 98,950 soldiers who actually 'took to the field', little wonder that the VC winners were regarded with considerable awe in New Zealand. A VC winner was indeed a rarity. The comparison with Australia is revealing. With the number of Australian soldiers who saw military action given as 331,781[2], if all things were equal, the Australian number of VCs awarded should have been just over three times that of the New Zealand figure. It was in fact six times higher. To express this another way: one VC was awarded for every 8995 New Zealand soldiers serving in the field while the Australian figure is one VC for every 5027 soldiers. This is a significant difference. The Canadian figures, while not as pronounced as the Australian ones, confirm that New Zealand soldiers were hard done by with regards to the VC. Canadian soldiers won 69 VCs during the war, 26 of which were awarded posthumously. With the number of Canadian soldiers who actually took to the field given as 422,405, the Canadian ratio for this award is one per 6122 soldiers, still a significantly higher proportion than the New Zealand figure.

THE NEW ZEALAND AWARDS IN THE FIRST WORLD WAR

The pattern of the New Zealand awards is also unusual. New Zealand winners of the VC and the date of the action that led to the award are listed below:

Date of action	Recipient	Place
August 1915	Cyril Bassett	Chunuk Bair, Gallipoli
September 1916	Donald Brown	High Wood, the Somme, France
June 1917	Samuel Frickleton	Messines, Belgium
31 July 1917	Leslie Andrew	La Basse Ville, Belgium
3 December 1917	Henry Nicholas	Polderhoek, Belgium
24 July 1918	Richard Travis	Hebuterne, France
24 August 1918	Samuel Forsyth	Grevillers, France
26 August 1918	Reginald Judson	Bapaume, France

1 September 1918	John Grant	Bancourt, France
12 September 1918	Henry Laurent	Gouzeaucourt Wood, France
30 September 1918	James Crichton	Crevecouer, France

There are some remarkable features about the timings of these awards. Only one VC was won in 1915 and another in 1916. Yet these were the years in which New Zealand soldiers established a formidable reputation during some difficult and bloody campaigning. The period includes the nine months of protracted warfare on the Gallipoli peninsula and the New Zealand Division's first major engagement on the Western Front — on the Somme in September 1916. While three awards were made in 1917, the worst year of the war for the Allies and the New Zealand Division, they were all for separate military actions. The most surprising revelation of this data is that over half of the VCs won by New Zealand in the First World War were for actions in the last five months of the war. This is also worthy of investigation as it is strongly related to the paucity of awards made to New Zealand soldiers in the course of the war.

GENERAL GODLEY'S INFLUENCE

In order to be successful, a recommendation for the VC or any other bravery award for a New Zealander fighting on the Western Front had to have the endorsement of two senior officers. They were Major General Sir Andrew Russell, the New Zealand divisional commander, and Lieutenant General Sir Alexander Godley, the commander of the New Zealand Expeditionary Force (NZEF). For different reasons both men had firm views on bravery awards and they did not rate the VC that highly.

General Sir Alexander Godley was a British regular officer who had been seconded to New Zealand prior to the war to organise New Zealand's defence force following the review undertaken by Lord Kitchener in 1910. It was Godley who commanded the New Zealanders on Gallipoli during their time there and, upon the formation of a New Zealand Division, retained command of the NZEF for the duration of the war. While he was an efficient administrator and trainer, Godley was not a success as a battlefield commander, and the New Zealand troops came to loathe him. From an impoverished background, Godley was acutely aware of how tenuous his hold on his exalted position was. He was therefore very concerned with ingratiating himself with the powerful, to cultivate useful social links and to cement himself firmly into his current position. With this in mind, Godley had little time for bravery decorations like the VC, nor did he have any incentive to ensure that New Zealand received its fair share of awards. In his voluminous correspondence to those in positions of influence, the VC was scarcely mentioned. What were mentioned on many occasions are the awards that really mattered to Godley: the 'K' awards, as they were known, that conferred a knighthood on the recipient. These included: the Order of the Bath Knight Commander (KCB), the Order of the Bath Companion (CB) and the Order of St Michael and St George Knight Commander (KCMG). Godley's correspondence is full of references to these awards (including his own KCB for his services on Gallipoli).

Nowhere is this trend more evident than in Godley's letters to the Minister of Defence, Sir James Allen, after the Battle of Chunuk Bair in August 1915. This was the battle where New Zealand won its first VC of the war, yet the award is mentioned only once in Godley's letters to Allen. This was in spite of the fact that Godley informed Allen just days after the fighting: 'I cannot speak too highly of the gallantry of all officers and men, and am so desperately grieved that they should have suffered such heavy casualties.'[3] On 20 October Godley wrote to Allen that: 'We are all very pleased at a New Zealander having got a Victoria Cross, and at the new List of Honours.' Godley then mentions several of the recipients of those honours: Colonel Plugge, General Walker, and Brigadier Richardson are mentioned by name; Corporal Bassett, the VC winner, is not.[4] The pattern is repeated in another letter a month later. Russell's KCMG is 'richly deserved . . . as he stands out prominently as a leader above all the rest'. Johnson's and Findlay's CB and Begg's CMG 'have all been earned'. No mention is made of Bassett's winning of the VC.[5] Nor is any mention made of Bassett's or any New Zealand VC in Godley's autobiography, *Life of an Irish Soldier*.[6]

Godley's focus on the knighthood or 'K' awards and the perceived uneven distribution of them became a serious political issue in New Zealand in 1917. This and other aspects of his behaviour were the subject of a vicious attack made on Godley in the New Zealand House of Representatives in August 1917. Ironically, even though he also had serious doubts about Godley's use of honours and awards, Allen was forced to defend Godley in the House.

In a letter to Godley on 10 April 1917 Allen had tried to alert him to the pending crisis:

> I feel sure that neither you or your staff will allow anything to stand in the way of selection of the very best men: neither rank, nor position, nor money, nor anything except efficiency will, I am sure, be your guide. Similarly with the honours that are being bestowed. There is some feeling in New Zealand that officers have received honours who are not much entitled to them as others.

In the letter Allen mentioned two people by name who had recently received honours but who he felt did not deserve them. He also mentioned a senior New Zealand officer who he felt had not been fairly treated in regards to honours.[7] Godley stoutly defended his actions in regards to honours and awards:

> I am afraid it is impossible to please everybody as regards Honours. But ours have been so liberally bestowed that really there are few that deserve them who have not got them.[8]

Allen's next letter conceded this point to Godley, but again warned of the ill feeling in New Zealand:

> I know you cannot please everybody with respect to honours but there is a good deal of criticism, as I have told you before, in

New Zealand, which is difficult for me to answer. I have never heard a grumble about Richardson's honours or Chaytor's or many others, but people here feel that there are some who have received honours who have deserved them as much as others who have got nothing.[9]

This disquiet peaked in the House of Representatives on 17 August 1917 when the Member for Eden, C.J. Parr, attacked the character and performance of General Godley. Parr opened his address by stating that he believed it was 'a most unfortunate thing for this country that General Godley is still in command of our Army at the front'. Accusing Godley of failing to win the regard or respect of the New Zealand soldiers, Parr believed that what really rankled with New Zealand soldiers was Godley's use of staff appointments and his use of military awards as a means to curry favour. As Parr stated:

I think he should have given New Zealand men most of the [staff] appointments, and not kept them for young Englishmen of good family connections. That is the thing that galls our men today. In just the same way the recommendations made by General Godley for decorations and honours have given grave dissatisfaction to the men at the front.[10]

Allen mounted a staunch defence of Godley in the House four days later. Declaring Parr's attack to be 'subversive of discipline' Allen then went on to refute all of the charges against Godley except the charge that he was unpopular with the New Zealand troops, which Allen knew to be an established fact. But as Allen pointed out, Napoleon was also unpopular with his men and 'unpopularity is not always a sign that a man is not a great commander'. When it came to refuting the charge about imperial honours Allen was on shaky ground and he knew it. He tabled a list of all awards that had been made to the NZEF as at August 1917, beginning with the three VCs. Including military decorations granted by allied nations as well as the imperial ones, they amounted to 1398 honours and decorations. This, according to Allen, meant that New Zealand 'has something to be proud of' and that New Zealand soldiers had not been neglected.[11]

'Can the Minister give us ranks?' asked Mr Witty.

'I am sorry I have not those details at present,' Allen replied.

'How many recommendations have been turned down?' asked Mr Parr.

'I am unable to give this information, but that is not the point,' replied Allen.

The point was the number of awards that had been made which, according to Allen, was greater per capita than had been awarded to the Australians:

> As far as I can make out, the decorations that have been given to New Zealand are at the rate of 1.7 per cent, or 17 in 1000; whereas to Australia the average is 1.2 per cent, or 12 in 1000.[12]

'The returns are wrong,' interjected an honourable member. Allen did not dispute this interjection, instead moving on to deal with the other issues concerning Godley that could easily be defended. These included the matter of Godley's unpopularity, which Allen admitted was true, but did not affect Godley's efficiency. They also included the charge that Godley lacked courage and that he gave preference to English staff officers instead of New Zealand officers. Allen resolutely defended Godley against the latter charges. That such a defence of the most senior officer of the NZEF was needed at this time is truly remarkable.

Despite Allen's defence of Godley in relation to honours and awards the House was still not convinced and opposition members were determined to exploit the issue. On 28 August, the Honourable Mr David Buddo, the Member for Kaiapoi, moved that the government produce before the House:

> . . . a return showing what decorations, orders, or medals have been issued to our military Forces, combatant or non-combatant, from the declaration of war to date.[13]

The motion, which was successful, required the government to produce a detailed breakdown of who had received the decorations. This was to be done by rank, by combatant or non-combatant status, by whether or not the receiver occupied a staff appointment, as well as those awards given for home service in New Zealand. The report, running to some 14 pages, was duly presented. The House was still not satisfied and on 11 September, the Member for the Bay of Islands, the Honourable Vernon Herbert Reed, was successful in having another motion on honours and awards passed in the House. The government was directed:

> . . . that there be laid before this House a return showing the number in each case of the following decorations which have been won by members of the New Zealand Expeditionary Force from the beginning of the war until June last: V.C. (with names of recipients), K.C.B. (also with names), K.C.M.G. (with names), C.B. (with names), C.M.G. (with names), D.S.O., Royal Red Cross, M.C., bar to M.C., M.M., D.C.M., bar to D.C.M., and M.S.M.: and also the name of the New Zealand officer who gives the final recommendation for the bestowing of such decorations.[14]

The return was duly tabled and contained all honours and awards made to members of the NZEF up to 16 August 1917. Leading the return were the three VC winners: Bassett, Brown and Frickleton. Then came all the 'K' awards made to 33 senior officers of the NZEF ranging in rank from lieutenant colonel to lieutenant general. The one KCB award made to General Godley headed the 'K's. The award most given was the Military Medal, with some 500 being awarded. There was a huge gap then to the Military Cross, with only 161 of these awards made, and finally 123 Distinguished Conduct Medals had been awarded. Surprisingly, no one had been awarded a bar to the Military Cross nor had a bar to the Distinguished Conduct Medal been won.[15] The report confirmed that:

The name of the New Zealand officer who gives the final recommendation for the bestowing of decorations is Lieutenant-General Sir A.J. Godley, K.C.B., K.C.M.G., General Officer Commanding New Zealand Expeditionary Force.

After three years of war, the low numbers in the return must have produced considerable alarm in many circles, as there was a huge increase in honours and awards in the last year of the war. While the number of VCs rose to 11 at the end of the war, the number of MMs reached more than 2000, with a further 62 bars being awarded. Similarly, the MCs reached a total of 506, with a further 25 bars being awarded. The Distinguished Conduct Medal, while not experiencing the same level of growth, more than doubled in number, reaching a total of 389 plus four bars being awarded.

Alarmed and hurt by the attack in Parliament, which several sources forwarded to him, Godley defended his actions in a handwritten letter to Allen:

. . . as regards honours and awards, I have exercised no favouritism and have been fortunate in obtaining for the Force a number of rewards considerably disproportionate to its size. General Russell said to me yesterday that he could think of no one who to our knowledge has conspicuously earned reward who has not obtained it.[16]

And in a letter dated 2 November 1917 Godley informed Allen that:

. . . owing to the very large numbers of honours and rewards that have been given to the New Zealanders, I have the credit, or discredit, whichever you like to call it, at General Headquarters and with the Military Secretary of being, if anything, rather lavish with my recommendations for rewards.[17]

Aware, however, of the damage he was causing to the New Zealand government over this and other issues, Godley offered his resignation in the letter of 27 October and again in another letter on 24 November. Allen replied that Godley's resignation was not required and that 'I must express my regret that you should have been troubled by criticism which appears to me to be so unjust'.[18] Godley, however, continued to justify his awarding of honours and rewards in further letters, sometimes going to extreme lengths to do so. A letter sent to Allen dated 1 March 1918 contained all the honours and awards made to members of the NZEF since the start of the war. Allen was informed:

There is no doubt but that honours have been given to it [the NZEF] more freely, and in a larger proportion to its numbers, than to any other such Force or Unit of the British Empire employed in this war.[19]

The list as at 15 February 1918 now included a total of 2843 imperial decorations and a further 140 foreign ones — a massive increase, more than 100 per cent, in the five months since the previous August. The VC, which headed the list, had increased from three to five, MCs now numbered 295, with an additional four bars being presented, DCMs numbered 202 and the MM had reached 1089. The floodgates for awards and honours were now well and truly open.

In a reply to Godley's correspondence of 1 March 1918, Allen allegedly stated that he had the list of honours read in the House of Representatives. Allen then informed Godley that 'I think every Member was gratified to know that the New Zealand soldiers have so distinguished themselves as to earn so many honours.'[20] However, the House was not sitting at the time. The Third Session of the nineteenth Parliament ran from 11 October to 1 November 1917 and the Fourth Session, a short sitting of just six days, did not get under way until 9 April 1918. Godley's new list of awards was never read to the House.

There are several things highly unusual, even suspicious, about Allen's reply to Godley's letter of 1 March. First, there is the matter of the dates of the correspondence. Godley's letter and list of awards is dated 1 March 1918; Allen's reply is dated just over two weeks later on 16 March 1918. There is no way that Godley's correspondence, travelling via surface vessel from Europe, could have reached Allen in this short time. It usually took two months for their correspondence to reach one another. Second, the letter has the word 'Duplicate' typed in original on it, the only time this word is used in the file. All other non-original correspondence bears the word 'Copy'. Third, while the letter looks like a carbon copy with its blue typescript, some details such as the heading have been typed directly onto the letter. And finally, the letter is the only copy in Godley's collection of letters that has an original signature on it; one signed in blue fountain pen. These anomalies, plus the fact that the list of honours and awards was never tabled in the House, must cast serious doubts as to the veracity of this letter.

Godley's claim of 'lavishness' was an exaggeration and can only be applied to the period from August 1917 to February 1918 which followed the criticism made of him in New Zealand. From February 1918, the NZEF would go on to win another 903 imperial honours and decorations, making a grand total for the war of 3746. In relation to the highest imperial honour, the VC, Godley's claim of being 'lavish' certainly does not hold. On 22 March 1918, the New Zealand Division was rushed south to the Somme to help stem the German Spring Offensive, which had broken the British defences there. In doing so the New Zealand Division passed from Godley's XXII Corps to Lieutenant General Sir George Harper's IV Corps. During their advance from the Somme in the middle of 1918 while serving in this new corps, the New Zealand Division would win more VCs in six months than they had won during the previous three years. There are some combined causal factors for this, but a significant one has to be the change in corps commander.

GENERAL RUSSELL'S INFLUENCE

The other person primarily responsible for honours and awards for the New Zealand soldiers in the First World War was the divisional commander, Major General Sir Andrew Russell. Russell had been a British regular soldier for a number of years before resigning his commission in order to farm the family's sheep station in the Hawke's Bay. He had kept up the military connection by his service in the New Zealand volunteers, and later, in the Territorial Force. Russell was a highly competent military commander who was determined to produce the best infantry division on the Western Front. Taciturn, dour and ruthless, Russell was quick to criticise, but slow to praise. He had little time for honours and awards. His attitude to them is revealed in the fact that he refused to nominate any of his mounted riflemen for gallantry awards on Gallipoli, despite the fact that many of his soldiers had earned them many times over. One rifleman bitterly recorded:

> General Russell has refused to recommend any individuals for rewards as he says every man is worth a V.C. and it is sufficient honour to belong to the brigade.[21]

According to the historian of the Mounted Rifles Brigade at Gallipoli, Russell's attitude to gallantry awards meant that 'insult was added to injury'.[22]

Russell's disdain for honours and awards is also evident in a letter written to his father shortly after his being awarded a knighthood. Russell's KCMG, awarded for his service on Gallipoli, was one of only four given to New Zealanders in the course of the war. Russell, however, was dismissive of its significance:

> I am sure you are pleased with my KCMG. It is of course more due to the excellent work done by the Mounted Rifle Brigade than to anything I have contributed. As I think you know, I have not much use for these kinds of things, being as my schoolmasters used to say pityingly, devoid of ambition. But I hope it will please the family and Gertrude, and so it will have its use.[23]

With little interest in honours and awards, Russell rigidly applied the guidelines for divisional commanders issued by the British War Office. These guidelines recommended the awarding of just one VC for each battle in which a division fought. In November 1917, in response to the criticism by Mr Parr in the House of Representatives, Russell explained the system of allocation to Allen:

The question of rewards is evidently misunderstood by those who find fault with it. For each period of six months we get an absolutely definite number of awards allotted to the Division, and these are on an equality with those allotted to other Divisions. This number is by me subdivided between the Brigades and other units composing the Division . . . The recommendations then lie entirely in the hands of Officers Commanding the Units, Brigadiers as regards their staff and myself as regards the Headquarters staff. I have never cut out a recommendation in the case of the New Zealand Division . . . All recommendations almost as a matter of course are passed by myself to the Corps Commander and the rest lie in the hands of G.H.Q. or the War Office.[24]

While Russell rigidly applied the quotas, this was through choice rather than necessity. If the quota system was mandatory rather than a guide, it would have been impossible for one British unit, the Lancashire Fusiliers, to win 'six VCs before breakfast' on the day of the landing at Gallipoli. Similarly, it would have been impossible for the Australians to win seven VCs for the action at Lone Pine. And Russell was happy enough to relax the quota system at the end of 1918.

Allen was not happy with the quota system and expressed his views to Russell in his reply. 'What if some Divisions were larger than others?' asked Allen, knowing that the New Zealand Division was at the time the largest division on the Western Front. If this was the case then: 'this practice does not seem to me to be equitable, and it does not stimulate one Division to excel another'.[25] Russell defended the system in his next letter to Allen, stating that 'I do not think you could devise a fairer system of allocation of awards than is now in force' and that 'at any rate within the Division, there is no dissatisfaction'.[26] Allen let the matter drop after this letter.

But Allen's concerns had made their mark and must be seen as a contributing factor to the large number of awards, including that of the VC, made in 1918. It must been seen as the primary factor influencing Russell's relaxation of the quota system. There were other important factors too. As mentioned above, the new corps commander from March 1918 was the avuncular Lieutenant General Sir George Harper. Harper, unlike Godley, took a strong paternal interest in the well-being of his soldiers and he rated the New Zealand Division highly. Then there is the fact that the nature of the war had changed in 1918. From August 1918 the Allies were constantly advancing, pushing back a depleted, exhausted German Army. For the Allies the war was now one of open warfare with plenty of pace and manoeuvre. The New Zealand Division excelled at this new type of warfare and from 21 August 1918 they were constantly in action, being used as one of the spearhead divisions of the British Third Army. All of these changed circumstances account for the six VCs won in the last months of the war.

There is another important issue regarding the VCs won by New Zealand soldiers in the First World War. Not one was awarded to an officer, despite the fact that commissioned officers were recommended for the VC from the very first campaign. There is no documentary evidence that explains this exclusion, but according to Chris Pugsley and others it was because 'both Russell and Godley believed that no matter what bravery an officer displayed he was only doing his job'.[27] If this is the case, and it remains the only logical explanation, it is a great injustice to the officers of the New Zealand Division. From its inception the VC was meant to be a 'democratic' award, one that recognised outstanding feats of gallantry regardless of rank. Had Bernard Freyberg or Alfred Shout, the most decorated Australian soldier of the Gallipoli campaign but a New Zealander by birth, been serving with the New Zealand Division they would not have won their VCs. Ormond Burton made this point in his autobiography when he compared Freyberg with an outstanding officer in his battalion. Burton wrote:

The difference between George Tuck, captain with a M.C., and Lord Freyberg was that George was intellectually more able, probably stronger, just as brave, but one was with Auckland, a Main Body private, and the other a 2/Lieutenant with the R.M.L.I.[28]

Similarly, had Charles Upham, VC and bar, been born 20 years earlier, he would not have joined that elite club of double VC winners. This gross injustice is further compounded by the fact that every surviving New Zealand VC winner was subsequently commissioned from the ranks and became an officer.

The Gallipoli campaign of 1915 was New Zealand's first true taste of twentieth century warfare. While it is acknowledged that New Zealand first felt the stirrings of nationhood on those far-off Aegean shores, the Gallipoli campaign was also where the pattern of stinginess, neglect and ignorance as regards the VC first became evident. It is the subject of the next chapter.

Chapter 5　The Gallipoli Victoria Cross

On 4 August 1914, Britain formally declared war on Germany. As part of the British Empire, New Zealand and the other self-governing dominions were also deemed to be at war with Germany. New Zealand's entry into the war of 1914–18 was enthusiastic and immediate, reflecting a mixture of ties of kinship with Britain, idealism about the protection of smaller nations and a degree of national self-interest. The war that embroiled most of the major European powers that August was the culmination of a crisis that had followed the assassination of Archduke Franz Ferdinand, heir to the Austro-Hungarian throne. The assassination produced a chain reaction of sabre rattling, military mobilisations, ultimatums, and finally, declarations of war. The alliance system then in place meant that the war, when it came, could not be isolated to just two protagonists. It would involve most of the nations of Europe as well as their far-flung colonial possessions.

It was meant to be a short war, one that produced decisive results, but wars seldom go according to plan. By the end of 1914 a stalemate had developed on the Western Front, which was the crucial theatre of operations in this war. Both sides had entrenched themselves across northern France and through the centre of Belgium. The complex trench systems stretched some 750 kilometres from the Swiss frontier to the English Channel. There was no outflanking the trenches nor was there any easy way of breaking through them. It became a siege, albeit a siege fought with modern weapons.

In an effort to break the deadlock and obtain some advantage over Germany without incurring the casualties that a frontal assault on the trenches in France entailed, Britain looked to other theatres of war. To British leaders in 1915, a campaign against the Ottoman Empire, Germany's ally, or in the Balkans, seemed an ideal way to outflank those German forces entrenched in France. In early 1915, the British, with French support, attempted to capture the Ottoman capital Constantinople via The Narrows with the aim of knocking them out of the war. This was the original aim of the Gallipoli campaign, an aim the Allies never came close to fulfilling.

In terms of its origins, planning and execution, the Gallipoli campaign remains one of the most controversial episodes in the history of the First World War. Initially the Dardanelles campaign was meant to be purely a naval affair. This was a mistake because, as historian Correlli Barnett has commented:

> A pre-war staff study had concluded that only a combined sea and land assault could hope to defeat the forts that commanded the Dardanelles from each shore. Such an amphibious operation demanded well-trained, well-equipped troops with experienced task force headquarters, and all the specialised equipment and communications necessary to put an army on a hostile coast and maintain it there.[1]

An amphibious operation of this magnitude also needed joint army and naval rehearsals, an adequate reserve force and high levels of secrecy. All of these essentials were lacking in the Gallipoli campaign.

The attempt to force The Narrows as the gateway to Constantinople began on 19 February 1915. It immediately ran into problems. On 18 March a great armada of 16 battleships, flotillas of cruisers and destroyers, and hundreds of minesweepers set out to force The Narrows. Great things were expected of this combined British/French fleet, but when they failed to penetrate the Turkish minefields and lost six capital ships in one day the navy had to face a painful reality. They were incapable of dealing with the combination of the dense minefield laid across The Narrows and the Turkish artillery batteries on both sides of the straits. The need for a land force of well-trained soldiers was readily apparent as it should have been from the beginning of the operation. The only solution was to stage a belated landing to clear these shores.

The Mediterranean Expeditionary Force under General Sir Ian

Hamilton was given this task and it was a formidable one. The Mediterranean Expeditionary Force consisted of the 29th, the Royal Naval, 1st Australian, and Australian and New Zealand Divisions and the Corps Expéditionnaire d'Orient, French troops of about division strength. The Turkish forces numbered six weak divisions of about 84,000, who had to guard about 150 miles of coastline. General Hamilton had nowhere near enough troops for the size of the task ahead. It was known at the time that the Australians and New Zealanders were only partially trained, inexperienced and, it was felt, of doubtful quality. As a result they were given a subordinate role in the initial landings; a sideshow within a sideshow. The ANZAC Corps, as they were now designated, were to land to the north of Gaba Tepe while the British and French made the main assault at Cape Helles.

The Australians and New Zealanders landed on the Gallipoli peninsula in the early hours of 25 April 1915. For reasons never satisfactorily explained, they went ashore a mile north of the gentle beach that had been selected as their landing area. High cliffs dominated the area and overlooked the beach on all three sides of what became Anzac Cove. The Australian and New Zealand soldiers who landed that day knew they had to get as high and as deep into the hinterland as they could. Unfortunately, when darkness fell, they had only penetrated to a depth of a mile and a half, still one mile short of the summit of the dominating Sari Bair ridge. Owing to their exhaustion and the fierce opposition of the Turkish defenders organised by Mustapha Kemal, they could get no further.

The landing on 25 April had gained no more than a tenuous foothold on the Gallipoli peninsula. General Hamilton's Mediterranean Expeditionary Force was penned into two narrow lodgements: the British and French forces at Cape Helles and the Australians and New Zealanders at Anzac Cove. There was to be no swift victory here for the Allies. Instead:

There ensued stalemate and trench warfare perhaps even more ghastly than the Western Front, in which the stench of corpses rotting in the blazing sun of May, June and July blended with the perfume of wild thyme, and the very narrowness of the front and rear areas added a dreadful claustrophobia.[2]

After the initial landing, the rest of the campaign involved trying to consolidate and expand the lodgement made on the first day. This peaked in the major offensive of August 1915 in which the Anzac forces played a leading role. It was during this attack that the New Zealanders briefly captured the Chunuk Bair ridge, the furthest point inland that the Allies penetrated. By September though, with the failure of the August offensive, it was evident that the troops on Gallipoli were exhausted and should be evacuated. The troops were withdrawn three months later in what proved to be the best planned and well-executed operation of the whole campaign. It had lasted eight-and-a-half months. With over 200,000 casualties and nothing to show for these losses, the Gallipoli campaign was a costly failure.

THE GALLIPOLI VCS

The majority of the 663 VCs awarded in the First World War were won on the Western Front. Of the awards won away from the European mainland, the Gallipoli campaign is predominant with 39 VCs being awarded during it. In the history of the Victoria Cross, the Gallipoli campaign is especially significant. It was at Gallipoli that the first VCs of the war were awarded to an Australian and to a New Zealand soldier and to a member of the Royal Marines. Units of the British Army took the lion's share of VCs with some 18 being awarded. With 11 awards the Royal Navy could also be well pleased with the recognition it received during the campaign, especially as some VCs were won by their newest elements. Submariners received two VCs, members of the Royal Naval Division (in which a young Bernard Freyberg was then serving) won another two, and one award went to a navy pilot. The remaining 10 VCs were Anzac awards: 9 won by Australian soldiers and 1 by a New Zealand soldier. Of the 39 Gallipoli VCs, 11 were posthumous awards, including seven given to men who died in the act of gaining the award. In keeping with the democratic traditions of the VC award, recipients ranged in rank from private to lieutenant colonel. Most, though, went to commissioned officers. The breakdown of awards is: 22 awards to officers, ten to NCOs, and seven to private soldiers or naval ratings.[3]

Regarding the Anzac VCs, unlike previous awards, not one was for rescuing wounded comrades. While some names were put forward for recognition of 'very special work re wounded men' the practice was actively discouraged. It was regarded as being far too dangerous to both the rescuer and the wounded man.[4]

The Battle of Chunuk Bair

After three months of trying to break the deadlock of trench warfare the British 8th Corps at Helles and the two French divisions were exhausted. Something new was clearly needed and in August 1915 General Hamilton attempted it. General Birdwood's Anzac Corps would now make the main effort to break out from their besieged foothold above Anzac Cove. Birdwood's corps was increased to 25,000 and ordered to make a left hook to the north by seizing the high ground of the Sari Bair Range. As part of this new attack two British divisions would be landed on the Anzacs Corp's left flank at Suvla Bay where they would secure a new beachhead prior to advancing up the Sari Bair Range from that direction and linking up with the left flank of the Anzac force.

The task of capturing the vital heights of Sari Bair, the strategic key to the peninsula, was allocated to General Godley's New Zealand and Australian Division. It was a tough objective to have. The sprawling heights of the Sari Bair ridge line consisted of sharp, rocky ridges, a maze of narrow gullies (or deres) that had been cut by years of torrential rain, sheer cliffs, and limited cover. To make up its depleted numbers, Godley's division was reinforced by the troops of a New Army division that had recently arrived at Gallipoli. All told Godley had some 45 battalions of infantry allocated to him for this attack, which was an exceptionally wide span of command.[5] Godley planned a two-phased attack. First, Brigadier Andrew Russell's Mounted Rifles Brigade and a British brigade would open a path to the heights by seizing the foothills in a silent night attack. Then two columns would advance up two separate gullies that night and storm the heights. On the left, a two-brigade force consisting of the 29th Indian Brigade and the 4th Australian Brigade would seize Hill 971 (Koja Chemen Tepe) and Hill Q. On the right, Brigadier Francis Johnston's New Zealand Infantry Brigade were to capture the vital high ground of Chunuk Bair, the dominant feature of the Sari Bair ridge line and some 860 feet high. These objectives had to be taken in the six hours of darkness on the night of 6–7 August.

To assist Godley's attack the Australian Division planned to carry out a series of diversionary attacks. The main one was to be made at Lone Pine, but another was planned by the Australian Light Horse at The Nek. This was, as most writers acknowledge, 'a highly ambitious plan'.[6] To have any chance of success it needed detailed planning, tight coordination, a skilled, decisive battle commander calling the shots and a modicum of luck. All of these essential factors were missing from this offensive.

As the New Zealand soldiers moved into position for the attempt on the heights, the Australians launched themselves at the Lone Pine trenches. Although meant as a feint, the fighting here was savage and the subterranean battle lasted for several days. In this epic struggle seven Australian soldiers won the VC. But the price was high: the Australians suffered over 2000 casualties, and the Turks more than 5000. The attack at Lone Pine served its purpose though, drawing in the immediate Turkish reserves and focusing the attention of the Turks for three days. It had created the ideal conditions for the left hook north of Anzac Cove.

The next phase of the attack also went well. After some hard fighting Russell's Mounted Rifles captured the foothills by 1.00 a.m. on 7 August. The Australian official historian Charles Bean described Russell's capture of the foothills as a 'magnificent feat of arms, the brilliance of which was never surpassed, if indeed equalled during the campaign'.[7] The door to Chunuk Bair and the Sari Bair heights had been kicked open. It now needed speed, decision and determination to seize the opportunity before it was slammed shut again.

But speed, decision and determination were lacking in the New Zealand senior commanders the morning of 7 August. Tragically the New Zealand infantry attack was delayed. It did not happen during the hours of darkness nor in the early morning of 7 August. The Australian 3rd Light Horse Brigade attacked the Turkish positions at The Nek in the early light that morning. This attack was meant to be coordinated with the New Zealand thrust towards Chunuk Bair. There was no coordination, though, as Johnston, his soldiers scattered and tired, hesitated to make the final assault on the heights. The delay was a fatal mistake and, as a result, four waves of Australian Light Horsemen were massacred at The Nek. According to historian Chris Pugsley, the New Zealand delay at Chunuk Bair meant that 'a priceless opportunity had been lost'.[8] It is easy to see why this was so. At dawn on 7 August Chunuk Bair was virtually deserted, held by an artillery battery and about 20 infantry. Most of the Turkish defenders on the heights had been rushed to Lone Pine. By 8.00 a.m., however, the men on Chunuk Bair had been reinforced by two companies of infantry from Kemal's 19 Division. At 9.00 a.m. a complete battalion of infantry arrived.

As mentioned above, the New Zealand senior commander responsible for this delay was Johnston. Pressured by Godley, who was some considerable distance away, his judgement affected by sickness and the liberal use of alcohol, Johnston altered his behaviour from caution to extreme recklessness. Ignoring the requests of his subordinate commanders to delay the New Zealand attack until nightfall, or to even delay it by half an hour so that machine-gun support could be arranged, Johnston ordered the Auckland Battalion and the 10th Gurkhas to attack Chunuk Bair at 11.00 a.m. Attacking uphill in broad daylight without the element of surprise and without artillery or machine-gun support is a poor military tactic. Little wonder that this mid-morning attack was shot to pieces and made little headway. The Auckland Battalion alone lost more than 300 men for an advance of less than 100 yards. Johnston was undeterred by these losses and ordered the Wellington Battalion, supported by half of the Canterbury Infantry, to make another daylight attack on Chunuk Bair. Its commander, Colonel William Malone, in an act of supreme moral courage, refused to make the attack. He told Johnston:

> My men are not going over in daylight — but they'll go over at night time and they'll take that hill . . . I will take the risk and any punishment. These men are not going until I order them to go. I'm not going to send them over to commit suicide.[9]

The attack was delayed until nightfall, and Malone was as good as his word. Following hard on the heels of an artillery barrage, the Wellington Battalion and soldiers from the 7th Gloucesters advanced to Chunuk Bair at 4.15 a.m. on the morning of 8 August. They found the crest almost deserted and occupied the trenches there. They were soon reinforced by soldiers from three New Zealand battalions including soldiers from the New Zealand Maori Contingent. Taking Chunuk Bair on the morning of 8 August had proved surprisingly easy. Keeping the position was an entirely different matter. When he learned that Chunuk Bair had been taken General Hamilton was elated, writing in his diary; 'Chunuk Bair will do: with that, we win!' He regarded its capture as 'a brilliant stroke of arms'.[10]

However, the soldiers on Chunuk Bair were in a very exposed position and from 6.30 a.m. they were constantly counterattacked by Turkish infantry, who recognised the importance of the hill's summit. The flat ground on the ridge was extremely narrow, being only 15 feet at its widest point, and the steep hills meant that the Turks had a relatively safe approach march — that is, they would be right on the New Zealand positions at Chunuk Bair before being detected. The front-line trenches became death traps. It was a fierce struggle and the fighting was savage, at times hand-to-hand.

Both sides suffered heavy casualties and Chunuk Bair and the features below it — The Apex and saddle — were littered with New Zealand bodies and discarded equipment. Conditions on the ridge were dreadful. It had been an exceptionally hot day and the soldiers soon used up their meagre water supplies. At the end of the day the Wellington Battalion had just 70 left of the 760 men Malone had led onto the ridge that morning. Malone too was amongst the fallen on Chunuk Bair, killed during a Turkish attack launched just after 4.00 p.m. Little wonder then that Fred Waite, the first New Zealand historian of the Gallipoli campaign, stated that for New Zealand, 8 August 1915 was 'the blackest day on the Peninsula'. He writes:

> A portion of Chunuk Bair was undoubtedly ours, but at what a cost! Many of the finest men of the Dominion lay dead upon the crest.[11]

That evening more New Zealand soldiers from the Otago Battalion and the Wellington Mounted Rifles were pushed onto Chunuk Bair to reinforce the few survivors that remained. They would do the bulk of the fighting on Chunuk Bair the next day and they too would pay heavily for it. By the evening of 9 August, the Otago Battalion had lost 17 officers and 309 men and the Wellington Mounted Rifles were left with just 73 of the 183 with which they had started the day.[12] There were no more New Zealand reinforcements left. After two days trying to hold Chunuk Bair in the face of desperate counterattacks by the Turks, the New Zealanders were spent. As Godley wrote afterwards, the New Zealanders 'had been fighting incessantly for three days and nights, with little food and practically no water, were completely exhausted and it was imperatively necessary to relieve them'.[13]

That evening two New Army battalions — the 6th Loyal North Lancashires and the 5th Wiltshires — replaced the few survivors of the New Zealand battalions. The relief on the evening of 9 August commenced at 8.00 p.m., but it was not completed until 2.00 a.m. on the morning of 10 August. At daylight a Turkish force of four regiments hurriedly thrown together by Mustafa Kemal attacked the two British battalions, which withdrew from the heights. Although New Zealand machine-guns at the Apex inflicted massive casualties on the advancing Turks, once again they were in possession of this crucial piece of ground. The Apex looked likely to fall too, but it was held through the actions of a New Zealand machine-gun officer, Major Jesse Wallingford. By 10 August both sides had fought themselves to a standstill on the Sari Bair ranges and had suffered grievous casualties. The Turks, however, again held the high ground.

The fight to take and hold Chunuk Bair was an epic struggle, 'one of the outstanding feats of arms in New Zealand history' according to Christopher Pugsley.[14] Those who survived the fighting believed that many New Zealanders deserved to win VCs that day. Only one New Zealander did though — Cyril Royston Guyton Bassett.

CYRIL BASSETT'S VC

Cyril Royston Guyton Bassett was born in Mount Eden, Auckland, in 1892. After leaving school in 1908 he worked as a bank clerk. Bassett was a short man, being only 5 feet 4 inches tall, and in 1915 weighed a wiry 9 stone 7 pounds. Bassett joined the Territorial Force when he was 17, but because of his height and slight build the army would only accept him as a bugler. He served with the Auckland College Rifles from 1909 to 1911 and with the Divisional Signal Company in Auckland from 1911 until the outbreak of the war in 1914.[15] In August 1914 Cyril Bassett was keen to join the Royal Navy, but his mother, 'a strongminded woman with four generations of the Army behind her', persuaded him to settle for the army instead.[16] His small stature almost saw him rejected for military service. As he recalled many years later:

When I went to join up, the Doctor said to me 'well, you're too small'. So I went to the end of the line and came up again. He put the tape around my chest and said 'no'. So I went around again. The third time he let me in.[17]

After the war Bassett used to joke that it was his short stature that was responsible for his survival, stating: 'I was always too close to the ground to be hit.'

Bassett had taken part in the landing on 25 April. Watching the soldiers going ashore and knowing that it would be his turn soon, Bassett experienced the concern that affects nearly all soldiers. He was worried about how well he would perform and later recalled:

The only thing that occupied my mind was 'I wonder how I'm going to behave when I get under fire. I wonder if I'm going to maintain my honour and integrity.'[18]

Bassett left a vivid account of his experience of the landing:

When I got ashore at Gallipoli there was a line of dead and wounded as far as the eye could see. Our troops hadn't got far inland and we were having a hell of a time from the Turks, who could see everything that was happening and were well entrenched.[19]

There was little time for introspection though and Bassett was immediately put to work laying telephone cables with the other signallers. Just over a week later on 2 May he had his name taken in consideration for a bravery award. It was not to be the last time this would happen.

On 7 August Cyril Bassett, who was then a corporal, kept communications working between the Auckland Battalion on the Apex and New Zealand brigade headquarters further down on Rhododendron Spur. It was dangerous work as the spur, the key to the approaches of Chunuk Bair, was heavily enfiladed by the Turkish defences and was almost devoid of cover. It was vital that communications be maintained from Rhododendron Spur to the forward positions of the Apex and Chunuk Bair. While attempting to do so on 7 August, Bassett was hit in the boot by a bullet, but it did not penetrate to his foot. The next day, 8 August 1915, was to be Bassett's moment of glory. On learning that Malone had taken Chunuk Bair, Brigadier Johnston at brigade headquarters, now on the Apex, sent forward a small section of signallers to establish communications with the force on the ridge. Bassett was in charge of this section of signallers. Communication with the ridge was considered so vital that an hour later Johnston sent out another team of signallers under command of Sapper Brian Dignan.

Upon reaching the Wellington Battalion on Chunuk Bair, Bassett could see the situation was desperate. He sent a man back to brigade headquarters with an urgent request for reinforcements. Meanwhile, Bassett stayed on Chunuk Bair attempting to establish communications with the headquarters.

The laying and repairing of telephone cables was dangerous work. Bassett and the other signallers had to climb the exposed slopes of the Sari Bair Range and carry out their vital task while under rifle and machine-gun fire from the heights. They had to carry coils of telephone wire and their repair kits with them and were armed only with a revolver and bayonet. For three days the signallers worked under constant threat of death or injury. On 9 August, for example, Bassett made three repairs to the damaged wire while under fire and less than 100 yards away from the Turks. A former schoolmate lying wounded in a crater recalled: 'I dreaded his [Bassett's] approach because I knew it would bring all hell from the Turkish guns.'[20] Sergeant George Skerrett was a battalion medic in the Otago Battalion on Gallipoli and witnessed the rare sight of a VC being won in action. In 1991, aged 98, he recalled:

I saw that chap win his Victoria Cross. I didn't know at the time that that's what it was. He was laying telephone wires under fire. Why he didn't get hit I don't know — but he wasn't still for a second. He was moving around all the time fixing wires, running them clear and getting them in the right place. Later I heard that he got a VC for that — I saw it.[21]

Bassett described his actions in an interview in 1965:

We were there practically until the morning of August 10th on those lines. Well, what we should have done really was to run out new lines but we didn't have [any] . . . All day on the 8th we were working on those lines, mending breaks, and on the 9th we did a bit of mending, but we were really tired. We were really worn out.

One of the signallers who'd been allotted to look after the telephone on the CB was badly wounded. We got that news, and then on the night of the 9th we laid a new telephone wire across to the Wiltshires, who had relieved our boys, and then we brought this wounded boy in. We couldn't get a stretcher and we had to bring him in on a blanket — four of us — and he had been wounded from the waist downwards . . . He had been out there a day and a night.[22]

It was a miracle that Bassett survived this four-day ordeal. As well as a bullet hitting his boot, another passed through his tunic collar and yet a third tore off the tunic's right-hand pocket. Bassett had to deal with his fear at the time too. He admitted being scared on the slopes of Chunuk Bair, so much so that at one time he wished he were one of the many flies buzzing around instead of a soldier so dreadfully exposed to harm. But Bassett conquered his fear as most soldiers do, believing that 'if the lines hadn't gone through, the losses would have been even greater'.[23]

For their heroic action on Chunuk Bair, Bassett and the five other signallers had their names recorded by Major Arthur Temperley, the brigade major, so he could recommend them for decorations. Bassett received a special mention for his earlier actions at Pope's Post in May, which resulted in him being awarded the VC for his actions at Chunuk Bair.

It was, and remains, an important award for a number of reasons. First, his was the only VC won by a New Zealander at Gallipoli, a point that irritated and embarrassed him in later life. Second, no one who was there or who knows the history of the Gallipoli campaign can doubt that Bassett earned this award many times over. As Fred Waite has written:

No V.C. on the Peninsula was more consistently earned. This was not for one brilliant act of bravery, but for a full week of ceaseless devotion.[24]

Third, Bassett's VC remains the only award made to a signaller in any Commonwealth army. Finally, Bassett's citation may be unique in that it carries the wrong date. Bassett was recommended for the VC for 'most conspicuous bravery and devotion to duty on the Chunuk Bair Ridge' while trying to maintain communications 'after the New Zealand Infantry Brigade had attacked and established itself on the ridge'. Chunuk Bair was not taken by the New Zealanders until the morning of 8 August yet the date mentioned in the citation and engraved on the medal is 7 August 1915, one day out.

On 13 August, Bassett was evacuated from Gallipoli. His health had broken down and he needed nine months of recuperation in England. In October 1915, while in an English hospital recovering from dysentery an 'astounded' Bassett learned he had won the VC.

Bassett did not rejoin his unit in France until June 1916. He served with it on the Somme in September 1916. One year later Bassett was commissioned as an officer. While in France Bassett was wounded twice: in October 1917 at Passchendaele and in March 1918 on the Somme. In France Bassett was also recommended for a Military Cross but it was not awarded. A confidential report written in January 1918 stated that Bassett:

Knows his work well, is keen and reliable. Inclined to worry himself unduly . . . Handles men well and is popular.

The report recommended Bassett for promotion.[25]

Bassett returned to New Zealand in December 1918 and was demobilised the following month. His last medical examination gave him a clean bill of health but recorded that there was 'some nervousness, result of being buried'.[26] Bassett returned to banking but again volunteered for military service in the Second World War. In 1940 Bassett resumed service with the National Military Reserve and was mobilised with the Royal New Zealand Corps of Signals in January 1941 with the rank of captain. He was promoted to the rank of major in February 1942 and then to lieutenant colonel in April 1943. When his active service ceased in December 1943 Bassett was the commander of the Northern District Signals.

Cyril Bassett died in 1983 aged 91 — he was the last surviving Gallipoli VC winner.[27]

When he returned from the war Bassett put his VC in the back of a drawer and there it stayed. He did not speak of it and rarely took it out. In fact his eldest daughter, Cherry, first learned her father had won the VC at primary school when her class studied Gallipoli.[28] There are two reasons for this reticence. Bassett was an exceptionally modest man and he was always uneasy about being awarded a VC. As he stated on the few occasions he spoke of his VC:

> When I got the medal I was disappointed to find I was the only New Zealander to get one at Gallipoli, because hundreds of Victoria Crosses should have been awarded there . . . All my mates ever got were wooden crosses.[29]

It is unfortunate that such a brave man and one so deserving of the VC should have felt uneasy and embarrassed at his award. But Bassett is right in one regard and his unease is understandable. Many more VCs should have been awarded to New Zealand soldiers at Gallipoli.

The New Zealand Army still commemorates Bassett's achievement at Gallipoli. Each year the Corps of Signals awards the Bassett Memorial Trophy to the corporal in the corps who demonstrates the most outstanding effort and achievement. The trophy is a kauri statuette of Bassett on Chunuk Bair. Bassett, who also regarded himself as a signaller rather than an engineer, was a lifetime member of the Corps of Signals Association. In his will Bassett bequeathed his VC to the Corps of Signals. The corps has given the VC to the Auckland War Memorial Museum on long-term loan.

OTHER CONTENDERS

If we look just at the Battle of Chunuk Bair, it is evident that many more VCs could and should have been awarded. General Hamilton acknowledged this in the New Zealand history of the campaign. Hamilton wrote that as he watched the New Zealand and Australian attack on the Sari Bair Range he recorded in his diary:

> They are not charging up into this Sari Bair Ridge for money or by compulsion. There they are — all the way from the Southern Cross — earning Victoria Crosses, every one of them.[30]

Acknowledging that at Chunuk Bair the New Zealanders 'had fought with rare heart', Australian historian Les Carlyon is right when he states that: 'It seems a denial of what they [the New Zealanders] did that only one Victoria Cross was awarded for their time on the summit.'[31] So who were the leading candidates from the actions on Chunuk Bair? There are quite a few.

For a start there were the signallers who worked alongside Cyril Bassett and who also demonstrated conspicuous bravery. Birkett, Whittaker, Edwards, McDermott and Dignan were also recommended for their actions. As we know from above, Bassett was selected as the only New Zealand recipient of the VC because it was the second time he had been recommended for a bravery award. Of the other five signallers, one, Sapper Dignan, received the Distinguished Conduct Medal; the other four received nothing.

Four officers have been singled out for their exceptional performances on Chunuk Bair. They were Lieutenant Colonels Malone of the Wellington Battalion and Arthur Bauchop of the Otago Mounted Rifles and Majors James Elmslie of the Wellington Mounted Rifles and J.A. Wallingford, the brigade's machine-gun officer. In the case of both Malone and Bauchop their omissions defy all explanation as both General Hamilton and Godley recognised their performances on Chunuk Bair as being exceptional. Hamilton wrote:

I lay a very special stress on the deeds of Bauchop and Malone. These two heroes were killed while leading their men with absolute contempt of danger — Bauchop after having captured what was afterwards known as Bauchop's Hill, and Malone on the very summit of Chunuk Bair. Both Bauchop and Malone were soldiers of great mark and, above all, fearless leaders of men.[32]

Godley was no less effusive in his praise of Bauchop and Malone. Writing to Allen just days after the battle Godley singled them out for their performances. Bauchop had been mortally wounded while leading his men on the night of 6 August 'under the most extraordinary difficult conditions, and in a country where nothing but the most gallant troops could possibly have succeeded'. Malone had been killed after taking Chunuk Bair 'which only a leader of most exceptional valour and determination would have captured'. Both Malone and Bauchop, he wrote, 'have throughout proved themselves to be born leaders of men'.[33] It is extraordinary that, if he really believed what he had written, Godley did not consider recommending both officers for the VC. However, his prejudice against officers receiving the award prevented this.

The case of Malone is particularly baffling. It was well known by all New Zealanders who served on Gallipoli that Malone had been instrumental in taking the heights of Chunuk Bair and that his performance while defending it had been inspirational. As one soldier later recorded: 'There [on Chunuk Bair] I saw the bravest man I ever saw, Colonel Malone, who was doing the jobs from Lance Corporal to Brigadier General.'[34] When Malone's performance on Chunuk Bair went unrewarded, a deep bitterness took hold amongst the New Zealand survivors of this battle.

One New Zealand officer — Major Elmslie — was recommended for the VC for his actions on Chunuk Bair. He was a South African war veteran and the second in command of the Wellington Mounted Rifles. Elmslie had inspired and rallied his battalion on Chunuk Bair despite being critically wounded. As one mounted rifleman later recorded:

Jim proved himself a splendid soldier and a first class officer. He was the idol of the regiment. Old Mr Elmslie ought to be the proudest man in the country to think he had such a son.[35]

Elmslie's commanding officer, Lieutenant Colonel William Meldrum, wrote out a VC citation for him but it is certain that Russell did not recommend it and Godley refused to forward it. In a small army nothing remains secret and the New Zealand soldiers became increasing embittered towards Godley. They saw officers whose performances had been questionable, such as Johnston's, being rewarded and those who performed exceptional feats of courage ignored or, in the case of Malone, unfairly blamed for the loss of Chunuk Bair by those who never set foot on the summit. As Christopher Pugsley has written:

> The belief grew that Godley would not hear of recommendations for VCs to officers as they were only doing their jobs, and by the end of August the men were prepared to believe anything of their Commander.
>
> The New Zealanders saw the mediocre rewarded and the dead blamed. They laughed bitterly at Johnston's 'excellently conducted' operations and spoke of the VCs that should have been awarded.[36]

Little wonder then that Cyril Bassett was embarrassed to be singled out for the VC when so many others had missed out.

Gallipoli veteran and historian Ormond Burton made a short list of VCs that he believed should have been awarded at Gallipoli. He was especially impressed with the performance of Chaplain Thomas Fielden Taylor. Burton wrote after years of reflection:

> He [Fielden Taylor] it was who gave courage at a time when it was running low after the fearful losses and the strain of drawnout suffering. Four of the men to whom the award of the Victoria Cross at Anzac would have been very popular were Richard Warden, the great scout of the Auckland Battalion, killed on Chunuk Bair . . .

the unknown soldier who was the heart and soul of the Wellington forward trench on Chunuk; Major Wallingford M.C. the hero of Anzac, and Fielden Taylor, the chaplain.[37]

There were many New Zealand heroes on Chunuk Bair in August 1915. That only one VC was won there is a gross injustice, one that leaves a bitter taste even so many years later.

CAPTAIN ALFRED SHOUT

Another New Zealander did win the VC at Gallipoli. He was Captain Alfred John Shout of Wellington, who was serving in the 1st Battalion of the Australian Imperial Force. It is a little ironic that the New Zealand-born Shout, described as 'one of Anzac's most legendary and popular characters',[38] became Australia's most decorated soldier of the Gallipoli campaign.

Shout won his VC at Lone Pine on 9 August 1915, where seven VC awards were made for actions that occurred during 7–9 August. Of the seven VCs awarded, three were won by commissioned officers.

Shout was a military veteran. He had served with the New Zealanders in the Boer War, where he had twice been wounded. Shout emigrated to Sydney in 1907 where he worked as a carpenter and joiner. Upon the outbreak of war in 1914 Shout immediately volunteered his services and, because of his previous military experience, he was commissioned as a junior officer. Shout was one of the first officers ashore during the landing on 25 April and had fought all day on Baby 700 and Walker's Ridge. Two days later he carried more than a dozen wounded men out of the firing line, though he was repeatedly wounded himself while doing so. For this action Shout was awarded the Military Cross and was also mentioned in despatches. Recovering from his wounds, Shout was promoted to Captain 11 days before the attack at Lone Pine. Throughout his service on Gallipoli Shout became renowned for both his cheerfulness and courage.

The Australian infantry took Lone Pine in less than an hour on 6 August, but was then subjected to five days of continuous counterattacks by the Turks. Losses on both sides were heavy. At Lone Pine Alfred Shout was truly inspirational. He was always in the midst of the action and led several bayonet charges on the first two days of attack. It was on 9 August that Shout won the VC while attempting to clear a Turkish lodgement from one of the saps at the Lone Pine position. He was fatally wounded while attempting to clear some trenches when one of his own bombs exploded prematurely, causing horrific injuries. Both his hands were blown to pulp, his left eye was blown out, his check gashed and his chest and one leg burnt. Shout remained cheerful to the end, reluctantly being taken away on a stretcher, stating that he would soon recover. It was not to be. Captain Alfred Shout died of his wounds three days later, just after his 33rd birthday. He was buried at sea from the hospital ship *Euralia*. Later, in one of those terrible clerical mix ups all too common in war, his wife Rose was informed that the report of his death was wrong, that Shout was only wounded and that he would be shortly be returning to Australia. The press in Australia then published news of his return, stating that he would be arriving in Sydney in mid-September. Things did not improve when the Australian government awarded Shout's family a reduced pension. Rose Shout had to remind the government that Shout had been a captain, not a lieutenant, at the time of his death and that he was also the holder of the VC.[39]

Australian historian, Les Carlyon, has recently written of Shout:

Myths were constructed around Simpson and his donkey [John Simpson Kirkpatrick, renowned for transporting wounded men on the back of a donkey], but not around Shout, who died from his wounds at Lone Pine and became Australia's most decorated soldier at Gallipoli. Shout was the casual hero with the cheery manner; he made hard things look easy and made men around him feel better. He deserves to be seen as one of the larger figures of the Gallipoli campaign, and it doesn't much matter whether Australia or New Zealand claims him.[40]

Alfred Shout was a commissioned officer, and had he been serving with his fellow New Zealanders at Chunuk Bair he would not have been awarded the VC, no matter how well he fought. It is therefore inappropriate for New Zealand to stake any claim on Alfred Shout as a VC winner, as tempting as this might be.

DUE RECOGNITION?

On the Gallipoli peninsula in 1915 over a million men fought each other for eight months. For the combatants Gallipoli was a hell on earth. In September, for example, 78 per cent of the Anzacs in seven battalions examined by medical authorities were suffering from dysentery and 60 per cent had skin sores.[41] It was an experience that changed these men for ever. Those who were lucky enough to survive this ordeal by fire were never the same again. As many commentators have noted, New Zealand lost more than just many of its soldiers at Gallipoli. It also lost its innocence. The campaign highlighted the natural talents of the New Zealand soldier, especially in his ability to adapt to the difficult circumstances, and it revealed his potential. The campaign also highlighted the courage of all the combatants involved. In the case of New Zealand, though, exceptional feats of courage tended to go unrewarded. But courage and natural ability were not enough in this war. They could not compensate for failures in planning, leadership, logistics and administration, and no soldiers in this war could afford to be committed to battle only partially trained. For the Allies and for the Anzacs, Gallipoli was a steep and costly learning curve.

The feeling that New Zealand soldiers had not received due recognition for their performances on Gallipoli was not just confined to those who fought there. The feeling was widespread in New Zealand, too, and the question of addressing this injustice was raised in the House of Representatives at the end of 1918. The member for Dunedin South, Thomas Sidey, asked Sir James Allen whether, in view of the lack of awards bestowed on New Zealand soldiers at Gallipoli that 'he will obtain a review of the records of the Gallipoli campaign with the object of having further honours (posthumous if necessary) conferred for meritorious services during that campaign'.[42] Allen replied:

> I regret that the honourable member's suggestion cannot be acceded to. Honours are awarded on the recommendation of senior officers on the spot, who can personally testify to the value of the service rendered. It necessarily follows that many gallant acts escape notice and many brave men go unrewarded. This, of necessity, is common to all campaigns. I do not think it would be possible or desirable to review the records of the Gallipoli campaign in the manner suggested, but a proposal to award a star to those taking part in the first campaigns of the war has been approved.[43]

Eighty years later some members of the New Zealand Parliament were still trying to gain more gallantry awards for New Zealand Gallipoli veterans. Most attention and energy was focused on trying to obtain a VC for Malone. The lack of adequate recognition for their gallantry, especially at Chunuk Bair, has become part of the New Zealand legend about the Gallipoli campaign, reflecting its special place in the nation's history and in its collective consciousness.

CHAPTER 6 The Western Front: 1916

During the First World War, for the combatants of the British Empire, the Western Front was where the numbers of Victoria Crosses grew. In New Zealand's case this was inevitable, as it was here that New Zealand made its main contribution to the war. More than 80,000 New Zealand soldiers served on the Western Front in France and Belgium over a period just short of three years. A further 17,000 New Zealanders served in the Mounted Rifle Brigade, the Imperial Camel Corps and a Wireless Corps in the Middle East. Surprisingly, given the hard fighting experienced in the Sinai-Palestine campaign, no New Zealander (and only one Australian airman) won the VC in this theatre of war despite the fact that several mounted riflemen were nominated for the award.[1] Sustaining a division on the Western Front was a mammoth effort for such a small nation as New Zealand — one that was to cost it dearly in terms of human life and suffering.

The Western Front was where the British and French Armies made their main effort of the war, and it was ultimately where the war was won and lost. From the time of their arrival in early 1916, the New Zealanders were part of the bloody attritional struggles here. The imagery of trench warfare is haunting. It includes waterlogged trenches, muddy wasteland and cruel barbed wire, nerve-shattering artillery barrages, incompetent generals and massive casualties. These powerful images have endured into the twenty-first century. One reason for this is because Britain and her empire lost nearly one million dead in the war, mostly on the Western Front. Of New Zealand's casualties in the 1914–18 war, 84 per cent of them — nearly 15,000 dead and 35,545 wounded — were experienced in the trenches of France and Belgium.

After Gallipoli the New Zealand Expeditionary Force underwent considerable reorganisation. In Egypt the Gallipoli veterans linked up with the newly formed Rifle Brigade and three batches of reinforcements to form an infantry division, the New Zealand Division. For the first time in its history New Zealand had a complete infantry division abroad on active service.

Almost immediately upon its formation the New Zealand Division sailed for France, landing at Marseilles in April 1916. There was little time for the New Zealanders to admire the charms of this new country though, as the men were marched straight from the Marseilles docks to waiting trains for the move to the front.

The New Zealand Division was initially committed to a quiet sector of the front at Armentières. The area was regarded as a 'nursery' and was used for the blooding of new divisions arriving in France. Armentières was also a location where the 'live and let live' system functioned. The advice many of the New Zealand soldiers received from their British counterparts on arriving there was 'Don't fire at him, chum, and he won't fire at you.' The New Zealanders were having none of this. They spent considerable time in repairing the trenches about Armentières, which had been allowed to fall into disrepair. They began actively patrolling No Man's Land. They conducted much reconnaissance so that they became familiar with their frontage and fired on the Germans whenever they could. They also initiated several trench raids that took prisoners and did considerable damage. In those first few months in the front line, the New Zealanders established the routines that they would carry with them throughout their time in France. In the process a raw, inexperienced division began its transformation into an effective fighting formation.

It was during the time at Armentières that the first recommendation for a VC award to a New Zealander was made in France. On the night of 2–3 July, Company Sergeant Major William Edward Frost of the 2nd Wellington Battalion was recommended for the VC for his part in extracting soldiers from No Man's Land after a raiding party from the battalion had got into difficulties. Not only did Frost help cover the withdrawal of the hard-pressed raiding party but he then went into No Man's Land on two separate occasions to rescue wounded soldiers. The recommendation states:

When the withdrawal to their own trenches had been completed Company Sergt Major Frost twice returned to the enemy lines through the German wire and under heavy fire rescued and brought back two wounded men who were lying within a few yards of the enemy's parapet and so prevented them from being taken prisoners.[2]

The recommendation was endorsed by Brigadier William Braithwaite and Major General Russell before being forwarded on to corps headquarters on 28 July 1916. Ignoring its similarity to many other acts that had been recognised with the VC, Frost's recommendation was denied. Instead he was awarded a DCM on 7 August and a Croix de Guerre three weeks later.[3] Frost died three days after receiving this later award from wounds sustained while trying to unhitch an injured horse from a wagon in Armentières.[4]

THE CASE OF PRIVATE JOHN DOUGLAS STARK

Private John Douglas Stark (Starkie) became one of New Zealand's most well-known soldiers of the First World War. One reason for this is that he was made the subject of a best-selling book by Robin Hyde with the evocative title of *Passport to Hell*. The sequel, *Nor the Years Condemn*, was much less popular. During the war years Stark was notorious in the New Zealand Division both for his reckless courage when in action and for his total lack of military discipline when out of the line. This ill discipline, combined with a love of alcohol and serious violent tendencies, meant that Stark was always in trouble with the military authorities. It saw him eventually sentenced to a lengthy sentence at Le Havre military prison from where he later escaped.

According to popular mythology, and recorded in a number of books, Stark was recommended for the VC for his actions on the night of 11–12 July 1916.[5] This was for rescuing more than a dozen wounded men from No Man's Land after a failed trench raid and for destroying two German machine-gun posts in the process. Instead of receiving the award though, the prison sentence, which had been hanging over Stark's head for his previous ill discipline, was commuted. He had been given a five-year suspended sentence at his court martial after being found guilty of drunkenness and attempting to strike a superior officer.

Stark was again recommended for a gallantry award, this time the Military Medal, at the end of the year. In this incident he retrieved a dead New Zealand soldier from No Man's Land in broad daylight and then returned to bring in missing equipment. The Military Medal was not awarded either because, since his court martial in July, Stark's conduct had not improved. He had continued his pattern of being absent from parade and in September had undergone Field Punishment Number 1, being tied to a wagon wheel, for one such infringement. Once again Stark's gallantry in the front line was used to offset his poor disciplinary record.[6]

Despite being badly wounded on two occasions in 1918, Stark survived the war and returned to New Zealand in 1919. He had not changed his ways and was soon in trouble with the authorities, serving time in prisons in New Zealand and Australia. During the Depression of the 1930s Stark worked on various relief projects around New Zealand. James Douglas Stark, the 'wild man' of the New Zealand Division, died of pneumonia in Auckland in 1942. He was 48 years old.

THE SOMME 1916

The main action of 1916 was the Battle of the Somme, in which the New Zealanders were committed to its third phase. The Battle of the Somme was the first real test for the New Zealand Division. On 15 September 1916, the same day that the newly invented tank made its appearance, the New Zealand Division attacked the German front-line trenches along with nine other British divisions. The New Zealand attack occurred between High and Delville Woods in the direction of Flers village. Ahead of them were three formidable and intact German trench systems. It was during the opening day of this attack and for his subsequent actions on 1 October that a New

Zealand sergeant, Donald Forrester Brown, won the VC. In keeping with the strict adherence to the War Office guidelines, Brown's VC was the only one awarded to the New Zealanders in 1916. Even then, it was only awarded after considerable lobbying by the officers of his battalion.

In its attack on the Somme, the New Zealand Division took almost all its objectives. It was in the line for three weeks, fighting without a break from 15 September until 2 October 1916. In hard fighting, often in thick mud and atrocious weather conditions, the division captured two miles of enemy territory and more than 1000 German prisoners. When the New Zealanders were withdrawn the division was in a sorry state. The men were exhausted, having reached the limits of their physical endurance. They were caked in mud, unshaven, and their clothes were ruined. They had the appearance of walking skeletons. The casualties on the Somme were heavy, some 7408 — the equivalent of seven of the division's 12 infantry battalions. Some units suffered losses in excess of 80 per cent of their personnel. Numbered among the dead was Sergeant Brown, killed in action on 1 October.

The New Zealand Division passed through its first offensive on the Western Front and established a formidable reputation while doing so. But its success came with a very high price tag. It would be many months before the New Zealand Division was in a fit state to be committed to a major action again.

THE SOMME VC:
SERGEANT DONALD FORRESTER BROWN

Sergeant Donald Forrester Brown, New Zealand's first VC winner on the Western Front, was born in Dunedin on 23 February 1890. Brown was educated in South Dunedin and at Waitaki Boys' High School, Oamaru. Prior to 1914, Brown had been farming at Totara for three years. He sold his farm and enlisted in the NZEF on 19 October 1915. He sailed with the 9th Reinforcements, arriving in Egypt in January 1916. Four months later Brown was in France serving with the 2nd Otago Battalion, part of the newly formed New Zealand Division. He left a revealing account of the division's arrival in France:

On arrival we had to wait about 24 hours before disembarking, but once off we entrained straight away for our place in the north. We passed through some great country, and were altogether some 55 hours in the train, and as we were all in a great mood, styled ourselves Massey's tourists. We reached our destination about 10.30 p.m., and found to our disgust that we had ten miles to march to reach our billets. That perhaps might not have been so bad, but it was cold as cold could be, and raining cats and dogs, and after the heat of Egypt we were feeling it pretty bad. Well, on we marched in full pack, then the Colonel lost his way, and we had to retrace our steps, and arrived at our destination at 4.30 a.m. Some were so beat that they lay down by the way, not caring what became of them. Where we are now we can see the cannon sending their shells to the enemy lines. Aeroplanes of all sorts and sizes fly about.[7]

At the end of August 1916, the New Zealand Division moved south to Picardy in preparation for its attack on the Somme. As another of Brown's letters shows, most New Zealand soldiers knew they would soon be in the thick of the action:

We have been relieved from the trenches, and are now further south, just behind where the fighting is going on. This country is a great place, and travelling down to here was as good as a month by the sea. The crops all over are just lovely, and France can hold her own for beauty. Shortly you will be hearing of us New Zealanders making an attack, as from what has been said and done, and the solid training we have been putting in, all leads to our making an attack shortly.[8]

Brown's last letter home, written just days before the New Zealand attack, shows he realised the likelihood of death or injury:

Just where we are at present things are going 'Somme'. We expect to get up very soon, and the noise is something deadly, and just here divisions go in and come out in a day or two reduced to less than company strength; so don't be surprised if I manage a trip. We are all in great spirits at being able to have a hand in this big push.[9]

The New Zealand Division fought in three major engagements during its three weeks on the Somme. These were on 15 September, the opening day of this third phase of the battle, followed by subsequent actions on 25 September and 1 October. Sergeant Brown won his VC for the heroism he displayed on two of these days.

On the evening of 14 September the New Zealand Division was in the front-line trenches between High and Delville Woods ready to launch a dawn assault. Their objective was to capture a large slice of the German front-line trenches around the villages of Flers and Gueudecourt, an advance of around three kilometres. The attack involved an uphill advance to capture the first German trench — named Switch Trench, or the Green Line — which sat atop the ridgeline there. The advance would continue in its next stage downhill to capture two more German trench lines, including the heavily fortified Flers Trench network — the Brown and Blue Lines respectively. The final stage of the advance would see one battalion advance to the Red Line or Grove Alley on Flers' northern outskirts.

As the New Zealanders moved into position an artillery barrage that had commenced three days earlier was pounding the German trenches. After a hasty breakfast, which included a tot of rum, New Zealand soldiers from the 2nd Infantry and 3rd Rifle Brigades climbed out of their trenches at 6.20 a.m. and moved gingerly forward behind the protection of a creeping barrage. The New Zealanders were on the left of the corps' line, the 41st Division was in the centre, a sector that included the troublesome feature of Delville Wood, and the 14th Division formed the corps' right flank. Facing the New Zealanders were two German divisions. They were the 3rd Bavarian Division, defending Crest and Switch Trenches, and the 4th Bavarian Division at Flers. Soldiers from both these divisions had been on the receiving end of the intense artillery barrage and had sought safety in their deep shelters.

In the 2nd Brigade sector, eight companies from the 2nd Otago and the 2nd Auckland Battalions advanced in four waves. They closed in on the German trenches and easily passed through the broken wire. In a well-coordinated venture the New Zealand infantry reached the German trenches just as the barrage lifted. The first two trenches, Coffee and Crest Trench, were easily taken with many Germans being killed in the process. Taking the next trench, however, was not so easy.

Switch Trench was 250 yards behind Crest Trench. As they advanced towards it the New Zealanders realised that one of their flanks was exposed. In their advance the New Zealanders had outpaced the 140th Brigade of 40 Division, now held up by stubborn German resistance at High Wood. The German defenders were able to pour enfilade fire into the Otago Battalion and this they did with a vengeance. Many Otago soldiers were hit and the advance was held up. It was during this crucial moment that Sergeant Brown and Corporal Jesse Rodgers swung away from the men on the flank and crept to within 30 yards of a machine-gun. They rushed it, killed the crew of four and brought the gun back. The two New Zealand battalions reformed in preparation for an assault on Switch Trench which they would charge as soon as the artillery barrage lifted. While waiting for the barrage to lift they came under fire from the rear by a machine-gun. Brown was again in the thick of the action. He and other soldiers rushed the gun and killed the crew. Then the barrage lifted and the New Zealand survivors rushed through the shattered barbed wire and stormed the trenches ahead of them. It was a successful assault. By 6.50 a.m. the New Zealand infantry were in complete control of the Switch Trench system.

The soldiers immediately set to work improving the defences of the trench in preparation for a counterattack. Brown was instrumental in organising this defence and rallying the men. The weary Otago soldiers remained in the Switch Trench until they were relieved at 2.00 a.m. the next day. Brown's company, which had started the morning with 180 men, was down to just 57. One of those wounded on 15 September later wrote of Brown:

> We advanced on 15th Sept., and to me it looked as though the men in our platoon would have followed him anywhere, for the simple reason that he would never ask a man to go anywhere, or do anything, that he wouldn't do himself.[10]

The 2nd Brigade was not involved in the attack on 25 September, but relieved the 1st Brigade in the Gird Trench on the night of 28–29 September in preparation for another attack on 1 October. The weather was atrocious and there was heavy German shelling.

On the morning of 1 October an eight-hour British artillery barrage began in preparation for the attack, which was timed for 3.15 p.m. that afternoon. The signal for the attack on the 2nd Canterbury's front was to be a barrage of 36 oil mortars, a terrible weapon that would smother the German trenches with flame and thick smoke. As the German trenches disappeared under a wall of flame and black cloud, the New Zealand infantry attacked. There was heavy opposition from the start and within minutes the two Otago companies on the right had lost all their officers. Sergeant Brown's company suffered heavily when attacking the Circus Trench. The attack was again held up by a machine-gun. Brown went forward, alone this time, located the gun, shot the crew with a German Luger pistol, and captured it.[11] This was the third time in two military actions that Brown was primarily responsible for restoring the momentum to a brigade attack. Once Brown had dealt with the troublesome machine-gun the New Zealand infantry attacked and captured the trench. Unfortunately though, Brown, who was in the vanguard of the attack, was hit in the head by long-range machine-gun fire and killed.

For a time it seemed as if Brown's repeated acts of gallantry on the Somme would not receive recognition. His company commander wrote to Brown's father that:

In the first trench we took he did some very good work, and I sent forward a recommendation for a D.C.M. to Headquarters. I enclose a copy of my recommendation, but I regret that owing to his untimely end nothing further came of it.[12]

Brown's battalion commander confirmed this when he wrote to his father that 'if he had lived I had hoped to recommend him, at least for the D.C.M., and he might have got a Victoria Cross'.[13] The officers of the 2nd Otago Battalion, however, would not let the matter rest. They lobbied their senior officers incessantly until a VC was finally approved. This accounts for Brown's recommendation for the VC being dated 14 April 1917 and its final appearance in the *London Gazette* on 14 June 1917, some eight months after the action it described.[14] On 30 August 1917, the Governor-General of New Zealand, the Earl of Liverpool, presented the nation's second VC of the war to Brown's father at Oamaru. The VC is still held by the Brown family. Sergeant Donald Forrester Brown VC is buried in the Warlencourt British Military Cemetery, France.

ANOTHER RECOMMENDATION

It is worth noting that a New Zealand officer was recommended for the VC for his actions on the Somme. He was Captain Frederick Starnes of 12th Nelson Company, 2nd Canterbury Battalion. During the attack on 20 September, 2nd Canterbury Battalion had secured their objective when, at 10.00 p.m. they came under a ferocious counterattack. The battalion's blocking positions were overrun, the Germans were able to encircle both flanks and the battalion was in danger of being isolated and destroyed. The history of the Canterbury Regiment describes how the situation was saved:

At this juncture Captain F. Starnes arrived with the remaining platoons of the 12th Company. Finding men of all companies mixed together, and in many cases without leaders, he organised small parties and set them to clear the enemy out of definite areas.

Captain Starnes personally led party after party, and after some very desperate fighting he at length cleared the trench from our right flank to the northern end of Drop Alley. He then led attacks on Drop Alley, till by 4 a.m. the whole of it was in our hands, and he was able to hand it over to the Black Watch.[15]

It was an impressive feat of military leadership and gallantry for which Starnes was recommended for the VC by his commanding officer, Lieutenant Colonel Hugh Stewart, and supported by Brigadier William Braithwaite. As his recommendation acknowledges:

Throughout these operations Captain Starnes displayed under extremely trying circumstances the greatest courage, coolness and energy, and set a magnificent example to all ranks.[16]

The VC was denied Starnes but on 1 October 1916 he received the 'immediate award' of the DSO instead.[17]

OTHER VCS OF SIGNIFICANCE

Four VCs that had strong connections to New Zealand were won on the Western Front. New Zealand-born soldiers serving with the Australian Imperial Force (AIF) won three of these VCs, while Bernard Freyberg, who was serving with the 63rd (Royal Naval) Division in France, won the other. Two were won in 1916 and two in 1918.

Private Thomas Cooke of the 8th Infantry Battalion, AIF, won the first of these VCs. Private Cooke, a builder born at Kaikoura in 1881, had moved to Melbourne a few years before the outbreak of the war. He won the award at Pozieres, in the Somme region, on 24 July 1916. When the Australians attempted to consolidate their hold on Pozieres, Private Cooke was ordered to take his Lewis gun team out into a dangerous part of the line. It was a machine-gun post that had been badly sited. Cooke and his team set off and quickly established their gun in the position. Its fire soon cleared the immediate area of German resistance but the post remained vulnerable to long-range machine-gun fire. One by one Cooke's men were hit and the Germans launched a counterattack. Cooke remained at his post, firing the gun until it ran out of ammunition. Still he remained at the post, pretending that it was still operational until he was killed. Like many Australian soldiers who fought on the Somme in 1916, Thomas Cooke has no known grave. His name, along with those of 10,700 other Australian servicemen, appears on the Villers-Bretonneux Memorial some 16 kilometres east of Amiens. Cooke's posthumous VC was gazetted on 9 September 1916 and is on public display at the Queen Elizabeth II Army Memorial Museum in Waiouru.

Captain (Temporary Lieutenant Colonel) Bernard Cyril Freyberg also won his VC in the fighting on the Somme in 1916. Freyberg was born in Richmond, Surrey, in 1889, but his family moved to Wellington, New Zealand, in 1891. Freyberg trained as a dentist and was commissioned as a junior officer in the Hauraki Regiment. Unable to obtain a commission in the New Zealand Staff Corps, Freyberg left New Zealand in 1913 and travelled to London at the outbreak of the war where he accosted Winston Churchill, then First Lord of the Admiralty, for a commission in the Royal Naval Division. He served at Gallipoli, where he won the first of four DSOs, and in France soon after. During the attack on Beaucourt village by two brigades of the 63rd Division, heavy German fire had decimated the attacking force. Freyberg's Hood Battalion, like the others in that attack, had been cut to pieces, but under his inspiring leadership it still managed to take its objectives. Unfortunately it was the only battalion that did and the survivors of the Hood Battalion plus some assorted stragglers were occupying a position embedded more than a mile into the enemy lines. Despite being hit twice during the attack Freyberg rallied his battalion and the survivors of the other units, and prepared to attack the Germans again on the following day. This they did, capturing the village of Beaucourt. Freyberg was hit again in this attack but stayed to organise his defences against a counterattack. While making a final inspection of the new defences Freyberg was hit a fourth time, this time severely. He still managed to issue his final instructions while being carried from the field on a stretcher. The village of Beaucourt was held.

Freyberg had provided inspiring leadership throughout this attack. A fellow VC winner, Major General Sir Henry de Beauvoir de Lisle, rated Freyberg's performance on the Somme in November 1916 as 'probably the most distinguished personal act of the War'.[18] During the next war Freyberg would continue to provide inspiring leadership as the general officer commanding the 2nd New Zealand Division and of the 2nd NZEF. He would also serve two terms as governor-general of New Zealand during 1946–52. Freyberg is regarded as one of New Zealand's finest military commanders. He died in 1963 when one of his Gallipoli wounds ruptured.

CHAPTER 7 The Western Front: 1917

The year 1917 was, without doubt, the worst year of the war for the United Kingdom and the dominions. For the New Zealand Division, 1917 was a long, hard year — the only full year of service for the division on the Western Front. Brought up to full strength after the Somme fighting and having to spend considerable time integrating the new arrivals, the New Zealanders faced their first large-scale offensive in the middle of the year. On the morning of 7 June 1917 the New Zealanders and Australians stormed the Messines Ridge in the Ypres salient in Belgium. Their job was made much easier by the meticulous planning of General Sir Herbert Plumer and the Second Army Staff. This included the detonation of 19 huge mines under the German front-line trenches. The New Zealand attack at Messines went very well and, apart from the attack on 4 October, was the only success the New Zealanders were to experience in 1917. In fact Messines was, according to the British Expeditionary Force commander, Field Marshal Sir Douglas Haig, the finest success in the war to that time.[1] It was at Messines that the second New Zealand VC on the Western Front was won, by Lance Corporal Samuel Frickleton. Just over a month later Corporal Leslie Wilton Andrew won another VC at La Basse Ville, also in the Messines sector.

The New Zealanders returned to the Ypres salient in October to take part in two great attacks. The first, launched on 4 October 1917, was a stunning success and all the allocated objectives were easily taken. The next attack, made just over a week later, on 12 October, was a tragic failure. It remains New Zealand's worst ever military disaster. More New Zealanders were killed and maimed on this morning than on any other day since the European settlement of New Zealand. It is surprising then, given the British guidelines and the gallantry displayed, that no VCs were awarded for either of these actions.

In December came another failed attack, this time at Polderhoek Chateau by the 2nd New Zealand Infantry Brigade. It was at Polderhoek that Private Henry James Nicholas won his VC, one of only two New Zealand VCs ever awarded to a private soldier. Although only a minor action, the attack at Polderhoek Chateau was a costly failure for the two battalions involved. It capped off a hard, difficult year for the New Zealanders.

A VC AT MESSINES RIDGE: LANCE CORPORAL SAMUEL FRICKLETON

Samuel Frickleton was born in Slamannan, Scotland, on 1 April 1891. He immigrated to New Zealand in 1913 and worked as a miner in the West Coast's famous Blackball coal mine.

Frickleton enlisted in the NZEF on 12 February 1915 and sailed for Egypt with the 5th Reinforcements in June as a corporal in the Canterbury Battalion. Upon his arrival in Egypt Frickleton became so seriously ill that he was forced to return to New Zealand, where he was discharged as medically unfit on 11 November 1915. His personal file reveals that he was suffering from tuberculosis.[2] Recovery must have been swift though because Frickleton re-enlisted in April 1916, this time embarking for the United Kingdom with the 15th Reinforcements. He was sent to France in late 1916 as a rifleman in the 3rd Battalion, 3rd New Zealand (Rifle) Brigade.

On that cold June morning in 1917 Frickleton was one of many soldiers ready to assault the Messines Ridge following the detonation of the huge mines under the German trenches. While only 19 of the 21 mines exploded, the one million pounds of ammonal and gun-cotton caused massive destruction and the shock waves were felt as far away as London. This eruption stunned the Germans, but there was more to come. An artillery barrage from 2266 field guns and howitzers and the fire of 144 machine-guns immediately followed the explosion. Behind the barrage at 3.10 a.m. came British and Anzac infantry attacking on a ten-mile front with the aim of snatching the Messines Ridge from the

Germans. This ridge was a vital piece of ground offering superb observation over the British lines around Ypres.

Just after 3.00 a.m. the New Zealand infantry moved forward in darkness and into the smoke caused by the explosions. They moved down into the valley, crossed the shallow Steenbeek Stream and started advancing up the ridge. The two forward infantry brigades easily took the trenches on the slopes of the ridge and then another brigade following up on this success passed through the new positions and captured a line beyond Messines village.

On the reverse slope of the Messines Ridge the first effective German resistance was encountered when the Rifle Brigade ran into a well-defended second line of trenches on the outskirts of Messines. Machine-gun fire inflicted heavy casualties, forcing the brigade's 3rd Battalion to take cover. The New Zealand advance was momentarily stalled. The fire was intense and many New Zealand soldiers were hit, including Lance Corporal Frickleton's company commander, who was killed.

It was at this moment that Frickleton, already slightly wounded in the right arm, decided to deal with the most troublesome of the machine-gun posts. He signalled his section to follow him, and together they advanced into their own artillery barrage and attacked the machine-gun post in open order. Being concealed by the noise and debris caused by the barrage, Frickleton was able to get within a few yards of the post before he lobbed in a Mills bomb. When it exploded, he rushed the machine-gun and bayoneted the surviving crew. He then went on to deal with a second machine-gun post about 20 yards away. While his men provided covering fire, Frickleton crept up to the edge of the post and destroyed the gun and crew single-handed, accounting for some 12 German soldiers in total. As a result of Frickleton's action the advance was able to continue and the final objective was reached.

Frickleton continued to rally and led his men until he was wounded again, this time in the hip. He was then caught in a German phosgene gas attack. Severely affected, he had to be carried from the battlefield, being later evacuated to the United Kingdom. The 3rd Battalion had taken all its objectives, plus 100 prisoners and three machine-guns. Its own casualties were heavy: 21 killed and 75 wounded.[3]

Frickleton's VC citation appeared in the *London Gazette* on 2 August 1917 and King George V later presented him his VC.

Frickleton returned to France in July 1917, but in October was again evacuated to the United Kingdom through illness. He was promoted to sergeant and then attended the Officer Cadet Training Unit (OCTU) in Cambridge, where he graduated as a second lieutenant in March 1918.

A recurrence of his earlier illness, compounded by the lasting effects of his gas inhalation, prevented his return to active service. In June 1918 he was returned to New Zealand as medically unfit and ceased service with the NZEF in December 1918.

This was not the end of Frickleton's military service though. He was commissioned as a lieutenant in the New Zealand Staff Corps in October 1919 and served until April 1927 when he was retired on medical grounds. His health during these years was poor and he suffered a nervous breakdown in 1925. At the end of 1926, with 'my health and nerves . . . giving way', Frickleton requested that he be paraded before a medical board. The board met in November 1926 and concluded that Frickleton was 'permanently unfit' and recommended that he be discharged from the service.[4] He was retired on 30 April 1927 with a miserly pension of £45 10s a year.

In 1934 Frickleton resumed service in the Territorial Force and was promoted to captain. His health was still poor and a letter he wrote in May of that year seeking an extension to his sick leave indicates some of his health problems. A doctor had to examine Frickleton's nose twice weekly 'and after he has probed around, my nose usually bleeds for a day or so after, and I would not like to take any unnecessary risk'.[5] In 1937 Frickleton was a member of the New Zealand Coronation Contingent that travelled to the United Kingdom for King George VI's coronation. Frickleton ceased service with the Territorial Force in 1937.

In 1939 Frickleton again volunteered for service overseas. A confidential minute by the assistant director of Medical Services indicates why Frickleton's offer of service was turned down:

The Medical History of Captain Frickleton, V.C. shows that he has been pensioned for Pulmonary Tuberculosis following his war service, and his last pensions report in 1927 stated that he had Pulmonary Fibrosis.[6]

Despite his illness Samuel Frickleton lived until he was 80 years old. He died on 6 August 1971. He is buried at the Taita Servicemen's Cemetery, Lower Hutt, and his VC is on public display at the Queen Elizabeth II Army Memorial Museum in Waiouru.

RECOMMENDATIONS BUT NO AWARDS

Two soldiers in the Rifle Brigade were recommended for the VC for their actions at Messines. The first was Corporal Henry John Jeffrey of the 1st Battalion, New Zealand Rifle Brigade. At Messines on 7 June Corporal Jeffery found himself alone facing an enemy dugout. Inside the dugout was a German machine-gun team firing on the Australians advancing in the valley. Corporal Jeffrey did not hesitate and rushed the dugout. His recommendation for the VC states: 'For conspicuous bravery and gallantry in action, single handed he attacked an enemy machine-gun position killing five of the enemy, wounding one and taking twelve prisoners.'[7]

Corporal Jeffrey was recommended for the VC by his commanding officer, and the brigade commander endorsed it. General Russell did not agree though, drawing three lines through the letters VC and writing DCM above and below it. Corporal Jeffrey was duly awarded the DCM but unfortunately did not live long enough to receive it. He was killed in action less than a fortnight later.

Later that day Rifleman Alfred Dunthorne, a stretcher-bearer with the Rifle Brigade's 4th Battalion, was also recommended for the VC for 'very conspicuous gallantry' while on Messines Ridge. Dunthorne had witnessed three men of a neighbouring company buried by German artillery rounds. 'He at once rushed to the place and amid thickly falling shells, heedless of his own danger, at the cost of great effort, he personally dug out two of the three men who had been almost completely buried.' This was risky business and another artillery shell buried all four men. Dunthorne, although 'badly shaken and dazed' worked on. 'Through his great personal bravery, fearlessness and grit under the most trying circumstances, he undoubtedly saved three men's lives.'[8]

This time Russell was happy to endorse the recommendation of the battalion commanding officer, Major Edward Puttick, and the brigade commander, Lieutenant Colonel Hugh Stewart. General Godley did not think the action worthy of a VC though and downgraded it to a DCM.

It is interesting to note that according to Hugh Stewart, the historian of the New Zealand Division, two NCOs of the Rifle Brigade were also recommended for the VC. Stewart records of the 4th Battalion New Zealand Rifle Brigade on 7 June:

> Splendid feats of arms were performed by 2 n.c.o.s, Sergt. J.W. Penrose and L-Sergt. J.E. Thomson, both of whom fell. With Dunthorne they were recommended for the VC.[9]

The recommendations for neither of these NCOs has been found.

A SPECIAL MISSION: CORPORAL LESLIE WILTON ANDREW

Leslie Wilton Andrew was born in Ashhurst in the Manawatu on 23 March 1897. The family moved to Wanganui where Andrew's father, William, was headmaster of Wanganui East School. Leslie Andrew was educated at Wanganui Boys' High School and later at the Wanganui Collegiate. After leaving school Andrew worked as a railway clerk until he joined the NZEF in October 1915. To ensure that he saw overseas service Andrew gave his age at enlistment as 20 and left New Zealand with the 12th Reinforcements in May 1916. On board the ship was another young man who had also lied about his age to get overseas. His name was Howard Karl Kippenberger and he would, in the next great conflict, become one of New Zealand's most well-known military commanders. Both men would play a key role in the Battle of Crete in May 1941.

The 12th Reinforcements spent an unwelcome three months in Egypt before sailing for France in August 1916. Eight days after joining the 2nd Wellington Battalion Andrew was wounded in the neck by shrapnel on the Somme in September 1916. Nine months later and still some months shy of his twenty-first birthday, Leslie Andrew won the VC for his actions at La Basse Ville.

On 31 July 1917, the British Second Army carried out a dawn attack as part of the battle to extend its hold on the Messines Ridge. In this attack, two New Zealand infantry battalions had been allocated three tasks. They were to take and hold La Basse Ville village, then clear a hedgerow system 500 yards to the north of the village and set up outposts there. Finally they were to raid the German defences between their newly established front and the railway line. The 2nd Wellington Battalion was to take and hold La Basse Ville and clear the hedgerow system, and the 1st Auckland Battalion was to raid the German defences to the north.

The New Zealand infantry were roused from their rain-flooded trenches at 3.30 a.m., given a tot of rum and prepared to move forward at 3.50 a.m. Right on time the British artillery fired a creeping barrage and the New Zealand infantry advanced behind it.

The village of La Basse Ville had been taken in an earlier New Zealand attack on 26 July. However, a successful German counterattack had retaken it the next day. During the attack of 26 July a German machine-gun post in an *estaminet* (or inn) on the Warneton Road had inflicted heavy casualties on the attacking infantry and had been instrumental in preventing the New Zealanders from thoroughly securing the village against a counterattack. In this attack on 31 July the attacking New Zealanders had made plans to deal with this troublesome position. That cold, wet morning Lance Corporal Andrew was leading two sections from the Wellington-West Coast Company on a special mission to attack and destroy the German machine-gun post in the two-storeyed *estaminet*.

On the way to their objective Andrew saw that a platoon from the Ruahine Company was having difficulty in reaching the railway line. It had run into heavy machine-gun fire coming from a flank. Andrew spotted the machine-gun and decided to help out the beleaguered platoon. With one section providing covering fire he led the other along the railway line and took the German machine-gun crew by surprise.

Andrew then regathered his men and proceeded on to the *estaminet*. While conducting a reconnaissance the German defenders spotted the New Zealanders and opened fire on them with the machine-gun. Andrew halted the attack, reorganised, and then attacked the Germans from a new direction, making a detour through a patch of thistles to do so. Andrew's small force, now down to just four men, was able to reach the rear of the building without being detected. They then threw in Mills bombs and stormed the building. It was easily captured. Having taken his objective, Andrew was not satisfied with the result. He and Private L.R. Ritchie undertook a reconnaissance towards Warneton and advanced as far as the British standing barrage would let them. This was a distance of about 300 yards, which brought them to the outskirts of the village. During this reconnaissance Andrew attacked and destroyed another machine-gun in an open trench. He and Ritchie also attacked German soldiers sheltering in a cellar and adjoining dugouts before returning to the *estaminet*.

An account of Andrew's action written by the official New Zealand correspondent appeared on 13 August 1917:

In all the recent fighting in which New Zealanders took part there was nothing finer than the heroism and leadership of a Wellington regiment sergeant, detailed to attack and capture an enemy machine-gun position in an isolated estaminet. He led his men forward, only to come unexpectedly upon another gun that was sending out a continuous stream of bullets and stopping the advance on the left. He immediately attacked this position, killed several of the crew, and put the rest to flight. After this adventure he was able to get only three of his men together.

With these three he proceeded to gain his ultimate objective. Observing that frontal attack would mean the destruction of his little band, he led the party through some thistles and attacked from the rear. As soon as they were close enough the intrepid four threw bombs at the crew and rushed upon the Germans, killing four, putting the rest to flight, and capturing the gun and the position. Leaving behind two men to remove the gun, the sergeant took the remaining man with him and advanced on a reconnoitring expedition as far the British barrage would permit. He brought back valuable information. Throughout the whole of these operations enemy shells were pounding into the position, and there was much machine-gun and rifle fire.[10]

Andrew's VC citation appeared in the *London Gazette* on 6 September 1917.

Les Andrew continued to serve on the Western Front and was promoted to sergeant on 1 August 1917. In March the following year he was commissioned. When his service ceased with the NZEF in October 1918, Andrew was an acting captain. He was lucky to survive the war, having been wounded twice and buried three times in the debris caused by exploding German artillery shells.

After the war Andrew secured a commission in the New Zealand Staff Corps, the equivalent of today's Regular Force. He returned to New Zealand in 1919, bringing with him a war bride from the United Kingdom. He was lucky to obtain a commission in the Staff Corps, as at least one senior officer had not been impressed by his leadership qualities. Brigadier A.E. Stewart wrote in reply to an enquiry from New Zealand:

> Captain Andrew proved an able instructor but lacks force and has no administrative abilities. I have already recommended officers who I consider more suitable for appointment to the New Zealand Staff Corps.[11]

As with most serving officers of the New Zealand Staff Corps, Andrew occupied many staff appointments in New Zealand. He was fortunate, however, to be one of three New Zealand officers chosen for a two-year exchange with the Indian Army from 1927 to 1929, where he served with the Highland Light Infantry. Like his fellow VC winner Frickleton, Andrew travelled to the United Kingdom with the Coronation Contingent in 1937. When the Second World War broke out in 1939 he was a major. In January 1940 Andrew was promoted to lieutenant colonel, seconded to the 2nd New Zealand Expeditionary Force (2nd NZEF) and given command of the 22nd Battalion, which became part of the Fifth Infantry Brigade.

As commanding officer of the 22nd Battalion, Andrew soon established a reputation as a strict disciplinarian. The nickname bestowed on him by the soldiers of the battalion was 'February' because of his habit of handing out 28-day detentions whatever the infringement. Andrew's 22nd Battalion saw little action in Greece, but it occupied the vital Maleme airfield and Hill 107 on Crete. Although told by General Freyberg to hold these positions 'at all costs', Andrew did not do so. The loss of Maleme airfield led to the loss of Crete and after the war Andrew drew much criticism in accounts of the Battle of Crete for this failure.

Andrew continued to command the 22nd Battalion in the early North African campaign. During Operation CRUSADER he temporarily took over 5 Brigade when Brigadier James Hargest was captured and he succeeded in attacking a German force at Menastir on 3 December 1941. For this action he was mentioned in despatches. However, as a result of his earlier performance Freyberg 'had lost faith in Andrew after the debacle of Crete'[12] and in February 1942 Andrew was returned to New Zealand.

Back in New Zealand Andrew commanded the Wellington Fortress Area and received a DSO in 1942 for his war services. In 1946 he commanded the Victory Contingent to London and attended the Imperial Defence College from 1947 to 1948. He was promoted to brigadier in 1948 and later commanded the Central Military District until his retirement in 1952. Leslie Wilton Andrew died in Palmerston North on 8 January 1969. He is buried at the Levin RSA Cemetery and his VC is on public display at the Queen Elizabeth II Army Memorial Museum in Waiouru.

Attacking a chateau:
Private Henry James Nicholas

Henry James Nicholas, the first soldier from Canterbury to win the VC, was born at Lincoln, about 20 miles south of Christchurch, on 11 June 1891. A carpenter by trade, Nicholas enlisted in the NZEF on 8 February 1916. He sailed for the United Kingdom with the 13th Reinforcements in May 1916, arriving in France as a private in the 1st Canterbury Battalion in September of that year. He was still a private soldier when he won the VC for his actions in the New Zealand attack at Polderhoek Chateau, near Gheluvelt in Belgium, on 3 December 1917.

The New Zealand attack aimed to dislodge the Germans from the chateau on the Polderhoek spur. The spur was a vital piece of high ground that overlooked the trenches then occupied by the 2nd New Zealand Infantry Brigade. It was planned to attack this position in the early afternoon of 3 December.

The attack started at noon when three brigades of artillery commenced firing a creeping barrage. Unfortunately, the attack was plagued with difficulties from the outset. Owing to the muddy conditions, many rounds of the opening artillery barrage fell short, causing heavy casualties amongst the 1st Otago Battalion, one of the two lead battalions in the attack. As soon as the attack began an icy wind sprung up from the west, dispersing the protective smoke barrage that had been fired.

The 1st Otago and 1st Canterbury Battalions set off in two waves abreast of each other. The ground was muddy and torn up with shell holes, which considerably slowed their progress. There was little German resistance at first until the two battalions reached the rise of the spur. Then heavy machine-gun fire coming from all directions halted their advance. This curtain of fire inflicted heavy casualties on the advancing New Zealanders. The 12th Nelson Company of 1st Canterbury was particularly affected, but its momentum was restored when the company commander, Captain G.H. Gray, rushed one of the machine-gun positions in a ruined pillbox, attacking it with Mills bombs. He captured eight Germans and the gun.

The German defenders then launched a frontal attack supported by enfilade machine-gun fire from the flanks. The New Zealand infantry faltered but Captain Gray rallied the men and they pushed the Germans back past several concrete pillboxes which the New Zealanders wrongly assumed were abandoned. Captain Gray was later awarded a Military Cross. Had he not been a commissioned officer, Captain Gray probably would have won the VC for his actions on this day.

One German machine-gun post in a well-defended strongpost was proving to be particularly troublesome. Its machine-gun opened up on the New Zealanders at close range. A section of infantry tried to storm the post but the section commander and several of the men attacking it were killed.

Private Nicholas was on the right of the New Zealand line with a Lewis gun crew attempting to form a defensive flank against the deadly machine-gun fire. He witnessed the fate of this infantry section and decided to intervene. Nicholas signalled the gun crew to follow him and then rushed forward undetected towards the post, reaching the parapet before the Germans realised it. Nicholas was actually alone now as he had a 25-yard head start on his section. At the parapet Nicholas shot the German officer in command of the post at point-blank range and then overcame the remainder of the garrison, some 16 men, using Mills bombs, German stick grenades and the bayonet. Four wounded Germans survived Nicholas' attack and he took them prisoner along with the captured machine-gun.

Nicholas' actions ensured that the advance could continue and the New Zealanders managed to get to within 150 yards of the chateau before the Germans halted them just after 1.00 p.m. With over 50 per cent of the attacking force now casualties, including most of their officers and senior NCOs, the New Zealand infantry could do little but dig in where they were. Immediately the Germans put in a series of counterattacks. During this time Nicholas went up and down the company line, collecting and redistributing ammunition. The counterattacks were driven off and the new line held until the two New Zealand battalions were relieved on 4 and 5 December. Private Nicholas' VC was gazetted on 8 January 1918.

Nicholas remained with his company, being promoted to sergeant in 1918. In October 1918 he was awarded the Military Medal for gallantry in the field. Tragically Sergeant Nicholas was killed only 19 days before the armistice in a minor skirmish. On the evening of 23 October 1918, Nicholas was on guard duty at a bridge over the St George River near Le Quesnoy when a German patrol stumbled onto the position. In the firefight that followed the German patrol suffered heavy casualties and one New Zealand soldier was killed — Nicholas. The history of the New Zealand Division in France records that Nicholas 'was in every respect a particularly fine soldier and man . . . setting always an invaluable example of steadfastness and faithfulness'.[13] His death was indeed a sad loss to his battalion and to New Zealand. Nicholas was buried in the Vertigneul Churchyard, Romeries, France. His mother bequeathed his VC and MM to the Canterbury Museum in 1932.

ANOTHER RECOMMENDATION

One further New Zealand soldier was recommended for the VC in 1917. He was Sapper William James Frederick Taylor, serving away from the New Zealand Division with the Tunnelling Company of the Royal Engineers. On the night of 15 June 1917 a German artillery round landed on a British ammunition dump, causing a massive explosion. Sapper Taylor ran into the flames of the explosion to rescue a wounded man. The recommendation states:

> Without hesitation he went into the flames and smoke . . . the wounded man will probably recover and if so Sapper Taylor undoubtedly saved his life at the great risk of his own.[14]

Major Henry M. Hudspect, commander of 171 Company, Royal Engineers, signed the recommendation and forwarded it on to the New Zealand Division for further action. Unfortunately no further action on the recommendation was taken and Sapper Taylor received no recognition at all for his gallantry.

Chapter 8 The Western Front: 1918

The heavy casualties of 1917 and a dwindling manpower pool forced the British at the beginning of 1918 to reduce the strength of their divisions from 12 infantry battalions to nine. While the Australians soon followed this reorganisation, the Canadians and New Zealanders did not. With its 12 infantry battalions plus an additional three entrenching battalions formed from the rump of the disbanded 4th New Zealand Brigade, and with an adequate reinforcement pool back in the United Kingdom, the New Zealand Division in 1918 was the strongest division in the British armies in France. In infantry strength it was the equivalent of a British corps.

For the New Zealand Division 1918 began with it recovering from the catastrophic defeat at Passchendaele the previous October. When spring finally arrived the fine weather offered the chance to scrub off the mud and blood of the Ypres salient. The men's spirits and health began to revive.

It was only the briefest of respites. Towards the end of March came news of a great disaster for the allied cause. The German Army had launched a massive offensive, the Kaiserschlacht, or the Kaiser's battle, aimed at winning the war before the armies of the United States joined their allies on the battlefield. The German offensive began well for them and broke the entire front of the British Fifth Army, who fell back 20 miles to the Somme with the Germans hard on their heels. The Germans aimed to take the vital junction town of Amiens, which would cut the northern railway system and isolate the Channel ports. To help stem this advance the New Zealand Division, along with other rested formations, was ordered to entrain for the Somme. Those New Zealanders who had survived the horrors of Passchendaele little imagined that they would soon be playing a crucial role in halting

Germany's last attempt to win the war. However, despite playing such a critical part in halting the German offensive in some ten days of heavy fighting, surprisingly not one VC was awarded to the New Zealanders, although one officer was recommended and another may have been.

The German Spring Offensive was eventually halted, although smaller scale offensives continued until May 1918. The failure of the offensive was the result of the stormtroops outrunning their artillery and logistics support and then coming up against determined, fresh opposition. With its failure there remained little potential for offensive action by the Germans for some time to come. It was now the turn of the allied armies to strike.

On 8 August 1918, the British armies in France launched their great offensive that became the 'Hundred Days'. This offensive eventually ended the war in France. From August to November 1918 the New Zealand Division, along with the British 37th Division, was almost continuously in action as part of the spearhead of the British Third Army. During this time it never experienced a reverse and came to be regarded as one of the best divisions in France. Morale in the division was high during these months as its soldiers were convinced they had the measure of their German opponents. The reasons for the outstanding success of the New Zealand Division during this time were its training, leadership and sheer size. The division also showed an aptitude for open warfare, the soldiers much preferring to be on the move rather than confined to the trenches where they were at the mercy of enemy artillery and snipers. Little wonder, then, that given these circumstances, along with a change in attitude of the GOC and a new corps commander, some six VCs were won in the last six months of 1918.

While 1918 was ultimately a successful year for the British and dominion armies, this success came at a high price. During 1918 these armies experienced their greatest number of casualties — some 830,000 between March and November 1918, with more than 300,000 casualties in the last three months of the war alone. In 1917, the worst year of the war for the Allies in terms of military disasters, the casualty figure was 818,000 in total. While the New Zealand Division suffered some 6500 casualties at Messines and a further 7500 for the Passchendaele battles in 1917, their role in halting the German offensive in March–April 1918 cost some 5000 casualties, and the 'Hundred Days' resulted in more than 9000 casualties. Winning the war proved an expensive business for all concerned, particularly for those at the forefront of the action, as the New Zealand Division was in 1918.

AN EARLY RECOMMENDATION?

According to several publications, a New Zealand officer may have been recommended for the VC for his actions during the German Spring Offensive of 1918.[1] He was Major Reginald Miles, who later served as a senior artillery commander during the Second World War. The source for this claim is a summary of Miles' military career prepared by army headquarters in 1965. It states:

> On 25 March 1918 he [Miles] was transferred to command 6th (Howitzer) Battery, NZFA, and for conspicuous gallantry near Ploegsteert Wood on 10 April 1918 when his Battery was overrun he was awarded the Distinguished Service Order after having been recommended for the award of the Victoria Cross.[2]

There are several reasons for doubting the validity of this statement. First, it is based on an earlier note that appears in Miles' personal file. That note, seeking to have Miles' military seniority increased, gave as a reason his impressive record of service in the First World War. It stated that Miles 'did extremely good service in the Field, gained the D.S.O. and Military Cross and was recommended for the V.C., also twice wounded'.[3] The note did not state for which action the VC recommendation was made nor did it state that the VC recommendation was downgraded to that of a DSO. Second, the New Zealand history of the division has a description of the action in which Miles was awarded his DSO but makes no mention of a VC recommendation.[4] Where VC recommendations were known to its author, Colonel H. Stewart, he included them in his history. Third, Miles' original DSO recommendation cannot be found, so conclusive evidence that he was recommended for the VC is missing. Therefore, if Major Reginald Miles was recommended for a VC, it is impossible to determine with any certainty the relevant action.

Miles returned to active service in the Second World War and from 1940 was commander of the Royal Artillery of the 2nd New Zealand Division. During the CRUSADER offensive in November 1941, Miles was one of many New Zealand soldiers taken prisoner by the Germans when their defensive positions on Belhamed Ridge were overrun. He was a prisoner of war in Italy until March 1943 when he and Brigadier James Hargest escaped through a tunnel with four other senior allied officers. Both Miles and Hargest succeeded in reaching neutral Switzerland and were awarded bars to their DSOs for their successful escape. The two men were then separated after some months of internment. Miles crossed into Vichy France and with the aid of the French Resistance travelled alone to reach Spain where he reported to the British authorities at Barcelona. Then, in one of the great mysteries of this war, with his passage to the United Kingdom now assured, Brigadier Reginald Miles took his own life on 20 October 1943. He is buried in the Municipal Cemetery, Figueras, north of Barcelona.

AN UNSUCCESSFUL RECOMMENDATION

An officer of the 1st Battalion of the Auckland Regiment was recommended for the VC for his actions during the German Spring Offensive. He was Captain Henry Ray Vercoe and he was recommended not for one single act of gallantry but for three over a very short space of time. The 1st Auckland Battalion, like most of the infantry units of the division, had been rushed south to the Somme district in order to plug the large gap in the line that had appeared between Hebuterne and Hamel. For the Aucklanders this had meant a five-day journey, covering more than 30 miles on foot, with only two nights of sleep. Thrown into the front line on the morning of 26 March, the 1st Auckland Battalion was committed to halting an advancing enemy just south of La Signy Farm. They would remain in the line for the next five days. It was during this time that Captain Vercoe performed his deeds 'of the greatest personal valour and daring'.[5]

On 26 March, as the battalion was moving in to fill part of the gap in the line, Vercoe's company commander was wounded and could not continue to lead it. Vercoe took over and led the company 'through a hail of machine-gun fire to a final success', which was the high ground of the Serre Ridge. Pushing the Germans off this vital ground was a significant achievement and, as one historian has written, this attack led by Vercoe 'demonstrated the fighting spirit and great courage of the New Zealand officers and soldiers'.[6]

The next day, 27 March, witnessed another impressive feat from Captain Vercoe. He ran out into No Man's Land, braving machine-gun and mortar fire, to rescue a wounded man. Then on 28 March came yet another daring act. A German artillery shell landed on the 1st Auckland Battalion's position, burying several men. Captain Vercoe did not hesitate, and despite the fact that the position was still being shelled, he ran over to where the men lay buried and 'with his bare hands and by himself dug out two of his buried men'.[7] For these three acts of incredible bravery, his battalion commander recommended Vercoe for the VC and Brigadier Charles Melvill supported it. Six eyewitness statements, including those by the company CSM, two sergeants and two corporals, supported the recommendation. Captain Joseph Gordon Coates, a future New Zealand prime minister, provided the officer witness statement. They were not enough to convince those higher up the chain of command, however, and Vercoe's officer status denied him the VC. 'Victoria Cross' was scratched out on the recommendation form and replaced with DSO.

A LEGEND IN HIS LIFETIME:
SERGEANT RICHARD CHARLES TRAVIS

Sergeant Richard (Dick) Travis, VC, DCM, MM and Croix de Guerre (Belgium), has solid claims to being regarded as 'New Zealand's greatest soldier'.[8] One of those few men immune to fear and fatigue, Travis was a resourceful, ruthless soldier who had a natural talent in his ability to read and use terrain. He was also a very unusual soldier in that he could operate as an individual in this war of mass participation while feeling completely at home in the carnage of the Western Front. As one writer recalled:

> Dick had no relations but many friends, real friends. He loved the game: he's the only man I ever met who did, but he truly did.[9]

Little wonder then that Travis was described by his peers as the 'King of the Raiders', or 'The Prince of No Man's Land'.

Dickson Cornelius Savage (as Dick Travis was originally known) was born at Opotiki on 6 April 1884. The Savage family owned Melrose Farm, Otara Road, Opotiki. His father, James Savage, was born in Ireland and had served in the Armed Constabulary during the New Zealand Wars. Dickson's mother, Fanny, was Australian born and it is claimed that she doted on Dickson, her fifth child and eldest son. Dickson was one of nine children born to James and Fanny, seven of whom were daughters. After quarrelling violently with his family, Dickson left Opotiki for Gisborne in 1905 and never returned. His last letter to his family in Opotiki, written when he learned his father was gravely ill, gives some indication of the cause of this separation:

> I am very sorry to hear about poor old Dad been so ill, it was a great shock to me to hear of him been so bad. It does not matter how he treated me or any of us, for we must remember that he is our father just the same . . . and for my part I reckon I was as much to blame as poor Dad for I had the same temper as he had

and therefore I was every bit as much to blame as he was for the rows we had.[10]

Three years later Dickson Savage was forced to leave Gisborne for Southland, where he worked as a horsebreaker. His reason for leaving is outlined in a number of written statements contained in his personal file. According to one:

He told me he changed his name on account of being accused of getting a girl into trouble in Gisborne, the father of the girl chased him off the [railway] station with a loaded gun.[11]

In August 1914 Dickson Savage, now calling himself Richard Travis, a matter that was to vex the military authorities after the war, enlisted from Ryal Bush, Southland, as a trooper in the Otago Mounted Rifles. In keeping with the mystery that surrounds this unusual man, Travis stated he was from Seattle in the United States. He gave his next of kin as Miss E. Letitia (Lettie) Murray of Ryal Bush, a young lady who, according to his biographer, he scarcely knew.[12] Miss Lettie Murray was also named as his beneficiary and next of kin in a will made by Travis on 22 May 1918. During the war years Lettie Murray had been sent Travis' medals for safekeeping and had also been receiving allotments from his pay, so the two must have formed some relationship. For her part, Lettie Murray, in correspondence after the war, stated that her relationship to Travis was 'his intended wife'.[13] Unfortunately though, after the war the secrecy surrounding this relationship and his estrangement from the Savage family in Opotiki resulted in a lengthy, acrimonious series of correspondence about who had the right to keep Travis' medals. This correspondence eventually came to involve the Army Department, the Prime Minister, the Minister for Defence and the Governor-General. However, as a result of the will made by him in May 1918, Miss Lettie Murray retained control over all of Travis' personal effects. Travis' medals, including the VC still in its original case, were eventually donated to the Southland Museum.[14] A close friend of

Travis, A.D. Swainson, gave the Savage family some of Dick's personal possessions, including his prized German binoculars and his identity disc.[15]

Travis left New Zealand with the Main Body of the NZEF in October 1914, bound for Egypt. During the Gallipoli campaign the Mounted Rifles were sent to the peninsula just prior to the large-scale offensive of August 1915 as dismounted reinforcements. Travis did not go with them but remained at Lemnos to tend the horses. He did manage to sneak away to Gallipoli, but not on official duty. Perhaps it was for this reason that in March 1916 Travis transferred as a private to the 2nd Otago Battalion and sailed with the battalion for France the following month.

From the moment the New Zealand Division first experienced the horrors of trench warfare on the Western Front at Armentières, Travis began to distinguish himself as a scout, sniper, patrol leader and raider. Travis' reputation was established at Armentières by his habit of leading many daytime patrols close up to the German wire. It was during this period too that Travis went out on patrol in No Man's Land for 40 successive nights seeking information or prisoners. For the next two years Travis had a remarkable career as a virtual free agent operating in No Man's Land. In France he was awarded the three highest military decorations that a non-commissioned officer could win: the DCM, the MM and the VC.

When the New Zealand Division moved to the Somme in September 1916 Travis continued to distinguish himself. On 15 September the 2nd Otago Battalion was one of the lead battalions in the attack at Flers when German artillery and snipers firing from their left flank harassed it. As the New Zealand history of the division explains: 'These snipers were dealt with by the redoubtable Pte. R.C. Travis . . . who now went out voluntarily into the open and silenced them.'[16] For his actions on the Somme Travis was awarded the DCM. He was also promoted to sergeant on 4 November 1916.

During the winter in Flanders in 1916 and early 1917, Travis was put in charge of the sniping and observation section of the 2nd Otago Battalion. He assembled a tight-knit, impressive team with equally impressive results. The 'Travis gang', as they became known, were conspicuous by their casual dress and the array of weapons they used. Travis himself never wore a helmet, but was always seen wearing a khaki balaclava. The weapon he carried during the day was a sniper's rifle equipped with telescopic sights. At night he carried a Luger pistol or revolvers, bayonet and a number of Mills bombs. Around his neck was his prized possession, a set of German Zeiss binoculars. A padre with the 2nd Otagos recorded:

As of old he came back with the balaclava stuck on the back of his head, a cigarette in his lips and two revolvers strapped on in front . . . It cannot be easy to be the recognised pride of the battalion and yet remain unaffected. Nevertheless right till the end Dick Travis was unspoiled.[17]

At Passchendaele on the night of 10–11 October Travis led a patrol from the 2nd Otago Battalion out into No Man's Land. He wrote a brief but accurate account of the deplorable conditions there and detailed the strength of the German positions:

No-man's-land is in very bad order — one mass of huge shell holes three parts full of water, a large amount of old wire entanglements scattered about makes it very awkward for patrolling. It is very heavy to patrol on account of the ground being so ploughed up by shell holes. It is very hard to keep your feet as it is so slippery . . . The enemy posn just below sky line commands a great field of Machine Gun fire and the observation is excellent.

In addition Travis had detected eight undamaged pillboxes in the 2nd Otago sector alone, the nearest only 150 yards from their start line for the attack.[18] Little wonder that the New Zealand attack of 12 October 1917 resulted in the inevitable massacre of those who took part in it.

After the New Zealand Division was rushed south in March 1918 to help stem the German breakthrough on the Somme, Travis and his 'gang' were active in undertaking patrols and raids once the position had stabilised in April. They were especially adept at bringing in prisoners for identification and interrogation. It was during this time that Travis was awarded the Belgian Croix de Guerre and an MM, the latter for a daylight reconnaissance which resulted in the elimination of a German machine-gun post.

In July 1918 the New Zealand Division faced the Germans at Rossignol Wood where the Germans occupied the east and southwest corner of the wood. The New Zealanders planned to renew pressure on the Germans here on 24 July. In front of the 2nd Otago Battalion were two massive barbed-wire blocks that the preliminary artillery barrage had failed to destroy. Travis volunteered to eliminate them and was as good as his word. He went out alone and in broad daylight to do so, crawling right up to the enemy positions. Once he reached the blocks he placed two Stokes mortar shells in the middle of the wire and calmly waited until one minute before zero hour before he detonated the shells. The blocks were destroyed.

In the infantry attack that followed Travis was soon in the thick of the action. Two machine-guns on the right flank opened fire and checked the battalion's advance. Travis located the position of the guns and rushed them, killing seven Germans from the two crews with his revolvers. Then a German officer and three men attacked him but he shot all four as they advanced down an open sap towards him. An eyewitness statement recorded:

> While we were attacking near Rossignol Wood on July 24th I saw Sergeant Travis rush into an enemy post from which two Machine Guns were holding up the attack on the right. By the time I could reach him, he had shot all the crew with his revolvers.[19]

Travis' actions allowed the rest of the Otago infantry to advance and take the German position where 'they found Travis reloading his revolvers, a line of corpses lying huddled at his feet'.[20] The battalion's war diary records:

The operation was quickly carried out according to plan, and resulted in the capture of 4 prisoners, 6 machine guns and one trench mortar. About 50 of the enemy were killed. In the actual attack we lost one killed and one man wounded.[21]

For his actions on 24 July Travis was recommended for the VC and it was duly gazetted on 24 September 1918. Unfortunately though, a German shell fragment had killed Travis less than 24 hours after his VC-winning action. The 2nd Otago war diary on 26 July 1918 recorded:

Between 8 a.m. and 9 a.m. the enemy put down a very heavy barrage all round our new positions. We suffered about 20 casualties including 2/Lt C.A. Kerse and Sergeant R.C. Travis D.C.M., M.M. killed. No counterattack materialised.

A day later the diary recorded one of the saddest events in its history:

2/Lt. C.A. Kerse and Sergeant R.C. Travis were buried with full military honours at the cemetery of Couin at 8 p.m. Brigadier General Young, 2nd Brigade Staff and the officers and men of the Battalion attended. The death of Sergeant Travis cast a gloom over the whole battalion. Only those who have been with us for any length of time can realise what a loss his death means to us. He left New Zealand with the Main Body and had never missed an operation. He went over the top 15 times and always did magnificent work. He won the D.C.M., M.M. and Croix de Guerre, and has been recommended for the V.C. His name will live in the records of the Battalion as a glorious example of heroism and devotion to duty.[22]

The padre quoted earlier movingly recorded:

Even the downpour of rain as the bodies were committed to earth seemed strangely appropriate. Unfortunately we become accustomed to death, yet that night we went home subdued.[23]

Another soldier wrote after the war:

> The companies marched away, the mourners dispersed, but the name of Dick Travis will live on while soldiers have memories and tales to tell, and will be an inspiration as long as the world honours courage, kindliness and self-forgetfulness.[24]

Sergeant Richard Travis was certainly a remarkable soldier whose fame spread well beyond the 2nd Otago Battalion. There is much about him that was and remains a mystery. What is undisputed, though, is his effectiveness as a scout and raider, which was unsurpassed in the New Zealand Division. There is little doubt, too, that all of his gallantry decorations were well deserved. It is a measure of his influence and fame that to date Dick Travis is the only VC winner of the NZEF to have a full-length biography.[25] In 1957, Walter Rowan visited Travis' grave at the cemetery in Couin. His stone bears the representation of the VC. 'In the adjoining fields cattle graze knee-deep in pasture after a lush spring. A more peaceful scene or a greater contrast from 1918 would be difficult to imagine.'[26]

In 1965, as a final tribute to his friend, A.D. Swainson, MM and bar, arranged for the New Zealand RSA to send four wreaths of Anzac poppies to Travis' grave in the Couin cemetery. Swainson stated that the wreaths of poppies were 'just a tribute from his pals before it is too late. We consider he was the greatest soldier New Zealand has ever produced.'[27] Certainly many New Zealand soldiers of the First World War shared Swainson's opinion.

THE VCs OF THE 'HUNDRED DAYS': 21 AUGUST TO 11 NOVEMBER 1918

Between 21 August and the end of September 1918 five New Zealand soldiers on the Western Front won VCs. This figure represents almost a quarter of all the VCs won by New Zealanders. It is indicative of the hard fighting and the high skill levels that the New Zealand soldiers had achieved in 1918. It also indicates the more relaxed attitude of their hierarchy towards approving gallantry awards.

Sergeant Samuel Forsyth

The first New Zealand soldier to win the VC during the 'Hundred Days' was Sergeant Samuel Forsyth of the New Zealand Engineers. Forsyth was a gold amalgamator from Wellington who had left New Zealand with the Main Body in 1914. He had served on Gallipoli where he had been slightly wounded and was twice evacuated sick. In August 1918 he was seconded to the 2nd Auckland Battalion for a spell in the front line prior to receiving a commission in his own unit. On 24 August 1918 the 2nd Auckland Battalion was ordered to capture the village of Grevillers as a prelude to the New Zealand Division's drive on Bapaume. By early morning the Aucklanders had reached the southern outskirts of Grevillers village, where they were pinned down by heavy machine-gun and rifle fire. For a time it seemed as if their progress was halted. Then two British tanks appeared in the distance but they made no effort to assist the New Zealanders despite the Kiwis' desperate attempts to attract the attention of the tank crews. Forsyth, who had carried out a reconnaissance of the German positions, ran under fire to the nearest tank and led it forward to assist the beleaguered New Zealanders. While doing so he was wounded in the arm but he continued to direct the tanks to a position where they could attack the German machine-gun positions. The Germans, aware of the danger, scored a direct hit on the lead tank with an artillery round. Forsyth then assisted the crew from the wreck, formed them and several New Zealand soldiers into a section, and led them forward to outflank the German machine-guns. The machine-gunners did not stay to face an attack from their flanks but withdrew, allowing the high ground around Grevillers to be taken.

Forsyth next helped to organise a new line of resistance on a bare exposed slope. While doing so he was killed by a German sniper. He is buried at Adanac Military Cemetery at Miraumont, France.

Ormond Burton was a close friend of Samuel Forsyth and was wounded in the arm by the same sniper that killed Forsyth. Also decorated for his part in this attack, Burton regarded Forsyth's VC as:

. . . one of the best of those that went to the New Zealanders. At Grevillers Sam was head and shoulders above us all — a most valorous exhibition of imaginative daring sustained through a long and dangerous advance. Behind it was a record second to none in the Division.[28]

After the action at Grevillers Burton wrote immediately to Forsyth's widow, Mary. She received his letter before the official death notification arrived. Mary Forsyth's reply is revealing:

My dear husband's last letter was very sad and I believe he must have felt it must be a farewell letter as he spoke of things in it that he never said to me in his life before. My dear brave husband how I loved him dearly and I was so looking forward to him coming over so soon.[29]

Forsyth's VC was gazetted on 18 October 1918. His VC medal was presented to Mary by King George V. Mary Forsyth had intended that, upon her death, the VC would be given to family members still resident in New Zealand. This did not happen and, sadly, the VC went into an American collection of medals. It was eventually offered for sale at Sotheby's in the United Kingdom. Despite the fundraising efforts of the New Zealand RSA and the members of New Zealand Clan Forsyth, the VC was sold to a Melbourne dealer on 26 January 1982 for $20,900. At the time this was the second-highest price ever paid for a VC.[30]

Sergeant Reginald Stanley Judson

Two days after Forsyth's VC-winning action, Sergeant Reginald Stanley Judson also won the award. Reginald Judson was an engineer and boilermaker from Auckland. He joined the NZEF in October

1915 initially as a rifleman, but transferred to the 1st Auckland Battalion in February 1916. He was 38 years old when he enlisted. Judson was present during the New Zealand attack on the Somme on 15 September 1916, where he suffered a severe abdominal wound. In fact Judson's wound was so severe that he remained in the United Kingdom in hospital or convalescence until the middle of 1918. He did not rejoin his unit in the field until June 1918. Like Travis, he was one of the very few soldiers on the Western Front to win all the major gallantry awards available for non-commissioned officers. Judson, however, is unique in that he won all three awards in a little over a month.[31]

This remarkable achievement began on the night of 24–25 July 1918, the same day that Travis won his VC. Judson rescued six New Zealand soldiers stranded near Hebuterne during a German counterattack. For this action Judson was awarded the DCM. Three weeks later, on 16 August, Judson led a fierce bayonet charge at Bucquoy that captured two machine-guns and 16 German soldiers. For this action he received the MM. Ten days later came the action that would lead to his winning the supreme award for gallantry.

In the attack on the town of Bapaume on 26 August German machine-gun fire had inflicted heavy casualties on the leading New Zealand infantry battalions forcing them to take cover. About noon the 15th Company of the 1st Auckland Battalion was ordered to assist the 2nd Wellington Battalion clear the machine-gun positions to their front in order to restore momentum to the attack. No sooner had the company commenced its move forward than it too was forced to take cover from the withering machine-gun fire. Sergeant Judson then led a small patrol through the fire and along a sap where they captured one machine-gun and attacked two more machine-gun crews with Mills bombs. The Germans tried to make a hasty withdrawal but Judson jumped out of the sap and ran fully exposed along its edge to head off the fleeing Germans. He managed to get in front of them, pointed his rifle at the group of 12 Germans and called upon them to surrender. There was a moment's hesitation and then the two

German officers ordered their men to fire on Judson, which they did. Judson threw a Mills bomb at the group, waited for it to explode and then leapt into the trench and fought the survivors hand-to-hand. He killed two of the Germans in this struggle; the rest fled, leaving behind their two machine-guns. The advance towards Bapaume continued unopposed. For this remarkable action Judson was recommended for the VC, which was duly gazetted on 29 October 1918. That same edition of the *London Gazette* also featured his DCM citation.[32]

After the war Judson remained in the army as a commissioned officer. Though his progress through the ranks was slow, Judson established a reputation for hard work, diligence and honesty. His character is summed up in one of his early annual reports that described Judson as 'conscientious . . . hard working . . . a man of fine feeling and high ideals though lacking in education'.[33]

Like a significant proportion of the veterans of the First World War, Judson's health had been seriously affected by his war service. He was so ill in 1924 that he was granted six months' sick leave by the army. While his medical report diagnosed that he was suffering from 'toxic vertigo', Judson had the classic symptoms of someone suffering from post-traumatic stress disorder. A 1924 medical report summed up his symptoms. It said Judson:

> Feels jumpy and not normal. Easily irritated and depressed at times. Easily fatigued. States he has palpitations at times. Sleep irregular. Gets to sleep and wakes up. Feels unable to do justice to his work.[34]

While Judson recovered from this illness he was unwell again in 1934. After losing consciousness on the afternoon of 16 August 1934, he reluctantly agreed to take more sick leave. As he explained, his doctor:

> . . . states that I must have rest otherwise the heart, owing to the presence of shrapnel in an old abdominal wound and the effects of gas poisoning will not stand the strain. He says that I must rest

completely for a month, but I will try and come down to the office each day and carry out the most essential part of my Area duties.

A doctor's certificate attached to the letter stated that Judson was experiencing pain in the wound site and was suffering from pulmonary emphysema caused by the inhalation of phosgene gas at Bapaume in September 1918.[35]

Judson again recovered and continued to serve in the New Zealand Army. He was granted an extra year beyond his retirement age for rank, finally retiring in 1937. The presence of eight pieces of shrapnel near his heart and the effects of the poisonous gas meant he could not return to the heavy work of the engineering trade.[36] Judson's miserly pension of just over £2 a week meant that he needed to find additional employment. He took up the position of secretary/bursar at Mount Albert Grammar School. A member of the public was so incensed with the treatment of Judson upon his retirement that he wrote to the Prime Minister:

> As a comparatively young man with a wife and family and a body too frail to take up again his work as an engineer, he is cast adrift on the beggarly income of £2-10 a week. Nothing I say can be an adequate comment on this . . . I feel New Zealand is guilty of gross injustice to this man, and it is only necessary to bring it before the proper authorities to have it remedied.[37]

Prime Minister Michael Savage expressed concern in his reply to V.F. Maxwell, but passed the matter onto the Defence Minister, Fred Jones, who was less than sympathetic. Jones pointed out that as well as his service pension Judson was also in receipt of a war disability pension of £1 1s. 3d. per week. He also pointed out that, of Judson's five children, only one could be classed as a dependant. Therefore: 'In view of the foregoing I am afraid I cannot agree with you that Captain Judson has suffered any injustice.'[38] Judson's circumstances did not change.

On the outbreak of war in 1939, Judson again volunteered his services. He was taken into the army and served for five years in charge of the Guards Vital Points Battalion in Auckland. Owing to a shortage of officers in the battalion, Judson did not take any annual leave from 1940 to 1945. Judson finally retired from the army in September 1946 with the rank of major. He died in Auckland on 26 August 1972 and is buried at the Waikumete Cemetery in Auckland. His VC is on public display at the Queen Elizabeth II Army Memorial Museum in Waiouru.

Sergeant John Gildroy Grant

Less than a week after the action that saw Sergeant Judson win the VC, another New Zealand sergeant, this time from a Wellington unit, won the VC on the Western Front. He was John Gildroy Grant, a builder and contractor from Hawera who had joined the NZEF in June 1915.

After taking the town of Bapaume, the New Zealand Division, part of a big allied push to keep pressure on the Germans, planned to advance to the village of Bancourt and on to Bancourt Ridge, the high ground some 800 yards east of the village. By 8.00 a.m. on the morning of 30 August two New Zealand battalions from the 1st Brigade had cleared the Germans from Bancourt and began their advance towards the ridge. The fight for the ridge proved much more difficult and just short of the crest the New Zealanders could make no headway. Here they were forced to dig in for the night. The following morning at 4.30 a.m. the German infantry launched a counterattack with some tanks in support and advancing behind an artillery barrage. The New Zealand line was pushed back some 300 yards where the men reformed and, in a four-and-a-half-hour running battle, fought their way back to their original line. Further attacks were made on the German positions on top of the ridge but they still could not be dislodged.

That night two New Zealand brigades were ordered to launch a dawn attack with the object of securing the top of the ridge. The 1st Wellington Battalion was to lead the attack for the 1st Brigade. When the New Zealand infantry reached the top of the ridge they came under heavy fire from five machine-gun posts but they pushed on and reached to within 20 yards of the guns before they were forced to take cover. It was then that Sergeant Grant and Lance Corporal C.T. Hill crawled towards the guns, leapt up in front of the machine-gun fire in the centre post and attacked the position. The German machine-gunners fled, then Grant turned his attention to the post on the left which he also subdued. The German resistance then died away. It was an impressive feat and, as the history of the division comments on Grant's actions:

> No one but the panic-stricken Germans at the gun could tell how the fire missed him. He leapt into the post, demoralising the gunners. His men were close on his heels.[39]

Lance Corporal Hill received the DCM for his actions this day, while Grant received the VC, which was gazetted on 26 November 1918.

During the 1930s John Grant, like so many other veterans, fell on hard times. He was discharged from the Territorial Force in 1929 as an officer who was over age and unable to attend camp. A report noted that he was 'apparently indifferent as regards training'.[40] Then in 1935 the *Star* newspaper reported the case of 'V.C. on Relief. Case at Paeroa. Surprise Discovery.' The officer in charge of the Northern Command was asked to investigate to find out who the VC recipient was at this relief camp and what his circumstances were. The report written by Colonel John Duigan was unsympathetic:

> I am given to understand that one J.G. Grant V.C. is working at a relief camp at Paeroa Race Course . . . As far as I can find out, Grant has on several occasions been provided with permanent employment, but is alleged to be unable to hold it, owing to his erratic habits. It appears that he is extremely unreliable, and it is to this factor alone that he owes his present position.[41]

The symptoms outlined in Duigan's report suggest that Grant was suffering from some form of post-traumatic stress as a result of his combat experience. Grant's situation did not immediately improve. He survived the Depression and the war that followed it. In 1956, Grant was one of the New Zealand VC winners to attend the Victoria

Cross Centenary Celebrations held in London. On the first evening of their arrival the VC recipients were to attend a function hosted by Lord Louis and Lady Edwina Mountbatten. Grant did not do too well. He arrived at the function drunk and upon seeing Lady Mountbatten he approached her, slapped her heartily on the back and asked 'How are you, Edwina?' After shaking hands with Lord Mountbatten Grant went up to the bar, threw some money on the counter and stated loudly: 'I'll shout the bar!' He then fell over a table. A horrified Lord Freyberg had Grant discreetly removed from the function.[42]

Grant died in November 1970, aged 81, and is buried at the Waikumete Cemetery in Auckland. He has a street named after him in Hawera, the town of his birth — the Grant VC Avenue. His VC is also on public display at the Queen Elizabeth II Army Memorial Museum in Waiouru.

Sergeant Harry John Laurent

Eleven days after the New Zealanders stormed Bancourt Ridge a sergeant in the New Zealand Rifle Brigade won another VC. Henry John Laurent (known as Harry), a grocer's assistant and commercial traveller from Tarata in Taranaki, joined the NZEF in May 1915. Prior to his enlistment, Laurent had served for four years with the Taranaki Rifles, a territorial unit.[43] Laurent fought at the Battle of the Somme, where he was wounded in October 1916.

By the end of the first week of September 1918 the retreating German armies were thoroughly demoralised and some units were in a state of disarray. The Allies were determined to exploit this condition by maintaining as much pressure as possible on the Germans. One of the formations in the vanguard of the Allies' advance was the New Zealand Division, which had followed up the retreating Germans after taking Bapaume. However, on 9 September German resistance suddenly stiffened when they established a well-defended defensive line running between Gouzeaucourt and Trescault and along the Trescault Ridge. Two attempts by the New Zealanders to crash through these positions failed. Overnight on 11–12 September a number of fighting patrols were sent out to regain contact with the Germans.

Sergeant Laurent led one such patrol of 12 men from the Rifle Brigade's 2nd Battalion. Laurent's patrol did more than contact the enemy. Owing to some faulty map-reading they actually overshot the German front-line trenches and penetrated the German lines to a depth of about 700 yards. Laurent realised his mistake when he hit the German artillery gunline, but he decided to take advantage of it. He quickly organised his men and they launched a daring attack right in the heart of the German position. It was spectacularly successful, killing some 20 Germans and capturing a further 112. One man from Laurent's patrol was killed in this exchange and three were wounded. It is a tribute to Laurent's skills as a leader and an indication of how demoralised the Germans were that he was able to extract his patrol and the prisoners under the most difficult of conditions. This involved having to fight a vigorous rearguard action while preventing over a hundred German prisoners from escaping — all of which had to be done by just eight men. It was an outstanding achievement, one that was recognised by the award of a VC, gazetted on 12 November 1918.

Laurent also has a street named after him in his parents' home-town of Hawera — Laurent VC Avenue. Harry Laurent served in the Home Guard during the next war, eventually reaching the rank of lieutenant colonel. He died in Hastings in 1988 and was New Zealand's last surviving VC winner of the First World War.[44] His ashes were interred in the Memorial Wall at the Servicemen's Cemetery at Hawera and his VC is on public display at the museum in Waiouru.

Private James Crichton

At the end of September 1918 Private James Crichton became the last New Zealand soldier to win a VC in the First World War. Private Crichton was an unusual soldier. Born in Carrickfergus, Ireland, in 1879, Crichton had served with the Cameron Highland Regiment in the South African war. After quitting his job as a cable splicer in Auckland, Crichton joined the NZEF in 1914, sailing from New Zealand with the Main Body. In April 1918, after serving with the 1st Field Bakery at Gallipoli and France, Crichton requested a transfer to an infantry unit. Although nearly 40 years old, Crichton relinquished his rank of warrant officer to join the 2nd Auckland Battalion as a private soldier.

It was during the crossing of the Scheldt River near Crevecoeur that Crichton's platoon ran into serious trouble. It became trapped on an island in the middle of the river when German machine-gun fire swept the stone bridge leading from the island, killing several men, including both the platoon commander and senior NCO. To make matters worse the bridge leading from the island to Crevecoeur had been prepared for demolition with explosive mines. The platoon needed to communicate its desperate situation back to company headquarters.

Despite having been wounded in the foot by machine-gun fire Private Crichton volunteered for this dangerous task. He swam the river fully clothed, hauled himself up onto an exposed bank in full view of the Germans and sprinted over the 100 yards of broken ground to report to company headquarters. As if this wasn't enough he then returned back to the isolated platoon, carrying the company commander's message to hold on.

On his own initiative Crichton then located the explosive demolitions and, although under fire from machine-guns and snipers, he managed to remove the fuses and detonators, which he put in his pocket; the explosive mines he placed in the water. Crichton was then told to report what he had done to the company commander so he completed the dangerous trip a third time. He was about to rejoin the platoon when his company commander ordered him to remain at his headquarters. While at the company headquarters Crichton helped the stretcher-bearers there with their heavy loads until the pain of his wound became too obvious. He was then sent, under protest, to a field hospital.

As a result of these incredible actions Crichton was recommended for the VC. Four eyewitness statements supported the recommendation, the one written by Captain James Evans outlining Crichton's actions:

I consider he [Crichton] showed the greatest courage in crossing the ground to deliver his messages as others were killed or wounded in doing the same, and I would not allow men to cross it.[45]

The recommendation was successful and was duly gazetted on 12 November 1918.

James Crichton was discharged from the NZEF in September 1919, with his final medical report stating that he was 'no longer physically fit for war service on account of wounds received in action'.[46] Crichton returned to his pre-war career as a cable splicer. In 1937, as a sergeant in the New Zealand Coronation Contingent, James Crichton, along with other VC winners, attended the coronation of King George VI .[47] He died in Auckland in September 1961 and is buried in the Waikumete Memorial Park Soldiers' Cemetery in Auckland. Crichton's immediate family donated his VC to the Auckland War Memorial Museum.

ANOTHER RECOMMENDATION BUT NO AWARD

At the end of 1918 another New Zealand officer was recommended for the VC. He was Captain Patrick Augustine Ardagh MC, the regimental medical officer of the 1st Auckland Battalion. Captain Ardagh was recommended for the VC for his 'conspicuous gallantry and devotion to duty' during 1–3 October 1918. Captain Ardagh had set up an advanced dressing station in an exposed portion of the front line, where he worked non-stop treating the wounded from four battalions for 36 hours. The eyewitness statement of his commanding officer says it all:

I personally observed Capt Ardagh on the 1st Oct. 1918 east of Masneeres dressing wounded in the open whilst shells were falling continuously in his vicinity. On two occasions to my own knowledge wounded awaiting attention were killed by falling shells. Even when portions of a man blown to pieces were scattered upon this officer, outwardly calm, he continued his work. No other Medical Officer was in the vicinity for 36 hours, and New Zealand, Scotch, English and German wounded were treated by him. The casualties were heavy and evacuation continued day and night, with the result that this officer was denied sleep for the first two nights.[48]

Lieutenant Colonel W.W. Alderman, who wrote this statement, recommended Ardagh for the VC. Three eyewitness statements, including one written by another officer, Second Lieutenant J.A. Jones, supported the recommendation, as did Brigadier C.W. Melvill. In the history of the VC award you would be hard-pressed to find a more deserving action, but General Russell did not support the recommendation and downgraded the award to a DSO.

OTHER VCs OF SIGNIFICANCE

Lieutenant Percy Valentine Storkey
On 7 April 1918 Lieutenant Percy Valentine Storkey, a law student from Vaucluse, New South Wales, but born in Napier in 1891, won the VC for his actions at Hangard Wood on the Somme. During a dawn attack Storkey's company of the 19th Battalion AIF came under heavy machine-gun fire that killed or wounded about a quarter of them, including the company commander. Storkey then took command. He ordered the company to take cover and then led a small party of 11 men around the flank of the German machine-gun position. Here they were able to get to the rear of the German position undetected until one of the Australians, upon seeing the backs of about 100 German soldiers, 'let out a string of traditional Australian oaths in a loud voice'.[49] With the element of surprise gone Storkey immediately led a bayonet charge against the nearest German post and easily overcame it. He then called upon the rest of the Germans to surrender. They did not, so Storkey threw some Mills bombs at them, which produced the desired result. About 30 Germans had been killed

or wounded, while the remainder, comprising three officers and 50 men, surrendered. With few of the original attacking force left the new position could not be held, so Storkey led what remained of his company and the prisoners back to the start line. For his actions on this day Storkey was recommended for the VC, which was duly gazetted on 7 June 1918.

The fate of Storkey's VC caused something of a minor scandal in Hawke's Bay in the early 1980s. Upon his death in 1969, Judge Percy Storkey bequeathed his VC to Napier Boys' High School where he had been a former pupil and dux of the school. In 1983 the school's Parents' League decided to sell Storkey's VC and use the money to provide some student scholarships. This caused a storm of outrage, forcing the Parents' League to back down. The VC was subsequently given on long-term loan to the Queen Elizabeth II Army Memorial Museum in Waiouru.

Corporal Lawrence Carthage Weathers

On 2 September 1918 Corporal Lawrence Carthage Weathers of the 43rd Battalion AIF won a VC for his actions at Allaines, north of Mont St Quentin on the Somme. Lawrence Weathers, born in Te Koparu in 1890, was an undertaker from Parkside, South Australia. Weathers' battalion had been ordered to clear a small triangle of German resistance east of Allaines village. Despite being surrounded, the Germans put up a ferocious resistance and Weathers' battalion made little progress against it. Weathers then went forward alone right up to the German position and attacked it with Mills bombs. He killed many Germans in this attack, including the commander of the besieged force. Weathers then returned to the Australian lines for a further supply of bombs and went forward again, this time with three companions. While his companions provided covering fire with their Lewis gun, Weathers crawled up to the parapet of the German position and commenced bombing it again. This distracted the Germans long enough to allow a platoon of infantry to rush the position and capture it along with 180 German prisoners and three machine-guns. Weathers was recommended for the VC for this action but never learned that it had been awarded. He was critically wounded on 26 September 1918 and died three days later. His VC was not gazetted until 26 December 1918. Weathers is buried in the Unicorn Cemetery at Vend'huile, France, and his VC is held in private hands.

The VCs of the Western Front

The number of VCs won on the Western Front reflects its importance in New Zealand military history. For the first time in the country's history, New Zealand soldiers fought in a decisive theatre of war against the main enemy of their allies. It was on the Western Front that New Zealand made its main contribution to the war effort and that contribution, along with that of its trans-Tasman neighbour, was substantial. As mentioned in Chapter 6, the price to pay for this substantial contribution was staggering.

There is little doubt that all ten New Zealand VCs were well-deserved awards. They involved acts of exceptional bravery, almost reckless courage, in the face of the enemy, where the risk of death and danger was ever-present. In the case of the VC winners, such acts of gallantry were usually undertaken by NCOs in order to get a stalled offensive moving again. Only the Crichton, Laurent and Travis VCs differ from this pattern. And strangely, given the pattern established in previous conflicts, all acts of gallantry that involved rescuing fallen comrades were not seen to be good enough to earn a VC. Acts of this type that were recommended for the VC usually resulted in the granting of a lesser award, but not the VC itself.

There is little doubt too that many more such awards could and should have been made. This is especially the case of those junior officers who, like their NCOs, took exceptional risks in order to achieve their allocated objectives. Some of them were recommended for the VC, but their officer status denied them access to this, the ultimate of gallantry awards. That many great deeds went unrecorded and unrecognised also goes without saying. It is just one of the many injustices that accompanies war. In some ways the ten VC winners of the Western Front were fortunate. Their feat of arms was witnessed and then recorded later by a commissioned officer. It was then passed up several layers of the chain of command with each in turn supporting that the award be made. Many other New Zealand soldiers were not as fortunate.

This takes nothing away from the New Zealand VC winners of the Western Front. That their acts of tremendous gallantry were seen, recorded and then rewarded is just one of the many fortunes of war. Their achievements are an important part of New Zealand's military history and deserve to be recognised as such. That so few VCs were awarded is a tragedy and an injustice, but it serves to highlight how much was achieved by those who did receive them.

CHAPTER 9 The First World War: air and naval VCs

The First World War was the first full war of the industrial age and therefore saw the introduction of much new technology. The internal combustion engine had made powered flight possible in 1903 and from the outset of hostilities the major combatants all included aircraft in their forces. At sea the developments in munitions and communications that contributed so greatly to the lethality of land warfare were also to be found. However, the greatest developments had been in the construction of all-metal fighting vessels, including submarines. The latter had been employed in various guises before, but by 1914 they had been developed into the basic form that would allow their utilisation as effective weapons of warfare.

On the declaration of war, New Zealand possessed neither an air component to the army nor a true navy of its own. Those young New Zealanders who were engaged in the early air war did so in the fledgling aviation elements of the British services. Similarly, those who were to fight at sea did so as members of the Royal Navy. In neither case were the numbers of personnel large, but in both environments an individual with strong New Zealand connections was to win the VC.

THE AIR WAR

The initial phases of the air war in the First World War were relatively benign. The aircraft types were primitive, reflecting the very recent development of powered flight, and were essentially of civilian design. The basic role of these air elements was reconnaissance and scouting ahead of the conventional forces. Once an enemy was spotted this would then be reported by dropping a message or delivering a verbal report after landing. The aircraft had relatively short endurance, could carry only one or two men and were not armed.

However, the young aviators of the new air services were as aggressive as any of their contemporaries in the ground or naval forces and markedly innovative. They soon set to developing their machines into more aggressive roles, in order to attack the ground targets they had hitherto only observed, as well as the enemy aircraft they encountered trying to observe their own forces. Later in the war, this would lead to the development of quite specific roles, with aircraft designed to undertake these functions. The individual scout plane, reliant on speed and manoeuvrability, was developed into the armed fighter with the primary role of destroying enemy aircraft. To improve the speed and ability of the reconnaissance aircraft to report their sightings, some were fitted with radios, which in turn then allowed them to direct the fire of friendly artillery onto hostile targets.[1] However, one of the first and simplest offensive roles undertaken by these airmen was to drop something — usually an explosive — on enemy targets as the aircraft flew over them.

As well as being a simple concept, the original bombers were also quite basic. In essence the pilot or crewmember of a standard aircraft simply dropped a bomb or grenade, often something they had carried in their laps, out of their cockpit. As this practice became more common, small racks were added locally, either inside or outside the airframe, in order to make carriage easier and if possible to take more bombs. At this early stage of the war, the crews were effectively attacking troops or targets of opportunity that they encountered on their patrols. They therefore continued to fly mostly unmodified airframes and to undertake a variety of tasks.

Once the war became more static, however, genuine targets of opportunity became less common. The movements of the opposing forces became more circumspect, and concentrations of troops or artillery were dug in and increasingly protected by anti-aircraft fire from machine-guns and cannons.[2] The same static conditions increased the importance of key nodes of communication, which each side needed to develop their own combat power. These included railways, roads, bridges and supply areas, as well as military targets like artillery concentrations and airfields.[3] However, in order to make an impact on these larger, dispersed and often protected targets, heavier and more effective bombs were required to be dropped on them with better accuracy. Thus the specialist bomber aircraft rapidly emerged.[4]

By the middle of the war, the majority of the specialist military aircraft types we are familiar with today, with the exception of personnel transporters, had emerged. More powerful engines and better construction techniques allowed for the production of heavier airframes capable of carrying greater loads, or lighter machines of greater speed. The scout/fighter became effective once mechanisms were developed to stop the flow of bullets from a machine-gun, firing straight ahead down the axis of the aircraft, from destroying the propeller.[5] Increasingly these specialist aircraft were concentrated together by the air services into groups specialising in the fighter, bomber or reconnaissance roles, according to the design of their machines.

To attack larger targets even deeper in the enemy's rear, larger bombers were required. The Germans in particular made use of the Zeppelin airship — a gas-filled buoyancy bag in a rigid frame with engines for propulsion, which they used to attack British cities. These airships themselves, and their bases, became targets for allied bombers. Many nations also developed increasingly large aircraft with two or more engines, capable of travelling yet further distances with larger bomb loads. From these the concept of strategic bombing was to emerge. In Britain's case the Independent Air Force, set up to coordinate the bomber offensive, was later to subsume the army and naval air services and emerge, by the war's end, as the Royal Air Force.[6]

Throughout this period of rapid technological, organisational and tactical development, it must be remembered that aviation was effectively still in its infancy, and flying itself was fundamentally dangerous. Add to this the lethal impact of combat and it is hardly surprising that many of the young men who took part in this new form of warfare were killed. They also established a romantic aura as the new knights of the skies, with much of the attention focusing on the exploits of the fighter pilots later in the war. However, the earliest exploit to attract the award of the VC to a member of Britain's Royal Flying Corps (RFC) went to a pilot for his gallantry during a bombing mission.

THE ATTACK ON COURTRAI

In mid-April 1915 the fighting around Ypres was particularly heavy. The Germans had just employed gas for the first time and were attempting to exploit a breakthrough at St Julien. In order to restrict their ability to bring up reserves, the RFC's 2 Squadron was directed to bomb three targets on 26 April. These were key communication centres in the enemy rear at Roubaix, Tourcoing and the railway at the Courtrai–Menin junction. The squadron was equipped with the BE2b, an unarmed two-seat observation aircraft that could carry up to 100 pounds of bombs without adversely affecting performance so long as the pilot flew alone, but even so the top speed was 70 miles per hour.[7]

Second Lieutenant William Rhodes-Moorhouse of the RFC was assigned the target at Courtrai. It took only 35 minutes to fly there from 2 Squadron's airfield at Merville, but he did not attack the target immediately. First, he circled the target at altitude to ensure he was in the right place. Then, despite having been advised to drop his single 100-pound bomb from altitude, Rhodes-Moorhouse commenced a shallow dive onto the target. He knew that a bomb dropped from higher up with no aiming assistance stood little chance of hitting anything. Therefore, he planned to release the bomb where he could better judge its trajectory, but this would necessitate flying the slow aircraft on a straight course low over the target. In doing so he knew he would be flying within easy range of small-arms fire from the ground, to say nothing of probably being within the lethal radius of his own bomb's explosion.

Rhodes-Moorhouse's initial pass over the target alerted the German troops in the area and the ground fire that greeted his actual attack was indeed hot, including from a machine-gun in the church belfry.[8] The aircraft sustained bullet and bomb shrapnel damage in the bomb run. Rhodes-Moorhouse was badly wounded by a bullet through the thigh, but he achieved a hit on the line west of the station. Then, in pain from his wound, in a damaged aircraft, and straining to gain speed he had to cross the general target area again, now at only 100 feet, in order to get away. The aircraft was hit again and Rhodes-Moorhouse was wounded in the stomach and hand.

Losing blood and in considerable pain, Rhodes-Moorhouse managed to fly his aircraft back to the British lines and land at his own airfield. On landing he had to be assisted out of his cockpit, which was described as being 'awash with blood'.[9] Instead of allowing himself to be taken for immediate medical attention, Rhodes-Moorhouse insisted on making a full report of the action. However, there was little that could be done for him. In addition to a severe loss of blood, the wound in his stomach was beyond the medical skills of the time. Knowing he was going to die, he asked to be buried in England. Rhodes-Moorhouse passed away at 2.30 p.m. the next day, 27 April 1915.

His backdated promotion to lieutenant was announced posthumously. Then on 22 May 1915 the *London Gazette* published notification of his award of the VC, following the recommendation of the Officer Commanding 1st Wing RFC, Lieutenant Colonel Hugh Trenchard (later Marshal of the Royal Air Force, Lord Trenchard).[10]

WILLIAM BARNARD RHODES-MOORHOUSE

William Rhodes-Moorhouse was not actually a New Zealander, having neither been born nor ever lived here,[11] but he had strong family connections to the country. William's father, Edward Moorhouse, was an Englishman and younger brother of William Moorhouse, after whom Moorhouse Avenue in Christchurch is named. Edward lived for some 24 years in New Zealand where he worked with his brothers, though with not quite their success. William's mother, Mary Ann, was a much stronger character, however, and she is the primary source of this country's claim to the first-ever air VC.

Mary Ann was the illegitimate daughter of William Barnard Rhodes, a Yorkshire-man who, from 1836, had made a prosperous position for himself as a grazier in Canterbury and then the North Island. He subsequently became a member of the Legislative Assembly and in 1869 married for the second time, to Sarah Ann Moorhouse, the sister of William and Edward. Mary Ann had been born in 1852 and her mother was a Maori woman, reputedly 'given' to Rhodes as a mark of respect by a North Island chieftain. Apart from her race, all detail about this poor woman is conjecture and it seems that Mary Ann was quite successful in suppressing any information about her.[12] Regardless of the woman's real status, William Rhodes legally took responsibility for Mary Ann and after his death she successfully contested his will to become his sole heiress, inheriting a considerable fortune. Afterwards, following their marriage at St Paul's, Wellington, in 1883, Edward and Mary Ann moved to England.

William Barnard Moorhouse was born in London on 26 September 1887 and was the couple's second child. He was educated at Harrow and then went briefly to Cambridge. However, he was more interested in cars and motorcycles than study. In 1906 he knocked down and killed a boy while racing, though he was only fined for the offence. In 1909 he left Cambridge and used his significant resources to participate in various races before developing an interest in flying. He could be described as somewhat of a playboy, but he appears to have applied himself to aviation. By 1911 he had his pilot's certificate and was involved in the design and construction of aircraft. On a long visit to America he won a number of aviation prizes and was the first man to fly under the Golden Gate Bridge. Following his marriage in 1912 he flew his new bride and a journalist across the English Channel, the first such flight with more than one passenger. In 1913 he changed his surname to Rhodes-Moorhouse in order to be eligible to inherit his maternal grandfather's estate.

As the holder of the Royal Aero Club Certificate 147 it was small wonder that on the outbreak of war Rhodes-Moorhouse immediately joined the RFC. However, he was initially assigned to administrative and instructional duties in England. Desiring a more active role, he eventually managed to obtain a posting to a front-line squadron. In March 1915 he flew a BE2b across the channel and joined his new unit on the twentieth of that month. He had only been with 2 Squadron five weeks when he undertook his final flight, becoming the first airman and the first Maori[13] to win the VC. Rhodes-Moorhouse's body was taken back to England as he had requested and was buried at his family home at Parnham House. Twenty-five years later the ashes of his son, Flight Lieutenant William Henry Rhodes-Moorhouse DFC, who was killed flying a Hurricane in the Battle of Britain, were interred alongside his father. In 1990 a private collector purchased Rhodes-Moorhouse's VC by auction for a then record price of £125,000.

THE WAR AT SEA

One of the several issues that had helped precipitate the First World War had been the competition between the European powers to build new warships, especially after the 1906 launch of HMS *Dreadnought* had made all previous battleships obsolete overnight. However, it was not to be major actions between battle fleets that characterised the conflict at sea — it was to be maritime commerce.

In the opening stages of the war at sea, there was a brief phase of movement. These were smaller fleet actions in which the Royal Navy pursued and sunk the colonial cruiser squadrons of the German Navy. The German High Seas Fleet itself, though superior in design on a ship-to-ship basis to their equivalent vessels in the Royal Navy, was numerically inferior. Additionally, the Germans were restricted in their access to the open oceans as they effectively only had one route from their base in Kiel through the Baltic and then into the North Sea. The one major battle, at Jutland on 31 May

1916, was effectively a draw, though the Germans sunk more British vessels than they lost. From that time on the German fleet remained confined, mostly to the Baltic, and largely restricted to port.[14] Bored and underfed, the sailors of the High Seas Fleet eventually mutinied in 1918 — probably their greatest contribution to the end of the war, though not the one their architects envisaged.

The same geographic dictates of Germany's coastline meant that her seaborne trade was also channelled. From its recent inception Germany was a continental power, predominantly reliant on its army to wield influence. Her colonial ambitions and the resource needs of a modern industrial nation, however, required the commercial elements of maritime power as well as its naval components. By comparison Britain had long been a maritime nation with a strong tradition of naval power and sea commerce. With a depth of experience in dealing with continental powers through maritime means, she commenced the war by instituting a naval blockade of Germany, as she had 100 years earlier against Napoleon.

However, the new technology of the industrial age did necessitate changes in methodology. The use of aircraft allowed vessels to be spotted from greater distances and the new artillery could fire further. Radio allowed fleets to be concentrated more effectively in response to sightings, and steam-turbine propulsion gave the vessels greater speed. Finally the new menace of submarines meant an unsuspecting warship could be attacked at any time, as happened on several occasions in the war's early months. This meant that, despite their numerical superiority, the Royal Navy could not undertake a close blockade of the German ports or fleet, but now needed to achieve this effect at a distance. The distant blockade also necessitated changes in practice, in that it required the interception and inspection of neutral vessels on the open seas, in order to ensure they were not carrying contraband that would eventually find its way to Germany. Although initially resisted, the British were eventually successful in regulating the routes of these neutral vessels and restricting German access to materials.[15]

After the destruction of German surface warships outside the blockade, and with the exception of some quite effective commerce raiders, the remaining element of naval power that the Germans possessed was their small force of submarines. As mentioned, these had scored some successes against isolated British battleships, which were legitimate targets for attack.[16] Attacking the sea trade Britain was reliant on was a different matter, because it depended upon interpretations of what was allowed by the laws of the sea regarding commerce raiding and the potential impact of ignoring those rules. The basic rules were that merchant vessels should only be sunk if they were carrying war material, which generally could only be established through stopping and searching them. Even if the attacker's intelligence was good enough to make a search unnecessary, the ship still had to be warned and its crew and passengers given time to evacuate.[17] These were characterised as cruiser tactics, but did not really make best use of the submarine's qualities of stealth and surprise attack. However, even after declaring the waters around Britain part of the war zone, simply sinking all ships risked angering neutral nations, upon whose cooperation Germany's own remaining access to imported materials was reliant. Further, the small number of submarines available, compounded by the relatively low number of torpedoes they each carried, meant that the blockade that could be achieved was relatively limited.[18] After the international outcry following the sinking of the liner *Lusitania* on 7 May 1915, the first phase of the submarine blockade was effectively suspended.[19]

In early 1916, before the Battle of Jutland, with the German Army having been pressured by Russian offensives and contemplating their own attack at Verdun on the Western Front, the General Staff managed to convince the Kaiser and his chancellor to allow another phase of submarine operations.[20] There were now more U-boats available and these were now fitted with deck guns, providing another method of destroying intercepted vessels. The submarine's method was to surface near a suspicious vessel and fire warning shots. The crew of the ship could then leave it, and the submarine would then sink it by shellfire or torpedo from the surface. This required the submarine to be on the surface and within gun range of its target, at danger from any weapons the vessel might possess, or at risk of attack by ramming if the U-boat was not careful. In effect the submarine had to surrender its inherent advantages for the duration of the attack. However, these tactics were relatively successful and placed significant pressure on the British and neutral commercial shipping entering the exclusion zone.

Presenting these new tactics as continued breeches of the laws of war, the British worked on a campaign of international condemnation, whilst instituting a few dirty tricks of their own. One of their major tactics was the development of Q-ships. These vessels looked like unremarkable merchant vessels, from which, in fact, most of them were converted. However, they were equipped with concealed weapons and crewed by naval personnel. Their method was to sail under either the merchant or neutral flags in areas where submarines were known to be active. If a submarine did fire on them, they had a range of decoy methods to make it appear the crew was abandoning them and that damage was greater than was in fact the case. The submarine would thus be lulled into a false sense of security and, once it came close enough, the Q-ship would unmask its guns, unfurl the naval white ensign, to attack and sink its persecutor. These tactics were, of course, highly risky, as they were reliant on the Germans not suspecting anything. Once the Germans became aware of the tactic, they were necessarily more wary of any vessel and more careful in their attack. Also, any vessel that was identified as a Q-ship itself became a specific target for the Germans.

In the end the U-boat threat was defeated by the introduction of the convoy system. Groups of merchant ships were gathered together and sailed with escorting warships. This reduced the number of potential targets to the Germans and increased their own risk if they attacked. A successful response to convoy tactics by the submarines had to await a later conflict, where they were to again face new types of countermeasures. From the perspective of New Zealanders winning the VC, the two new technologies of submarine warfare and airpower would coincide in that later war. However, the first New Zealander to win the award for the destruction of a U-boat did so commanding a Q-ship.

HMS PRIZE

HMS *Prize* was one of the later Q-ships, converted to the role in February 1917. A three-masted topsail schooner, she measured 112 feet, weighed 200 tons, and was originally German. As she had been the first enemy vessel seized at the outbreak of the war, she was registered as the *First Prize*, before being renamed again when she was taken into the navy. She had been chosen for the role because of her design — a wooden schooner looked less dangerous and not quite worth a torpedo to a potential attacker.[21] By 1917 the Germans were well aware of the Q-ship tactic and had transitioned anyway into the final, unrestricted phase of their use of submarines, where all suspected shipping could be attacked from below without warning. The latter had been allowed out of desperation, as the German leadership believed that the USA was soon bound to join the Allies. They therefore reasoned that they needed to knock Britain out of the war before either the American forces could make an impact, or the British blockade undermined their own war-making capacity any further.

The *Prize* was equipped with two concealed 12-pounder guns as well as machine-guns. Like many of her ilk, her crew were naval reservists, predominantly ex-merchant seamen or fishermen, familiar with the types of vessels being employed in the Q-ship role. Command of HMS *Prize* had been given to Acting Lieutenant William Edward Sanders of the Royal Naval Reserve (RNR). After completing conversion and a brief workup, she departed Milford Haven on 26 April 1917 for her first patrol. The first four days were completely uneventful, with no hostile sightings and the vessel was about 180 miles southwest of Ireland.

Nearing the end of the patrol area, Sanders had already directed a change of course for midnight 30 April when the alarm was sounded at 8.45 p.m. The schooner was now being stalked by U-93, itself on its maiden cruise, but with a veteran crew under the command of U-boat ace, Kapitänleutnant Georg Freiherr (Baron) von Spiegel. The U-93 was ending a successful cruise, having already sunk 11 vessels but in the process having exhausted all her torpedoes.

However, as a larger submarine displacing 1000 tons, U-93 had 105-mm deck guns mounted both fore and aft of her conning tower. Von Spiegel found the *Prize* too tempting as a target but, unknown to Sanders, was making a surface attack out of necessity.[22]

Initially, from the German perspective, everything looked to be going well. Their warning shots, one ahead and one behind, resulted in the schooner's crew immediately taking to their boats. The next few shots were telling, as they resulted in visible damage to the ship and caused fires to start. Von Spiegel scanned the vessel's deck carefully, but sighted no sign of life through the smoke. After firing 16 rounds in 20 minutes of bombardment, and seeing that the *Prize* was obviously taking on water, he finally ordered his submarine to move in and deliver the killing shots from closer range.[23]

The trap that von Spiegel was wary of was, of course, precisely the one that had been set for him. The personnel who had 'abandoned' ship were the panic party and they had deliberately approached the U-boat in such a way as to force her to change course, thus presenting a better target when Sanders unmasked his guns. Similarly, the fires that had first started were controlled and deliberately lit to create smoke. However, the bombardment of the *Prize* had been intense and there was also real damage by now. Although the crew had remained unhurt to this point, the engine room was flooding and on fire, while the hull had been holed twice below the waterline. Sanders had been able to move about the ship concealed to ensure his men were all right, but it took a collective effort of nerve for the crew to remain under cover until the vital moment.

Sanders and his men held their nerve. He waited until U-93 was only some 70–80 yards away when, at 9.05 p.m., he ordered 'down screens and open fire'. Simultaneously Sanders broke the white ensign to indicate that HMS *Prize* was a naval combat vessel. At that moment the Germans fired again and the *Prize* took her first casualties. Their own opening volley was immediately effective, however, when the rear gun scored a hit on the submarine's forward 105-mm gun, destroying it and decimating the crew. At the same time the Lewis machine-gun killed and wounded several of the enemy deck party. The after gun of the *Prize* managed to score ten hits on the submarine in short succession, while the forward gun found its mark a couple of times as well. The submarine then commenced to manoeuvre in a way that initially led Sanders to suspect she was going to ram him or try to bring a torpedo to bear. However, at that moment the German's rear 105-mm gun was hit and von Spiegel, who had joined it to direct the fight, having already been driven from a similar role at the forward gun when it was destroyed, was knocked into the water by the body of a wounded man. In the confusion following the disappearance of its commander, the submarine took further hits, badly damaging the conning tower. Both vessels then continued on diverging courses, until the submarine apparently came to a halt 600 yards away. At that distance she was then judged to sink by the stern and a white vapour seen rising was ascribed to seawater reaching her electric batteries.[24]

By now Sanders could not come about to mount a pursuit of U-93, or further verify her destruction. He and his crew had the more immediate job of trying to keep the *Prize* afloat. The panic crew had rescued von Spiegel and a couple of his men, who gave their parole and assisted in helping to keep the ship afloat. Eventually, by shifting all the weight to one side, they were able to get the worst holes above the waterline sufficiently that they could be patched. It then took Sanders until 2 May to bring his ship into port, where she required three weeks of repairs before she was ready to resume her patrol area.

For his actions and leadership against U-93, on 22 June 1917 the *London Gazette* notified the award of the VC to William Edward Sanders. Awards were also made to his second in command, Lieutenant Beaton, who received the DSO; the warrant rates received the DSC and all remaining crew got the DSM. Because the actions of the Q-ships were still secret, no detail of the action was published. By this time HMS *Prize*, with her captain and crew, was back actively patrolling. However, unbeknown to them all, U-93 had not in fact been sunk, but had reached Kiel after an epic surface journey necessitated by the damage she had sustained in the fight. HMS *Prize* was now a marked ship.

WILLIAM EDWARD SANDERS

William Sanders was born in Auckland on 7 February 1883. His father was a bootmaker and he and his wife had emigrated from England. Edward had gone to sea in 1897, aged about 14, and by the time he was 26 had worked his way up to become a first mate and held an extra master's ticket. Shortly after war was declared the sailing ship on which he was serving was wrecked and Sanders showed considerable skill and coolness in bringing survivors ashore through difficult surf in the ship's boats. The sinking allowed him to join the Union Steamship Company, where he was employed as an additional officer on troopships going to the Middle East. However, the duty of transporting other men to war soon palled for Sanders and as early as June 1915 he started making approaches to the Admiralty to join the Royal Navy.[25] Having been accepted, he completed his current appointment and then worked his passage to England. On 19 April he was commissioned sub-lieutenant in the RNR.

Given his maturity and previous experience in sailing ships, Sanders was immediately assigned to the Q-ship force. After a naval gunnery course he was appointed as second in command and gunnery officer of the SV *Helgoland*. This vessel was a two-masted Dutch brigantine, armed with four 12-pounder guns and a machine-gun. His work aboard was evidently very good and his standing was further enhanced by his coolness in action during encounters with U-boats in September and October. During the latter contact a gun screen jammed, but Sanders managed to free it while under fire from the enemy.[26] This led to his promotion to acting lieutenant and appointment to command of HMS *Prize*.

Once the *Prize* had resumed her patrols in late May 1917 she was, as already stated, a marked vessel, and various ruses were carried out to vary her appearance, including sailing under false neutral flags. Ten days before the publication of his VC, the newly promoted Lieutenant Commander Sanders noted, when the *Prize* encountered a submarine on 12 June, that the vessel could not be enticed within a mile of his ship. Having used all the normal subterfuges without success and after being wounded himself, Sanders was eventually forced to return fire at this distance, at which point the submarine disengaged. For this action he was to be awarded the DSO.[27]

HMS *Prize*'s next encounter with a U-boat was to be her last. On 13 August 1917 she was again patrolling off Ireland, this time in conjunction with the British submarine D6. The plan was for the *Prize* to act as the bait to lure a U-boat, and if she could not destroy it herself to hold it long enough for D6 to make an attack. The basic concept worked when a U-boat was sighted, but D6 could not find its target and the German vessel slipped away. D6 rendezvoused with the *Prize* at 9.00 p.m. and was told that the U-boat had come to within 200 yards and had been hit before making its escape. Unfortunately the submarine commander was persistent and HMS *Prize*, now confirmed as a decoy ship, was a priority target.[28] At 1.30 a.m. on 14 August the second officer on D6 saw the *Prize* blow up and sink, as the second of two torpedoes fired by UC-48 found its target. William Edward Sanders and his entire crew were lost.[29]

Sanders' VC was presented to his father by the governor of New Zealand and it, along with his DSO and other memorabilia, are now displayed in the Auckland War Memorial Museum.[30]

William Sanders stands alone as the only New Zealander ever to have won the VC while serving in the navy, though one man was subsequently to be awarded the Albert Medal for an act of bravery not in the presence of the enemy. However, three more men were to be awarded VCs for bravery in air combat and, like William Rhodes-Moorhouse, these men all did so as pilots in bomber aircraft, including one for sinking a U-boat.

CHAPTER 10 The Second World War: problems and issues

B arely 20 years after the signing of the armistice that ended hostilities on the Western Front, New Zealand was at war once more. And yet again New Zealand made 'a disproportionately significant contribution . . . to the Allied war effort'.[1] Some 205,000 men and women served in the New Zealand armed forces during the Second World War, with about 140,000 of them being despatched overseas to serve in fighting formations. A further 250,000 served in the Home Guard and other emergency organisations in New Zealand. This remains New Zealand's 'greatest national effort to date'[2] and such an experience was a pivotal event in New Zealand's history. Those New Zealanders killed during the conflict numbered 11,671, the highest per capita in the Commonwealth.[3]

In regards to the number of VCs awarded during the Second World War, unlike the war of 1914–18, New Zealand servicemen proportionately did very well. Far fewer awards were made in this second great conflict, despite the fact that it lasted two years longer than the previous world war, involved more people and included an additional military service. However, New Zealand won a similar number of VCs in the war of 1939–45 compared to its record in the First World War. This was certainly not the case for other Commonwealth nations involved in both conflicts. Before looking at the figures for VC awards during 1939–45, an explanation of why so few were awarded is required.

In May 1920, through the means of a consolidating warrant, the criterion for winning a VC was redefined. The key criterion of 'in the presence of the enemy shall have then performed some signal act of valour, or devotion to their country' was changed. It now read: 'For most conspicuous bravery or some daring or preeminent act of valour or self-sacrifice or extreme devotion to duty in the presence of the enemy.'[4] The 1920 warrant also made formal provision for posthumous awards and extended eligibility to the merchant marine, to women of the nursing and hospital services and to civilians serving with the forces. The warrant for the first time standardised the colour of the medal ribbon to maroon for all services. Previous to this, the navy's ribbon had been blue and the army's red.[5]

These changes, together with the creation of several other categories of gallantry awards, had the net effect of making the VC harder to win. This can be seen in the figures for awards made during the Second World War. Only 182 awards were made during 1939–45, less than one-third of the 663 awards made during the First World War. The same number of VCs were awarded from 1939 to 1945 as were awarded during the Indian Mutiny of 1857–59.[6] Of significance, too, is the high number of posthumous awards made during the Second World War. As John Percival has written:

> Many, too many, of the men who won the Cross during the Second World War died winning it. The award has grown progressively more difficult to achieve as other medals have proliferated and as the nature of modern warfare has reduced the opportunity for outstanding courage 'in the presence of the enemy'. Only those actions so evidently heroic that they carried more than a high chance of death in battle could hope to qualify in the struggle with Germany and Japan.[7]

The changes meant that actions that probably would have won a VC in earlier conflicts, if they were recognised and recorded, were, more often than not, given a lesser award. This was usually the DSO if the person was an officer, or the DCM if they did not hold the King's Commission.

During the First World War, the great majority of VCs were won on the Western Front. In the war of 1939–45 they were spread across the globe, with no one theatre of war predominant. The VCs were awarded in the following theatres of operations or campaigns:

Burma	31	
North Africa	27	(including 21 won by the Eighth Army)
Northwest Europe (1944–45)	22	
Italy	21	
The Pacific	11	
Dunkirk (1940)	6	
Dieppe Raid	3	
Crete	3	

Of the individual services, 24 VCs were won by the navy, 26 by the air forces of Britain and the dominions, and the rest (132) by the army. Nearly half of the VCs of the Second World War, some 88 in total, were posthumous awards.

Individual nations of the British Empire won the following number of VCs:

United Kingdom	106
Indian Army	30
Australia	20
Canada	12
New Zealand	9
South Africa	3
Rhodesia	1
Denmark (serving with UK)	1
Fiji	1[8]

With nine VCs for this conflict, New Zealand's count is similar to the 11 awards made for the 1914–18 war. Those for Canada and Australia are remarkably different. Australian VCs for the Second World War numbered 20, with half of these being posthumous awards — significantly fewer than the 66 VCs won by Australian soldiers in the First World War. Unlike the previous conflict, none of the Australians awarded the VC during 1939–45 were New Zealand born. The case of Canada is even more striking. Canadian soldiers won the lion's share of the dominion awards in the 1914–18 war, with 69 VCs being awarded. In addition Newfoundland, part of

Canada in 1939 but a separate dominion in the First World War, also won a VC. However, from 1939 to 1945 Canadian servicemen won just 12 VCs.

What of the New Zealand awards for the Second World War? The total of 9 VC awards is made up of 6 army awards (including one bar to Charles Upham) and three to New Zealand airmen. Only two of the awards were posthumous awards: those made to Moana Ngarimu and Lloyd Trigg. The New Zealand winners of the VC and the date of the action of the award appear in the table below:

Date of action	Recipient	Place
28–29 April 1941	Jack Hinton	Greece
20–28 May 1941	Clive Hulme	Crete
22–30 May 1941	Charles Upham	Crete
5 July 1941	James Ward	Over Germany
14–15 July 1942	Charles Upham	North Africa
15 July 1942	Keith Elliott	North Africa
26 March 1943	Moana Ngarimu	North Africa
3 May 1943	Leonard Trent	Over Holland
11 August 1943	Lloyd Trigg	Over the Atlantic

Despite New Zealand being well represented in the VC awards for the Second World War, several important problems and issues exist.

The most glaring omission from the above is an award for a New Zealand sailor. In 1939 New Zealand's navy consisted of three ships and just over 1300 sailors, half of them on loan from the Royal Navy. By 1945, more than 10,000 New Zealand sailors were manning some 70 ships and they had served in some of the fiercest naval engagements of the war. In addition, another 8000 men served in the Royal Navy, the Fleet Air Arm and the Mercantile Marine. As Peter Dennerly has commented:

> After six years of war many of its [New Zealand Navy] number had been decorated for gallantry in all parts of the world, and they had earned a reputation for getting the job done, no matter what the difficulties or dangers involved.[9]

It is hard to believe that, given its record of service in this long war, not one New Zealand sailor deserved a VC. It is worth noting too that no Australian sailor has ever won the VC.

One New Zealand sailor did come close. He was Commander William James Lanyon Smith, known as 'Kiwi', a noted midget submariner of the Second World War. In July 1945 Kiwi Smith was part of a four-man crew of the midget submarine HMS *XE3* which attacked a Japanese heavy cruiser in Singapore Harbour. After attaching mines to the cruiser's hull, the submarine became trapped under its intended prey. The submarine crew persevered with their mission though and after a nerve-racking 15 minutes the submarine was able to wriggle free. Two of the submarine's crew were later awarded the VC for this action, while Smith received the DSO.[10] This disparity in honours for an action in which the whole crew equally shared the dangers and demonstrated 'most conspicuous bravery . . . extreme devotion to duty in the presence of the enemy' seems inequitable.

Another obvious omission is that of a New Zealand fighter pilot. Those New Zealand airmen who won the award were part of Bomber or Coastal Command. A significant proportion of the 12,078 New Zealand airmen who served in the Royal Air Force (RAF) during the war were part of Fighter Command. In fact, during the Battle of Britain in 1940, 127 New Zealand fighter pilots took part, the largest dominion contribution and the third-highest national component after the British and the Poles.[11] However, the nature of a fighter pilot's war service makes it nearly impossible for them to be a contender for this highest gallantry award. Aerial combat for the fighter pilot is usually an individual type of engagement done at great speeds. The actual engagement usually lasts only a few seconds and is, more often than not, all over before anyone can witness it. Yet a VC recommendation now demanded eyewitnesses, written testimony and careful scrutiny. Little wonder then that of the gallant 'few' who fought in the Battle of Britain, only one of the RAF fighter pilots involved won the VC. He was Flight Lieutenant James Nicholson who, on 16 August 1940, was seen attacking a squadron of German planes over the New Forest area in Southampton while his own plane was engulfed in flames.[12] Surprisingly, Flight Lieutenant Nicholson survived this encounter, bailing out of his wrecked Hurricane after shooting down the Messerschmitt that had caused the damage. He was, however, badly burned and needed months of rehabilitation before he could fly again. Sadly though, Nicholson did not survive the war. He was killed in an air crash in the Bay of Bengal in early 1945. James Nicholson was the only fighter pilot to win the VC during the war.[13] When it comes to VC awards of the Second World War, New Zealand fighter pilots are part of a much larger neglected group.

Yet New Zealand proportionately did well in the VCs awarded to airmen during the war. Of the 25 awards made to airmen in Bomber and Coastal Commands, New Zealanders were awarded three.

Though the New Zealand army appears to have fared well in the VC awards for this war, there are still significant issues that need to be highlighted. While the 2nd New Zealand Division was almost constantly in action from April 1941, the army VC awards are for just four actions: Greece (Jack Hinton), Crete (Charles Upham and Alfred Hulme), Ruweisat Ridge (Keith Elliott and Upham again), and Tebaga Gap (Moana Ngarimu). This leaves out many actions and a whole campaign where New Zealand soldiers fought with distinction. It also leaves out the contributions of the 3rd New Zealand Division operating in the Pacific. Two examples of these significant omissions appear below.

According to C.E. Lucas Phillips, one of the most important VC battles of the war was 'the fascinating and curiously neglected CRUSADER operation'.[14] During this first great test for the newly created Eighth Army, British soldiers won five VCs. Lucas Phillips has written of this: 'For CRUSADER, with five VCs in its 19 tempestuous days, was very much a soldiers' battle.'[15] The distinguished soldier-historian Major General Howard Kippenberger believed that the 2nd New Zealand Division had been at its finest during the CRUSADER battles. He wrote soon after the campaign:

Don't think New Zealand Troops ever fought quite so well. Auchinleck [General Sir Claude, commander in chief, Middle East] came to see me in hospital and said we'd done the finest fighting he'd ever known and he meant it.[16]

It is ironic then that the 2nd New Zealand Division, which did the bulk of the infantry fighting during CRUSADER and which even the Germans acknowledged as being responsible for the ultimate victory,[17] did not get a single VC during the campaign.

Of greater significance and almost impossible to explain is the lack of a New Zealand VC during the Italian campaign. From October 1943 until the end of the conflict the 2nd New Zealand Division fought in this theatre of war. There they participated in some of the most protracted and bitter fighting of the war. This included the slogging match at Cassino in February and March 1944 — the one battle of the war that most approximated the conditions of the stalemated bloodbaths of the Western Front. Towards the end of 1944 the 2nd New Zealand Division participated in a series of textbook river-crossing operations that won them much praise from their allies and routed the enemy in front of them. Then, on 1 May 1945, the New Zealanders crossed the Isonzo River, something that had eluded their Italian allies in the previous war despite 11 great battles to do so. They entered Trieste the next day just ahead of Josef Tito's Yugoslav partisans, thus preventing that city from falling under the Iron Curtain. The fighting on the Italian peninsula had been hard and protracted. The terrain of Italy was well suited to defensive warfare and the Germans had again proved to be skilful soldiers. The New Zealanders had played a significant part in the defeat of the German forces in Italy and it cost them 2003 dead and another 6705 wounded to do so.[18] That no New Zealand soldier features amongst the 21 VCs awarded during the Italian campaign defies explanation. It is inequitable and perhaps inexcusable.

There is something peculiar about the army VCs. Upon close examination of those who drafted the recommendations and those who signed them off and pushed them up the chain of command, it is impossible to ignore the influence of a senior New Zealand officer in all but one of the awards. That officer is Howard Kippenberger, quoted above, and who has been described alternatively as 'the most respected man in the New Zealand Army' and 'the emerging talent of the Division'.[19] Kippenberger's influence can be seen in the table below:

Army VC winners

Name	Commanding officer	Brigade commander
Hinton	*Kippenberger*	Puttick
Hulme	Leckie	Hargest
Upham	*Kippenberger*	Puttick
Elliott	Russell	*Kippenberger*
Upham's bar	Fountaine	Burrows (consulted *Kippenberger**)
Ngarimu	Bennett	*Kippenberger*

* King George VI also consulted with *Kippenberger* before awarding the bar to Upham's VC in 1945.

Although Kippenberger was Hinton's commanding officer, the circumstances surrounding the Greek campaign meant that he had little to do with this VC recommendation and award. Kippenberger was, however, intimately involved with four of the remaining five VC awards. Of the senior New Zealand army officers, only Kippenberger had made a lifelong study of military history. This detailed study ensured that Kippenberger understood the needs of posterity and he knew that New Zealand soldiers during the war were creating an enduring legacy. This understanding meant that Kippenberger appreciated the importance of adequate recognition for gallantry and he was determined that his soldiers received their fair share. It is unlikely that other New Zealand commanders had the depth of military knowledge possessed by Kippenberger and they perhaps did not push their soldiers' cases for recognition as much as he did. It is probably significant, too, that Kippenberger did not serve long during the Italian campaign — he was seriously wounded on

2 March 1944. Had he served on beyond this date the New Zealand VC record in this campaign may well have been different.

So although New Zealand's record of VC awards for the Second World War is proportionately much better than that for the previous conflict, there are still several important problems and issues which this chapter has highlighted. With the VC being much more difficult to win in this conflict, there is little doubt that all of the New Zealand awards that feature in the next three chapters were well deserved. But what this chapter has shown is that, despite the impressive record for the Second World War, more VC awards should have been made. The chapters that follow highlight some recommendations for the VC which were rejected, often for the most spurious of reasons. There is little doubt, too, that New Zealand sailors and airmen are definitely under-represented in the chapters that follow and that more army awards should have been made, especially in the last two years of the war.

CHAPTER 11 Greece and Crete 1941

The rundown state of the New Zealand army during the 1930s meant that it was more than 18 months before an army formation was ready for combat. The 2nd New Zealand Division was together as a complete entity for less than a month before it was committed to its first major campaign of the war. This was the ill-fated Greek campaign of April 1941.

The 2nd New Zealand Division was deployed to Greece along with the 6th Australian Division and a British armoured brigade in March 1941. This force was totally inadequate to face the German onslaught of more than 20 divisions when it came on 6 April. In the air, the disparity was even greater: some 1100 Axis aircraft against 80. The deployment of W Force, as it was designated, was in reality, little more than a political gesture.

There was little serious fighting for the Commonwealth forces, but for three weeks they conducted a series of difficult rearguard actions against the advancing Germans. These were fought over a distance of 300 miles along the mountain passes and crowded roads of central Greece. As Howard Kippenberger later recorded of the campaign:

> We had a certain amount of fighting but not very much. We were bombed and many difficult and hazardous moves were executed extremely well in the rearguard retreat.[1]

The parallels between the Greek campaign and Gallipoli 26 years earlier are striking. New Zealand troops were again committed to an expedition in the Mediterranean that owed its origin to Winston Churchill's strategic vision and to his powers of persuasion. This thought occurred to the New Zealand divisional commander (and VC winner), Major General Bernard

Freyberg, while on his way to Greece. He recorded in his diary on 6 March:

> I have been in all Mr Churchill's military ventures — Antwerp, Gallipoli and now this Greek War. The third venture will, I trust, be the one that which redeems all the others.[2]

Freyberg's hopes were to be cruelly dashed in this third venture which, like the Gallipoli campaign, also ended in an ignominious defeat and a military evacuation. Unlike the Gallipoli campaign, though, the evacuation was only a partial success — more than 14,000 Commonwealth soldiers were left behind and forced to surrender. The Greek campaign was also the prelude to an even greater military disaster for New Zealand in the Battle of Crete that followed soon after.

As with Gallipoli, New Zealand won just one VC for the fighting during the Greek campaign. There is a substantial difference though. The VC awarded to a New Zealand soldier here was the only one given for the fighting on the Greek mainland.[3] The soldier who won this VC — the first New Zealand VC of the Second World War — was a nuggety sergeant from Southland serving in the 20th Battalion. He was John (Jack) Daniel Hinton.

JACK HINTON'S VC

John Daniel (known as Jack) Hinton was born at Colac Bay, near Riverton, on 17 September 1909. His father had served as a sergeant with the New Zealanders during the Boer War. Hinton ran away from home when he was 12 years old. He initially worked delivering groceries for five shillings a week. A year later, only 13 years old, Hinton sailed to the Ross Sea on a Norwegian whaling ship, the *C.A. Larsen*. The vessel was a factory ship, and at 15,000 tonnes was then the largest whaling factory ship in the world.[4] Jack Hinton worked on board as a galley hand and was the youngest member of the crew. He spent nine months on board the vessel for which he was paid the princely sum of £381. As Gabrielle McDonald has commented, this amount of money in the hands of a 13-year-old was 'a small fortune in those days'.[5]

After signing off the *C.A. Larsen*, Hinton worked as a farm hand around Lake Wakatipu. He later moved to the West Coast of the South Island where he spent all of the 1930s. In that rugged part of the country Hinton worked initially as a gold miner on the black sands of the West Coast beaches, and then as foreman-driver in the Public Works Department.

When war broke out in 1939 Jack Hinton was one of the first men to enlist. He volunteered at Greymouth and was the twenty-second man to enlist from that town. The 'bush telegraph' must have been very active at the time as, according to his biographer, while at Greymouth Hinton received a telegram from his father urging him to 'do his duty'. There was also a small package containing his father's sergeant's stripes from the Boer War and a note that said 'Here — sew these on!'[6]

Hinton joined the 20th Infantry Battalion in 1939 as it was being formed at Burnham Military Camp. Howard Kippenberger was its original commanding officer. The 20th Battalion was to be the only New Zealand infantry battalion in the Second World War to win more than one VC (it actually won three of them). Jack Hinton was put in C Company, but being 30 years of age he was somewhat older than the rest of the recruits and within a few weeks he had been promoted to corporal. He sailed with the 20th Battalion in January 1940 and was promoted to sergeant in August of that year. It is not known whether he sewed on his father's sergeant's stripes upon his promotion.

Hinton has been described as 'a man of strong, rugged features',[7] a dry and earthy character with a real dislike for humbug. Although he was known as a quiet man, he was not afraid to speak his mind or challenge military authority when it was called for. The 20th Battalion's official history describes one such incident that soon became part of its folklore. In Egypt in the first few weeks of 1940 the troops were on the British Army ration scale and were receiving no food parcels from home. They found the British rations 'rather light' and were constantly hungry. General Freyberg only learned of this situation when he was visiting C Company of the 20th Battalion while it was doing a field firing practice at Abbassia. On this visit Freyberg asked a senior NCO how the men were progressing, and received a very blunt reply:

'How are the men shooting?' Freyberg asked Hinton.

'How would you expect them to bloody well shoot,' he [Hinton] replied briskly, without stopping to think. 'Not enough bloody rations, stinking heat and sand.'

'Repeat that,' said the General.

Hinton repeated it.

'What's your name, sergeant?'

'Hinton, sir.'

'Oh yes, Hinton,' replied the General. 'Carry on.'

Freyberg then had a few words with the company commander who in turn spoke to his sergeant about how to speak to senior officers in future. It was noted though that the men's rations were soon being supplemented from divisional funds.[8]

As mentioned above, the 2nd New Zealand Division was part of the Western Desert Force sent to Greece as a grand political gesture. Initially the New Zealanders were in the north of Greece in the Katerini region preparing a defensive position known as the Aliakmon Line. When the Germans launched their attack on 6 April from the north and from the west through Yugoslavia, the 2nd New Zealand Division had to abandon the Aliakmon Line and withdraw to the south. The division moved back to guard the Olympus Pass where they remained for three days and managed to halt the initial German thrust south. Another withdrawal was required when the Germans seemed likely to outflank the New Zealand position so the division was pulled back to the Thermopylae Pass, and then further south again to the evacuation beaches. The fighting was brief and sporadic, but by 14 April the reality was that the Allies in Greece were in full retreat.

Jack Hinton had seen little of the fighting in Greece, as he had not been with the battalion during its long withdrawal. Hinton had been with the division's reinforcement unit, initially at Athens and then further south at the port of Kalamata where he and thousands of other allied troops awaited evacuation. It was at Kalamata that Hinton won his VC in the 'last fire of allied resistance in Greece'.[9]

On 26 April 1941, Hinton and the rest of the New Zealand reinforcements were camped in some olive groves several kilometres north of Kalamata (formerly known as Kalámai). The port of Kalamata, a picturesque fishing village on the southern shore of the Peloponnese peninsula, was surrounded by hills. It was now crowded with thousands of British, Australian and New Zealand troops all awaiting evacuation. In charge of the evacuation from Kalamata was an English officer, Brigadier Leonard Parrington. During the night of 26–27 April, some 7000 Australian troops were taken off in Royal Navy destroyers. The New Zealanders had been warned to be ready to embark on ships the next day.

On 27 April, though, there was much disorganisation in the village. 'No one seemed to know what was going on — there was much confusion, and there were people milling around,' recalled Albie Thompson from 4th Field Artillery Regiment.[10] No evacuations occurred on 27 April and the troops just had to wait. The situation was tense as a squadron of British warships was expected to arrive at any moment and it was known that the Germans were not that far away. Of the 6000-odd troops awaiting evacuation at Kalamata only a small handful were equipped to fight.

On 28 April, a German advance guard from 5 Panzer Division reached Kalamata at dusk. This force pushed through to the quay, where a large group of allied soldiers were lined up, and opened fire on the defenders with two machine-guns and two self-propelled six-inch guns. In the fading light, there was much confusion and during the firefight that followed many soldiers remained inactive. As the New Zealand official history makes clear, the situation was chaotic and 'there was no overall command'.[11] One of the

German troops' first successes was to capture the naval liaison officer, which ensured that contact with the approaching navy ships was now impossible. There was no organised fighting, but several small firefights developed, usually under the leadership of an officer or NCO. As Pringle and Glue state:

> There had been plans for two companies to defend the road entrances to the town, but there seems to have been some hitch somewhere and the brunt of the fighting fell on little assorted groups who hurtled into the fray as they came down from the hills in response to the sound of the firing that so irresistibly called them.[12]

One of the NCOs to become involved immediately was Sergeant Jack Hinton. At the sound of firing, Hinton went forward to the headquarters and attempted to find out what was happening. No one there had any idea at all about the situation. While at the headquarters Hinton again spoke bluntly to a senior military officer — amazed to hear Brigadier Parrington order the men around him to surrender, Hinton immediately challenged the brigadier's decision:

> 'Surrender?' said Jack incredulously. 'Go and jump in the bloody lake!'
> 'I'll have you court martialled for speaking to me like that!' said Parrington.
> 'If you're not careful I'll have you court martialled for talking surrender!'[13]

Hinton then set off to find out for himself what was happening. He was armed with a .303 rifle, bayonet fixed, and had several hand grenades in the pockets of his shorts.

He ran along Beach Road towards the town and met up with Major B. Carey of 3 Royal Tank Regiment in command of a machine-gun post near the beach. Carey assured Hinton he could provide covering fire for an advance so Hinton retraced his steps, collected about 12 New Zealand soldiers and led them back into the town of Kalamata. According to his biographer, Hinton was experiencing a mad feeling of excitement:

He was scared, shit-scared really, but over-riding these feelings, he had a sense of crazy excitement, almost as if there was some invisible force egging him on, and he was caught up in it. It was telling him to do these mad things, throw his life to the wind. Suddenly, he knew without a doubt why he had travelled thousands of kilometres. Everything he had done in the last year was in preparation for this moment. It was so clear to him he almost laughed out loud.[14]

Hinton's first target was the big gun which had commenced firing on the port. Heading towards the guns, he ran into two men sheltering in a doorway. Hinton was on the point of bayoneting them when one spoke to him in English. It was the medical officer, Major George 'Two-Pill' Thomson who, according to Hinton's biographer, later wrote the VC recommendation for Hinton. Hinton's party then came under fire from German infantry, hitting one of the New Zealanders in the arm. An order was shouted for the advancing New Zealanders to 'retire to cover', to which Hinton shouted 'To hell with this! Who'll come with me?' Apparently his actual words were much stronger than this and were unfit for recording in the *London Gazette* announcing the award.[15]

Hinton and Private A.M. Jones set off in the direction of the waterfront and towards the German guns. Hinton dealt quickly with a machine-gun post that was blocking the way, using a grenade to kill all of its crew. Then while Private Jones' Bren gun provided covering fire, Hinton reached the waterfront and attacked the first of the big guns. He was only several metres from the nearest gun when its crew noticed him. The gun fired at him but missed. Hinton threw two grenades at the gun and crew. With Hinton's advance, the machine-gun fire from Carey's post and supporting fire from the other New Zealand attackers, the surviving crew members abandoned the gun and fled into nearby buildings along the waterfront.

Hinton had just one grenade left. He threw it at the remaining gun, which the Germans also abandoned, fleeing into nearby houses. Followed by a crowd of eager New Zealand soldiers, Hinton attacked them and cleared both houses, killing all the Germans who had taken shelter there. At the end of this action, a German rushed out from behind a building and fired a short burst with his submachine-gun. Hinton was hit in the stomach, which ended his involvement in the fighting.

The allied soldiers had recaptured the town and control of the vital quay but unfortunately no evacuations took place that night. The Royal Navy, witnessing the fight from the sea, believed that the town and quay had been lost and there was no naval liaison officer on shore to tell them otherwise. In the early hours of 29 April the trapped soldiers at Kalamata heard the sound of German tanks and lorries arriving. Brigadier Parrington formally surrendered at 6.00 a.m. that morning. The fighting at Kalamata had lasted only a few short hours. It had been a chaotic mess. As Hinton's biographer has aptly commented:

> The tragedy of Kalamata was that there was little direction, little ammunition and medical supplies, many of the troops were unarmed, and by the time it was decided to cease fire in the early hours of 29 April, there was little darkness left for anyone to escape to the hills through the surrounding German posts.[16]

The wounded Jack Hinton was now a prisoner of war (POW), just one of thousands taken in this Greek tragedy.

After the fighting was over, letters from other New Zealand prisoners mentioned Hinton's courage and leadership and, as stated above, Major Thomson drafted a recommendation for the VC. The actual recommendation held at Archives New Zealand, however, states that Hinton was 'recommended by various British Officers who are now P.W.'[17] The end result was an investigation and the eventual awarding of the honour, which was gazetted on 14 October 1941. At the time of the gazetting Hinton was in solitary confinement in a German POW camp as a punishment for attempting to escape. The commandant of Stalag IXC, near Bad Sulza, paraded the prisoners and announced the news to them. Hinton was pulled out of his cell, presented the VC ribbon and was then marched back to solitary confinement.

News of Hinton's VC was received in Egypt a week after Upham's VC had been confirmed. Upham and Hinton were in the same company of the same battalion. A notice appeared in the battalion lines: 'Join the 20th and get a VC.'[18] Lieutenant Colonel Jim Burrows, the second in command of the 20th Battalion before his promotion, was commanding the New Zealand Training Depot at Maadi in Egypt. He sent Kippenberger the following memorandum as a joke:

Honours and awards
Reference our communication 11/1/4630 dated 15th October 1941, for 2nd Lieut. Upham read 2nd Lieut. Upham and Sergeant J.D. Hinton.

It would be a convenience to this Headquarters if in future, the names and members of the Twentieth Battalion who win VCs were published in one list and not on different days as appears to be the present practice.[19]

While the memo was sent in jest, much to Burrows' surprise it was later quoted in a British war anthology as if the memo had been written in earnest.[20]

Jack Hinton spent many weeks in a German POW hospital at Kokkinia near Athens recovering from his stomach wound. He was listed as 'Missing in Action' until August 1941.[21] When he was deemed well enough, Hinton was sent to the POW camp in Germany.

Hinton hated being a POW and made life difficult for the Germans whenever he could, escaping twice, albeit only briefly. On his second escape attempt Jack Hinton was at liberty for a couple of weeks. Interrogation and beatings by the Gestapo followed his recapture. A report on his conduct as a prisoner states:

Sgt Hinton in Stalag 9c kept the boys in a good state of morale, made himself unpopular with the Germans as a result of constant consideration for the men, especially New Zealanders. Sgt Hinton also made one escape but unfortunately through a railway accident he was recaptured before being able to leave the country.[22]

When his prison camp was liberated in April 1945 Hinton borrowed an American uniform and fought briefly with them before his nationality was discovered.

Hinton was sent to the United Kingdom and was presented with his VC by King George VI at a Buckingham Palace investiture in May 1945. It was the same ceremony where another former POW from the 20th Battalion, Charles Upham, received the first of his VCs. A year later Hinton, also like Upham, now back in New Zealand, was awarded a delayed mentioned in despatches for his escape attempts.

After the war Hinton managed or leased Dominion Brewery hotels, initially in Auckland, and at one stage owned his own hotel at Cobden on the West Coast. In 1953 Hinton was part of the New Zealand Coronation Contingent for Queen Elizabeth II. He returned regularly to the United Kingdom to attend the VC and GC celebrations held in London. The last year he did so was in 1993, when he was the sole New Zealand VC representative as Charles Upham was too ill to travel that year.

Hinton, like most VC winners, was always reticent about having been singled out for the distinction. As with Charles Upham, it bothered him that he had been taken prisoner while many of his friends had gone on to fight in other battles:

> They were wonderful men. Congratulate them, not me. I had my war cut short. My mates went on to fight more battles. They are the real heroes.[23]

In 1964 an unfortunate incident occurred to this reluctant war hero. Jack Hinton was set upon and robbed in Latimer Square, Christchurch, by three thugs. They took his money, passport and watch.

Jack Hinton died on 28 June 1997 — New Zealand's last surviving VC winner. Just before he died a biography was published about him, written by Gabrielle McDonald. Jack Hinton was at its launch, where the Deputy Prime Minister, Winston Peters, presented him with a walking stick carved by the people of the Far North as a tribute.

Jack Hinton received a full military funeral, including a 100-strong honour guard and a eulogy delivered by the Chief of Staff, Major General Piers Reid. More than 800 people attended the funeral. On 1 July 1997, the House of Representatives observed a minute's silence in honour of Jack Hinton. Then the Prime Minister, Jim Bolger, made a short speech stating that Hinton's death 'closed a major chapter of New Zealand's participation in World War 2 ... Mr Hinton's citation made extraordinary reading. It is the stuff of heroes.'[24]

Jack Hinton is buried in the returned services section at the Ruru Lawn Cemetery in Christchurch. Hinton's VC remains in the care of his family, who have loaned it to the Queen Elizabeth II Army Memorial Museum at Waiouru until December 2028. The restaurant at the Christchurch RSA is named after him: the John Daniel Hinton Restaurant. Above the doorway of the entrance is a photo of Hinton in a soldier's uniform taken in 1940. On Anzac Day 2002 a plaque was unveiled at Colac Bay in memory of Jack Hinton. The Riverton Community Board chair, Ms Carina Kingipotiki, unveiled it, stating that Jack Hinton was like the canopy of the forest 'protecting the rest and giving them something to look up to'.[25] It was a fitting tribute to this modest war hero, who only towards the end was accorded the full recognition he deserved, having lived much of his post-war life in the shadow of Charles Upham.

THE CASE OF DONALD JOHN STOTT

While Hinton's VC was the only one awarded during the Greek campaign, another New Zealander was recommended for this honour for military service in that country. He was Donald John Stott and his case is most unusual.

Stott joined up in 1939, serving as a gunner in the 5th Field Regiment. He fought with this unit throughout the Greek campaign in the rank of sergeant. In May 1941, Stott was wounded and captured during the Battle of Crete. The Germans did not hold him for long though. On 6 August 1941, he and his close friend, Robert Morton, made a spectacular escape by pole-vaulting over the prison fence in broad daylight.[26] Both New Zealand soldiers evaded recapture until they were finally able to reach North Africa in November 1941.

In May 1942, Stott was commissioned and volunteered for service with the clandestine British Special Operations Executive (SOE). In March 1943 he parachuted into Greece to join the SOE mission there, which was primarily concerned with aiding the Greeks against their German occupiers. One of his tasks was to assist a resistance group with the destruction of the Asopos railway viaduct, which would sever the important rail link between Salonika and Athens. The destruction of this viaduct had been considered an impossible task but Stott's courage and determination were instrumental in seeing it completed. For his actions at the Asopos viaduct, Stott was recommended for a VC by the head of the British Military Mission in Greece, Brigadier E.C.W. Myers. The VC award was downgraded to that of the DSO because, according to Brigadier Myers, 'not a shot had been fired'.[27] If this was the reason for the downgrading of the honour, then it was extremely short-sighted. The viaduct and its approaches were well guarded by the Germans, and if shots had been exchanged the mission would have failed and Stott's guerilla band most likely would have been destroyed.

Stott later received a bar to his DSO for his further services in Greece and returned to New Zealand in May 1944. He married in June, and in July was sent to Australia to undertake special operations behind the Japanese lines. Operating with the Z Special Unit and now promoted to major, Stott led a 12-man team on a recon-naissance mission near Balikpapan on the Japanese-occupied island of Borneo. Dropped by submarine near the island, Stott set off for the Borneo shore in a two-man rubber dingy. The weather was rough at the time and the coast of the island was infested with crocodiles. Stott and his companion were never seen again. Extensive investigations conducted after the war found no trace of either man. The official verdict was that Major Donald John Stott, DSO and bar, 'was presumed to have been drowned on the night 20/21 March 1945, while engaged on special active service duty off Balikpapan, Borneo'.[28] Thus ended the life of one of New Zealand's most notable special operations officers.

THE BATTLE OF CRETE, MAY 1941

To save time and to rescue more troops from the Greek mainland, most of the allied soldiers were taken from Greece to the island of Crete about 100 kilometres away. This, they believed, would merely be a staging point on their way back to Egypt. Some 32,000 Commonwealth soldiers were dropped on Crete at the end of April 1941, including one Australian infantry brigade and the bulk of the 2nd New Zealand Division. It came as a considerable surprise to many of them to learn that they would remain in Crete for some time and that they were expected to repel a German invasion of the island within weeks. On 30 April 1941 Major General Bernard Freyberg reluctantly accepted command of the allied forces in Crete and warned them that a German attack was imminent.

The reason for Freyberg's reluctance and the troops' surprise is not hard to see. Most soldiers had arrived in Crete carrying their personal weapons and little else. The most basic of military equipment was lacking, including entrenching tools, tripods for machine-guns, artillery, signals equipment, blankets, medical stores and so on. There was no air support available for the soldiers on Crete either, yet ironically they would be forced to deploy a significant number of their best troops defending Crete's airfields, which were obvious targets for the German invasion. From start to finish, Crete was 'a pauper's campaign'.[29]

There was a month's respite before the German air attack came on 20 May 1941. The New Zealand soldiers, numbering about 9000, were responsible for the western sector of the island, including

Maleme airfield, the towns of Platanias and Canea, and the village of Galatas. After the usual unopposed morning aerial bombardment came a mass drop of German parachutists and troops landing in gliders. The sight of so many men slowly drifting to earth under silk canopies has been described as being 'hypnotically beautiful'.[30] The hypnosis, as powerful as it was, did not last long. The defenders sprang into action and the vulnerable parachutists were cut to pieces. Their losses were heavy and not one of their objectives had been taken by nightfall of that first day. Back in Athens, the Germans were convinced that their airborne invasion had failed and they were on the verge of a humiliating defeat. But overnight the position was transformed by several New Zealand command failures which enabled the Germans to capture and hold Maleme airfield and Hill 107 overlooking it. Belated counterattacks by the New Zealanders to recapture these vital positions failed. The Germans were quick to capitalise on this success, flying in much-needed reinforcements, supplies and equipment to Maleme airfield. They had gained a substantial foothold on the island and, unlike the defenders, were quick to exploit any advantage, however slim.

A week of heavy fighting followed during which two highpoints of action occurred for the New Zealanders. These were the retaking of Galatas village after it had been captured by the Germans on 25 May, and the long bayonet charge of 42nd Street (so nicknamed by the 42nd Field Company of the Royal Engineers who bivouacked there) two days later, which destroyed an entire German battalion then in pursuit of the allied soldiers. Yet such highpoints could not delay the inevitable. On 26 May Freyberg communicated his belief to Cairo that the troops on Crete 'had reached the limit of their endurance and the position was hopeless'.[31] Freyberg then began preparations for an evacuation from the fishing port of Sphakia on the southern coast and received official permission to do so the next day.

From 27 May onward, the New Zealand soldiers, along with their Australian and British counterparts, began the long, arduous trek over the mountainous spine of Crete down to Sphakia, fighting several rearguard actions as they went. Evacuations from Sphakia commenced after dark on 28 May and continued for the next three nights. Not all troops could be taken off from Crete, however, and about 6500 men were left behind to become POWs, including some 2180 New Zealanders. The Battle of Crete was a tragic end to the Greek campaign and another serious military defeat for the Allies. It is a battle, however, that holds a special place in the public imagination of New Zealanders. As Michael King has commented:

> Of all the battles in World War II, none engraved itself more deeply on the national consciousness than that for Crete. It was the Gallipoli of its era.[32]

There are several reasons why Crete holds this special place in New Zealand's military history. One is that, but for the loss of Maleme airfield, a scratch force made up largely of Australians and New Zealanders would have inflicted on Nazi Germany its first land defeat of the war. Another reason is that during the fierce fighting against what was the elite of the German military machine, most New Zealand (and Australian) units fought with distinction. Two out of the three VCs awarded for this battle were won by New Zealand soldiers. The New Zealand honours included the first of Charles Upham's two VCs. On the same day that the award was announced in the *London Gazette* the VC citation for Sergeant Alfred Clive Hulme of the 23rd Battalion was also published.

ALFRED CLIVE HULME'S VC

Alfred Clive Hulme was born in Dunedin on 24 January 1911. A farm labourer from Motueka, Hulme joined the 2nd NZEF just two days before his thirtieth birthday. He was described as being a powerfully built man with broad shoulders and as having 'an astonishing gift for initiative and leadership, a cool head and remarkable skill at arms'.[33]

At the time of the Crete campaign, Hulme was the 23rd Battalion's provost sergeant and was detached to the 2nd New Zealand Division's field punishment centre at Platanias under the command of Lieutenant W.J.G. Roach. At this centre were those soldiers who had committed crimes or misdemeanours since leaving Egypt. Being a senior NCO of a military field punishment centre was a tough job, certainly not one for the faint-hearted. On the morning of 20 May, the prisoners were having breakfast when the German airborne attack began. There was no time to finish eating:

'I think it's it,' said Sergeant Hulme. 'Get rifles, grab gear and move to 23 Battalion as in orders,' said [Lieutenant] Roach.[34]

The prisoners were issued with their rifles, which had been stored close by for just such an event and were released to fight the Germans. They all fought hard and those who survived the battle won the remission of their sentences.

At Platanias Sergeant Hulme, operating alone, dealt with a number of snipers. When the prisoners had rejoined the 23rd Battalion, Hulme led several groups of soldiers and succeeded in destroying some of the German forward positions. After two days at Platanias, Hulme, and the small parties of men he led, had killed over 100 Germans.[35] However, one such killing haunted Hulme for many years. He had returned to the field punishment centre to find a German paratrooper rummaging through papers there. The paratrooper was huge, well over six feet tall, with broad shoulders and fair hair. Hulme shot him just below the brim of his steel helmet and later stated that 'he had never felt so sorry to kill a German'.[36]

Sergeant Hulme had by now acquired a German paratrooper's camouflage blouse and cap that he wore to deceive the Germans. He was also using a German Mauser sniper's rifle equipped with telescopic sights and carried Luger pistols. According to the 23rd Battalion's history, these items of clothing 'gave him some protection on his stalking patrols and may possibly have misled the Germans'.[37] Such a ruse, however, was against the rules of war at the time, being defined as a 'perfidious act'. Any soldiers perpetrating such a ruse, if caught, risked summary execution. Many German soldiers were shot in late 1944 and early 1945 for just such an offence. Regardless of this risk, Hulme continued using this ruse in his campaign against the German snipers.

On one occasion at Platanias, Hulme came across a small party of New Zealand engineers taken prisoner, being guarded by only one German sentry. He did not want to shoot the sentry for fear of hitting one of the New Zealanders. Instead, Hulme silently crept up behind him, killing him with a short German bayonet, safely freeing the captives.

Hulme was one of the New Zealand soldiers who took part in the famous attack on Galatas organised by Kippenberger. During that attack a platoon from the 23rd Battalion was held up by machine-gun fire and grenades coming from a building described in the official history as a schoolhouse. Sergeant Hulme went forward alone and attacked the schoolhouse with grenades, which put the Germans to flight.

It was just after clearing this building that a most unfortunate incident occurred. Shots were fired from another house at the New Zealanders and Hulme saw a German run into it. He and another New Zealand soldier set off in pursuit. They went into the house but could see nothing. Then they noticed a trapdoor in the floor open slightly and assumed the Germans were hiding in the cellar. While the other New Zealand soldier lifted the trapdoor, Hulme threw two German grenades through the opening. The people sheltering there were Cretan women and children and they were killed and injured by the grenades the New Zealanders had thrown. As they left the house the German soldier was found hiding behind a door and the New Zealand soldier grabbed Hulme's rifle and bayoneted him in a furious rage. Hulme had great difficulty extracting the bayonet from the wall behind the German and was haunted by this incident for many years to come.[38]

That night, again disguised as a German parachutist, Hulme stalked around the outskirts of Galatas, killing several more Germans.

The next day, 26 May 1941, Sergeant Hulme learned that one of his brothers, Corporal H.C. 'Blondie' Hulme of the 19th Battalion, had died of wounds. This news deeply affected Hulme, one writer recording that he 'felt a cold need to avenge his brother's death'.[39]

It started almost immediately. During the withdrawal from Galatas, Hulme dropped behind his battalion and took up a sniping position that covered a food dump. He waited until the Germans arrived, shot three of them and forced the remainder of the German patrol to withdraw.

Later in the withdrawal the 23rd Battalion provided the rearguard. After a gruelling night march the battalion reached Stylos and the exhausted men threw themselves to the ground to snatch some much-needed rest. Two officers of the battalion made a quick reconnaissance before settling down. It was fortuitous that they did. When they reached a stone wall on top of the ridge they spotted a party of Germans emerging from the creek bed about 400 yards away. The Germans saw the two New Zealanders and fired at them. It was a desperate situation and the weary men were ordered to the ridge. Major H.H. Thomason, the company commander, barked out an order: 'Sergeant Hulme! Get men on top of that hill! Whoever gets men there first wins!'[40]

Hulme, still in a cold fury over his brother's death, did not need much encouragement. He was one of the first to reach the hill and immediately opened fire on the Germans, who were now only 15 yards away. When some grenades had been primed, Hulme threw these at the enemy. After shooting several Germans, Hulme was hit in the arm, but he kept shooting. The Germans, soldiers from II Battalion, 85 Mountain Regiment, beat a hasty retreat. Hulme had been inspirational throughout the encounter. The battalion's history records:

Hulme was to be seen sitting side-saddle on the stone wall, shooting at the enemy on the lower slopes. His example did much to maintain the morale of men whose reserves of nervous and physical energy were nearly exhausted.[41]

The next day was also a day of action for Hulme. During a conference of senior officers at 5 Brigade headquarters behind 42nd Street, German snipers concealed among rocks in the hills opened fired on the officers. Hulme volunteered to deal with them. Wearing the camouflage blouse again he climbed up behind the Germans and pretended to be part of their group. He shot the leader first, and as the four other snipers looked around to see where the shot had come from, Hulme also turned his head as if searching for the shooter. Then he shot and killed two more in quick succession. The other two snipers, knowing something was amiss, began to leave, but Hulme shot them too. Major Thomason, watching through his binoculars, witnessed most of these actions.[42]

Later during the withdrawal, the Germans brought a mortar into action. Hulme, on his own initiative, penetrated the German position, killed the mortar crew of four and put it out of action. On the same day he killed three more snipers who were causing trouble. Hulme had now killed 33 German soldiers. He was in the process of stalking his next victim when he was shot through the shoulder and disabled. Ordered to the rear, Hulme stayed in the Stylos area, directing traffic and organising stragglers into section groups. Hulme travelled with the 23rd Battalion to Sphakia on 30 May where he was evacuated to Egypt.

For his actions on Crete his battalion commander, Lieutenant Colonel D.F. Leckie, recommended Hulme for the VC. Lieutenant W. Roach, Lieutenant G.H. Cunningham, Major Thomason and Brigadier James Hargest provided the eyewitness statements. Brigadier Hargest's statement recorded that:

Sgt Hulme, during the whole of the fighting up till the moment of being wounded, conducted himself with such courage that the story of his exploits were on everybody's lips. From my own personal observation I know he showed such a complete contempt for danger that it amounted to recklessness . . . The effect his actions had on all the men in his unit is incalculable, and he at once became almost legendary. I sincerely hope that the recommendation will be accepted.[43]

Angus Ross, the author of the 23rd Battalion's history, concluded of Hulme's performance on Crete:

With the prescience of a mystic and the assured self-confidence of a man who trusted his intuition or 'sixth sense' in the special kind of fighting in which he engaged in Crete, Sergeant Hulme established something of a record for an infantryman.[44]

Hulme's VC was gazetted on 10 October 1941 by which time he was back in New Zealand. As a result of his wounds on Crete, Hulme was discharged in February 1942 as medically unfit. The gunshot wound to his shoulder had resulted in a wasting of the forearm and a limitation of his wrist movement. Hulme's disability caused by his wounds worsened over the years. In September 1951 he received a 60 per cent disablement pension, and in May 1960 this was changed to a 100 per cent disablement pension.[45]

Despite the disability caused by his wounds, Hulme resumed service with the home defence establishment from May 1942 through to September 1943 when he was discharged, having reached the rank of warrant officer class II. He rejoined the army briefly in 1946 so that he could be an official member of the New Zealand Victory Contingent sent to the United Kingdom.

Upon leaving the army in 1943, Hulme bought a trucking company at Te Puke which he ran until his retirement. Like most VC winners, Hulme rarely spoke about the war and would wear the VC only on Anzac Day. It is clear, though, that he suffered from post-traumatic stress after the war and the incident of the grenades in the cellar at Galatas particularly played on his mind.[46] In his later years, though, Hulme, like a lot of old soldiers, felt the need to talk about his war to someone. According to his daughter Anita:

There was a period when the war years really got to my father, to the point where he had to talk about it. I used to love listening to his stories. They'll certainly be with me on Sunday [Anzac Day, 1999] when I hand over Dad's medal.[47]

Alfred Clive Hulme died on 2 September 1982, aged 71. He is buried at the Dudley Cemetery, Vercre Drive, Te Puke.

Hulme's VC is owned by his family, who have loaned it to the Queen Elizabeth II Army Memorial Museum at Waiouru until

January 2009, where it is on public display. As mentioned above, Anita Hulme, his daughter, presented his VC to the museum on Anzac Day 1999. This presentation by Ms Hulme meant that the museum now holds five of the six army VCs of the Second World War.

Anita Hulme's brother was the late Denny Hulme, a Formula One racing driver who in 1967 had been the Formula One world champion. Denny Hulme completed 112 Grand Prix races, being placed 61 times with eight victories. He was inducted into the New Zealand Sports Hall of Fame in 1993, a year after he died while racing a V8 car at the Bathurst 1000 in New South Wales.

Upham's first VC

During the Second World War, only one soldier obtained the rare feat of winning the VC twice. As C.E. Lucas Phillips has commented: 'It is quite impossible to write any book about the Victoria Cross without the inclusion of this rare and superlative achievement.'[48] That soldier was the New Zealand officer Charles Hazlitt Upham.

Charles Upham was born in Christchurch on 21 September 1908, where he attended Christ's College as a boarding student during 1923–27. The college then had a compulsory cadet system and Upham served five years with the cadets, rising to the rank of sergeant.[49] Following his graduation from high school, Charles Upham was sure that he did not want to enter a profession like his lawyer father. He wanted to go farming instead. So Upham enrolled at Canterbury Agricultural College (which later became Lincoln College, then Lincoln University) and graduated with a Diploma in Agriculture in 1930. From 1930 to 1936 Upham worked as a musterer, shepherd and farm manager in the backblocks of Canterbury. In March 1937 Upham joined the Valuation Department as a land valuer and was still with the department when war was declared in 1939. He immediately joined up.

Charles Upham was a foundation member of the 20th Battalion, where he soon came to the notice of its commanding officer, Howard

Kippenberger. Upham was promoted to sergeant six days before he sailed from New Zealand with the advance party in January 1940. After several months' training in the Western Desert, in August 1940 Upham was sent to the Officer Cadet Training Unit (OCTU) as 'a reluctant candidate'. At the OCTU, Upham attained a C pass and passed out bottom of his class.[50]

In 1941, Second Lieutenant Charles Upham was a 33-year-old platoon commander, which is quite old for a subaltern. He had established a reputation for taking great care of the men under his command and for his proficiency in all types of infantry weapons. It was known that he led by example, something that earned him the respect of the men he commanded. Upham had also developed a reputation for being 'obstinate, pugnacious, independent, blunt, tactless, hard-swearing, highly strung, careless in his dress',[51] qualities that often drove his senior commanders to despair. They recognised, however, that beneath the rather gruff exterior Upham was developing into 'a superb junior leader'.[52]

Upham sailed to Greece with the rest of the 2nd New Zealand Division in March 1941. His platoon saw little fighting on the mainland but it was there that Upham contracted a severe bout of dysentery that was to plague him throughout the Greece/Crete campaign. At times Upham was so weakened by the ailment that he could barely walk. For several weeks the only thing he could eat was condensed milk.[53] As expected, his physical condition rapidly deteriorated, and by the time of the Battle of Crete Charles Upham was a mere shadow of his former self. However, it soon became apparent that even in a poor state of health Upham could still provide inspirational leadership and fight with tremendous courage.

On Crete, on the day of the invasion, Upham's platoon was sent to clear out some paratroops who had landed between the 20th and the 19th Battalions. This it did without much trouble. Then, when news of the capture of Maleme airfield reached them, the 20th Battalion was warned that it would be used in the counterattack.

The counterattack to retake Maleme was launched much too late. It did not get under way until 3.30 a.m. on 22 May. Parts of two battalions — the 20th and 28th (Maori) Battalions — were used. Charles Upham was leading 15 Platoon of C Company towards the airfield when, about a mile past the startline and while crossing an open field, the men came under fire from a German heavy machine-gun concealed behind a tree about 60 yards to their front. Four members of the platoon were hit. The platoon went into an immediate action drill, diving to the ground and crawling forward under the vocal encouragement of their commander. The sections crawled forward until they were only 25 yards from the machine-gun, from where they kept up a steady fire on the German position. Meanwhile, Upham moved around the open right flank of the machine-gun position and attacked it with grenades from the rear. He threw three grenades and then ran forward, firing his pistol. Upham stormed the position, killing eight Germans in the process. An eyewitness recorded:

> We edged forward on our stomachs until we were within 20 yards of the Nazis, who were tucked away behind a large tree, and then opened fire with our one Tommy gun, one Bren gun and eight rifles. As we kept up the fire the platoon officer [Upham] cautiously crawled round to the side and slightly to the rear of the tree. Although it was still dark, we could tell by the way the Jerries were shouting to each other that they didn't like the look of the situation. When he got round behind the tree the platoon officer jumped to his feet and hurled three Mills bombs, one right after another, into the nest and then jumped forward with his revolver blazing. Single-handed he wiped out seven Jerries with their Tommy guns and another with a machine-gun . . . Two machine-gunners managed to hobble away in the darkness, but we got them later.[54]

After attending to their wounded, Upham's platoon moved on. They soon came under fire again, this time from two machine-gun positions. One was concealed in a house, the other in a shed nearby. While the platoon's Bren gun gave him covering fire, Upham, bending as low as he could, dashed ahead and reached the safety of the shed. He pulled the pin from a grenade, placed it in a dead German's hand and pushed the German back into the shed. Upon the explosion Upham ordered his men forward and the half-dozen unwounded Germans in the shed surrendered. Inside the shed eight more wounded Germans were captured. Then the second machine-gun firing from a window in the house opened up and hit one of his men in the stomach. Upham ran towards the house carrying a grenade in his hand which he threw through the window. The platoon moved on.

When they reached the village of Pirgos, still half a mile from the airfield, they found some 200 Germans present from the 2nd Parachute Regiment. Upham's platoon had to clear this village house by house. As Private Hill-Rennie later recalled:

> Jerry had taken up vantage points in the houses. We slowly blasted our way from house to house, wiping out one nest after another, while the snipers kept up a constant, deadly fire.[55]

At Pirgos village, near the airfield, the platoon could hear a captured Bofors gun firing. Upham's platoon moved towards the gun until they could fire at the gunner. While his men kept the gunner's head down, Upham crawled around on his stomach to within ten yards of the gun, where he lobbed a grenade that killed the gunner and damaged the gun. Upham left a vivid account of this action:

> Went on meeting resistance in depth — in ditches, behind hedges, in the top and bottom stories of village buildings, fields and gardens on road beside drome. The wire of 5 Bde hindered our advance. There were also mines and booby traps which got a few of us. We did not know that they were there.
>
> There was T.G. [Tommy gun] and pistol fire and plenty of grenades and a lot of bayonet work which you don't often get in war. The amount of M.G. [machine-gun] fire was never equalled. Fortunately a lot of it was high and the tracers enabled us to pick our way up and throw in grenades. We had heavy casualties but the Germans had much heavier. They were unprepared. Some

were without trousers, some had no boots on. The Germans were hopeless in the dark. With another hour we could have reached the far side of the drome. We captured, as it was, a lot of MGs, 2 Bofors were overrun and the guns destroyed. The POWs went back to 5 Bde.[56]

The village was finally cleared and the airfield lay ahead but it was now broad daylight. The remnants of the two New Zealand battalions had reached the edge of the airfield but they could get no further. The counterattack had failed.

At the airfield that morning Upham could see 'planes were landing (some leaving drome too) and the parachutists were jumping out and getting straight into the battle for the Germans were counterattacking on the right flank'.[57] The New Zealand attackers could not stay where they were in the open and further progress was impossible. The inevitable order to withdraw was given.

During the attack on Maleme, D Company had become isolated from the rest of the 20th Battalion, which had been ordered to withdraw. Directed by Lieutenant Colonel Jim Burrows, acting as the commanding officer, to send 'two very good men' to warn this isolated company that it was time to leave, Upham and his sergeant, David Kirk, set out on this dangerous mission. In order to reach D Company, Upham and Kirk had to advance through 600 yards of enemy territory. The ground they had to cross was open and exposed, with pockets of Germans everywhere. Upham killed two more Germans along the way and found that D Company had already withdrawn. On the way back he located some isolated men from B Company and brought them back to the battalion's new position. But Upham was still not finished. He, Kirk and others from his platoon went into Pirgos village again to retrieve their wounded. They carried several badly wounded men back on wooden doors and other improvised stretchers. Upham and his team went into Pirgos village twice that morning to bring in wounded soldiers.

Charles Upham had certainly had an eventful 24 hours and his performance had been inspirational. As one historian has noted,

'Throughout the whole night's fighting Upham had shown first-class junior leadership in a most impressive display of aggressive infantry action, and he had begun to win his VC.'[58] Indeed, this was only the beginning.

That afternoon, at about 4.00 p.m. during the withdrawal from Maleme, Upham was wounded in the left shoulder by mortar shrapnel. He refused to let it incapacitate him and asked his platoon sergeant to cut the shrapnel from his shoulder. Dave Kirk later recalled:

Upham handed me his pocket knife and insisted that I extract the offending shrapnel. After carrying out what I thought was rather a neat bit of surgery, though it must have been rather painful for the patient, I tried to persuade him to go and have it dressed at the RAP [regimental aid post]. As he refused to go I went and reported it to Captain Den Fountaine who then came down to us and ordered Charlie to the RAP for treatment.[59]

On the sixth day of fighting on Crete, Upham's platoon was involved in the attack on Galatas, where he was again wounded, this time in the leg. During the attack Upham was hit in the ankle by a spent machine-gun bullet. The bullet lodged in his ankle, where he left it in order to stop any bleeding. He squeezed the bullet out from his ankle a fortnight later in Egypt.[60]

When the New Zealanders were ordered to retire from Maleme to a new defensive position, Upham placed his platoon under the command of his sergeant and went forward to warn the other troops. Along the way Upham faced — and shamed — death yet again. He came upon two Germans, who fired on him. After his battlefield surgery Upham had the use of only one arm, and he needed to be accurate and fast in drawing the rifle bolt back and chambering the second round in order to return fire. Upham crawled to a position where he could rest his rifle in the fork of a tree, using it to support his weapon, from where he shot both Germans, the second having got so close that he actually fell onto the muzzle of Upham's rifle.

After Galatas, the long retreat to Sphakia began — a trek of over 40 miles over mountainous terrain. Upon reaching the fishing village, Upham was instrumental in resolving a significant threat to the allied evacuation there. On 30 May, a force of about 50 heavily armed Germans managed to outflank the New Zealand rearguard and travel down a ravine towards the evacuation beach. Just short of the beach the Germans began shooting at everything they could see, hoping to throw the New Zealanders into a panic. Brigadier Inglis and Colonel Kippenberger moved into action. The 18th Battalion was to send men along the eastern slope of the ravine, while A Company of the 20th Battalion blocked the ravine's mouth. Upham was to lead C Company onto its western slope in order to attack the enemy party on its flank.

Upham's company, exhausted though they were, was the one forced to do the bulk of the climbing onto the ravine's west shoulder. Then they had to send a firing party to the very top of the ravine, a climb of a further 600 feet over a distance of just on two miles. It took Upham and his men more than two hours to get into position. They worked above and around the Germans and then fired down on the infiltrating enemy. The Germans below them were caught by the plunging fire and were wiped out. The four men of the firing party accounted for 22 of the Germans, and the other company on the east ridge killed the rest. One man who took part in this action recorded:

> The going was hard and the men were very tired, but, led by Lt Upham, they toiled up the steep slope until they observed Germans running between rhododendron bushes in the bed of the ravine which was otherwise devoid of cover . . . The sides of the ravine were so steep that one man . . . had to be held by the legs so that he could lean over far enough to fire with his Bren.[61]

The situation had been restored and the evacuations could continue that night. A reluctant but very sick Charles Upham, weeping from exhaustion, illness and bitter frustration at leaving some of his men behind, was evacuated to Egypt. After nine days of superb leadership, courage and endurance he was reduced, in the words of Howard Kippenberger, to 'a walking skeleton'.[62]

When the dust settled from the Crete debacle Kippenberger drafted the VC recommendation for Charles Upham. Twelve pages of documentation, including eyewitness statements from Captain D.J. Fountaine, Sergeant Kirk, a corporal and two private soldiers, supported it. Fountaine's statement is typical:

During the whole of the operations in Crete Mr Upham showed a total disregard for his own safety, very seldom used cover as he was always moving around his platoon cheering them on and his coolness, leadership and unremitting attention to his men were an inspiration not only to his men but to the whole company and every one with whom he came in contact.

For a man in good physical condition the 10 days operations in Crete were strenuous. Mr Upham had diarrhoea from the time we left Servia Pass in Greece on April 18 until we arrived back in Egypt but he remained on duty throughout.[63]

The recommendation progressed rapidly up the chain of command and the citation appeared in the *London Gazette* of 10 October 1941. It was an immensely significant award, as Upham was the first New Zealand commissioned officer to win the VC since Heaphy. Kippenberger, extremely proud of this 'grand soldier', regarded Upham's Crete VC as 'one of the best of the war'.[64]

General Sir Claude Auchinleck presented Charles Upham with his VC ribbon at a ceremonial parade by 4 Brigade in early November 1941 — the same presentation at which Kippenberger received the DSO and Major R.J. Lynch the MC. As he pinned the award to Upham's tunic General Auchinleck had the following exchange with Upham:

Auchinleck: 'Congratulations, Upham. New Zealand will be very proud that you have won this decoration.'
Upham: 'I didn't win it, sir.'
Auchinleck: 'Then if you didn't, Upham, I don't know who did.'[65]

It caused Kippenberger and several other senior officers some concern when they noticed that Upham was wearing yellow socks at the presentation. That concern increased when Upham almost forgot to salute Auchinleck as he marched off the parade ground. He had marched away 20 paces before he remembered that a salute was necessary. Upham's denial to Auchinleck was genuine. He was embarrassed at receiving the VC and felt that he had only been part of a much larger team effort. As his biographer has noted, 'Charles Upham has never really overcome that first feeling of embarrassed defensiveness. It has remained with him throughout the years.'[66]

As an indication of this, Upham was too self-conscious to wear the VC ribbon. Kippenberger had to order him to do so. And at one time, sick of Upham deliberately avoiding visiting New Zealand dignitaries who all wanted to meet the new VC winner, Kippenberger 'sent a warning to his oversensitive VC: "Next time I'll charge you with cowardice."'[67] Charles Upham never got used to, nor enjoyed, the publicity associated with winning this highest of honours. Unfortunately for Upham there was much more on its way.

THE LION OF CRETE: DUDLEY PERKINS

Similar to Don Stott on the Greek mainland, a New Zealand soldier also returned to Crete to work with the partisans and to be recommended for the VC. He also did not receive the honour. He was Staff Sergeant Dudley Perkins who, through his exploits on Crete, was named by his friends 'Vasili', which translates as 'the Lion'.

Perkins had been captured by the Germans at the end of the Crete campaign, but managed to escape. With the help of Crete's underground resistance movement, he managed to make his way to Egypt where he was recruited by the British SOE. Staff Sergeant Perkins' job was to return to Crete and help organise the Cretan resistance, which he did from July 1943.

Perkins proved to be an outstanding military leader and it

was this that earned him the nickname Vasili. Michael King has written of him (and it is a comment that could equally apply to Don Stott):

> He [Perkins] was but one of hundreds of examples of mild-mannered civilians who discovered that, faced with wartime conditions, he was possessed of great courage and considerable military skills.[68]

According to his biographer, Perkins was twice recommended for the VC, but 'nothing came of them'.[69] While several reasons have been given why both recommendations were unsuccessful, the most common is that no British officer had been present to witness the actions for which he had been nominated.[70]

Staff Sergeant Dudley Perkins was killed in February 1944, a few days after his twenty-ninth birthday, when the Germans ambushed his partisan team. His involvement in Crete's partisan operations further strengthened the links between New Zealand and the people of Crete and this has not been forgotten. Five years after the war a photograph was sent to the British Consulate in Canea showing a small girl laying a wreath of flowers on Dudley Perkins' grave. An inscription on the back of the photograph read:

> Grave of the most fearless of fighters ever to leave New Zealand, known to all Cretans as the famous Kapetan Vasilios. Killed over 100 Germans single-handed during the Occupation. Led a guerilla band, and fell from machine-gun fire in February 1944, near Lakkoi — the last gallant Kiwi killed in Crete. This man is honoured by all Cretans.[71]

It was quite a tribute to a man who certainly deserved the highest of gallantry awards.

Dudley Perkins is commemorated in Crete by a plaque. On 21 May 2003, the New Zealand Prime Minister, Helen Clark, unveiled another plaque to Perkins at the Wellington-Greece Memorial.

In relation to the VCs won during the Greece/Crete campaign there are some remarkable similarities amongst the three New Zealand VC winners. All three were early volunteers for overseas service and were older than most of their counterparts. All three were over 30 when war broke out in 1939. They all came from rural backgrounds. This age difference and the higher level of maturity that came with it saw all three men become senior NCOs very early in their military careers, despite having only rudimentary military experience prior to their enlistment. Upham did become a commissioned officer, but he never lost that common touch with his men that most successful NCOs develop. All three men were noted for the care and concern of their men and were proficient with all forms of infantry weapons. Unfortunately, though, Hulme and Hinton became casualties of the Greece/Crete debacle and, as will be revealed in the next chapter, only Upham survived this first campaign to fight another day.

CHAPTER 12 North Africa 1941–43

Upon their return from Crete in May 1941, the 2nd New Zealand Division spent the next two years in North Africa fighting against the Germans and Italians as part of the British Eighth Army. Campaigning in North Africa saw the New Zealanders fighting military actions in Egypt, Libya and Tunisia in an ultimately successful effort by the Allies to clear North Africa of enemy forces. It was a long, difficult campaign exacerbated by the harsh physical conditions of North Africa and by a combination of command, doctrinal and equipment failures in the first half of the campaign. In addition to enemy action, the New Zealanders soldiering in North Africa had to endure intense desert heat, flies, freezing cold nights, floods, shortages of equipment and several changes in the army commander over the two years of campaigning. They also experienced several serious military defeats which they learned from before success was eventually attained.

The first major action for the 2nd New Zealand Division was Operation CRUSADER, which was also the first battle for the newly titled Eighth Army. The battle commenced in November 1941 and saw the New Zealanders doing the bulk of the infantry fighting. Despite this, as stated in a previous chapter, New Zealand soldiers were not among the five VC winners of this battle. It was a battle marred by serious command failings, chronic confusion and lost opportunities for the Eighth Army. While the battle was an eventual success for the Allies, this 'success' cost the New Zealanders more casualties than the two previous military disasters. New Zealand casualties in CRUSADER numbered 4620, 'making it the most costly battle of the war for New Zealand'.[1]

After a brief pause in Egypt to refit and take on reinforcements, the 2nd New Zealand Division moved to Syria in February 1942 where it would remain until hastily summoned back to Egypt in

June. The time spent in Syria was invaluable as it gave the division time to absorb the lessons of recent fighting and to change its war-fighting doctrine. Prime amongst these changes was General Freyberg's recognition of the brigade group as an ineffective fighting formation and his retention of the larger divisional structure for this role. These changes were then reinforced by a period of hard training. Most significant of the changes was the concentration of the artillery regiments into one single divisional unit rather than being dispersed, as previously happened. Prearranged fire patterns were also trialled and proved to be so effective that the British Army later adopted them.

In mid-June 1942, the Eighth Army was in disarray as a result of Erwin Rommel's latest offensive campaign. Within weeks Rommel captured Tobruk and bundled the British out of Libya. The New Zealanders, hastily recalled to the Western Desert, encountered the Eighth Army in full retreat. It was like March 1918 again. 'You're going the wrong way, chum,' British soldiers told the New Zealanders as they advanced towards the Egyptian border. Eventually taking up a defensive position on an escarpment at Minqâr Qaim, the 2nd New Zealand Division narrowly averted disaster. As the British forces melted away at the approach of the Afrika Korps, the 2nd New Zealand Division was left isolated at Minqâr Qaim and was soon surrounded. Only a daring night breakout prevented a catastrophe. It was during this breakout, which was one of the epic events of the North African campaign, that Charles Upham again distinguished himself. His actions during the breakout contributed to the awarding of his second VC.

The 2nd New Zealand Division then joined the rest of the Eighth Army on the Alamein Line running from the coast in the north to the impassable Qattara Depression at its southern end. The Alamein Line was the last defensive position before the Nile Delta. In the fighting on the Alamein Line the 2nd New Zealand Division was involved in two serious military disasters. The first of these was the Battle of Ruweisat Ridge on the night of 15–16 July. Here, five of the six infantry battalions involved in the fighting suffered such heavy casualties that they were unfit for further military action.

The Battle of Ruweisat Ridge resulted in more than 1400 New Zealanders being killed, wounded or captured in a single night of fighting. Not even the two VCs won during the fighting here could redeem this battle from being an unmitigated disaster. Less than a week later though, a similar disaster occurred at the El Mreir Depression and a further 900 New Zealand soldiers became casualties.

With a change in command and the arrival of Lieutenant General Sir Bernard Montgomery at the helm of the Eighth Army, the military situation in North Africa improved dramatically for the Allies. Repulsing Rommel's last attempt to break through the Alamein Line in August, Montgomery launched his own attack on the Axis forces in North Africa two months later. On 23 October 1942 the Battle of El Alamein began, and it proved to be the turning point of the campaign. Rommel was defeated and began a long retreat across North Africa, with the Eighth Army in a rather slow and muddled pursuit. During the Battle of El Alamein and the pursuit of Rommel across Egypt and Libya, the 2nd New Zealand Division played key roles.

At the end of January 1943 the Axis forces had fallen back into Tunisia. The 2nd New Zealand Division played a small part in defeating Rommel's last attack against the Eighth Army at Medenine on 6 March. Then, reinforced to corps size, including the addition of an armoured brigade, the 2nd New Zealand Division prepared to carry out a giant left hook in order to outflank the formidable Mareth Line defences. This move led to the hard-fought Battle of Tebaga Gap, which broke through the Axis defences there, forcing the Germans and Italians to conduct a hasty retreat. It was during the fighting at Tebaga Gap, in the struggle to take Point 209, that a Maori subaltern won a posthumous VC.

After the fall of the Mareth Line and following the successful Operation TORCH landings of British and American forces on the northwest coast of Africa, the Axis forces were squeezed into a small defensive perimeter in Tunisia. The last major action of the campaign by the New Zealanders was the fight for a steep hill called Takrouna, on the coastal plain south of Enfidaville in Tunisia. The fighting to take this feature was vicious, sometimes hand-to-hand, and the casualties on both sides were heavy. During the fighting, several New Zealand soldiers distinguished themselves and at least one was recommended for a VC.

On 13 May 1943, Axis resistance in North Africa collapsed and more than 238,000 Axis troops became prisoners of war. It was an important strategic victory for the Allies, one in which the New Zealanders had played a significant part. But New Zealand's contribution came at a heavy cost: 2980 New Zealanders dead, another 7000 wounded and 4041 taken as POWs.[2] It was the most costly land campaign of the war for New Zealand and the three VCs won here during the fighting hardly seem to do this fighting justice. And in May 1943 the end of the war was still two long years away.

Upham's second VC

Charles Upham did not participate in the CRUSADER battle. He had been deliberately left out of it by his commanding officer, Howard Kippenberger. It was just as well, as the entire 20th Battalion was overrun by Axis forces on Belhamed Ridge, and Upham would certainly have been amongst the casualties. When the battalion was reformed from the pool of reinforcements and those 'left out of battle' (LOB), Upham was promoted to captain and placed in command of C Company.

When Rommel broke through the Eighth Army's defences in June, the 2nd New Zealand Division was summoned from Syria back to the Western Desert. By 21 June the division was in the desert again, moving against the steady stream of an army in retreat. It occupied a defensive position at Minqâr Qaim some 25 miles south of Mersa Matruh. There they were to operate as a mobile force in conjunction with other formations of Eighth Army. It did not work out that way, and on 26 June 1941 the 21st Panzer Division and the 90th Light Division of the Afrika Korps had all but surrounded the 2nd New Zealand Division at Minqâr Qaim.

Throughout 27 June Upham was again inspirational, at one stage standing on the cab of a truck to attract the fire of nearby German infantry so that the New Zealand mortars could target them. As the battalion history records:

> Upham, with characteristic coolness, moved around his company on foot, crossing open ground swept by small-arms and mortar fire, steadying one platoon which was under shellfire and encouraging his men; he set an example appreciated by all who saw it, except perhaps the field gunners, whose 25-pounders were firing over C Company's positions over open sights.[3]

When Freyberg was wounded that afternoon, Brigadier Lindsay Inglis took command. The situation was desperate. The 2nd New Zealand Division was surrounded on three sides, had no tank support, the guns were down to 35 rounds a piece, one brigade had become separated from its transport vehicles, and their general had been seriously wounded. Inglis decided to attempt a breakout spearheaded by 4 Brigade on the night of 27–28 June. To break out of the encirclement 4 Brigade was to punch the hole through which the rest of the division would drive. The 19th Battalion was to be the point of the spearhead, with the 20th Battalion on the left and the 28th Battalion on the right.

The hasty withdrawal from Minqâr Qaim was a savage affair, with much hand-to-hand fighting needed in order to break through the German encirclement. Charles Upham and C Company were in the thick of the action. Upham was armed with his pistol and a haversack full of grenades, which he used with deadly effect. He attacked vehicle after vehicle with his stock of grenades and used his pistol liberally. It is not known how many vehicles he destroyed that night, nor how many Germans he killed. On one occasion Upham noticed a truck full of German soldiers trying to escape the carnage. He ran up to the truck, ignoring the heavy fire from automatic weapons, and destroyed the truck and all its occupants with grenades.

Upham was later somewhat derisive about the German troops and their performance at Minqâr Qaim:

In the advance the enemy were completely taken by surprise and many were killed at point-blank range without their trousers or boots on. I have never seen trained soldiers so bewildered or 'flap' so much.[4]

The New Zealanders smashed through the German lines at Minqâr Qaim 'leaving behind chaos and destruction'.[5] Charles Upham had been responsible for a fair amount of this destruction.

It was at Minqâr Qaim that Upham's performance was again regarded as being exceptional and this set him on the path towards obtaining a second VC recommendation. After Minqâr Qaim Brigadier Jim Burrows, now commanding 4 Brigade, went to see Kippenberger and stated emphatically that Upham deserved another VC for his conduct during the breakout.[6] Although Upham's bar to his VC was not given for his actions at Minqâr Qaim alone, as the official historian of the battle for Egypt has noted, Minqâr Qaim started the process:

> For an action in which so many men distinguished themselves, decorations had to be sparingly awarded. But there were no two minds in the Division that it had the right to claim on behalf of one of its officers the most jealously guarded award, a bar to the Victoria Cross . . . The highest award for bravery, however, was not made for this action alone. It came for like conduct at Ruweisat. But the foundation of the Division's claim to the signal honour was laid at Bir Abu Batta [Minqâr Qaim].[7]

The breakout from Minqâr Qaim saved the division from certain captivity and completely disorganised the advancing Germans, delaying their arrival at the El Alamein position for three days. This delay provided Eighth Army the brief respite it needed to occupy this last line of defence in Egypt.

In mid-July, whilst on the Alamein Line, the 2nd New Zealand Division received orders to take Ruweisat Ridge as part of an attack by 30 Corps. Ruweisat Ridge was a prominent, gently sloping ridge in the southern portion of the line. It ran in an almost dead-straight line from east to west for a distance of ten miles. Although it was nowhere more than 35 feet high, the ridge dominated the desert for some miles around. The job of capturing Ruweisat Ridge was given to the New Zealanders and to 5 Indian Brigade. The 1st Armoured Division was ordered to give tank support. As one historian has noted about this operation: 'The notice was minimal, the proposition formidable.'[8] He might have added two more descriptors. Planning for the operation was abysmal, cooperation between the formations taking part non-existent.

For their part in the operation, the 2nd New Zealand Division carried out a silent night advance of more than six miles, over broken ground in the dark, through the enemy positions. Two brigades of infantry set off at 11.00 p.m. on the night of 14 July. Enemy resistance was fierce and there was considerable depth to the enemy line. But the New Zealand and Indian infantry pushed through the Axis positions and by dawn on 15 July they had possession of the ridge. As Lucas Phillips has commented, to advance six miles at night at an angle to the main objective while having to fight through to the position for the last four miles 'was an exceptionally fine infantry achievement'.[9] At dawn though, there was no sign of the armoured protection that had been promised and which was soon to be vitally needed.

The 20th Battalion was one of the battalions held in reserve. Before he could commit it to action though, Brigadier Burrows had to know what was happening up on Ruweisat Ridge. He asked Upham to send an officer to find out. Upham refused to send an officer from his company, but instead went forward in a jeep himself. He was soon under heavy fire but set up a German machine-gun on the jeep and returned as good as he was receiving. Meanwhile his driver edged towards the ridge. The jeep ran into German tanks and skirted around them, still trying to find the lead battalions. Upham found what remained of them and made an important discovery. The main enemy positions were actually well forward of the ridge and the battalions on the ridge were now deep in enemy territory and cut off from support. The scene on the ridge was chaotic. Upham later reported:

Captain Charles Heaphy.
Surveyor, artist, explorer and
the first New Zealand serviceman
to win the Victoria Cross.

003062, Alexander Turnbull Library,
Wellington, New Zealand

A wedding photograph of Captain
William James Hardham, VC taken
in March 1916. Hardham was the
first New Zealand serviceman to
win the VC on overseas service.
The only New Zealand VC winner
of the Boer War, he served with the
Wellington Mounted Rifles in the
First World War.

024506, Alexander Turnbull Library,
Wellington, New Zealand

No VC was more consistently
earned. New Zealand's only
VC of the Gallipoli campaign
was awarded to Corporal Cyril
Royston Guyton Bassett.

PA Coll-6001-05, Alexander
Turnbull Library, Wellington,
New Zealand

William Rhodes-Moorhouse, the first ever Air VC, whose maternal grandmother was Maori.

Air Force Museum, Christchurch

Captain George Tuck, MC of 1st Auckland Battalion. The equal of Freyberg in courage according to Ormond Burton.

Auckland Weekly News

Major Frederick Starnes, DSO, OBE. As a captain with the 2nd Canterbury Battalion, Starne's incredible gallantry earned him a recommendation for the VC. His officer status denied him the award though.
Auckland Weekly News

Sergeant Donald Forrester Brown. New Zealand's only VC of the 1916 Somme battle was made posthumously to Brown only after constant lobbying by the officers of his Otago Battalion.
031677, Alexander Turnbull Library, Wellington, New Zealand

Lieutenant General Sir Alexander Godley. Much more interested in the 'K' awards than the more democratic VC.

2002.210, Kippenberger Military Archive, Army Museum Waiouru

Major General Andrew Russell. Russell had 'not much use for these kind of things' and believed that it was sufficient honour for a man to belong to the New Zealand Division.

H259, Kippenberger Military Archive, Army Museum Waiouru

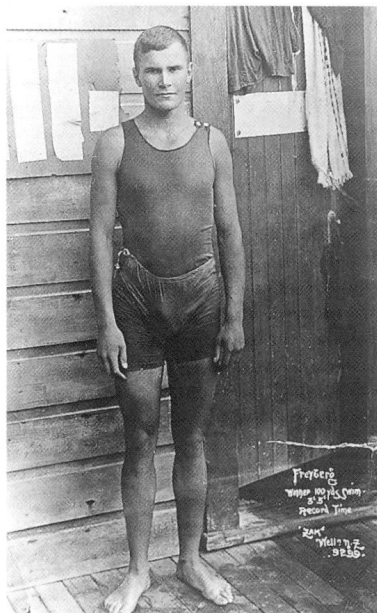

Bernard Cyril Freyberg.
Wellington Swimming
Champion.

1991.2106, Kippenberger
Military Archive,
Army Museum Waiouru

Lord Freyberg — his VC
all but hidden by the gold braid.
Freyberg's VC won in the First
World War was regarded by many as that
war's most distinguished act of courage.

2002.207, Kippenberger Military Archive,
Army Museum Waiouru

William Sanders, the only New Zealander serving in the Navy to win the VC.
Navy Bulletin

Leslie Wilton Andrew won the VC as a Corporal in the 2nd Wellington Battalion in July 1917. He continued to serve in the New Zealand Army until his retirement in 1952 as a Brigadier. Andrew's performance on Crete as a battalion commander has attracted considerable controversy.

Private Henry James Nicholas won the VC during a disastrous assault on the Polderhoek Chateau in December 1917. Sadly, Nicholas did not survive the war.

031673, Alexander Turnbull Library, Wellington, New Zealand

Sound claims to be considered one of New Zealand's greatest soldiers. He fought under the assumed name of Richard Charles Travis.

103803, Alexander Turnbull Library, Wellington, New Zealand

Sergeant Samuel Forsyth was killed in the action for which he won the VC. The current location of his VC is unknown.
031678, Alexander Turnbull Library, Wellington, New Zealand

Sergeant Reginald Stanley Judson won every gallantry award possible in the space of a remarkable six weeks.
025461, Alexander Turnbull Library, Wellington, New Zealand

Sergeant John Gildroy Grant won the VC for gallantry near Bancourt on 1 September 1918. He fell on hard times after the war.

031676, Alexander Turnbull Library, Wellington, New Zealand

Sergeant Henry John Laurent won the VC at Gouzeaucourt Wood in September 1918. He also served during the Second World War.

031672, Alexander Turnbull Library, Wellington, New Zealand

Boer War veteran Private James Crichton won New Zealand's last VC of the First World War.
031675, Alexander Turnbull Library, Wellington, New Zealand

Sergeant John Daniel Hinton of the 20th Battalion won the only VC to be awarded for military action on the Greek mainland. Unfortunately he was wounded and captured the day after his award-winning action and endured long years of captivity. This photograph was taken in 1953.
PA Coll-5469-059, Alexander Turnbull Library, Wellington, New Zealand

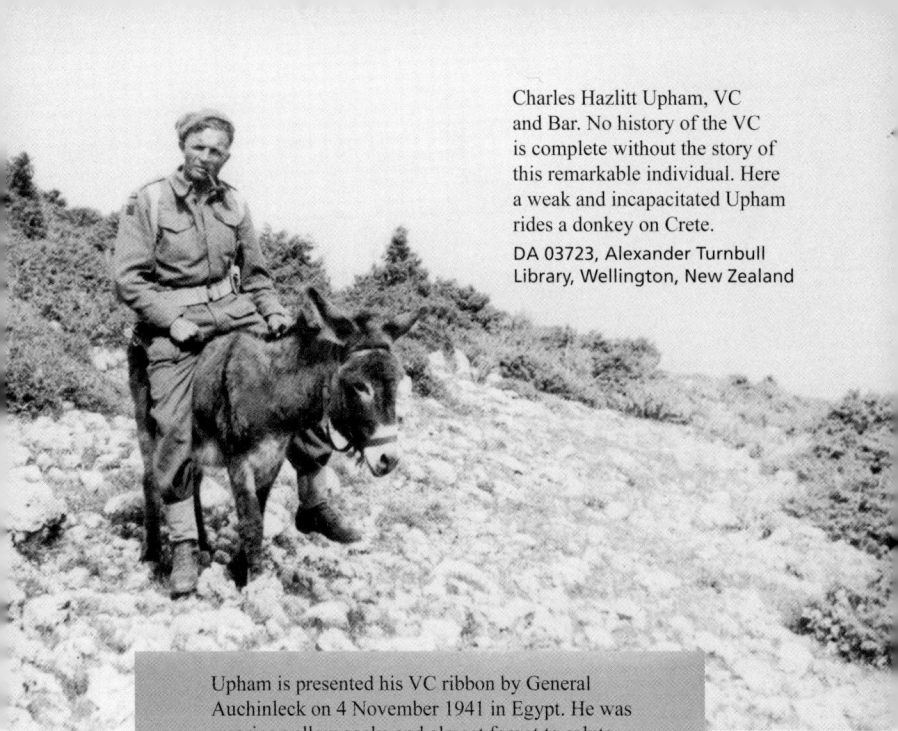

Charles Hazlitt Upham, VC and Bar. No history of the VC is complete without the story of this remarkable individual. Here a weak and incapacitated Upham rides a donkey on Crete.

DA 03723, Alexander Turnbull Library, Wellington, New Zealand

Upham is presented his VC ribbon by General Auchinleck on 4 November 1941 in Egypt. He was wearing yellow socks and almost forgot to salute Auchinleck when he marched off the parade.

DA 02165, Alexander Turnbull Library, Wellington, New Zealand

Sergeant Alfred Clive Hulme is surrounded by admirers from
Kowhai Junior High School in October 1941.

009623, Alexander Turnbull Library, Wellington, New Zealand

The wing-walker.
James Allen Ward in the cockpit
of an Airspeed Oxford Trainer.

017626, Alexander Turnbull
Library, Wellington, New Zealand

Brigadier (later Major General) Howard Kippenberger. This prominent and popular commander was intimately involved in most of the Army VCs of the Second World War. He later wrote an account of his wartime experiences that received international acclaim.

DA3721, Kippenberger Military Archive, Army Museum Waiouru

Sergeant Keith Elliott won the VC for his gallantry at Ruweisat Ridge in July 1942. After the war he became an Anglican minister.

DA 12682, Alexander Turnbull Library, Wellington, New Zealand

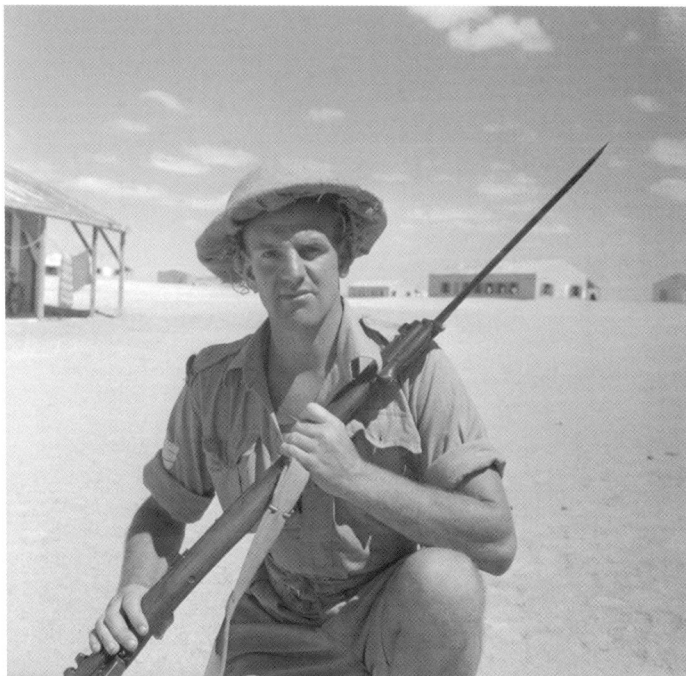

below: Second Lieutenant Moananui-a-Kiwa Ngarimu won the VC at Tebaga Gap in Tunisia in March 1943. It was another posthumous award.

DA 01990, Alexander Turnbull Library, Wellington, New Zealand

Flying Officer Lloyd Allan Trigg, the only recipient of the VC to receive it based on the testimony of the enemy he was fighting. It was a posthumous award.

DA 01988, Alexander Turnbull Library, Wellington, New Zealand

Leonard Henry Trent with his wife and daughter, Christine, on board the *Akaroa* in Auckland Harbour. Trent was lucky to survive the destruction of his aircraft and during his period of captivity was involved in the Great Escape.

021381, Alexander Turnbull Library, Wellington, New Zealand

Army Form W. 3121.

Date Recommendation passed forward.
Brigade. 2.4.43
Received 2.4.43 / Passed 2.5.43
Division
Corps 7 May 43
Army

Schedule No. (to be left blank)	Unit	Regtl. No.	Rank and Name (Christian names must be stated)	Action for which commended (Date and place of action must be stated)	Recommended by	Honour or Reward	(To be left blank)
	28 NZ (MAORI) BN		MANAHI, Ngar, L/Sjt.	On the 6th to 7th Apr 43 during the attack upon the TAKROUNA feature L/Sjt MANAHI was in command of a Section. The objective of his platoon was the pinnacle, a platform of rock, right on the top of the feature. Early in the advance his platoon came under heavy enemy fire which caused many casualties, including the platoon commander, in which it in the end only amounted in the platoon reduced in strength to only a few found the platoon reduced in strength to only a few men. L/Sjt MANAHI continued the advance towards their objective, L/Sjt MANAHI leading a party of three up the WESTERN side. During this advance they encountered heavy LG fire from positions on the slope and extensive sniping by the enemy actually on the pinnacle. In order to reach their objective L/Sjt MANAHI and his party had to climb some 500 ft to the almost sheer and during the ascent they were under heavy fire. L/Sjt MANAHI whole time they were under heavy fire. L/Sjt MANAHI personally led the small party and silenced several LG posts in turn. Eventually by climbing hand over fist they reached the pinnacle and after a brief fight some 60 enemy, including an OP officer, surrendered. They were then joined by the remainder of the platoon and the pinnacle was captured. Within a short time the small area was subjected to intense mortar fire from the considerable array to be still holding the villa of TAKROUNA and the SOUTHERN and WESTERN slopes. The platoon Sjt was killed and continuous shelling. The platoon Sjt was killed and other casualties reduced the party then holding the pinnacle to L/Sjt MANAHI and two plus. An Arty OP offr who had arrived ordered L/Sjt MANAHI to withdraw but he and his men remained and held the feature. This action was confirmed by late 1Q as soon as communications were established. The end of the	[signatures] Lt-Col Comd 28 NZ (MAORI) Bn

to DCM.

[signature] Brigadier. Comd 5 NZ Inf Bde.

[signatures] Maj Genl Comd 2 NZ Div

[signatures] GOC 10 Corps

NZEF | to DCM. | |

MEMORANDUM for:

Army Headquarters (A.G.)
N.Z. Military Forces,
Featherston Street,
WELLINGTON.

5th June, 1946.

DETERMINATION OF CASUALTIES.

20681 Major D. J. STOTT
64785 Capt. L. T. McMILLAN.

In November last Lieutenant Colonel H. O. Rigg, who was then serving with the Services Reconnaissance Department, Melbourne, visited Army Headquarters and Base Records and discussed the position regarding the two above-named officers who were reported missing while engaged in special operations with the Australian Forces.

As pointed out in my memorandum to you of the 27th November, there was no definite evidence that Major Stott and Captain McMillan had lost their lives although the general belief held by the Australian Authorities appears to be that both were drowned before reaching shore while attempting to land at Balikpapan from a submarine.

In view of the lack of any real evidence of death it was decided that both officers should remain classified as missing meantime, but as it is now nearly fifteen months since they were reported missing and as there is no evidence to the contrary it is suggested that a presumption of death should be made on lapse of time and on what information is available.

Will you please give this matter your consideration and advise your decision to this office in order that the next-of-kin may be notified.

Director.

MEMBER INTERROGATED

Japanese area Commander and Natives

No.   Rank   Name   Unit

PARTICULARS OF CASUALTY AND BURIAL INCLUDING
MEANS OF KNOWLEDGE OF INFORMANT

Have personally searched all areas where the above was supposed to have landed; no natives of coastal or inland villages have heard of, or seen Major STOTT.

I interrogated the Japanese commander of the are at time of landing; they also had never heard of or seen the above. In my opinion he was drowned at sea while coming ashore in a rubber canoe. The whole coastline is heavily mangroved and heavily infested with crocodiles.

PERSONAL PARTICULARS OF MEMBER WHO
SUSTAINED CASUALTY

Maj STOTT was a New Zealander attached to S.R.D. He was in charge of a party which landed in Dutch BORNEO. Maj STOTT with Capt McMILLAN and two sergeants left a submarine about 3 to 4 miles offshore on the night of k May 45; their landing point was to be Capt TAMBANGONOT on the MAHAKAM river delta in Dutch BORNEO. They travelled in small rubber canoes, two men in each. He became separated in the darkness. The two sergeants reached shore and eventually joined up with the remainded of the party in vicinity of the village of SAMBODJA.

Maj STOTT and Capt McMILLAN have NOT been seen since leaving the submarine. No equipment or canoe has ever been found on the coast.

Signature of Interrogating Officer—

(Sgd) R Sapper Lt.

NZ Rapwi Contact Team

Signature of Informant—

(Sgd) R. Sapper Lieut

Date 5 Nov 45.

FOR USE AT 2nd ECHELON LHQ ONLY

Casualty Identified by O2E as

Related Interrogation
Serial Nos.

No.   Rank   Name

Unit

Lex Report

Classification to be changed to

Signature

Date

Forms from the enquiry into the disappearance of Major Donald John Stott. Recommended for a VC for his services with the Special Operations Executive in Greece, Stott and a companion disappeared off Dutch Borneo in May 1945.

Personal File of Major Donald John Stott, New Zealand Defence Force

I could not find 19th Battalion when going forward and 18th and 21st were in confusion. So were the Germans. They were getting trucks out, pulling guns back by hand. All this went on under cover of fire by tanks which in groups of three were covering the withdrawal. It was a very colourful show with flares going up, tanks firing red tracer bullets from machine-guns. Two German tanks were put out by 18th Battalion with sticky bombs [a form of hand grenade with a sticky outer coating]. They went up close to me. The German troops were being badly cut up while the Italians were surrendering in hundreds. They were out of all proportion to our people and really broke up the attacks with their crowds . . . All the time this was going on, and even before it, there was a rumble of tanks on our exposed left flank. We thought it came from our tanks which were supposed to be there.[10]

Upham, who had been away over an hour conducting this dangerous reconnaissance, and who had covered a considerable distance, reported the situation to Burrows then rejoined his battalion. It was soon thrown into the fray.

The 20th Battalion's objective was Point 63, an exposed rocky outcrop on the ridge, but it soon ran into a German artillery position sheltering in a depression. Upham's C Company was ordered to clear the enemy from the depression while another company raced on to Point 63. There was little time for finesse, so Upham led the attack against the enemy position in a direct frontal assault. While leading it Upham was seriously wounded in the left arm. It was 'a tearing wicked wound from machine-gun bullets that ripped through his biceps and smashed his arm at the elbow'.[11] The force of the bullets threw Upham to the ground, but he got up and staggered on. He continued to lead the attack even with his left arm smashed and dangling uselessly at his side.

After a bayonet charge of about half a mile into the depression, Upham's company took the position after a brief, violent action. Then Upham went to the RAP for treatment. His account of the action is as follows:

In the valley the Huns were making a stand. It was broken ground with a small rise or pimple in it and beyond that the rise on the far side of the valley. On the floor of the hollow were guns, trucks and Huns in confusion. So we went into it with a bayonet charge for half a mile past the slit trenches on the forward slope . . . and consolidated on the far side under intense fire . . . I remember saying to someone this was the greatest victory yet. There was everything a soldier wanted lying about — an enormous heap of rifles, another big heap of unopened mail, stores galore and loaded trucks, several half-tracked vehicles and six field guns (two of them 88s), and a group of German wounded.[12]

Upham's company had taken the position and 142 POWs but it now numbered less than 50 men and most of the officers had become casualties.

Ruweisat Ridge was taken, but the situation was precarious. The battalions on the ridge were isolated, lacked support weapons and couldn't dig in. There was no sign of the promised armoured support and that morning the Germans attacked the ridge using tanks and infantry. The 22nd Battalion was overrun except for a platoon which was extricated by Sergeant Keith Elliott, who features later in this chapter. Meanwhile, Upham tried to rejoin his company but had to return to the RAP. Later that day Upham again tried to rejoin his company but was wounded again, this time in the leg by a mortar shell. Now unable to walk, Upham was with the six survivors of his company when the German armoured cars and tanks arrived to take them prisoners of war. Upham's biographer recorded:

Upham lay on the ground watching it coming closer, savouring the bitterness of it. One arm, one leg, one man for whom the war was ending in pain and humiliation.[13]

The attack on Ruweisat Ridge had been a disastrous operation for the 2nd New Zealand Division. In the 20th Battalion all three rifle company commanders involved became POWs, including

Upham, and all the battalion's subalterns were casualties. Many New Zealand soldiers shared Upham's pain and humiliation at Ruweisat Ridge.

As with Jack Hinton, Upham hated being a POW. He was determined to escape as soon as he was well enough to do so. After receiving some rough, basic medical treatment where he narrowly escaped having the wounded arm amputated, Upham made his first escape attempt. He did not get far, only making it into the roof cavity of the prison. Upham's second escape attempt was slightly more successful. He leapt from a lorry while in transit from Northern Italy to Germany and remained free for a few hours before being recaptured. Arriving at the Weinsberg POW camp in Germany, Upham made two more unsuccessful escape attempts but he did not get past the camp's barbed wire.

Upham's fourth escape attempt was his most famous. He was scrambling over the barbed-wire fence in broad daylight when a staple on the fence broke and Upham was pitched head first onto a barbed-wire entanglement where he was stuck fast. Upham was soon discovered and an approaching guard unslung his rifle to shoot him. But Upham calmly smoked a cigarette while waiting to be shot. This display of raw courage so impressed the German guard that he couldn't shoot Upham. The camp commandant later berated the guard for not doing so. As punishment though, Upham was sent to Oflag IVC, more commonly known as Colditz Castle, near Leipzig, a special camp for particularly troublesome allied officers. On his way to Colditz, Upham tried another escape, jumping from a speeding train to do so. He was at liberty for a day and a night before he was caught again.

Charles Upham was the only combatant officer from the 2nd New Zealand Division to serve time in Colditz. The handful of others were medical personnel, including a doctor and a dentist. As his biographer acknowledged: 'Upham could not escape from Colditz. He knew it.'[14] Upham was still in Colditz at the end of the war when it was liberated by allied troops on 15 April 1945. After the camp's liberation Upham joined an American unit and fought as part of it for several days. His nationality was eventually discovered and Upham was made to return to England.

When in London after the war both Upham and Hinton attended an investiture at Buckingham Palace on Friday 11 May 1945. Later Upham, like Hinton, also received a mention in despatches for his many escape attempts. Upham returned to New Zealand in September 1945 and ceased service with the 2nd NZEF in November of that year. At this time he was unaware that he been recommended for a bar to his VC.

The recommendation for a bar to Upham's VC had been changed to that of a DSO in 1945. An explanatory note was added, which stated:

> This gallant officer has now been released from captivity and was recently presented with his VC at the hand of HM the King, and in support of this belated recognition for a DSO there is quoted below in full the original citation written for a bar to the V.C.[15]

Meanwhile General Freyberg, at the instigation of Inglis, went to the Army Council to have Upham's second recommendation examined 'in the cooler light of history'.[16] The papers were then sent to King George VI, who read them and then sought the advice of Major General Kippenberger, then resident in London. The King had examined the papers very carefully and said to Kippenberger that the award of a bar to a VC 'was a very, very unusual thing: in 90 years there had been only two cases'. Kippenberger's reply was immediate and direct: 'In my respectful opinion, Sir, Captain Upham won the Victoria Cross several times over.'[17] The King was persuaded and the award was approved. The recommendation for the DSO was amended to a 'Bar to VC'. Surprisingly, given the 12 pages of evidence for the Crete VC, no eyewitness statements supported this second award.[18]

Upham, the first combat soldier to receive the award twice, was back in Christchurch when he learned that the bar had been gazetted in London. He did not welcome the news, stating to a close friend: 'What about all the others? We all did exactly the same things. Why pick on me?'[19]

Upham was now a household name in New Zealand where the Minister for Defence, Frederick Jones, stated in a press release that the bar to the VC was 'a most exceptional honour. [It] stamps Captain Upham as one of our bravest and most outstanding leaders.'[20] Newspapers across the world carried the story of the double VC winner. The citation for the bar appeared in the *London Gazette* on 26 September 1945 and the Governor-General, Sir Cyril Newall, presented the bar to him in Christchurch the following year.

After this startling development the people of Canterbury started a collection for Upham in order to purchase a farm for him. It soon raised more than £10,000. Upham refused to accept the money, suggesting instead that it be put towards the children of ex-servicemen. The Charles Upham Scholarship Fund was formed to award education scholarships to the sons of servicemen tenable at either Lincoln College or Canterbury University.

After the war, Upham took up farming, something that he had wanted to do since childhood. He won a returned servicemen's ballot and farmed in North Canterbury on a 400 hectare block in the remote Conway Flats district. Always a modest man, Upham shunned publicity despite being one of the most famous of VC winners. He always refused to accept any monetary reward and even refused to accept a knighthood when it was offered.[21]

Unlike Dick Travis of the First World War, Upham had to live with the legend his deeds of valour had created. He did not find it easy, but the remoteness of Upham's farm provided some sanctuary from the intense publicity that dogged him. When Upham took over his farm, which he named Lansdowne, 'there was no road, no houses and the land was wild and unproductive'.[22] It was a challenge that Upham relished and his hard work slowly transformed Lansdowne. Upham cleared the scrub from the farm although he left a small area of native bush intact. He top-dressed the slopes with fertiliser, erected sheds and thoroughly fenced the property. Lansdowne soon became a very productive farm, running some 1600 sheep, 50 Hereford cattle and nine horses.[23] Such a transformation must have been very rewarding — and therapeutic — for Charles Upham. Together with his wife, Molly, Upham farmed in the one location for 47 years and raised three daughters along the way. As one writer perceptively noted:

> Charles Upham has found peace in which to live and work at
> Lansdowne; far away are the years of war and captivity in the
> camps of Lamsdorf, Weinsburg, Silesia and Colditz Castle.[24]

Upham reluctantly attended the allied victory parade in London in 1946 as an official member of the New Zealand Victory Contingent, but only after being pressured by the New Zealand Prime Minister, Peter Fraser, to do so. He also attended the VC centenary celebrations in London along with other New Zealand VC winners in 1956.

On 18 July 1955, after reading *Reach for the Sky* and *The Dam Busters*, Kenneth Sandford, a barrister and solicitor and the Crown prosecutor at Hamilton, wrote to Kippenberger, requesting assistance to write a book 'based on infantry heroism' using Upham as its subject. Sandford had previously published two works of fiction and had been a captain in the 34th Battalion, 3rd New Zealand Division. Kippenberger's reply was not encouraging:

> My own feeling is that it would be extremely difficult to 'write
> up' an infantryman. Infantry fighting is a hard brutal business
> . . . I am willing to give any help I can.

Kippenberger also warned Sandford that getting Upham's cooperation would be difficult: 'Upham is a very curious chap, not well at present and at no time easily predictable. You face a difficulty here.'[25] However, Upham did agree to cooperate with Sandford in the production of a book but only so long as Kippenberger was used to arbitrate on points of dispute. The end result was the book *Mark of the Lion: The Story of Capt. Charles Upham, V.C. and Bar* that appeared in August 1962. It has become one of New Zealand's most popular books and by the end of 1962 it was already into its fifth reprint. *Mark of the Lion* is still in print more than 40 years later and has sold more than 400,000 copies.

Charles Hazlitt Upham died on 22 November 1994 and was cremated. It had once been put to him that when he died he would have a state funeral. Upham, typically self-effacing, replied: 'A bugle will do.'[26] Upham's ashes are in the family plot in the churchyard of St Paul's Anglican Church, Papanui, Christchurch. His medals are on long-term loan to the Queen Elizabeth II Army Memorial Museum in Waiouru.

Upham is commemorated by the continuing scholarship that bears his name and in the 1990s a navy sealift vessel was named in his honour. The vessel did not prove to be suitable for New Zealand waters and was later sold. Molly Upham unveiled a bronze relief memorial at the Bridge of Remembrance in Christchurch on 26 March 1997 and in December that year the New Zealand Prime Minister, Jenny Shipley, unveiled a large bronze statue of Charles Upham at Amberley, in North Canterbury. Shipley stated that the statue was 'a lasting memorial to the man and his deeds'.[27]

Unfortunately, just a week after the unveiling, Upham's statue was attacked and damaged by an anti-war protestor who had arrived in Amberley driving a van with a painted slogan: 'Killers Aren't Heroes'. After a verbal altercation with the sculptor, Mark Whyte, who was putting the finishing touches to the statue, the protestor took to it with a chainsaw that also had a grinder attached. The man made a few scratches on the statue's right boot before some concerned locals overpowered him and then called the police. The protester, a 37-year-old Christchurch man, was charged with wilful damage and trespass. The attack devastated the local community, who were 'fiercely proud and protective of the statue'.[28]

It was an unfortunate incident, but one that did nothing to tarnish the reputation of one of New Zealand's greatest war heroes. Throughout his military service Charles Upham always led from the front, was always at the point of maximum danger and, as Kippenberger rightly commented, probably deserved to win the VC several times over. He really was a man possessed of exceptional courage and fortitude.

The final word here goes to fellow soldier and renowned sporting journalist, the late T.P. McLean:

Was he New Zealand's greatest soldier of the Second World War?

The question is unimportant. He was Charles Hazlitt Upham. Charlie Upham. Unforgettable.[29]

SERGEANT KEITH ELLIOTT

As previously mentioned, a second VC was won at the Ruweisat Ridge debacle. It was awarded to Sergeant Keith Elliott of the 22nd Battalion for a most unusual military action.

Keith Elliott was born in the small backblock settlement of Apiti, some 28 miles north of Feilding, on Anzac Day 1916. Elliott's family moved to Feilding soon after his birth, where Keith attended the Lytton Street school. He later attended the Feilding Agricultural High School (FAHS) where he played for the first fifteen. FAHS had an important influence on Elliott. He was particularly impressed by its motto, 'Kia toa, kia ngakau nui' (meaning 'be strong, be of good heart'). Unfortunately Keith Elliott had to leave FAHS in the third term of 1933 in order to work on the family farm when his elder brother became too ill to do so. Keith Elliott was 17 years old and for the next six years he worked as a farmer, spending most of that time breaking in new farmland at Marima, a farm of 96 acres halfway between Pahiatua and Eketahuna. It was hard, back-breaking work and at one point Elliott considered walking off the farm. He was prevented from doing so by a 'quiet rebuke' from his mother.[30]

Elliott persisted with farming until one morning in 1939, when he was feeding the cows, 'my father came running across the paddock, waving his arms and calling out that Britain had declared war on Germany'. Elliott's response was instant:

I must go. That was the only thought in my mind. Out of the simplicity of those three words was to arise something that was to completely change the course of my life . . . No time was to be lost.[31]

The 23-year-old Elliott tried to enlist in 1939 at Palmerston North. His personal file shows that he was five feet, four-and-three-quarter inches tall and weighed 10 stone 11 pounds. It also shows that he was classified as medically unfit as a result of his bad teeth.[32] Elliott eventually marched into Trentham Camp in January 1940 and was drafted into No. 11 Platoon, B Company, 22nd Battalion. Elliott was to serve with this platoon for his entire time in the army. The battalion's commanding officer was Lieutenant Colonel L.W. Andrew, VC, who some thought 'too much of a disciplinarian'.[33] Elliott later recalled:

> We arrived in Trentham, all very inebriated, you know, and we were rounded up by those barking lance-corporals, and I thought it was quite interesting, to see these fellows straggle into the place. Coming from the country we were pretty rough material. But we had a wonderful colonel. He had won the VC in the 1914– 18 war, Colonel Andrew VC, and he was a great soldier, a great disciplinarian. He would stand out there on the parade ground like a statue, tremendously well controlled and disciplined, and he was a fellow who never expected you to do something he wasn't prepared to do himself. But he expected the best, the tops . . . second rate was no good to him.[34]

The 22nd Battalion was part of the Second Echelon which sailed to the United Kingdom, arriving there on 16 June 1940. They would be there for the rest of the year. Soon after their arrival Elliott was promoted to lance corporal. While at Mytchett, near Aldershot, 5 Brigade — as the Second Echelon was now designated — was inspected by several important dignitaries, including Bill Jordan, the high commissioner; Lord Bledisloe, a former governor-general; King George VI; and the Prime Minister, Winston Churchill. After Christmas in the United Kingdom, 5 Brigade sailed for the Middle East on 4 January 1941.

The brigade had barely set foot in Egypt when it sailed for Greece in March 1941. After considerable moving around and confusion, it occupied a position at Mount Olympus where it had its first contact with the Germans. On the heights of Mount Olympus Elliott's battalion had a perfect view of the advancing German tanks and infantry. During the firefight that followed, Lance Corporal Elliott stood out for his calm manner and for his aggression towards the enemy. A badly wounded soldier, Alan Murray, later recalled:

> I saw him [Elliott] pumping away with a Tommy gun as though he was playing marbles in the middle of a school room. I was getting out of it. I was scared stiff myself, but he didn't look to be.[35]

The brigade stopped the German advance for one day and then withdrew under the cover of darkness.

Two days later 5 Brigade was on the road to Porto Rafti where the Royal Navy evacuated them to Crete. Elliott later wrote:

> I arrived in Crete still only a lance-jack with my talents, if any, not yet discovered. I was never what might be termed a brilliant soldier, or even a brave one, but one of the luckier fortunate type, who had the wind with me and a sort of guardian angel looking after me. I found this throughout my Army career — shining at nothing; and only by the grace of God in the right place at the right time.[36]

Arriving on Crete on Elliott's birthday, 25 April 1941, the 22nd Battalion was allocated to the defence of Maleme airfield. It would become the critical position in the defence of the island. Elliott's platoon took up defensive positions just above the aerodrome on a small riverbed. Then on 20 May — a beautiful clear day on Crete — while the troops were at breakfast, the German transport planes came over with their fighter protection. The invasion was on. Elliott recalled:

> My most vivid impression is that the invaders were squealing like pigs as they drifted down, which is understandable, because they must have seen the grim-faced Kiwis below them waiting with their weapons. And we had to deal with them like pigs, charging with our bayonets. It was horrible putting our training into first practice.[37]

That night Elliott's platoon received the order to abandon their defensive positions and move out. Keith Elliott was indignant:

> You know the Germans got the biggest hiding they'd ever had, up to that point in time . . . we defeated the finest fighting machine of the German Army . . . I suppose by ten o'clock in the morning it was all over in our area. And in the evening Major Leggitt came and said we were going to pull out, Lance Corporal Elliott said 'Why? Have you got the wind up, Sir?' He wasn't very impressed.[38]

After some brief skirmishing near Pirgos, during which Elliott was wounded in the arm, the 22nd Battalion commenced the long march over the mountains to the evacuation beaches at Sphakia.

Back in Egypt, Elliott was promoted to lance sergeant and then to platoon sergeant. He took part in Operation CRUSADER as part of the infantry platoon allocated to the protection of 5 Brigade headquarters at the Sidi Azeiz airfield. It was at Sidi Azeiz that the whole brigade headquarters was captured by the panzers of the Afrika Korps, Rommel himself turning up to inspect some of the POWs. There followed two months of captivity in Bardia under the most trying of conditions. The prisoners were kept on a near-starvation diet, there were no sanitary provisions and the prison pens were overcrowded with men. As Elliott recalled of these weeks in captivity: 'All we knew were moments of misery, hours of heartache, days of depression.'[39] Elliott had weighed nearly 12 stone when he was captured, but when released he was down to just seven stone, having lost nearly half his body weight.[40] He was more upbeat about the experience in a letter written to his old school:

> The force attacking us was mainly tanks, infantry coming up after we had surrendered. After our artillery and anti-tank guns had been knocked out there was only one more thing to do, and by surrendering, Brigadier Hargest saved many lives . . . The following weeks were tough on the men, but once again we came through and gained a great deal by our experience as prisoners of war.[41]

On 2 January 1942 Elliott and his fellow POWs were released when South African soldiers captured the prison camp.

When the 2nd New Zealand Division was in Syria, Elliott contracted malaria and had to spend some weeks in the New Zealand General Hospital in Nazareth. He missed the division's hasty return to Egypt and the breakout at Minqâr Qaim. Elliott rejoined his platoon on 13 July 1942 just in time for the attack on Ruweisat Ridge. In an unusual development — a result of sickness and a shortage of commissioned officers — Elliott found himself acting as the platoon commander for the forthcoming attack.

The 22nd Battalion was one of the lead battalions for the attack on Ruweisat Ridge, being part of 5 Brigade in the centre of the attacking force. The battalion moved off at 11.00 p.m. on 14 July, heading towards the ridge some six miles away. At midnight the 22nd Battalion hit serious resistance and fought the Germans and Italians for the next four hours until they reached the ridge. Just before dawn, Brigadier Kippenberger turned up in a Bren gun carrier. He took a quick look around and was pleased: 'Hurry up and dig in before light, boys.' Then he hurried away to look for his other battalions.[42] It proved to be very good advice because as Kippenberger left, he came under fire from several approaching German tanks.[43]

What the New Zealanders had not discovered in their night attack was that ten tanks of 8th Panzer Regiment, part of 15 Panzer Division, were laagered for the night in the middle of the division's new position. Three had been destroyed, but the rest soon sprung into action after first light on 15 July. They fell on the unprotected infantry of the 22nd Battalion, first attacking them from the south and east, making 'shrewd use of natural cover, the early, misty light, and a dust haze'.[44] The tanks, with their supporting infantry, soon captured all of the 22nd Battalion with the exception of Sergeant Elliott's platoon.

Elliott's 11 Platoon, now down to 19 men, was on the battalion's extreme right flank. In an interview given shortly before his death in 1989, Elliott admitted to having a premonition that 15 July would bring disaster for the battalion. His responsibilities weighed heavily upon him:

I prayed hard that night [14 July], you know. You get a feeling about an action like this. A bit like the 15th round and you're down and out. The Germans had us beaten, that's what it amounted to. I knew it was going to be a pretty rough ordeal . . . All of a sudden you find yourself right out in the middle of nowhere and you're a sergeant in charge of 30 men. That's what changed the whole thing . . . all in a matter of minutes.[45]

Elliott, keeping to his farming routine, was up well before dawn. Scanning the horizon, he noticed tanks and infantry approaching from the southwest and immediately recognised the black crosses on the tanks. He went to the platoon commanders of 10 and 12 Platoons to warn them of the approaching German tanks, only 'to be given the emphatic answer that they must be British tanks'.[46] But Elliott knew without a shadow of a doubt that they were German tanks and that 'the position was obviously untenable under tank attack'.[47] Having been a POW before, Elliott did not relish the prospect of a repeat experience. He put a question to his men that later became his catchphrase: 'What is it, boys — Stalag or the bush?' 'The Bush,' was the cry.[48]

Elliott decided to save his platoon and ordered his men to move forward and away from the approaching tanks. As he explained many years later:

But these [tanks] had the wrong jerseys. Yeah, they had big black crosses on them and they were coming around our flank . . . They [the two officers he reported the sighting to] had never been in action before. So I took a risk. I took my men forward and we watched the tanks come in and take our battalion.[49]

An eyewitness later recorded:

It was all very bewildering to have tanks coming in from the front and the rear and they now had their machine-guns going all the time to keep us down . . . One platoon on our right that was near a bit of a ridge made a run for it, they had of course to run a hell of a gauntlet of machine-gun bullets, and it was pretty grim to see these men running with dust being kicked up all round them as they fell or dived to the ground and then up and on again. These were Keith Elliott and his men, and as they began running men shouted: 'What the hell are you running for — they are our tanks.'[50]

As one historian has noted, Elliott's action was most unusual for a VC winner:

> To start with, he disobeyed orders and saved his men from certain capture by exercising his own initiative. If events had turned out differently he could have easily been charged with deserting his post.[51]

Elliott led the platoon to the slight cover offered by a ridge some 300 yards to the north. While doing so he was hit in the chest by a bullet fired from one of the German tanks. It was deflected by his paybook but it still took a chunk out of his chest. Elliott later explained how a soldier's disobedience saved his life:

> And the only reason I'm alive today is because of this fellow George Fletcher . . .George is lying in his trench and I'm walking down telling him to get going and run . . . and he questioned my birth, you know, he reckoned I was illegitimate, and I stopped to correct him in a nice way . . . and a bullet went across my chest, passed through one tit and out the other side. Now if I hadn't stopped for a moment it would have gone straight through me. I always thank old George for that.[52]

The platoon reached the ridge without loss, but then had to move on to another small ridge 400 yards further north to avoid being in the line of fire of their own anti-tank guns. From this new position Elliott's platoon saw the rest of their battalion being overrun and marched into captivity. Elliott's initiative and courage had saved his platoon. After having his chest wound attended to, Elliott linked up with two platoons of the 21st Battalion.

Later that morning a report reached the 21st Battalion of a badly wounded New Zealand officer lying out somewhere to the north, and in desperate need of medical attention. Elliott volunteered to look for the officer and bring him back. He took eight men and ventured out.

While searching for the officer, Elliott's small party came under fire from an enemy machine-gun post in a slight depression some 500 yards away and from another post to their right about 250 yards distant. While Corporal R.F. Garmonsway took four of the men to deal with the nearer threat, Elliott, although bleeding and in pain, led the remaining three men in a bayonet charge across 500 yards of open ground towards the depression. It seemed a foolhardy venture, but when they had reached to within 50 yards of the depression the Italians in the post, about 11 in number, ceased firing and stood up to surrender. There was an anti-tank gun and four machine-guns in the post, which Elliott set about dismantling. While doing so, two more enemy posts fired on them from about 100 yards to their north and directly ahead of them.

Elliott decided to press on and attack these posts, which he did, leaving his men to keep the POWs in order. Both posts were taken and Elliott's small party had now taken more than 50 POWs. There were more to come though.

Yet another post, this one on a gently rising slope directly ahead of them, opened fire on them. Elliott decided to deal with this fourth post in similar fashion. He sent one man back for reinforcements and with the other two men he started to attack the post on the slope. Once again they came under fire from a new post, this one to their rear from the west. Leaving his remaining two men to attack the post on the slope and look after the POWs, Elliott attacked the machine-gun post on the flank by himself. It meant another dash across 200 yards of open desert during which Elliott, not unexpectedly, attracted considerable fire from the post he was attacking. This unwelcome attention forced Elliott to shelter behind an abandoned water truck near the post. Elliott was wounded in the thigh when a machine-gun bullet passed through the truck. Another passed through the tank on the truck's back, showering him with refreshingly cool water. He rested for about a minute and then fought on. All the Italians except the machine-gunner had now laid down their weapons and were ready to surrender. Elliott shot a sniper, who had been hampering his soldiers at the previous post, hobbled over to a sand dune overlooking the machine-gun post and lobbed a grenade into it. He then attacked with the bayonet. With the machine-gunner killed, the rest of the men in the post, some 15 in all, surrendered to Elliott. Then, taking his POWs with him, Elliott returned to the post on the slope and helped his two men subdue it. Elliott was again wounded while doing so, this time in the knee and the back. The three New Zealand soldiers now had 80 POWs. They joined up with the rest of the platoon, which had captured another 62.

In summary, Elliott's platoon, under his superb leadership, had killed about 30 of the enemy and taken 142 POWs. Elliott had been instrumental in subduing five enemy posts, one of which he had to attack single-handedly. As Elliott later recorded with some degree of understatement: 'It had been an exhaustingly eventful four hours.'[53] Elliott's platoon had only two casualties, both wounded, of which his wounds were the most serious. The wounded officer, whose injuries had initiated the actions described above, was rescued by other reinforcements and survived the war.

When the action was over, the 21st Battalion had managed to link up with an Indian unit and Elliott was taken to its ADS (advanced dressing station). He was later evacuated to the New Zealand General Hospital where he spent the next three months. It was a remarkable performance by Keith Elliott, and Lieutenant Colonel T.C. Campbell, the battalion's commanding officer, initiated a VC recommendation. Five supporting eyewitness statements were included. One was by Captain Russell Richard Thomas Young, who had been captured by the German tank force on the morning of 15 July, but had managed to escape a day later. He stated:

> We were under heavy tank, machine-gun and mortar fire, hemmed in as it seemed on all sides with no effective anti-tank support, and for Sjt Elliott to have been able to bring out so many men

under such circumstances showed an amazing quick appreciation of the situation and outstanding qualities of leadership.[54]

And as the New Zealand official historian has commented: 'His exploits were all the more remarkable in that he was still suffering from the after-effects of a bad bout of malaria.'[55]

The notification of the VC appeared in the *London Gazette* on 24 September 1942. Elliott had only been told of it the previous day while at lunch in the sergeants' mess at Maadi Camp. As Elliott later described the occasion: 'Out of the whirling kaleidoscope of my mind, one thought registered above all others' — he felt an urgent need to go to the toilet.[56] After receiving the news, General Freyberg gave Elliott a field commission and the newly arrived Lieutenant General Bernard Montgomery presented his VC ribbon to him. The presentation of the VC proper had to wait for nearly two years when it was presented to Elliott on 2 August 1944 in Wellington by the Governor-General and Marshal of the Royal Air Force, Sir Cyril Newall.

Elliott was ordered to return to New Zealand shortly after the Montgomery presentation, something that always rankled with him. According to his biography, Brigadier Inglis explained the reason for his return over a drink in the officers' mess:

> There's not enough room in the Division for two Victoria Cross holders and the General isn't likely to retire in favour of you, sergeant . . . Well Keith, you know it wouldn't look too good if you were knocked out in the next battle. This war game isn't only fighting — politics come into it a fair bit.[57]

Inglis' explanation is unconvincing although Upham's recent capture may have put pressure on the military authorities to ensure Elliott remained safe. A strange note on Elliott's personal file may explain the real reason for his forced return to New Zealand. In it, Brigadier A.G. Conway, the adjutant general, explains:

> In a private letter to me dated 12th June, Brigadier W.G. Stevens

explains that early in May, 1943, the proposal to commission Sgt. Elliott was submitted to the G.O.C. [Freyberg] and it was decided that Sgt. Elliott was to be sent home as not being really fit for a commission.

The G.O.C. later having evidently forgotten this decision when at Maadi sent for Sgt. Elliott and commissioned him on the spot.

The G.O.C. was to explain the position when in N.Z. but did not mention it.[58]

Elliott remained bitter about being sent home from the war early while his friends had to fight on. He later asked Freyberg why it was done, but Freyberg's reply was simply, 'But, Keith, look at you today.'[59]

Keith Elliott arrived back in New Zealand on 12 July 1943, nearly a year after the action at Ruweisat Ridge. He experienced considerable discomfort with the publicity, ceremony and adulation of being a VC winner, later writing: 'It was an ordeal for which I was unprepared and I was thankful when I could escape from time to time to replenish my resources by working around the farm.'[60] Like Charles Upham, Elliott was always modest about the military exploits that earned him the VC. He used to joke with his friends, with some truth to it, that he won his VC while running away from the enemy.[61]

When his service in the 2nd NZEF ceased in December 1943, Elliott returned to farming and, like Upham, found a welcome respite there from the intense publicity that the VC generated. But Elliott was destined for a major career change. In February 1946 he began studying for the priesthood and was ordained an Anglican minister on 30 November 1947. As he later admitted, his VC probably was responsible for getting him into the church, as it compensated to some degree for his lack of education. Elliott stated:

It [the VC] opens all sorts of doors. Good doors as well as bad doors. It depends on which one you want to go through. I happened to go through the right one.[62]

Elliott served a year as a curate in Palmerston North before taking up a position as the first padre appointed to Linton Military Camp. This role was primarily for the initial intake of 18-year-old boys under the new Compulsory Military Training Scheme. As part of his ministry Elliott was attested into the New Zealand Territorial Force on 22 February 1950 with the rank of chaplain 4th class.[63]

Following on from this service as padre came several years at the Wellington City Mission, then service in a number of parishes around the lower North Island, including seven years with the Maori Mission. He was for some years the chaplain to Waikune Prison and eventually returned to the capital to serve again with the Wellington City Mission.

October 1954 marked an important occasion. The Reverend Keith Elliott travelled by air to Egypt with Kippenberger and 23 other New Zealanders for the unveiling of the El Alamein Memorial. General Freyberg and Field Marshal Montgomery also attended. While in Egypt, Elliott took the opportunity to travel out to Ruweisat Ridge. It was a moving experience:

> It was strange to stand again on a deserted ridge, with only a few familiar landmarks and the moving sand to remind one that this was a place where man had fought to and fro, and that this sterile ground had been lost and won again in the last desperate battle to defend the Suez Canal.[64]

In 1956 Elliott again travelled abroad, this time as one of the ten New Zealand VC holders to attend the VC centenary celebrations in the United Kingdom. As he later wrote of this visit: 'glittering occasions followed each other with bewildering speed'. The highlight, though, was a parade by about 1000 VC holders at Hyde Park.[65]

In 1960 came 'one of the most dramatic acts of his life' in the post-war years, according to T.P. McLean. At the 22nd Battalion reunion that year Keith Elliott refused to wear his VC as a form of protest against the All Black rugby tour of South Africa that was then taking place. Elliott received much criticism for his actions but stuck to his protest. As one of his old platoon members later explained with some sympathy, Elliott 'so much hated the idea of the rigid colourbar of South Africa that he couldn't allow himself to be associated, as a New Zealander, with people who so treated their black peoples'.[66] With the nation then gripped with rugby fever and the protest movement in its infancy, Elliott's protest was an act of tremendous moral courage.

In 1961 Elliott was due to be posted to either the Reserved or Retired List of Officers. He wrote to army headquarters and must have had his forced return to New Zealand in 1943 in mind:

> I have know [sic] objections to be posted to the Reserve List of Officers providing the Army will accept me without my Decoration in the time of war if they won't I have know other alternative but to be posted to the Retired List.
>
> I take Services regularly at Waiouru Military Camp and have know difficulties and am prepared to carry on.[67]

This letter infuriated the Assistant Military Secretary, who drafted an angry handwritten note for his commanding officer:

1. Decorations are conferred by the Sovereign and it is not within the prerogative of the individual as to whether or not he/her will accept it. Once conferred it can only be taken away by the Sovereign. The return of the physical symbol of the decoration does not alter this fact.
2. There is however no regulation which says that a decoration (or its ribbon) must be worn nor is there any compulsion in the use of 'letters' after the name.
3. Therefore, whether Elliott likes it or not, he is the recipient of the VC, but there is no requirement for him to wear the decoration or its ribbon, nor is it necessary for the letters VC to be appended to his name.
4. My personal view is that he should be posted to the Retired List.

The Military Secretary agreed and Elliott was duly posted to the Retired List for Officers on 17 August 1962.[68]

In 1967 Elliott published his autobiography (with Rona Adshead), *From Cowshed to Dog Collar*. It was a modest success. The Reverend Keith Elliott retired as the vicar of the Makara-Karori West parish on 26 April 1981. Just four years earlier he had walked from Cape Reinga to Bluff — the length of New Zealand, some 3400 kilometres — in order to raise money for a new church and community hall. As John Percival later wrote of this venture: 'For a man of sixty-one who was already overweight and took little exercise, it was a brave, not to say foolhardy venture.'[69] At the end of the first day Elliott had walked 40 kilometres and developed large blisters. By the third day his feet were red raw. Typically though, Keith Elliott finished the walk but did not raise as much money as he hoped. His walk and an art sale raised $45,000.

His three sons, two daughters and ten grandchildren ensured an active retirement. Until a year before his death he was the welfare officer for the Fire Service in Wellington and, always a keen bowler, he was also president of the Raumati South Bowling Club on the Kapiti Coast. In 1987 Elliott donated the VC Cup to the club. Nearly ten years later they returned the favour, making a special memorial garden for him complete with a plaque bearing his name that simply states: 'Soldier — Parson — Bowler'.[70]

The Reverend Keith Elliott died on 7 October 1989 at the Te Omanga Hospice in Lower Hutt after a long battle with cancer. He was buried with full military honours and, at the request of the Elliott family, two students from FAHS were honorary pallbearers. Elliott is buried at the Paraparaumu Cemetery in the returned servicemen's lawn section.

In 1972 the Reverend Keith Elliott had presented his VC to FAHS 'in recognition of the importance it had played in his life and education'.[71] It is currently on loan to the Queen Elizabeth II Army Memorial Museum in Waiouru until 1 May 2007.

In December 1942, shortly after winning the VC, Keith Elliott wrote to the school that had been such an important influence in his life. The letter reveals much about Keith Elliott's personal philosophy. It reads in part:

> I always remember being told by a certain person there was a job for you in the world — go out and find it and make a job of it. Our job has come in a very different line any of us ever expected, but if we can make a job of this, your future will come in the occupation you are now training for, and some of you may 'perhaps kick a goal from your try' and bring honour to our School in a better way than I — in a time of sanity. However, there are things that will face you all — hardships that must be overcome; and if this war can bring about peace evermore it will be worth the waste and destruction it is causing.[72]

THE MAORI BATTALION VC: SECOND LIEUTENANT MOANANUI-A-KIWA NGARIMU

Second Lieutenant Moananui-a-Kiwa Ngarimu won the VC for his actions at Tebaga Gap, Tunisia, on 26 March 1943. Unfortunately Ngarimu's VC was a posthumous award, the only army VC of this war to be so awarded. The young Maori warrior was killed in action after a night and morning of constant fighting, during which he performed many deeds of valour.

Moananui-a-Kiwa Ngarimu was born at Kokai Pa on Kokai Hill near Ruatoria, on 7 April 1918. With eight sisters and a brother, he came from a large family. His parents must have been of some standing in the Maori community, as Ngarimu was schooled at Te Aute College in the Hawke's Bay. He spent two years at Te Aute College as a boarder before leaving after the fourth form to work as a shepherd on his father's farm. Ngarimu volunteered early in 1940 for service overseas, enlisting in the 2nd NZEF on 11 February. He was two months short of his twenty-second birthday.

Prior to joining the 28th (Maori) Battalion then training in Palmerston North, Ngarimu became engaged to Miss Dah Walker from Tutumutai Station. After two years of military service overseas though, Ngarimu unexpectedly broke off the engagement with little explanation. He merely stated that the engagement was not fair on the girl he had left behind. Miss Walker was devastated and became withdrawn and solitary. She died almost a year to the day after Ngarimu, 'of a broken heart, her sisters say'.[73]

Ngarimu did not receive a commission until April 1942 and his initial appointment was as an intelligence officer. While working in the intelligence section, Ngarimu came to the attention of a future commanding officer of the Maori Battalion. Sir Charles Bennett later described the qualities he saw in Ngarimu:

He had qualities which indicated to me that here you have a chap who was solid, who can be relied upon and a man of good intelligence who was disciplined, a bit of an introvert, rather than an extrovert. He was in control of his situation all the time. And he was the kind of fellow I felt where, if you give him a job to do, you can be sure he will do it.[74]

In March 1943 though, Ngarimu was back in an infantry role as a platoon commander in C Company, the company filled primarily with men from the Ngati Porou tribe.

By then, the war was coming to an end in North Africa. In fact, the campaign had only a few more months to run. In an attempt to turn the Mareth Line in Tunisia, General Montgomery combined a frontal assault in the coastal sector with a giant left hook of armoured and infantry units under the command of Freyberg. This left hook aimed to break through the German positions at Tebaga Gap, a gap of six miles in mountainous terrain that formed part of the Mareth Line. There was a formidable force allocated to this left hook. The 2nd New Zealand Division would provide the bulk of the infantry but the division was bolstered to corps strength by the inclusion of several other units. These included 8 Armoured Brigade, a force of Free French under General Leclerc, a British armoured car regiment, a British artillery regiment and, later, the 1st British Armoured Division.

On 19 March, the New Zealand Corps set off, moving slowly and in great secrecy. Despite reaching Tebaga Gap two days later it was not until 26 March that Freyberg believed he had sufficient force to make a full-scale assault. In an unusual tactic, given that the New Zealanders nearly always attacked at night, a full-scale blitzkrieg attack was planned for the afternoon of 26 March. With total air supremacy and the Desert Air Force finally giving the close air support the infantry on the ground craved, the New Zealand Corps easily forced the gap open and drove through it in numbers. The only real opposition came from German units fighting in the gap's surrounding hills. Most troublesome was the 2nd Battalion, 433 Panzer Grenadier Regiment of 164 Light Division, dug in on Point 209.

Point 209 and its prominent underfeature dominated one side of the Tebaga Gap. The underfeature, on which most of the subsequent fighting took place, was later named Hikurangi, a spiritually significant mountain on the North Island's east coast. This was done as a tribute to the actions of the Ngati Porou company. On 26 March though, Point 209 and Hikurangi formed a bastion above the New Zealanders from which the German defenders continually poured mortar and machine-gun fire. The armoured support allocated to the attack on this feature had sheared away from it after five tanks had been knocked out in succession by a well-concealed 88-mm gun. The Maori Battalion therefore needed to clear this feature, relying only on its own resources to do so.

Captain Arapeta Awatere, the C Company commander, was ordered to swing his company to the right and capture the troublesome heights. The battalion's three other rifle companies were to dig in where they were to establish a firm base. Awatere sent 13 Platoon to work around to the right onto the feature's rear slope. Meanwhile, 15 Platoon was to attack the crest in the centre and Ngarimu's 14 Platoon was to attack on the left flank. The attack on Hikurangi commenced at 5.00 p.m.

The unusual topography and poor map reading had a significant influence on the fighting that followed. Throughout the evening and night of 26 March, the Maori Battalion thought it was attacking Point 209. They were, in fact, attacking the underfeature, Hikurangi, which was separated from the main peak by a saddle about 1000 yards long. So when brigade headquarters was informed that Point 209 had been taken, they confined their artillery support to the feature's reverse slopes in the belief that the summit had been captured. This meant that the Maori attack on Hikurangi had no effective artillery support.[75]

Meanwhile, Second Lieutenant Ngarimu, coming in from the left flank, moved his platoon by section rushes to reach the base of Hikurangi without suffering any casualties. While 15 Platoon was pinned to the ground at the foot of the hill by the fire coming from Point 209, Ngarimu led his men straight up the steep rocky slope, ignoring the machine-gun and mortar fire coming their way. During the climb, Ngarimu destroyed two machine-gun posts by himself and was the first soldier to reach the crest of Hikurangi. After a brief but fierce fight the crest was captured. Ngarimu consolidated his position there and the men of 13 Platoon joined him. The two platoon commanders (Ngarimu and Lieutenant S.F. 'Bully' Jackson), realising that they had not captured the high ground, then attempted to break through to Point 209, but they lacked sufficient strength to do so. They returned to Hikurangi and dug in. Firing from both sides was constant throughout the night with the crest of Hikurangi being continuously swept by machine-gun fire from Point 209. As the battalion's history records: 'the Germans were as determined to push the Maoris off the crest as the Maoris were determined to stay there'.[76] The situation had reached an impasse and a counterattack was needed to eject one side from their current position.

The Germans took the initiative and launched repeated counter-attacks on the night of 26–27 March. That they were all defeated was primarily due to Ngarimu's spirited leadership. Many Maori soldiers were wounded or killed in these attacks but still the remaining defenders fought on. After the failure of the first counterattacks the Germans then used their mortars, which on the rocky unprotected hillside had a devastating effect. After a particularly heavy mortar barrage, followed closely by a renewed German bayonet attack, Ngarimu bellowed with all his strength for the survivors to stand up and engage the enemy man for man. This they did and, although outnumbered, they threw back the German attackers. During one of these counterattacks Ngarimu was hit in the shoulder by a rifle bullet.

In the next counterattack some German soldiers penetrated the Maori position. Ngarimu rushed to the threatened area and shot several Germans with a submachine-gun. Those he did not hit fled for their lives. Ngarimu searched frantically for a grenade and, not finding one, he threw large stones instead. The effect was the same and the Germans hastened their retreat.

But still another German counterattack occurred and this one forced the Maori soldiers off Hikurangi's crest. Ngarimu, in a 'majestic fighting mood'[77] rallied the dislodged men around him and led them back onto the ridge in their own ferocious counterattack. They were successful and took Hikurangi a second time. While doing so, Ngarimu was wounded again, this time in the leg.

Lieutenant Colonel Charles Bennett, the battalion's commanding officer, climbed onto Hikurangi to inspect the situation. He immediately requested that the wounded Awatere and Ngarimu report to the RAP. Both refused to do so, with Ngarimu pleading: 'I'm alright, Sir. Let me stay a little longer with my men.'[78] Bennett relented and allowed him to stay. Awatere later did go to the RAP but only when 'his wounded leg had swollen so much that he could only crawl'.[79] Lieutenant Jackson took over C Company and would later provide one of the witness statements for Ngarimu's recommendation. Colonel Bennett stressed that the hill was to be held at all costs. Awatere replied: 'Have no fear, Sir. This hill will never be lost.'[80] Bennett then returned to his battalion headquarters, which he moved to within a few hundred yards of the foot of Hikurangi.

Dawn on 27 March found 14 Platoon still in possession of the hill but with only Ngarimu and 12 men left. Only two of these soldiers had not been wounded. Lieutenant Jackson reported to Bennett that he doubted if the remnants of the company could hold out much longer. Reinforcements — two sections from D Company — arrived and the soldiers on Hikurangi waited for another counterattack. It soon came.

Disregarding their losses, the Germans, reinforced by two

fresh platoons, launched a dawn attack in full view of the Maori Battalion's headquarters. From that location they saw Ngarimu lead another charge, firing his submachine-gun from the hip. They saw him reach the crest of the hill and stand there defiantly. He was silhouetted against the ridgeline when he was shot dead, his body falling amongst several Germans he had recently killed. The battle then raged around Ngarimu's body. Fresh waves of Germans arrived but the reinforced Maori routed them. The Germans fell back to Point 209 and remained there. Half of the German soldiers involved in this counterattack had been killed or wounded.[81]

Just after this dawn counterattack, Brigadier Kippenberger visited the Maori Battalion and immediately recognised that the battalion was not on Point 209 as they had reported. Kippenberger arranged for a heavy artillery barrage to be fired upon Point 209 immediately. According to the New Zealand official historian of the campaign, the artillery barrage by two field and two medium artillery regiments caused 'devastating damage'.[82] The artillery fire was kept up for most of the morning until the Germans surrendered.

It was agreed by all that it was C Company, especially 13 and 14 Platoons, that had won this tough battle. All told the 28th (Maori) Battalion lost 22 killed and 77 wounded in the fight for Point 209, but its members won every military bravery decoration then available in the action at Tebaga Gap, including the VC. Eyewitness statements from two lieutenants, one corporal and a private supported Ngarimu's VC recommendation. As Corporal P. Tamepo recorded:

During the night we were attacked many times. Some of us broke but Mr Ngarimu always stayed at his post yelling at us to come around him. When we ran out of hand grenades we used stones. Our officer was wounded twice. A lot of us told him to get out but he said he would wait until morning to see how he felt then.[83]

On 2 June 1943 General Freyberg sent a 'Secret Special Telegram' to the New Zealand Prime Minister, Peter Fraser. It advised Fraser that he had 'just been notified that His Majesty the King has approved posthumous award of V.C. to 39784 2nd Lt M.N. Ngarimu 28th

Maori Battalion for outstanding gallantry in Tebaga Gap during the battle of Mareth on 26th and 27th March'. According to Freyberg, Ngarimu's VC 'will give the greatest satisfaction to all ranks of the Division and the full citation . . . will, I know, be read with the greatest pride by Maori and Pakeha alike'.[84]

Ngarimu's VC citation appeared in the *London Gazette* on 4 June 1943. On this day, Ngarimu's father received an urgent telegram from the New Zealand Prime Minister. It stated:

> I desire to convey to you the Government's warmest congratulations on this great honour conferred on your son and deeply regret that he did not live to receive the award he had so gallantly won.[85]

On 6 October 1943 the Ngati Porou and Whanau-a-Apanui, the clan of Ngarimu's mother, gathered in Ruatoria. There they witnessed the Governor-General, Sir Cyril Newall, present Ngarimu's VC to his parents. As he had not made a will, a court appointed Ngarimu's mother as his next of kin and she received his war service gratuity.

After the service, Mr Hamuera Ngarimu spoke solemnly and sadly about his son's achievements:

> Mrs Ngarimu and I wished that Moana could be here to see the tribute, take pride . . . to all the Maori people because of what he did to win the Victoria Cross. He loved his country so well that he was glad to die for it.[86]

Second Lieutenant Moananui-a-Kiwa Ngarimu is buried in the British Military Cemetery, Sfax, Tunisia. He is commemorated by a scholarship. His family have loaned Ngarimu's VC to the Tairawhiti Museum in Gisborne.

THE TAKROUNA AFFAIR

By 13 April 1943 the New Zealanders had reached the outposts of the Enfidaville Line in Tunisia. Their role in the forthcoming attack, which would be their last major action of the campaign, was to capture Enfidaville and a series of rugged coastal foothills west of the village. The attack, codenamed Operation ORATION, commenced on the night of 19 April. While Enfidaville village was easily captured, the attack on the foothills was a bloody disaster with none of the designated objectives being taken. The first of the foothills, Takrouna, proved to heavily fortified with well-planned killing zones on either side of it. New Zealand's planning for the attack was poor. The objectives given to the attacking battalions were far too ambitious, coordination between units was non-existent and the senior commanders had underestimated the resolve of the enemy, who were well entrenched in the foothills. Takrouna was eventually taken, but only after two days of fierce hand-to-hand fighting by small parties of New Zealand infantry during which the New Zealanders suffered more than 500 casualties. Little wonder then that Kippenberger, the commander responsible for making many of the mistakes mentioned above, described it as 'a real soldier's battle in which the initiative and determination of the fighting troops won the decision'.[87] During this savage fighting many New Zealand soldiers distinguished themselves and two had solid claims for being considered for a VC. One of these claims caused considerable controversy in New Zealand, and still does to this day. This chapter will deal with the least controversial case first.

WALTER BABINGTON 'SANDY' THOMAS

A recent publication has claimed that a New Zealand officer earned a VC at Takrouna. He was Walter Babington 'Sandy' Thomas, who became the youngest battalion commander in the 2nd NZEF during the war. Sandy Thomas, from Motueka, enlisted in the 2nd NZEF in November 1939. On Crete as a young officer in the 23rd Battalion, Thomas won an MC for his conspicuous gallantry during the fighting. Wounded and left behind by the retreating New Zealanders, Thomas managed to escape captivity after several attempts and make his way to Syria where he rejoined the 2nd New

Zealand Division. This impressive feat earned him a bar to his MC. At Takrouna, with all of the 23rd Battalion's senior officers killed or wounded, Thomas took over command of the battalion and secured its startline, which had proved extremely difficult. The battalion then managed to capture a good defensive position well into the enemy lines. There Thomas effectively organised the battalion's defences, which prevented it from being overrun and suffering further casualties. For his bold leadership at Takrouna, Thomas was made an immediate DSO.[88] His DSO recommendation is impressive:

> Throughout the difficult day of April 20 when for many hours the Battalion was isolated, Major Thomas continued to exhibit high qualities of leadership and when relieved was still holding the vital ground he had gained.
>
> Throughout he showed tactical ability of the highest order, a quickly offensive spirit and an infectious enthusiasm and cheerfulness which were an inspiration to his Battalion.[89]

Years later, in 1951, after reading Thomas' best-selling account of his early years, entitled *Dare to be Free*, Howard Kippenberger wrote to Thomas expressing his regret that Thomas' book had not covered the later campaigns in North Africa nor the Italian campaign. Kippenberger's letter contained a surprising admission:

> Takrouna would have been difficult for you to write as you played the chief part in winning that affair and I have long been sorry that I didn't put you up for a VC. From what I now know, I believe you would have got it.[90]

Sandy Thomas served throughout the Italian campaign and then commanded the 22nd Battalion in Jayforce, the New Zealand contribution to the occupation of Japan after the war. He later married the widowed sister of an old Nelson friend: Leonard Trent VC. Finding service in the post-war New Zealand army rather dull, Thomas secured a regular commission with the British Army in 1947 and had a long, distinguished career before retiring with the rank of major general in 1971. Sandy Thomas now lives on Queensland's Gold Coast.

SERGEANT HAANE TE RAUAWA MANAHI

In the capture of Takrouna, no soldier played a more prominent role than Lance Sergeant Haane Te Rauawa Manahi. A member of the Te Arawa tribe, Manahi joined the 28th (Maori) Battalion in 1939 and served in Greece and Crete, where he was wounded. Manahi was promoted to lance sergeant in February 1942 and held this rank during the fight for Takrouna.

The night attack by 5 Brigade on Takrouna and three other foothills failed to secure any of the allocated objectives. The attacking battalions blundered into the killing zones on either side of Takrouna and withering fire from the hill pinned them down to just beyond their starting positions. But in the early morning of 20 April, a near-miracle occurred. Two sections of Maori soldiers, one led by Manahi, the other by Sergeant Johnny Rogers, attacked up the rear of the hill from different directions. They climbed up the steep slopes from the east and southwest. It was an incredibly difficult task as they had to fight their way up the first part of the hill 'running for shelter from rock to rock, and firing on the enemy positions'.[91] By first light the two groups were only halfway up the pinnacle, but they had climbed above and behind the main enemy positions so that they could fire down into the defenders' fighting pits. Many white flags appeared when they did so and Manahi sent Private Hinga Grant to take care of them. Grant 'rounded up sixty Italians and escorted them away from the war'.[92]

Meanwhile, Manahi and Rogers and their small band climbed higher towards the pinnacle. The last 20 feet was an almost sheer rock face, so that some of the soldiers had to use bunches of enemy telephone cable to assist themselves onto the peak of the precipice. Takrouna was taken.

If taking the Takrouna feature was hard, holding on to it was not any easier. As the battalion history records of Takrouna on this day:

> When the enemy realised that his observation post on Takrouna was lost, both the pinnacle and the ledge were subjected to fire of all types. It was kept up almost continuously during the day, and the events which follow must be pictured as occurring under a constant deluge of mortar and other shells.[93]

As a result of this shelling, casualties continued to mount during the day.

After two attempts to get messages back to his battalion failed, Manahi himself went back to the battalion headquarters and gathered reinforcements, ammunition, food and stretcher-bearers. These he led back onto the peak of Takrouna, ignoring a British artillery officer's advice that he should abandon the position. On Takrouna he was joined by 15 Platoon from the 21st Battalion under Lieutenant R.A. Shaw.

At 3.30 p.m., more than 15 hours after the New Zealand soldiers started this attack, Italian troops mounted a fierce counterattack that aimed to recapture Takrouna. Twelve truckloads of Italian infantry had arrived and launched an attack from the northwest. When part of the feature was lost in the afternoon, the enemy had to be driven from the feature again in fierce hand-to-hand fighting. At one stage all control was lost when an Italian grenade exploded in a building that sheltered the New Zealand wounded, killing most of the occupants. The response was 'swift and savage', as Manahi later recounted: 'That's when the boys turned around and started using the bayonet.' There were no survivors. Those who were not bayoneted or shot were thrown over the cliffs. As Ian Wards observed, this was one of those grim moments in war when all control is lost.[94]

That evening, after Manahi and his Maori soldiers had withdrawn from the summit, the Italians retook part of the pinnacle. A stalemate developed where no side could shift the other from its portion of the hill. Reinforcements were called for, with a special request that Manahi return on account of his local knowledge of the feature.

So Manahi returned to the summit a third time with a party of about 14 volunteers and once again led a counterattack to retake it. Then in the afternoon, he and two other NCOs led small groups of soldiers in an attack on the village at the base of the hill. Manahi took several enemy posts on the northeast slopes, which assisted a platoon from the 21st Battalion in their attack on the village. The Italian defenders, some 323 in all, and five Germans surrendered. The fight for Takrouna was finally over.

Lieutenant General Sir Brian Horrocks, the corps commander, witnessed most of the action and later wrote:

A few days later I visited Takrouna and it was all I could do physically to reach the top. How the Maoris did it wearing full equipment in the face of tough enemy opposition I simply did not know . . . I have mentioned this fight in some detail because in my opinion it was the most gallant feat of arms I witnessed in the course of the war and I was bitterly disappointed when Sergeant Manahi whom we had recommended for a VC only received the DCM.[95]

Horrocks later stated he could not 'to this day imagine how it was captured in the face of tenacious enemy resistance'.[96]

Manahi still had one more important task to perform after Takrouna was finally secured. He returned to the pinnacle of Takrouna a fourth time, this time at night, where he supervised the removal of the New Zealand dead. They were 'wrapped in blankets and lowered by rope down the rocky cliff face and laid to rest in a specially dedicated plot'.[97] Of the 319 Maori soldiers who had taken part in this battle, 124 were killed, wounded or missing. Other battalions suffered heavy casualties: the 21st Battalion lost 169 men, whilst the 23rd Battalion lost 115.[98] The New Zealanders' last victory in North Africa had exacted a heavy price.

Everyone in the 2nd New Zealand Division knew of the exploits of Manahi. As Ian Wards has written, 'In the Division as a whole the men who survived the struggle were regarded with something akin to awe.'[99] Kippenberger, aware of the tremendous heroism displayed by Manahi, sent his brigade major, Denis

Blundell (later Governor-General of New Zealand), to investigate the action and to draft a recommendation for Manahi to receive the VC. The recommendation was four pages long and was supported by three eyewitness statements. As Lieutenant Ian Hirst of the 21st Battalion recorded:

> But for the action of L/Sjt Manahi and his men the capture of the whole feature would have been delayed considerably. During these operations L/Sjt Manahi and his men were continually under shell and small arms fire.[100]

Kippenberger, Freyberg, Horrocks and Montgomery all supported the recommendation, but somewhere between Middle East Headquarters and the VC Committee of the War Office, Manahi's VC recommendation was downgraded to the award of the DCM. The original recommendation carries the stamp of Lieutenant General Henry Maitland Wilson as authorising this downgrading.[101]

In June 1943, Haane Manahi was repatriated to New Zealand and discharged from the 2nd NZEF. Throughout his life he never worried about missing out on the VC. According to his son Rau, Haane Manahi 'was a humble man and more concerned about his comrades not receiving recognition for their efforts than what happened to his VC recommendation'.[102] Haane Manahi was killed in a motor vehicle accident on 29 March 1986, aged 72.

After his death Manahi's relatives and his old comrades tried to have a VC awarded, but without success. Feeling amongst Maori ex-servicemen ran so strongly on this issue that Sir Charles Bennett formed a committee to lobby to have the Manahi case reconsidered. Three times the Queen was petitioned to reconsider the case of a VC for Manahi and each time she declined. Twice approaches were made through the Governor-General, and on the third time they were made directly by the New Zealand government.[103] Feelings and passions were inflamed by the conviction that Manahi had been denied his VC on the grounds of race alone — that is, because he was a Maori soldier. Sir Howard Morrison, Manahi's nephew, is typical:

Race is the reason why Maori soldier Sergeant Haane Manahi was not awarded a Victoria Cross for bravery . . . I was very close to Sir Denis [Blundell] and he was devastated about his recommendation being totally ignored. He told me the British had said there was no way two Maori could get a VC out of the same campaign.[104]

Sir Howard may have been referring to an account attributed to Blundell that appeared in Wira Gardiner's book on the Maori Battalion, *Te Mura O Te Ahi*. In a chapter entitled 'The Politics of Bravery', Blundell is alleged to have said:

Like the rest of the Division [I] was disgusted when he was awarded an immediate DCM. I feel sure that here was an example, that even in the realm of bravery, politics played a part, and that the award to 2nd Lieutenant Ngarimu only some three weeks previously influenced the final decision. This for me was confirmed when later at the Gejira Sporting Club in Cairo, our Military Secretary, Brigadier Rudd, asked me to tell the story to a senior British general. The General's comment was 'we did make a mistake'.[105]

Sir Charles Bennett reflected the bitterness and the strong sense of injustice felt by many Maori soldiers and relatives:

A grave injustice has been done to a great soldier, and indeed to the Maori people as a whole . . . as grave in my view as the confiscation of Maori lands in the last century.[106]

This last comment is probably overstating the case to some degree. It was always unlikely that Manahi would be awarded a VC so long after the event. Instructions issued by King George VI were quite specific on the subject. The King decreed that there should be no further awards of decorations for the Second World War after 1949.[107] In 1997, when New Zealand Prime Minister, Jenny Shipley, officially requested the Queen to upgrade the DCM to a VC, the

Queen followed her father's advice once more and declined to do so. In a letter to Jenny Shipley the Queen stated that 'it would not be right to review the award so many years after the relevant event'.[108]

While Manahi's actions at Takrouna were undoubtedly deserving of a VC, it is unlikely that this will ever happen. Manahi's family and supporters can take comfort from three important considerations. As this book has shown, Manahi's failed recommendation is not an isolated case at all. Several other New Zealand service personnel have deservedly been recommended for the VC, only for the recommendation to be downgraded or ignored entirely, sometimes for the most spurious of reasons. And Manahi did receive the DCM for his actions, the second-highest gallantry award then available to a non-commissioned soldier. Others who were recommended for the VC received less distinguished awards and some received no recognition for their bravery at all. Third, the publicity and controversy surrounding the case has meant that Manahi's deeds at Takrouna have not been forgotten. Most New Zealanders with an interest in military history are well aware of them. Many VC winners and certainly no other declined VC recommendation has received anything like the attention that the Manahi case has generated.

CHAPTER 13 The air VCs of the Second World War

B etween the end of the First World War and the outbreak of the second global conflict 21 years later, airpower had continued to develop in all aspects of technology and also in war-fighting doctrine. The glamour of aviation and its civilian applications had allowed it to progress as nations became increasingly 'air-minded'. The fabric-covered, wooden-framed, biplane aircraft of the earlier conflict had predominantly been replaced by monoplane airframes with much more powerful engines and stressed-metal skins. Endurance had also been greatly increased, so that aircraft had crossed the oceans and pioneered air routes around the globe. Commercial airlines had evolved and the movement of passengers was now routine. Many of these types, developed for the civil market, were taken virtually unchanged into military service as transport aircraft, or with slight adaptation formed the basis of reconnaissance or bomber types.

Other specially designed military aircraft sacrificed certain potential qualities for others such as endurance or higher speed, greater load carrying or increased robustness. The speed of the fighters and faster bomber types had increased from 130 miles per hour in 1918 to over 300 by 1939. Most aircraft were equipped with voice radio for easy communication with both their comrades in the air and their ground support elements or bases. Armament had gone from two machine-guns on fighters to eight in British machines, and a combination of machine-guns and high-powered cannons on the German aircraft. The larger bomber types could carry thousands of kilograms of bombs for hundreds of miles.

In doctrinal terms the inter-war airpower debate had mostly concerned bombers. The Royal Air Force had evolved from the Independent Air Force of 1918, which had been established for the role of strategically bombing German targets. The RAF's first commander, Lord Hugh Trenchard, was seized by the concept that bomber aircraft could attack the enemy's rear, over the static fortified lines that appeared to characterise ground warfare between modern industrialised states. He, and those who echoed his ideas, asserted that this was a more economical means of providing a nation's defence in both financial and human terms. As the RAF was the first autonomous air force in any country, established as a service in its own right equal to the navy and army, Trenchard's ideas were very persuasive to a new generation of airpower advocates in various militaries.

In Italy General Giulio Douhet and in the USA General William 'Billy' Mitchell advocated or developed very similar ideas. In addition, technology seemed to support their assertions. The emergence of multi-engined bombers able to fly above anti-aircraft fire, and faster and higher than the single-engined fighters available, was the catalyst. These men theorised that the bomber would always get through and therefore governments should concentrate their scarce defence resources on providing such aircraft types. Under Trenchard's 12-year command of the RAF, Britain concentrated on developing its bomber force to provide the advanced types necessary to police the British Empire and to carry any war into Europe.

Germany, however, had drawn other lessons from the First World War and when she was able to build a new air force — the Luftwaffe — she concentrated on developing one that could cooperate closely with her army, as did the Russians. Japan similarly provided air forces to operate in conjunction with her ground elements, but given the emphasis placed on the navy, Japan developed a strong carrier-based element of airpower as well. As world tensions grew and the lessons of smaller conflicts such as the Spanish Civil War emerged, the bomber myth was gradually exposed. Modern fighter types were being developed that could defend against bombers, while radio control allowed such defences to be coordinated. Also, as populations became accustomed to the concept of aerial bombardment, they proved not to be susceptible to the mass hysteria that the bomber theorists had asserted would result from its use.

Just in time, in the years immediately before the outbreak of hostilities, Britain started to develop the Hurricane and Spitfire. These modern, mono-wing fighters were capable of meeting Germany's Messerschmitt 109 on an equal footing. Britain also developed RADAR (RAdio Detection And Ranging), which allowed her to identify enemy aircraft formations approaching England and thus provide a warning to the defending fighter squadrons and anti-aircraft defences. However, the RAF's light bomber and ground cooperation elements remained weak and poorly equipped. The French were somewhat slower in investing in their air forces at all, relying instead on the Maginot Line, of concrete fortifications, tank obstacles, machine-gun posts and other defences that faced Germany and Italy, to forestall any attack.

Once war did break out in 1939, it demonstrated time and again that surface forces, naval or army, had extreme difficulty operating in a hostile air environment. This was not the only factor in the success of the German Blitzkrieg on Poland and then France, but it was a key element. The Luftwaffe was equipped with fighters in sufficient numbers and quality to seize control of the air over the advancing armies. This then allowed aircraft types optimised and trained for ground support, to speed the army's advance by destroying Allied troop concentrations and disrupting their transport and communications, to shatter their cohesion and coordination. In effect these aircraft provided aerial artillery support to the ground forces. This was all in conjunction with a better land-tactical doctrine, especially in the employment of concentrated armoured forces, and a plan that drove around the flank of the Maginot Line defences. Thus the battle for France was lost in six weeks and Britain stood alone, with a mauled and under-equipped army, the Royal Navy, and the RAF depleted in fighters but largely intact in its bomber command.

The Germans appreciated that, to invade England, they needed to cross the channel without allowing the Royal Navy to intercept their invasion fleet. Given their own lack of conventional naval forces, they could only do this by airpower, so the Luftwaffe needed to ensure the complete destruction of RAF Fighter Command. This was what the first phases of the Battle of Britain were designed to do. The Luftwaffe planned to destroy the British fighters first, to ensure its own bombers could prevent the Royal Navy interfering with a subsequent invasion, while their fighters would then deal with any residual British bomber forces. The plan very nearly worked, but broke down when the German leadership decided prematurely to switch their attack from the as yet undefeated Fighter Command to bombing population centres.[1]

The Battle of Britain drove home several lessons concerning the use of modern airpower. It was proven that the bombers did not always get through. Even when they did, the destruction they caused was insufficient to collapse either civilian morale or government resolve if it was not linked to the imminent arrival of ground forces. It showed that bombers flying in daylight were very vulnerable to attack by modern fighters, alerted by RADAR and coordinated from the ground, unless closely escorted by their own fighters. The Luftwaffe's fighters were limited in the escort role because of their short endurance time over England. The night blitz that followed proved less costly in bomber aircraft lost, but had far greater difficulty finding specific targets and was consequently restricted to area bombing.

Britain drew the correct lessons concerning their Fighter Command and also worked to develop the types and doctrine necessary to provide close support to army operations. Following the success of their attack at the Battle of Matapan and against the *Bismarck*, Britain also belatedly appreciated the offensive importance of airpower against surface warships, though not sufficiently to save its battleships HMS *Repulse* and HMS *Prince of Wales* from the Japanese. From the war's outset she had integrated aircraft into her anti-submarine operations. However, in the early stages of the war there was a critical shortage of trained aircrew as well as competing calls on the better aircraft types available. The only offensive element left to Britain for the direct attack of Germany was Bomber Command. Having already established that daylight raids were not possible, Bomber Command started its five-year night-bombing campaign against German population centres.

In 1942 the United States entered the war and the heavy bombers they had been developing now joined the attack. American doctrine had continued to advocate accurate attack on specific targets by day. To overcome the fighter defences, the American aircraft were much more heavily equipped with defensive weapons than the British, but consequently could not carry such heavy bomb loads. These aircraft, particularly the Flying Fortresses and Liberators, also possessed very long ranges, which reflected their intended use over the Pacific, making them ideal for anti-submarine operations over the Atlantic.

In the normal cycle of development and countermeasures, the Germans soon produced effective RADAR of their own. Both sides managed to make these small enough to fit into aircraft, providing eyes to the night fighters, navigation aids to the night bombers, and the ability for maritime aircraft to extend their effective search ranges and accuracy against submarines. The Allies also developed longer range fighters that allowed bombers to be escorted to hostile targets during daylight. The British, however, still tended to retain their heavy bombers for night missions on Germany, and used their lighter types for smaller, precision attacks.

By the war's end, Germany and Japan had been swamped by allied airpower. Their own defensive airpower had been decimated, with the majority of their best pilots killed, their aircraft industries obliterated and the key supplies, particularly fuel, brought to a standstill. Under this dominance of the skies, the Allies were able to advance their armies and navies into the enemy homelands. Germany was forced to surrender after her territory had been almost completely overrun by the Allies, while Japan's overseas forces were driven back and two of her major cities were bombed with the new nuclear weapons.

To achieve this preponderance of airpower, numerous personnel were required both to fly the aircraft and maintain them. Britain's empire provided several advantages in this. The same global expanse encompassed in the British Empire, which necessitating a geographic dispersal of some of her air combat power, also provided sources of recruits, safe skies in which to train and sources of aircraft production. Even before the war, the British had been recruiting dominion manpower into the RAF, in addition to the forces raised locally by the governments of the empire's constituent countries. Several New Zealanders had been in the RAF since the First World War and held key command positions. Air Chief Marshal Sir Keith Park commanded 11 Group of Fighter Command during the Battle of Britain and then was responsible for the defence of Malta in 1941–42 while the Germans attempted to neutralise that base through persistent air attack. Air Marshal Sir Arthur Coningham was responsible for developing the methods of close air support for the army and commanded the tactical air forces, first in North Africa and then in the invasion of Europe. Of those recently recruited, one of the first aces and heroes of Fighter Command was Flying Officer Edgar 'Cobber' Kain. The New Zealand Permanent Air Force had been established in 1923 but, because of the cost of aircraft, had remained comparatively small. However, numerous young New Zealanders were either to join the Royal New Zealand Air Force (RNZAF, established as a separate service in 1937) in its rapid expansion during the war, or either the RAF or Fleet Air Arm via such mechanisms as the Empire Air Training Scheme.[2] Twenty-six airmen were to be awarded the VC and three of these, following in the footsteps of William Rhodes-Moorhouse, were New Zealanders.

There could, of course, have been others. New Zealanders constituted seven per cent of the Fleet Air Arm,[3] and were particularly active in the campaigns against Japan. However, it was for flying a Hellcat divebomber in an attack on the German battleship *Tirpitz* that Lieutenant Commander 'Ron' Richardson was recommended for a posthumous VC by the commander in chief of the Home Fleet. Richardson was the commanding officer of 1840 Squadron flying off HMS *Indefatigable*. He had pressed home his attack on 24 August 1944, despite intense flak, until his aircraft was shot down and he was killed. This was the only known VC nomination made for a New Zealander serving in the navy in the Second World War. The recommendation was, however, declined and Richardson received a posthumous mention in despatches.[4]

Another officer who was definitely recommended but also only received a mention in despatches was 20-year-old Pilot Officer Frank Watkins. On 20 December 1942 he was on his thirtieth mission, his third as a pathfinder with 156 Squadron and one of the last this unit was to undertake in Wellingtons. Over the target, Duisberg, the aircraft was hit by flak and Watkins' friend, the bombardier Bill Brooke-Norris, was badly wounded. The remainder of the crew bailed out while Watkins and the navigator, Squadron Leader John Carter, attempted to sedate the wounded man and get him out of the aircraft, which was losing height and taking further flak hits. They could not manage it and at the last possible moment Watkins, as aircraft captain, ordered Carter to jump and stated his intention to attempt a crash landing in order to save his friend. In the event, both perished in the crash.

Carter wrote back to his squadron from prison camp in January 1943 and informed them of Watkins' deed, recommending his recognition. The squadron commander agreed and recommended the VC, which was supported all the way to Bomber Command. Sir Arthur Harris, commanding Bomber Command, forwarded the recommendation but felt additional supporting evidence would be required which could not be obtained until all the survivors were properly interviewed. The matter was held in abeyance until after Germany was defeated and the prisoners were repatriated. It is not known at that stage if the interviews were conducted, but in June 1946 Watkins, now buried in the Riechswald Forest Cemetery with Brooke-Norris, received a mention in despatches.[5]

THE WING WALKER: SERGEANT JAMES ALLEN (JIMMY) WARD, RNZAF

The first of the three New Zealand airmen to be awarded the VC was Sergeant James Ward, a pilot in 75 (NZ) Squadron of Bomber Command. This squadron was equipped with Wellington bombers, one of the most advanced operational types available to the RAF at the outbreak of hostilities. The squadron's first six aircraft and 20 personnel had all been provided by New Zealand on the declaration of war.[6] Designed by Barnes Wallis, who subsequently invented the bouncing bomb of Dambusters fame, the Wellington was a twin-engined machine with a range of 2000 miles, carrying 4000 pounds of bombs, at a speed of about 230 miles per hour. The aircraft had a crew of six and its normal protective armament was a forward turret with two machine-guns, and a tail turret with four.[7] The fuselage and wings were constructed from a geometric lattice frame, called 'geodetic', which was flexible and consequently could absorb a lot of punishment. Unusual for the time, when metal was predominantly being used for newer designs, the Wellington was fabric-covered, making it easy to repair. The design was so successful that the British produced Wellingtons throughout the war.

On the night of 7–8 July 1941 Ward was the second pilot of a Wellington returning from a raid on Münster. They had cleared the coast of Holland and were over the Zuider Zee at about 13,000 feet when they were attacked by a Messerschmitt 110 night fighter. Before Sergeant Box, the rear gunner, managed to shoot the attacker down it had hit the Wellington with cannon fire and incendiary bullets. These had ripped through the starboard wing and set the engine on fire, as well as destroying the radio, rupturing hydraulic pipes and wounding the front gunner.[8] This was a dangerous situation for a fabric-covered aircraft, but was made worse by a fuel pipe also having been broken, which was feeding the flames on the wing. The crew tried to put the fire out by knocking a hole in the side of the fuselage and using first their fire extinguishers and then even the coffee from their flasks, but to no effect.

The Canadian aircraft captain, Squadron Leader R.P. Widdowson, decided to abandon the aircraft, but Ward offered to make a last desperate attempt to stop the fire. He planned to climb out of the aircraft, through the astral navigation dome on top of the fuselage, and then climb down onto the wing, to crawl out to the engine and smother the fire with a canvas cockpit cover. His companions insisted that he be 'secured' with the line from the inflatable dinghy and persuaded him to retain his parachute, albeit on his chest.

Widdowson brought the aircraft speed down as much as he dared, but even so the Wellington was travelling at over 100 miles per hour when Ward managed to crawl out of the hole on top of the aircraft. He got down onto the wing by kicking holes in the fuselage's canvas sides and placing his feet in the geodetic framing. On the wing he got himself down as flat as possible, but this was made difficult by the parachute on his chest. He inched his way out towards the fire, creating handholds by kicking holes in the wing fabric in addition to those caused by the fighter's cannons. As he neared the engine the task was made more difficult by the increased turbulence from the propeller wash with which he had to contend, as well as the wind.

When he reached the fire in the wing, he managed to pull out the cover from inside his jacket and to smother the flames as planned. He then pushed on the short distance to the engine itself, in order to try to deal with the leaking fuel pipe. He pushed the cover into the hole in the wing caused by the fire near the leak, and held it there with one hand while holding onto the wing with the other. Hanging on with only one hand, he soon tired, but as soon as he removed his other hand from the cover the force of the moving air blew it out of the hole. Ward pushed the cover back into the hole a second time. However, shortly afterwards, when he was again forced to remove his hand in order to maintain his grip on the wing, the cover was carried away. Exhausted, and with nothing else to use to stop the fire, Ward returned to the aircraft. It was now that the rope around his waist came to his aid as, kept taut by his crewmates, it gave him the necessary assistance to complete his journey.

As it transpired, Ward had done enough. By putting out the fire on the wing fabric, he had prevented it from spreading. The leaking fuel had nothing left in the vicinity with which to ignite and spilled away into the night. Widdowson was able to resume course for England. Despite a brief flare-up caused by a pool of petrol, the fire did not prevent their landing at Newmarket airfield around 4.30 a.m. However, they did so with no brakes or flaps so that, after using the entire airfield, the aircraft was eventually arrested by a hedge and fence at the end. The damage, in conjunction with that caused by their brief combat and the fire, resulted in the aircraft being written off.

For his exploits that night Wing Commander C.E. Kay DFC, the commanding officer of 75 Squadron, recommended Widdowson for a DFC, the rear gunner Sergeant Box for the DFM and Ward for the VC.[9] Notification that the award had been approved appeared in the *London Gazette* on 5 August 1941.

Jimmy Ward was born in Wanganui on 14 June 1919, the son of English parents. He attended Wanganui Technical College and then trained as a teacher in Wellington, a classmate of Cobber Kain's. Qualifying in 1939 he had taken an appointment at Castlecliff School, Wanganui, but volunteered to join the RNZAF when war broke out.

He was not called forward for training and enlistment at Levin until 1 July 1940. He then completed elementary flying training at Taieri, before his advanced course at Wigram. He came third in his class for ground training and his ability as a pilot was described as of a high average standard. His reports variously describe him as very keen, with plenty of confidence and initiative as well as being physically strong, intelligent, temperate and generally reliable in all responsibilities.[10] Receiving his wings on 18 January 1941, he was promoted to sergeant before deploying overseas at the end of the month. From March he undertook operational training in Scotland, before being formed into a crew and posted to 75 Squadron.

Ward's first operation was not with the crew he trained with, however. The night after his arrival in 75 Squadron — his twenty-second birthday — he flew as Widdowson's second pilot on a raid on Düsseldorf. He undertook five more missions in this appointment before the Münster raid. Following that mission Ward was reunited with his original crew from Lossiemouth,[11] as captain of his own aircraft, and together they undertook three missions. On 13 September 1941 the RNZAF liaison office in London suggested Ward should be returned to New Zealand as an instructor,[12] but there was no time for this proposal to be followed up.

On 15 September 1941 he and his crew manned one of 12

aircraft from 75 Squadron participating in a raid on Hamburg. The conventional understanding is that the Wellington was hit several times by anti-aircraft fire whilst over the target, and crashed in flames.[13] However, the observer and wireless operator managed to escape, and one subsequently recorded what actually happened after he had been released from a German POW camp. The Wellington was indeed caught in the searchlights above Hamburg shortly after it had released its bombs but there was no flak, a sure sign night fighters were in the vicinity. Sure enough, some 20 miles outside Hamburg, they were bounced by a night fighter which shot them down. James Ward was last seen at the controls of his aircraft, having ordered the crew to bail out and the two who managed to do so saw the Wellington, with their four crewmates, actually hit the ground.[14]

James Allen Ward was originally buried by the Germans in a civilian cemetery. After the war his remains were identified and re-interred at the British Military Cemetery at Ohlsdorf, near Hamburg. His VC and other memorabilia were held on behalf of 75 Squadron (in suspension) and Ward family descendants by the Commander RNZAF Base Ohakea until early 2006, when they were returned to the family, who have since loaned the VC to the Auckland Museum.

THE VENTURAS

As well as 75 Squadron, there were to be six other New Zealand squadrons in the RAF, numbered 485 to 490. In 1942, 487 Squadron was formed and equipped with the Lockheed Ventura light bomber. This aircraft was one of those derived from pre-war civilian types, in this case the American-manufactured Lockheed Electra and Lodestar. An earlier military version of this twin-engined type, the Hudson, was in service with the RNZAF in the Pacific. The Ventura had a top speed of 322 miles per hour and a bomb load of 5000 pounds, both superior to the Wellington and with a similar range.[15] However, the night-bombing role was now being undertaken by aircraft such as the Lancaster, that had an 18,000-pound bomb load and superior defensive armament. The Ventura and other light bombers were therefore used for small, precision raids in daylight. The Ventura was not popular with crews as it was considered too slow, too tiring to fly, lacking in adequate defensive firepower and requiring strong fighter cover in order to achieve anything.[16] Essentially, there were faster and better-armed RAF aircraft available, such as the Boston or Mosquito, which aircrew would have preferred.

The squadron had been formed around a nucleus of New Zealanders with experience in light bombers, most of whom had been serving in the RAF. It was grouped with the similarly equipped 464 (Australian) Squadron at Feltwell, under the command of Group Captain R.L. Kippenberger.[17] Both 487 Squadron flight commanders already held the DFC, but most of the crews were new and required considerable work to come up to an adequate standard of formation flying. This was achieved and the first operational sortie, a raid on the Philips factory at Eindhoven, Holland, in December was a success but cost the squadron its commander, Wing Commander F.C. Seavill. In the next few months the squadron undertook several raids on targets along the Dutch, French and Belgian coasts.

On 3 May, the B Flight commander, Squadron Leader Len Trent, DFC, was preparing to lead the squadron for another raid on the docks at Flushing on the Dutch coast. He and his crew need not have been there, but they had been forced to return early from another raid by engine trouble a couple of days before and Trent had therefore tossed a coin with Wing Commander G.J. Grindell for who would lead this one. However, as the formation awaited takeoff, this target was cancelled.

A new plan, codenamed Ramrod 17, to bomb the electrical powerhouse outside Amsterdam, was delivered. The new raid was complex and, even though it was primarily a diversion for a raid by Bostons on the Dutch Steel Works, the crews were ordered to press on regardless.[18] The bombers were to rendezvous with a Spitfire escort of three squadrons and then fly at sea level to their target, before climbing at the last possible moment to their bombing height. Two more Spitfire squadrons were to provide top cover, following the same flight plan but arriving slightly ahead of the main formation in order to gain height and cover their run over the target. This complexity was necessary in order to avoid showing up on the German RADAR too early and so avoid alerting the fighter defences.

However, the late change of plan necessarily meant there was less time available to fully brief everyone involved. The bombers and their close escort worked well, but unfortunately the top-cover fighters left 20 minutes too early and climbed as soon as they got to Holland. The very thing that the plan was meant to avoid therefore happened. The top-cover Spitfires were detected by the German RADAR and Luftwaffe fighters were scrambled. Unfortunately for the approaching Ramrod 17 force, not only had they lost surprise, but more than just the usual defending fighter force was available. Some Luftwaffe VIPs were visiting the Haarlem area, near Amsterdam, and the fighter personnel from the Lowlands/ Scandinavia zones were holding a training session at Schiphol airport to coincide with this.[19] Consequently not only was the fighter strength higher than usual, so that fully 70 aircraft scrambled to meet the raid, but it included a concentration of expert pilots determined to show their prowess. Worse still, having alerted the enemy, the top-cover fighters, running short of fuel, returned to base before the raid arrived, allowing the Germans to gain height over their incoming prey. The escorts knew some of what was happening, but only Trent's aircraft had the VHF radio that could communicate with them. However, he couldn't speak to the fighters because of electrical interference from the other, unmodified, Venturas in his formation. Ten minutes out from their target, the bomber crews thought, wrongly, that everything was going to plan.

The German fighters then pounced out of the sun, with some 20 planes occupying the close escort while another 30 attacked the Venturas. The leader of the other flight of Venturas, Flight Lieutenant A.V. Duffill, was the first to fall out, his aircraft smoking as it went down. In short order six more Venturas were knocked out of the attack. After the first pass, Trent could see the dogfight with the close escort going on behind him, but was unable to locate the top cover, unaware that it had already gone. The German fighters then manoeuvred to keep the four remaining bombers away from Haarlem, unaware that they didn't know about the potential VIP target there and were in fact making for a different target.

The Germans came in again and again, so that one by one Trent's companions fell. Eventually one Luftwaffe pilot made a fatal mistake. Instead of diving under the Ventura as he completed his attacking pass, he banked in front of it. The Ventura had two 50 calibre and two 30 calibre machine-guns in its nose, fired by the pilot. Len Trent let the fighter have the benefit of all his firepower, causing it to fall in flames. Even so, there were only two bombers left as they came over Amsterdam and the flak started to rise, while the German fighters continued their attack. Trent then had to maintain a steady course through this gauntlet in order to drop his bombs, which he did successfully.

When his bombs were gone, Trent could see no other surviving British aircraft in the area and believed he was the last to be shot down.[20] As he was closing his bomb doors and contemplating how to escape, all the Ventura's controls were lost, though the aircraft remained in level flight. Trent ordered his crew to bail out, but they had not managed to do so when the aircraft went into a spin. Trent himself was thrown out and parachuted clear, as did his navigator.[21]

Of the 12 Venturas that commenced the raid, one had turned back over the English Channel with a loose cover. Ten aircraft had been destroyed or fallen over the sea after they had been driven back and only one Ventura returned from combat. Flight Lieutenant Duffill had actually managed to regain control of his plane and bring it back to base, with his wounded crew aboard. Of the 48 bomber aircrew on Ramrod 17, only eight returned to England, 12 were made prisoners of war, including Trent, and 28 were killed. The power station continued to function.

Squadron Leader
Leonard Henry Trent, RAF

Leonard Henry Trent was born in Nelson on 14 April 1915, where his father was a dentist. The family moved to Takaka in 1919, where he attended Nelson College as a boarder. He was fascinated by aviation from an early age, and was also a good golfer, winning the Nelson club championship while still at school.[22] His sport did detract from his study, however, and he had to take his matriculation exams twice.[23] After leaving school he worked in clerical jobs and briefly for his father.

On his own initiative he took his A pilot's licence at the Otago Aero Club in 1937 and then successfully applied for a short-service commission in the RAF. He undertook further flying training at Wigram, from which he received his wings in May 1938. He was described as 'Above average as pupil pilot, flies very accurately and smoothly. Has good grasp of ground subjects and is very keen and attentive at lectures.'[24] He arrived in England in July that year to start a five-year appointment with the RAF.

When war was declared the next year, Trent was sent to France, initially flying photo-reconnaissance in Fairey Battle aircraft with 15 Squadron before that unit converted to Blenheim bombers. From May 1940 the unit undertook numerous raids against the attacking German forces and for his part Trent was awarded the DFC. Posted to instructional duties in July, he also received a commendation for bringing down a Boston bomber that had an engine fire during a familiarisation flight. He spent nearly two years instructing, during which time he also married, before being promoted to squadron leader and posted to headquarters 2 Group of Bomber Command.[25] He was by then anxious to return to operational flying and had hoped to go to a Boston squadron. However, on the basis of being a New Zealander with experience in light bombers, he was posted as a flight commander to help form 487 (NZ) Squadron.

After being shot down over Amsterdam, Len Trent was taken as a POW and had a dramatic imprisonment, eventually being sent to Stalag Luft III at Sagan in Northern Germany (now in Poland). On the night of 24–25 March 1944 the inmates of the British compound in that camp managed a mass escape through a tunnel, nicknamed 'Harry', that they had dug under the wire. At 3.30 a.m. on 25 March it was Len Trent's turn and he was to be the seventy-ninth man through. In the film version of *The Great Escape*, the last prisoner through the tunnel alerts the guard by his impatience. As in the film, the tunnel did indeed come up short of the forest and there was a signal for the men to move when the guard wasn't looking. However, as Trent was crawling towards the trees a guard came towards the tunnel exit, probably in order to relieve himself. When he was very close he saw another New Zealander, Mick Shand, lying near the woods and was about to shoot when a further prisoner hiding in the tree line distracted him by yelling at him not to. The guard's shot went wide and Shand escaped with another man. Three remaining prisoners in the close vicinity, along with the man at the tunnel mouth, were forced to reveal themselves and were thus recaptured immediately.[26] Seventy-six men had by then managed to make good their escape. Of these only three managed to evade the massive German manhunt that ensued and return to England, while 50 of the escapees, including three New Zealanders, were executed on Hitler's orders after they were recaptured.[27]

Trent remained in captivity until released in May 1945, having endured a harrowing forced march as the Germans moved their prisoners away from the advancing Russians. He was immediately flown back to England and reunited with his family. He elected to stay attached to the RAF, having been transferred to the RNZAF in 1944, and was employed flying DC-3s in Transport Command. It was only now that a full debrief of Ramrod 17 could be undertaken by RAF authorities and as a result Len Trent was recommended for the VC. On returning from a flight after midnight one evening, he was directed to see the station commander immediately at his house. Over a sherry in the small hours of the morning Len Trent was informed that he had been awarded the VC.[28] The investiture by the King took place at Buckingham Palace on 12 April 1946.

Len Trent contemplated a permanent commission in the RNZAF, but eventually accepted one in the RAF instead. He served in various instructional posts and was then given command of a Valiant bomber squadron. His last post was as the British air attaché to Washington, from which he retired as a group captain in 1964. He and his family eventually settled in Auckland, where he died on 19 May 1986. His VC is held by the RNZAF Museum at Wigram, Christchurch.

THE NEW WAR AT SEA

As indicated in the introductory section of this chapter, the impact of airpower was felt not only on land but also at sea. The Germans entered the Second World War with a significantly better fleet of U-boats and with no scruples from the outset on how to employ them. The British had also learnt from past experience and employed convoys, undersea detection and patrols in order to restrict the freedom of the U-boats to attack, as well as move and resupply. A cycle of measures and countermeasures, mostly favouring the Germans, went on until 1943, while the British struggled to provide sufficient vessels, of the proper type, to adequately escort their convoys. At the same time air patrols proved effective at both detecting and attacking submarines if they were caught on or near the surface. The Germans extended the ranges of their patrols, and the British had to find means to close these gaps in their air coverage of the oceans.

By 1943 the aircraft of Coastal Command were equipped with RADAR, which could detect the submarines even if only small portions of them were above the surface. We now also know that the German's automated coding system, the Enigma cipher machines, had been compromised and their messages were being reliably broken on a regular basis so that consequently the Allies often had a very clear idea where the U-boats could be located. In addition to this technology, long-range aircraft were then available from the USA that could be freed for this task and bases had been developed, where necessary, in order to close 'the Atlantic gap'. One such base was at Rundum on the west coast of Africa, from where the RAF Coastal Command's 200 Squadron operated. In July 1943 the squadron converted from the Hudson to Liberator bombers. The patrol radius of the squadron thus increased from 900 to 1400 miles, with a larger payload of weapons and sensors, meaning patrols could be as long as 12 hours.

SUBMARINE HUNTER

On 11 August 1943 at about 7.30 a.m., Flying Officer Lloyd Trigg was piloting one of the squadron's two new Liberators that had been despatched on a targeted search for a U-boat off the West African coast, 240 miles southwest of Dakar.[29] It is apparent from the letter sent to Trigg's widow by one of his fellow squadron members after the war that the patrol was not routine. They had been given specific areas where they expected to find a craft. This therefore contrasts with the details in the official version of events, which portrayed the mission as a routine patrol.[30] This was driven by the perceived need to keep the secret that the German naval codes had been compromised through most of the war. Consequently the original version of events has Trigg spot a U-boat after eight hours of patrolling,[31] where the actual target U-468 was in fact sighted on the surface at 9.45 a.m.[32]

In order to make either a successful bombing or a depth-charge run on a submarine, the aircraft had to come in low and be straight over the target when it delivered its attack. The Liberator's size gave it greater range, but also made it considerably less manoeuvrable than a smaller aircraft like the Hudson, so its attack was comparatively slow and predictable. The Germans had also changed their tactics and instead of diving to avoid attacking aircraft, they were now armed with a significant battery of defensive guns in order to disrupt air attack and to prevent an aircraft from making an accurate run.[33]

U-468 was a smaller submarine of about 500 tons commanded by Oberleutnant zur See Klemens Schamong. It was his first command and it had not gone well. They had reached their patrol area from France without incident, but had made no attacks. They were only returning to base now because their resupply vessel, U-462, had been sunk in transit. Schamong's crew saw the Liberator in plenty of time to prepare themselves. While Trigg radioed his intention to attack, he commenced his descent from the patrol height of 6000 feet to the required attack altitude of 150 feet, but this took about four minutes.[34] After this nothing more was heard from the Liberator. A search was mounted the next morning that soon located seven men in a Liberator's rubber dinghy. A day later a British destroyer picked up the castaways, but in a twist of irony they were the captain and some crewmembers of the U-boat. They provided the description of the attack.

Schamong reported: 'It required courage I never thought I would see.' Having sighted the aircraft before it made its attack, they were ready to open fire when the Liberator came within 1000 metres. Their fire was accurate and they made hits along the aircraft's wing and tail, so that the fuselage burst into flames and one port engine was set ablaze. The Germans even saw their tracer rounds passing straight through the airframe. Blazing from hull to tail, the plane did not deviate from its route or fire on the submarine. Then, when it was 50 metres overhead, the Liberator released its load before flying straight on for a short distance and crashing into the sea.[35] The aircraft could have tried to evade, or attempt to ditch at sea once it was first hit, but Trigg had pressed home his attack regardless of the danger.

Oberleutnant Schamong and several of his crew were thrown into the sea or escaped the rapidly sinking U-boat. When they surfaced they found the Liberator's rescue dinghy, which had apparently broken loose when the aircraft impacted. It was on the basis of the testimony of Klemens Schamong, from his debrief of the action, that Lloyd Trigg was awarded the VC.

LLOYD ALLAN TRIGG

Lloyd Allan Trigg was born at Houhora near Auckland on 5 May 1914. His father, a farmer, was English but his mother was a New Zealander. He was educated at Whangarei High School where he was both a good student and a good sportsman. He had some military experience where he evidently displayed leadership, having been the company sergeant major in the School Cadets and also becoming a non-commissioned officer in the Mounted Rifles. When the war commenced he was working as a salesman and lived at Hamua, near Pahiatua, with his wife and two young sons. As a slightly older man with responsibilities, he did not join up until 1941.

Trigg chose the air force because he had always been interested in aviation. When he left for war he promised his wife he 'would not go looking for decorations'.[36] His squadron mates recorded that he hated the Germans and wanted to get the job done and go home.[37] Other reports in his personal file record that he was 'an above average pilot, inclined to be slow absorbing knowledge, but working extremely hard to achieve very good results'.[38] As early as his ground training he was noted for his marked keenness and he was recommended for a commission. Trigg initially trained in New Zealand before being sent to Branton, Manitoba, in Canada, under the Empire Air Training Scheme. By the time he left Canada to join RAF Coastal Command in October 1942, he had been promoted to flying officer and was the captain of a Hudson crew.

Trigg was posted to 200 Squadron on the West African coast and arrived there in January 1943. After numerous patrols he first engaged a U-boat in March, straddling its track with depth charges. Two days later he attacked another and is reported to have actually managed to hit it on its bow. For these actions and his consistent effort, on 16 June 1943, he was awarded the DFC. His commanding officer reported: 'During the course of a fine operational career this officer has set a conspicuously good example of keenness to fly under all conditions.'[39] As one of the squadron's more effective aircraft commanders, Trigg was therefore selected to be one of the first to do conversion training on the new Liberators and to ferry one to the unit from America.

The announcement of Lloyd Trigg's award of the VC was gazetted on 2 November 1943. In the message notifying this to New Zealand, the RNZAF liaison office in London also informed the government that his status should now be recorded as 'Missing believed killed'.[40] At his wife's request, special arrangements were made for the Governor to present her husband's posthumous award to her at home in the Victoria Valley, so that as many as possible of Trigg's family and friends could be present. This was done on 27 May 1944. Lloyd Trigg's medal group, including the VC and DFC, was sold by the family and is now in a private collection in the United Kingdom.[41]

Lloyd Trigg's VC is both unusual and important for several reasons. It is unusual as it is the only known case where the award was to all intents and purposes based solely on the testimony of enemy combatants. Oberleutnant Schamong and his first lieutenant, Leutnant Heimannsberg, provided the key eyewitness statements. Trigg's VC is the second for a New Zealander, after Sanders, for sinking a submarine, but the first for doing so from the air. His was also the last act by a New Zealander to be recognised by the award of a VC in the Second World War. Consequently, of greatest significance, this means that Lloyd Trigg's is the last-ever VC that a member of the New Zealand armed forces will ever win under the British administration of the award. Whenever New Zealand service personnel face the enemy in future wars or conflict situations, they are now eligible for gallantry awards that are specific to New Zealand, headed by the Victoria Cross of New Zealand. Lloyd Trigg is therefore the last of the list of New Zealanders recognised by the British with the award of Victoria Cross 'For Valour', that had started with Charles Heaphy only 79 years earlier.

CHAPTER 14 The George Cross and Albert Medal[1]

A s the previous chapters have explained and illustrated, the Victoria Cross was, from its inception, for valour in the presence of the enemy. In its earlier days, awards were frequently made for saving the lives of comrades, as in all three cases where it was awarded to New Zealanders in the nineteenth century. However, the problem existed throughout of how to recognise acts of bravery which were equally meritorious but where no enemy were involved. The latter was not, of course, solely a military problem, as many acts worthy of recognition occurred in civil life as well. There was a brief period, between 1858 and 1881, where the rules of the VC were structured to specifically allow awards for acts of bravery not in the presence of the enemy. However, only six such awards were made in 1866 and 1867. The first was in 1866 to Private Daniel O'Hea in recognition of his bravery for removing ammunition from a railway carriage that was on fire at Danville Station, Quebec. O'Hea subsequently served in the New Zealand militia. The remaining five such VCs were all awarded the next year for the one incident in the Andaman Islands, where members of the 24th Regiment (of Rourke's Drift fame) rescued colleagues through heavy surf, in the belief their lives were threatened by hostile tribesmen. These cases were deemed exceptional and also unsatisfactory from the perspective of administering the VC, so the warrant of 1881 was tightened to specifically preclude further such awards.[2]

The problem of how to recognise acts of bravery in non-warlike situations therefore persisted. Queen Victoria herself recognised this issue and in a warrant dated March 1866 instituted a gold medal for saving life at sea. She named this the Albert Medal after her husband, the Prince Consort. The next year, a further warrant created a bronze medal as a second class to this award. In 1877 the award was further developed so that the specific element of saving life at sea was removed, allowing the recognition of acts on land, but retaining the requirement to save life. Although the Albert Medal did not have a high precedence or profile, it was accepted that it rated as a civil equivalent of the VC. The medal is an oval shape, surmounted by a crown and suspended from a red and white striped ribbon. The centre of the oval has an intertwined capital A and V, and is surrounded by a heraldic belt containing a motto. On the medals awarded at sea the motto is 'for saving life at sea' and an anchor is incorporated into the A and V, while the land award has no additional motif and the motto is 'for saving life on land'.

On 24 September 1940, King George VI approved a warrant to institute the George Cross. This medal was placed behind the VC and ahead of all other awards, to recognise acts of the greatest heroism or of the most conspicuous courage in circumstances of extreme danger, where a military award would not be appropriate. This award was specifically intended to be predominantly for civilians and one of the most famous instances of its conferral was that made to the island of Malta in 1942. The design of this medal is a simple silver cross, with each arm of equal width. In the centre is a circular disc, showing St George slaying the dragon, with the words 'for gallantry' around the outside of this. On the outside of the disc and between each arm of the cross is a stylised G with the roman numerals VI inside, in recognition of the King. The medal is suspended from a plain blue ribbon, essentially the one previously worn by naval holders of the VC.

The creation of the George Cross caused some confusion over the status of the Albert Medal. The new warrant cancelled the Empire Gallantry Medal (EGM), which had been created in 1922, and directed that these awards be exchanged for the George Cross. The EGM was rated junior to the Albert Medal in precedence, but had now been made the equivalent of a George Cross, itself superior to the Albert Medal. In 1949 the King further directed that the Gold Award should cease and that the Albert Medal could only be awarded posthumously. Finally, on 21 October 1971, it was announced that the Albert Medal was to cease and that all surviving holders of the award would be required to exchange them for the George Cross, and warrants to that effect were produced at the end of the year.

It is not the purpose of this book to deal comprehensively with either the Albert Medal or the George Cross. However, as the non-combat equivalents of the Victoria Cross for acts of supreme valour it is appropriate that those awards made to military men deserve mention in this work. Three servicemen were awarded the Albert Medal, two in the First World War and one in the Second World War. Only three New Zealanders have ever been awarded the George Cross. All three awards were posthumous and two were to serving soldiers. The stories of each follow in chronological order of their act of gallantry.

James Werner Magnusson

The first New Zealand soldier to be awarded the Albert Medal for saving a life at sea was actually a soldier who had been born in Sweden. James Werner Magnusson was a 22-year-old merchant seaman, who joined the Auckland Mounted Rifles (AMR) at the outbreak of the First World War and served at Gallipoli. He was on the peninsula from the landing of the AMR until September, when he was evacuated with severe dysentery. He returned in November 1915 and was evacuated with the remainder of the Anzacs in December.

The AMR remained in Palestine as part of the New Zealand Mounted Rifles (NZMR) under Brigadier Edward Chaytor, when Major General Russell took the remainder of the New Zealand Division to France in 1916. Magnusson remained unwell and spent further time in hospital, before joining the Mounted Rifles training unit. On 16 May 1916 he was court martialled on charges of casting away his rifle and using insubordinate and threatening language to a superior while on active duty. The circumstances appear to be that on 13 May 1916 he was part of the guard of the camp, but took offence when the orderly officer questioned him as to his duties.[3] Having recounted what he did and said, Corporal Hanham stated that he had known Magnusson eight months, having served with him on Gallipoli, that he had done good work at Hill 60 as a bomber, and that Magnusson's weakness was a lack of self-control. He was sentenced to a year's detention, or military imprisonment. Three months of the sentence was later remitted.

Magnusson was returned to New Zealand to serve his sentence at Featherston and in Dunedin. At the end of his detention he was posted to the 21st Reinforcements in December 1916 and sailed with them the next month for England. From there, on 19 April 1917, he joined a draft of 36 men to rejoin the AMR in Egypt, along with some 4000 others aboard HMT *Transylvania*. On 4 May 1917, off the coast of Italy, the ship was torpedoed by a German submarine.

The NZMR draft commander, Lieutenant W.G. Lyons, forwarded a report of what then happened. Knowing that Magnusson was a seaman, he had tasked him to assist with getting some of the lifeboats away. Magnusson then saw a man who had fallen in the water and was in trouble. He promptly jumped into the water himself and swam to the drowning man in the very rough seas. He effected a rescue by getting the man into a lifeboat, before returning to the ship itself and reporting back to Lieutenant Lyons. His action was witnessed by several officers and he was later recommended for an award. However, the *Transylvania* sunk 50 minutes after she was struck and, despite the efforts of naval vessels, 413 people were lost at sea, including James Magnusson.

On 8 March 1918 a notice appeared in the *London Gazette* that James Werner Magnusson had been posthumously awarded the Albert Medal. This made him New Zealand's first-ever Albert Medallist. His father, however, still lived in Sweden and therefore his decoration and war medals were all forwarded to him there as next of kin.

Randolph Gordon Ridling

Nearly a year later, on 19 April 1918, at Brocton Camp in England, Randolph Ridling became the second New Zealand serviceman to be awarded the Albert Medal. Before joining the New Zealand Rifle Brigade in December 1915, Ridling had been a school teacher, having been educated at Auckland Grammar School and Auckland University College. Obviously a man of some aptitude, he was almost immediately made a corporal and within two months was a sergeant major; he was commissioned in May 1916. He was posted overseas in October 1916 with the 18th Reinforcements. Finally joining a rifle company in France as a platoon commander on 17 February 1917, Ridling had a brief tour at the front as he was severely wounded only four days later.[4] Even though he spent five months being treated and recuperating before returning to Sling Camp, his wounds had not healed and he required further treatment. After this Ridling was retained in Brocton Camp as a bombing instructor.

It was evidently a cold day on 19 April 1918, but instruction had to proceed, and after initial lessons a number of the men had successfully thrown the Mills bomb. Then Rifleman J.A. McCurdy came into the bay to throw his bombs. The witnesses at the subsequent court of inquiry described him as nervous and inattentive, while he himself said he was cold. Regardless of the reason, having pulled the safety pin on his grenade when instructed to do so, McCurdy then fumbled it, dropping the armed bomb inside the bay. McCurdy panicked and dived away from Ridling to the corner of the bay. Ridling had to move across the bay and bodily lift the cowering man, who fought him as he was dragged out of his corner and even kicked the grenade towards the entrance in his panic. Ridling had acted with sufficient speed and force, however, that he managed to get McCurdy out and was himself exiting the bay when the grenade exploded behind him. McCurdy was only slightly wounded, but Ridling received several shrapnel wounds in his groin.[5] Brigadier General George Richardson,[6] in charge of NZEF administration and training in

England, recommended Ridling for the Albert Medal and notice of its approval appeared in the *London Gazette* on 19 December 1919.

Ridling received his award from the King at Buckingham Palace, by which time he had completed his service with the NZEF and taken up a scholarship at Cambridge University. Before this he had been an acting captain, working as an education officer and dealing with troops before they were demobilised and returned to New Zealand. After the war, Randolph Ridling returned to teaching and eventually became the director of the Wellington Technical College, from where he retired in 1950. In 1971 he made a special request not to exchange his Albert Medal for the George Cross, on the grounds of its high sentimental value, which was approved. Randolph Ridling died in Wellington on 13 January 1975 and his medals are on display at the Queen Elizabeth II Army Memorial Museum in Waiouru.

DONALD WILLIAM DALE

The third and last New Zealand serviceman to be awarded the Albert Medal was Stoker First Class Donald William Dale of Timaru. Only a 17-year-old farm labourer at the outbreak of war, Dale, like many other under-age men keen to get away, employed the traditional mechanism of falsifying his age in order to join up early in 1940. Despite getting into the army, circumstances seemed to prevent him getting away, so that on 20 May 1942 he transferred to the navy, now giving his correct age. After several months' training, in November 1942 he was drafted to the crew of HMS *Achilles*, then under repair in Portsmouth.

This repair work was still continuing when, on 22 June 1943, there was a major explosion below decks in one of the main fuel tanks. The explosion killed 14 men and caused significant structural damage, as well as filling the vessel with thick, acrid smoke. A number of surviving workmen below decks were stunned and unable to find their way out to safety. Even men with breathing apparatus were overcome in the rescue attempts.

Dale was among a large number of the ship's company who joined the rescue efforts. Because all the breathing apparatus sets were in use, Dale's only aid was a handkerchief tied across his face. Regardless of this he managed to get down two decks and entered a smoke-filled compartment, not even knowing what condition it was in, in order to bring out four men whose cries for help he could hear. Not content with this effort, after a brief rest Dale moved to another section of the ship and this time had himself lowered three deck levels to the tank where the original explosion had taken place. To get around the distorted structures he had to wriggle into spaces he could only guess at because of the dark and the remaining smoke. Essentially he was working by feel alone to move towards the sounds made by the injured men. On one occasion he is known to have dropped through a hatch off a ladder, not knowing if there was anything below on which to land safely. In this second descent into the mutilated ship he managed, with assistance, to hoist out another two men.[7] For these actions Dale was gazetted with the Albert Medal on 23 November 1943. He was to have received his medal from the King, but his ship was forced to sail the day before the investiture, so it was finally presented in Christchurch on 11 November 1946 by the new Governor-General of New Zealand, Sir Bernard Freyberg, VC.

As the repairs to *Achilles* took time, Dale joined most of the crew when they took over HMS *Gambia* and he served on this ship until November 1945. During this time he saw active service in the Pacific, and HMS *Gambia* was part of the allied fleet present to witness the formal Japanese surrender in Tokyo Bay. Discharged in March 1946, Dale returned to South Canterbury where he eventually ran his own successful contracting business. In 1953 he briefly rejoined the Royal New Zealand Navy as a leading stoker aboard HMS *Black Prince* in order to be part of the New Zealand Coronation Contingent. Donald William Dale died suddenly at Waimate on 28 October 1969, aged only 47.

DAVID GEORGE RUSSELL

David Russell was in fact a Scot, who arrived in New Zealand in 1938, aged 27. He was working as a hospital orderly in Napier Hospital when war broke out a year later and he volunteered immediately. Called forward for training in January 1940, Russell left New Zealand with the Second Echelon. He was posted to the 22nd Battalion and fought with them in Greece and Crete, before serving in the Western Desert. He was wounded in the fighting on Ruweisat Ridge on 14 July 1942 and was among the large number of New Zealand troops captured there.

Russell was eventually moved to Campo PG 57 in Italy, north of Trieste, from which he successfully escaped when the Italians surrendered. He remained at large in the rear of the German forces and took the lead role in organising assistance and movement for other escapees through to Yugoslavia, despite only holding the rank of lance corporal. Eventually he was recaptured, but escaped again, this time from Campo PG 103 near Udine, along with several other servicemen.

At this stage in the war, the general Italian population were increasingly hostile to the Germans and many were quite willing to shelter and assist Allied escapees. Russell was taken in by Guiseppe Vettorello and his family, given clothing and shelter. Russell became part of the local community and again started organising other escapees, moving between groups by bicycle. However, on 22 February 1945 his luck again ran out and he was caught by Italian fascist troops still loyal to the Germans. His capture occurred in the vicinity of Vettorello's home, though it is believed he was trying to lead them away from it when he was caught. Nevertheless, Vettorello was also arrested by the fascists.

The young lance corporal was taken to the German command post, where he was vigorously interrogated in the hope he would firmly implicate Vettorello. Russell denied ever meeting the man, even after severe beatings and also remained silent regarding any other escapees or members of the resistance. Eventually the German commander, Oberleutnant Haupt, threatened that if

Russell did not confess he would be shot as a spy in three days and, to lend credence to the threat, Haupt had him chained to the stable wall.

Even now the beatings continued, but Russell remained resolute and said nothing. Haupt's interpreter subsequently stated that Russell's bearing won even his persecutor's admiration. An Italian civilian, tasked to take him food, urged Russell to save himself, but he only replied 'let them shoot me'. Haupt maintained his word and on the third day, 28 February 1945, at Ponte di Piave, Lance Corporal David Russell was executed by a firing squad.[8] The German warrant officer in charge stated: 'The prisoner died very bravely!' With Russell having maintained his silence to the end, the fascists had insufficient evidence against Vettorello and he was subsequently released.

Immediately after the war, Russell's story came to the attention of Middle Eastern Command and it was followed up thoroughly by the Mediterranean Special Investigation Branch in April 1945,[9] the information gathered forming part of the evidence in subsequent war crimes trials. As a result several credible eyewitness accounts were available. Their summation was that Russell 'in preferring death to dishonour, virtually surrendering his life to the ransom of the many, and that a more outstanding example of self-immolation in the face of extreme peril cannot be conceived'. Russell's body had been retrieved by the villagers of Ponte di Piave, who had buried it under a substantial memorial and they were not pleased when he was subsequently re-interred at the Commonwealth War Cemetery at Udine.

After the full story of Russell's gallantry and self-sacrifice came to light, a recommendation for the George Cross was initiated by army headquarters in New Zealand. On 24 December 1948 this award was published in the *London Gazette*. The medal was subsequently presented to Russell's father, by the King, on 26 July 1949. New Zealand's first George Cross was therefore personally presented by the sovereign after whom it was named. Of Russell's courage there can be no doubt, as it was intimately and premeditatedly in the presence of the enemy, over a period of days, in a way that no other award recorded in this book reflects. In previous periods Russell's gallantry may well have qualified him for the VC, but as his act did not occur within the context of an actual combat situation, as was then required to be eligible for that decoration, he had to be recognised with another award. David Russell was therefore the first New Zealander to be honoured with this new, non-combat decoration, of only very slightly less precedence but no less distinction than the VC.

MURRAY KEN HUDSON

The second New Zealander to receive the George Cross was Sergeant Ken Hudson of Opotiki. Of Maori descent and a regular soldier of 13 years' experience, he had seen active service with the infantry in Malaysia and Vietnam, as well as having served with the Special Air Service (SAS) in Borneo. A soldier of notable presence and physique, as a private he had been chosen to be the model for a regimental silver statuette being made for the 1st Battalion, Royal New Zealand Infantry Regiment (RNZIR). In 1974 he was serving as a member of the cadre staff attached to 7 RNZIR, a New Zealand Army Territorial Force infantry battalion drawn from Wellington and the Hawke's Bay, where he worked from Masterton.

On 13 February 1974 elements of 7 RNZIR were training in Waiouru and Sergeant Hudson was helping supervise a live grenade-throwing exercise. He was the throwing bay NCO and his friend, Sergeant Graham Fergusson, was the thrower. As he was taking Fergusson through the drill, Hudson became aware that the other NCO had already, in some way, armed the grenade. Perhaps it was a case of familiarity leading to inattention, but the result was that the grenade was now live. With short seconds to act, Hudson was heard to order Fergusson to throw immediately, but as this was not within the sequence of the drill the man expected to follow, he did not respond. Hudson then grabbed Fergusson's throwing hand, still holding the grenade, in both of his. In this way Hudson attempted to bodily throw the grenade himself, or at least get it over the parapet of the throwing bay, because he was aware what effect the weapon would have in the enclosed space of the bay. It is said that he was within inches of success, the difference between injury and death, when the grenade exploded. He could have saved himself when Fergusson disobeyed the order to throw, but he chose to remain and try to save his friend.

Like Riddling nearly 56 years earlier, Ken Hudson had about four seconds in which to make his decision and act, but he was not so lucky. When the grenade exploded, both he and Fergusson were killed instantly. There was no doubt regarding this selfless act above the call of duty as Hudson tried to save his fellow NCO, and he was recommended for the George Cross. The award was announced in New Zealand on 23 September 1974, but was published in the *New Zealand Gazette* on 26 September 1974, and the *London Gazette* a fortnight later on 11 October 1974. Sergeant Hudson's widow, Shona, received the medal from the Governor-General, Sir Denis Blundell (who as a member of Freyberg's staff had investigated the case for Manahi's VC recommendation in 1942) at Government House, Wellington, on 11 December 1974. All Sergeant Hudson's medals and his George Cross are on display at the Queen Elizabeth II Army Memorial Museum in Waiouru.

FOR THE SAVING OF LIFE

The common element to these five awards was thus the attempted saving of life, at extreme risk to one's own. It is therefore not surprising that most of the awards, including the first (Magnusson) and last (Hudson) were posthumous, but only Russell met his death as the direct result of enemy actions. The first New Zealand recipients of both the Albert Medal and the George Cross were foreign born: Magnusson in Sweden and Russell in Scotland. The remaining three men were native New Zealanders, with Hudson being Maori. Hudson thus joins those brave men of his race, recognised for their courage, including Ngarimu and Rhodes-

Moorhouse with the VC as well as Rapata, Te Keepa and Ahururu, who had all won the NZC. This last point is an interesting one, because it highlights a circular development. The five military men in this chapter will be the only New Zealanders recognised for their gallantry in non-combat situations by this system of honours and awards. Since 1999, the supreme award for gallantry for a New Zealander, other than in combat, is now the New Zealand Cross.

CONCLUSION: Ordinary men, extraordinary deeds

I n the early morning of 27 November 1941, the men of 5 Brigade headquarters, encamped around Sidi Azeiz in the Libyan desert, began to prepare breakfast. It was to be a breakfast that was never eaten, because just after 7.00 a.m. came news that 40 German tanks were approaching from the direction of Bardia. Before the headquarters could signal this unwelcome news to the division, the first German shells began falling on them. The men manned their defensive positions in a vain attempt to repel the armoured surge heading their way.

Amongst the defenders were four two-pounder anti-tank gun crews of the 7th Anti-tank Regiment with their small, ineffectual guns still hitched on the lorries that carried them. The four gun portees were driven to a slight rise some 200 yards beyond the brigade's defensive perimeter where they took up firing positions. From these exposed positions the four guns opened fire on the approaching tanks at a distance of about 1200 yards. While they hit some of the approaching tanks, most of their shells bounced harmlessly off the German armoured machines. The four anti-tank guns soon attracted the fire of nearly all of the tanks from ranges in excess of 1000 yards and soon all of the guns had received a direct hit. But as the official history of the campaign states, the anti-tank gunners kept fighting:

> Knowing full well the odds were hopeless, the gunners nevertheless carried out their drill in parade-ground order and the No. 1 of P4, Bombardier Niven, gave his orders quietly and calmly, allowing three rounds for each tank engaged, until the gun was hit and its traversing and elevating gears wrecked.[1]

When all the guns were hit and with most of the gunners now casualties, the unhurt Bombardier Michael Niven walked calmly around all the guns, collecting the wounded, who he drove to the ADS. When he had completed this task, Niven drove the lorry with the one serviceable gun back into action, which just happened to be in front of Brigadier Hargest's slit trench. Brigadier Hargest watched 'in wonder and admiration' as Niven single-handedly engaged the advancing tanks at close range, undertaking the work of four men to do so.[2] Niven's actions brought down a mass of fire on him and the truck and gun were hit, the third shell putting the gun out of action for good. But Niven's actions did not end there. He slid down from the burning truck, made his way to the nearest artillery piece in action and assisted the gun crew there until that gun was also damaged by shellfire. Then Niven assisted a Bofors crew until that gun was also put out of action and he was fighting with E Troop of 5 Field Regiment in the final stand of Hargest's headquarters. It was an impressive display of cool courage under fire, which as Hargest later wrote 'in other times would certainly have been rewarded'.[3]

Alas, it was not to be, and Niven's gallantry at Sidi Azeiz received no recognition at all. Yet this was not the end of Bombardier Niven's war and his further acts of incredible bravery. Taken prisoner at Sidi Azeiz, Niven was taken to Bardia but did not remain there for long. Because he had volunteered to undertake medical duties for the prisoners, Niven was sent to Italy and later to Germany. While a POW, Bombardier Niven made several escape attempts, at one point reaching Czechoslovakia where the Gestapo unluckily picked him up during a routine street check.[4] He suffered torture at their hands and remained in a Gestapo prison for two months before being transferred back to a POW camp. This experience still did not stop him. He escaped again on 1 April 1945 and made his way westward until he eventually reached the advancing allied armies.[5]

The odd thing is that despite Niven's gallantry at Sidi Azeiz being witnessed by several officers, including Brigadier Hargest, and its being recorded in the official history of the campaign, Bombardier

Michael Niven was not recommended for, nor did he receive, a single gallantry award. He was not even mentioned in despatches for his escape attempts.[6] Niven's case highlights a point raised in the introduction and one of the recurring themes of this book — that all gallantry awards are an unfair lottery. Tremendous acts of courage — like Niven at Sidi Azeiz, like Sergeant Kenrick in the New Zealand Wars, like Bassett's fellow signallers on Gallipoli — went unrecognised and unrewarded. It is one of the fortunes of war.

This inequity is especially prevalent for the VC award. A successful VC requires an act of gallantry to be witnessed, investigated by a commissioned officer, and written up so that it meets the requirements of the prevailing warrant. It must then pass successfully through several layers of military command and various committees until it finally reaches the sovereign for his or her approval. Unfortunately, as this book has shown, these approving authorities were rarely free from prejudice and misunderstanding, which has often had an adverse effect on the approval process. That New Zealand military personnel have been the victims of this complex process is clear, although more often than not it has been the New Zealand military authorities who have been responsible for this.

There is little doubt too that the VC has become progressively harder and harder to win. Since the Boer War, no New Zealander has won the VC for saving life under extreme danger, for which so many of the earlier VCs were given. The awards of the double VC winners — Dr Noel Chavasse (a distant cousin of Charles Upham) and Arthur Martin-Leake — and of the New Zealanders Heaphy, D'Arcy and Hardham all fell into this category. Instead, the exacting standards of the various warrants have been raised even higher so that the VC is now only awarded in the most extreme of combat situations, usually for aggressive action against the odds, where one's chance of surviving the VC action are slim indeed. In contravention of Queen Victoria's original intention, the VC has now become an award for the dead as much as for the living. Posthumous awards, originally not covered in the VC warrant, are now prevalent when VCs are awarded. These trends appeared to be well entrenched when both VC awards made in the Falklands campaign of 1982 were made posthumously to soldiers killed while directly assaulting the enemy. However, the latest VC, awarded to Private Johnson Beharry, from the 1st Battalion, the Princess of Wales's Royal Regiment, was given for saving the lives of 30 comrades in Iraq. This is in line with the older trend of recognising those who rescue their comrades under fire. Thankfully, Private Beharry survived his act of gallantry, making him the first living soldier to receive the VC since 1969.[7]

It is to be hoped that a New Zealand service member behaving in a similar way would be recognised in the same manner. As this most recent award should make clear, where the act is one of supreme gallantry in a direct combat situation, the VC is the most appropriate form of recognition. Where there is no direct enemy threat, then an act of bravery is best recognised by other awards, especially the NZC. The key tests remain the standard of the act of gallantry and the presence of the enemy.

This does not imply that those New Zealanders who did win the VC did not deserve them. Rather, it implies that there should have been more of them. All of the New Zealanders who won the VC deserved to do so. Looking at their feats of valour it is clear that these were ordinary men doing extraordinary deeds. This was something that Keith Elliott, who was also taken POW at Sidi Azeiz along with Bombardier Niven, admitted in an interview just weeks before his death:

> You see I don't think people who win the Victoria Cross are very different. When you're a sergeant, as I was, you have an added responsibility. The other fellows are pushing you, if you like. You can't falter or show you're afraid . . . courage has got nothing to do with war, but with life.[8]

And being ordinary men who experienced fear, hesitation and self-doubt during combat, and post-traumatic stress after it, makes their achievements even more remarkable.

There are some strong similarities amongst the New Zealand VC winners. With the exceptions of Ngarimu and Ward, they were all older, more mature men. Only Nicholas and Crichton were private soldiers, although Crichton had previously served in a different unit as a warrant officer and Nicholas was later promoted to sergeant. The rest were predominantly senior NCOs and junior officers, those men upon whom the burden of leadership on the battlefield falls. There is certainly something in Elliott's suggestion above that these men were pushed on to their great deeds of valour by those they were leading in battle. With the exception of Trent, who had secured a short-service commission with the RAF, all were non-regular, citizen soldiers or airmen.

The VC winners who returned to New Zealand faced a difficult period of adjustment. While all returning service personnel faced problems fitting back into society, the VC winners faced additional burdens. They were war heroes in a very small country where it was almost impossible to hide. The publicity spotlight was forever turned their way and most were uncomfortable with it. Upham, the double VC winner, experienced this unwelcome attention more than any other VC winner, and it is little wonder that he sought refuge from it on a remote farm in North Canterbury. But all the VC winners experienced it to some degree. Keith Elliott spoke of the strain of 'one engagement after another' as 'an ordeal for which I was unprepared'. He dreamed of escaping this ordeal, even though he knew he had no chance of doing so:

On occasions, even to this day, I wistfully indulge in the dream that VC holders should be given a home on a remote island with a special 'OC' — that is, 'Out of Circulation' — pension. That would be a far more comfortable life than having to cope with people who put one in a little niche as someone special, overlooking that one is an ordinary man doing ordinary things. If I try to remember that, why cannot they?[9]

While they were all ordinary men, their extraordinary deeds in the presence of the enemy had been recognised and they had been given the highest of gallantry awards. This fact marked them apart in New Zealand. It unfortunately meant they had to live with the legends they had created in a small country hungry for heroes. Unwelcome, intrusive publicity was to become a noticeable feature of their post-war lives.

It is now more than 60 years since a New Zealander has won the VC. If another 60 years are to pass before it is awarded again the decoration may come to lack relevance for this country. There is little point in having a gallantry award on the books that no one in the country is good enough to win.

As stated at the very start of this book, the VC is a special gallantry decoration. Its special nature ensures that any award of the VC instantly becomes an important part of a nation's military heritage. It also becomes part of a much wider heritage of the British Commonwealth of Nations. Sadly, for too long New Zealand neglected the military aspect of its history, although this is currently changing. People have come to recognise that New Zealand's military heritage is also a vital part of their family history, and that seeking knowledge of the military past does not equate to a liking for war or ignoring the pain and suffering it causes.

There is a definite resurgence of interest in New Zealand's military heritage. Witness the young New Zealanders flocking to Gallipoli every Anzac Day, for example, or the growing crowds at the dawn services around the country. It is also evident in the large number of books that have recently appeared on New Zealand's military history and which seem to enjoy considerable popularity. While we still have some way to go, most New Zealanders are aware that the nation has a long, proud military heritage, one that is well worth preserving.

An important part of this heritage is New Zealand's association with the Victoria Cross and those who won this highest of gallantry awards. While most New Zealanders have heard of Charles Upham, the most famous of the VC winners, few could name many more of this nation's VC holders. This is unfortunate because the gallant deeds of all New Zealand's VC winners should not be forgotten. We hope this book will ensure that this does not happen.

Rank and name:	Major Charles Heaphy
Unit:	Auckland Militia, NZ Military Forces
Date of act of bravery:	11 February 1864
Theatre of war:	Waikato, New Zealand

For his gallant conduct at the skirmish on the banks of the Mangapiko River, in New Zealand, on 11 February 1864, in assisting a wounded soldier of the 40th Regiment, who had fallen into a hollow amongst the thickest of the concealed Maoris. Whilst so doing he became the target for a volley at a few feet distant. Five balls pierced his clothes and cap, and he was wounded in three places. Although hurt, he continued to aid the wounded until the end of the day. Major Heaphy was at the time in charge of a party of soldiers of the 40th and 50th Regiments, under the orders of Lieutenant Colonel Sir Henry Marsham Havelock, Bart., C.B., V.C., the senior officer on the spot, who had moved rapidly down to the place where the troops were hotly engaged and pressed.

London Gazette, 8 February 1867

Rank and name:	Captain Henry Cecil Dudgeon D'Arcy
Unit:	Cape Frontier Light Horse, South African Forces
Date of act of bravery:	3 July 1879
Theatre of war:	South Africa

For his gallant conduct on the 3rd July, 1879, during the reconnaissance made before Ulundi by the Mounted Corps, in endeavouring to rescue Trooper Raubenheim of the Frontier Light Horse, who fell from his horse as the troops were retiring. Captain D'Arcy, though the Zulus were close upon them, waited for the man to mount behind him; the horse kicked them both off, and though much hurt by the fall and quite alone, Captain D'Arcy coolly endeavoured to lift the trooper, who was stunned, on to the horse, and it was only when he found that he had not the strength to do so that he mounted and rode off.

His escape was miraculous as the Zulus had actually closed upon him.

London Gazette, 10 October 1879

Rank and name:	1251 Farrier Sergeant Major William James Hardham
Unit:	Fourth New Zealand Contingent
Date of act of bravery:	28 January 1901
Theatre of war:	South Africa

On 28 January 1901, near Naauwpoort, this non-commissioned officer was with a section which was extended and hotly engaged with a party of about twenty Boers. Just before the force commenced to retire Trooper McRae was wounded, and his horse killed. Farrier Sergeant Major Hardham at once went, under a heavy fire, to his assistance, dismounted, and placed him on his own horse, and ran alongside until he had guided him to a place of safety.

London Gazette, 4 October 1901

Rank and name:	Second Lieutenant William Barnard Rhodes-Moorhouse
Unit:	2 Squadron, Royal Flying Corps
Date of act of bravery:	26 April 1915
Theatre of war:	Air operations, France

For most conspicuous bravery on 26 April 1915, in flying to Courtrai and dropping bombs on the railway line near that station. On starting the return journey he was mortally wounded, but, succeeded in flying 35 miles to his destination, at a very low altitude, and reported the successful accomplishment of his object. He has since died of his wounds.

London Gazette, 22 May 1915

Rank and name:	4/515 Corporal Cyril Royston Guyton Bassett
Unit:	New Zealand Divisional Signal Company, NZEF
Date of act of bravery:	7 August 1915
Theatre of war:	Gallipoli

For most conspicuous bravery and devotion to duty, on the Chunuk Bair ridge in the Gallipoli Peninsula on 7 August 1915. After the N.Z. Infantry Brigade had attacked and established itself on the ridge Corporal Bassett in full daylight and under a continuous and heavy fire succeeded in laying a telephone line from the old position to the new one on Chunuk Bair. He has subsequently been brought to notice for further excellent and most gallant work connected with the repair of telephone lines by day and night under heavy fire.

London Gazette, 15 October 1915

Rank and name:	Captain Alfred John Shout
Unit:	1st Battalion, Australian Imperial Force
Date of act of bravery:	9 August 1915
Theatre of war:	Lone Pine, Gallipoli

For most conspicuous bravery at Lone Pine trenches, in the Gallipoli Peninsula.

On the morning of the 9th August, 1915, with a very small party Captain Shout charged down trenches strongly occupied by the enemy, and personally threw four bombs among them, killing eight and routing the remainder.

In the afternoon of the same day, from the position gained in the morning, he captured a further length of trench under similar conditions, and continued personally to bomb the enemy at close range under very heavy fire until he was severely wounded, losing his right hand and left eye.

This most gallant officer has since succumbed to his injuries.

London Gazette, 15 October 1915

Rank and name:	No. 3055 Private Thomas Cooke
Unit:	8th Battalion, Australian Imperial Force
Date of act of bravery:	24–25 July 1916
Theatre of war:	Pozieres, France

For most conspicuous bravery. After a Lewis gun had been disabled, he was ordered to take his gun and gun-team to a dangerous part of the line. Here he did fine work, but came under very heavy fire, with the result that finally he was the only man left. He still stuck to his post, and continued to fire his gun.

When assistance was sent he was found dead beside his gun. He set a splendid example of determination and devotion to duty.

London Gazette, 9 September 1916

Rank and name:	8/3504 Sergeant Donald Forrester Brown
Unit:	2nd Battalion, Otago Infantry Regiment
Date of act of bravery:	15 September 1916
Theatre of war:	High Wood, France

For most conspicuous bravery and determination in attack when the company to which he belonged suffered very heavy casualties in officers and men from machine gun fire. At great personal risk this NCO advanced with a comrade and succeeded in reaching a point within thirty yards of the enemy guns. Four of the gun crew were killed and captured. The advance of the company was continued till it was again held up by machine gun fire. Again Sergeant Brown and his comrade with great gallantry rushed the gun and killed the crew. After this second position had been won the company came under very heavy shell fire, and the utter contempt for danger and coolness under fire of this NCO did much to keep up the spirit of his men. On a subsequent occasion in attack Sergeant Brown showed most conspicuous gallantry. He attacked single-handed a machine gun which was holding up the attack, killed the gun crew and captured the gun. Later, whilst sniping the retreating enemy, this very gallant soldier was killed.

London Gazette, 12 June 1917

Rank and name:	Captain, Temporary Lieutenant Colonel Bernard Cyril Freyberg
Unit:	Queens Royal Regiment (West Surrey), Commanding Hood Battalion, Royal Naval Division
Date of act of bravery:	13 November 1916
Theatre of war:	Beaucourt sur l'Ancre, France

For most conspicuous bravery and brilliant leading as a battalion commander. By his splendid personal gallantry he carried the initial attack straight through the enemy's front system of trenches. Owing to mist and heavy fire of all descriptions, Lieutenant Colonel Freyberg's command was much disorganised after the capture of the first objective. He personally rallied and reformed his men, including men from other units who had become intermixed. He inspired all with his own contempt of danger. At the appointed time he led his men forward to the successful assault of the second objective, many prisoners being captured. During this advance he was twice wounded. He again rallied and reformed all who were with him, and although unsupported in a very advanced position, he held his ground throughout the day and the following night under heavy artillery and machine gun fire. When reinforced on the following morning he organised the attack on a strongly fortified village, and showed a fine example of dash personally leading the assault, capturing the village and 500 prisoners. In this operation he was again wounded severely but refused to leave the line till he had issued his final instructions. The personality, valour and utter contempt of danger on the part of this single officer enabled the furthermost objective of the corps to be permanently held, and on this point d'appui the line was eventually formed.

London Gazette, 16 December 1917

Rank and name:	Lieutenant William Edward Sanders
Unit:	Royal Naval Reserve, Commanding HMS *Prize*
Date of act of bravery:	30 April 1917
Theatre of war:	Irish Sea

In recognition of his conspicuous gallantry, consummate coolness and skill in command of one of His Majesty's ships in action.

London Gazette, 22 June 1917

Admiralty, 20 November, 1918. With reference to the announcements of the award of the Victoria Cross to Naval Officers and men for services in action with enemy submarines, the following are the accounts of the actions for which these awards were made.

Action of HMS *Prize* on 30 April, 1917.

HMS *Prize* a topsail schooner of 200 tons under the command of Lieutenant William Edward Sanders RNR, sighted an enemy submarine at three miles range and approaching slowly astern.

The 'panic party' in charge of Skipper William Henry Brewer RNR (Trawler Section), immediately abandoned ship. The ship's head was put into the wind, and the gun crews concealed themselves by lying face downwards on the deck. The enemy continued deliberately shelling the schooner, inflicting severe damage and wounding a number of men. For twenty minutes she continued to approach, firing as she came, but at length, apparently satisfied that no one remained on board she drew out of the schooner's quarter 70 yards away. The White Ensign was hoisted immediately, the screens dropped, and all guns opened fire. A shell struck the foremost gun of the submarine, blowing it to atoms and annihilating the crew.

Another shot demolished the conning tower, and at the same time a Lewis gun raked the survivors off the submarine's deck. She sank four minutes after the commencement of the action in clouds of smoke, the glare of an internal fire being visible through the rents in her hull. The captain of the submarine, a warrant officer and one man were picked up and brought on board the *Prize*, which was then herself sinking fast. Captors and prisoners however succeeded in plugging the shot holes and keeping the water under pumps. The *Prize* set sail for land, 120 miles distant. They were finally picked up two days later by a motor launch and towed the remaining five miles into harbour. The award of the Victoria Cross to Acting Lieutenant William Edward Sanders was announced in the *London Gazette* No. 30147 dated 22nd June, 1917.

London Gazette, 20 November 1918

Rank and name:	6/2133 Lance Corporal Samuel Frickleton
Unit:	3rd Battalion,
	3rd New Zealand (Rifle) Brigade
Date of act of bravery:	7 June 1917
Theatre of war:	Messines, Belgium

For most conspicuous bravery and determination when with attacking troops which came under heavy fire and were checked. Although slightly wounded Corporal Frickleton dashed forward at the head of his section, pushed into the barrage and personally destroyed with bombs an enemy machine gun and crew which were causing heavy casualties. He then attacked the second gun, killing the whole of the crew of twelve. By the destruction of these two guns, he undoubtedly saved his own and other units from very severe casualties, and his magnificent courage and gallantry ensured the capture of the objective. During the consolidation of the position he received a second severe wound. He set, throughout, a great example of heroism.

London Gazette, 2 August 1917

Rank and name:	11795 Corporal Leslie Wilton Andrew
Unit:	2nd Battalion,
	Wellington Infantry Regiment, NZEF
Date of act of bravery:	31 July 1917
Theatre of war:	La Basse Ville, Belgium

For most conspicuous bravery when in charge of a small party in an attack on the enemy's position. His objective was a machine gun post which had been located in an isolated building. On leading his men forward he encountered unexpectedly a machine gun post which was holding up the advance of another Company. He immediately attacked, capturing the machine gun and killing several of the crew. He then continued the attack on the machine gun post which had been his original objective. He displayed great skill and determination in his disposition, finally capturing the post, killing several of the enemy, and putting the remainder to flight. Corporal Andrew's conduct throughout was unexampled for cool daring initiative and fine leadership and his magnificent example was a great stimulant to his comrades.

London Gazette, 6 September 1917

Rank and name:	24213 Private Henry James Nicholas, MM
Unit:	1st Battalion,
	Canterbury Infantry Regiment, NZEF
Date of act of bravery:	3 December 1917
Theatre of war:	Polderhoek, Belgium

For most conspicuous bravery, and devotion to duty in attack. Private Nicholas, who was one of a Lewis gun section, had orders to form a defensive flank to the right of the advance, which was subsequently checked by heavy machine guns and rifle fire from an enemy strongpoint. Whereupon, followed by the remainder of his section at an interval of about twenty-five yards, Private Nicholas rushed forward alone, shot the officer in command of the strongpoint and overcame the remainder of the garrison of sixteen by means of bombs and bayonet, capturing four wounded prisoners and a machine gun. He captured the strong-point practically single-handed, and thereby saved many casualties. Subsequently, when the advance had reached its limit, Private Nicholas collected ammunition under heavy machine gun and rifle fire. His exceptional valour and coolness throughout the operation afforded an inspiring example to all.

London Gazette, 8 January 1918

Rank and name:	Lieutenant Percy Valentine Storkey
Unit:	19th Battalion, Australian Imperial Force
Date of act of bravery:	7 April 1918
Theatre of war:	Bois de Hangard, France

For most conspicuous bravery, leadership and devotion to duty when in charge of a platoon in attack. On emerging from the wood the enemy trench line was encountered and Lieutenant Storkey found himself with six men. While continuing his move forward a large enemy party — about 80 to 100 strong — armed with several machine guns was noticed to be holding up the advance of the troops on the right. Lieutenant Storkey immediately decided to attack this party from the flank and rear, and while moving forward in the attack was joined by Lieutenant Lipscomb and four men. Under the leadership of Lieutenant Storkey, this small party of two officers and ten other ranks charged the enemy position with fixed bayonets, driving the enemy out, killing and wounding about thirty, and capturing three officers and fifty men, also one machine gun.

The splendid courage shown by this officer in quickly deciding his course of action, and his skilful method of attacking against such great odds, removed a dangerous obstacle to the advance of the troops on the right, and inspired the remainder of our small party with the utmost confidence when advancing to the objective line.

London Gazette, 7 June 1918

Rank and name:	9/523 Sergeant Richard Charles Travis, DCM, MM
Unit:	2nd Battalion, Otago Infantry Regiment, NZEF
Date of act of bravery:	24 July 1918
Theatre of war:	Hebuterne, France

For most conspicuous bravery and devotion

to duty. During 'surprise' operations it was necessary to destroy an impassable block. Sergeant Travis, regardless of all personal danger, volunteered for this duty. Before zero hour, in broad daylight, in close proximity to enemy posts, he crawled out and successfully destroyed the block with bombs, thus enabling the attacking parties to pass through. A few minutes later a bombing party on the right of the attack was held up by two enemy machine guns, and the success of the whole operation was in danger. Perceiving this, Sergeant Travis, with great gallantry and disregard of danger, rushed the position, killed the crew, and captured the guns. An enemy officer and three men immediately rushed at him from a bend in the trench, and attempted to retake the guns. These four he killed single-handed, thus allowing the bombing party, on which much depended, to advance. The success of the operation was almost entirely due to the heroic work of this gallant NCO, and to the vigour with which he made and used opportunities for inflicting casualties on the enemy. He was killed twenty-four hours later, when, under a most intense bombardment prior to an enemy counterattack, he was going from post to post, encouraging the men.

London Gazette, 24 September 1918

Rank and name:	4/400 Sergeant Samuel Forsyth
Unit:	New Zealand Engineers
	(attached 2nd Battalion, Auckland Infantry
	Regiment) NZEF
Date of act of bravery:	24 August 1918
Theatre of war:	Grevillers, France

For conspicuous gallantry and devotion to duty in attack. On nearing the objective, his company came under heavy machine gun fire. Through Sergeant Forsyth's dashing leadership and total disregard of danger, three machine gun positions were rushed and the crews taken prisoner before they could inflict many casualties on our troops. During a subsequent advance his company came under heavy fire from several machine guns, two of which he located by a reconnaissance. In his endeavour to gain support from a tank, he was wounded, but, after having the wound bandaged, he again got in touch with the tank which, in face of very heavy fire from machine guns and anti-tank guns, he endeavoured to lead, with magnificent coolness, to a favourable position. The tank, however, was put out of action. Sergeant Forsyth then organised the tank crew and several of his men into a section, and led them to a position where the machine guns could be outflanked. Always under heavy fire, he directed them into position which brought about a retirement of the enemy machine guns and enabled the advance to continue. This gallant NCO was at that moment killed by a sniper. From the commencement of the attack until the time of his death, Sergeant Forsyth's courage and coolness, combined with great power and initiative, proved an invaluable incentive to all who were with him, and he undoubtedly saved many casualties among his comrades.

London Gazette, 18 October 1918

Rank and name:	24/1699 Sergeant Reginald Stanley Judson, DCM
Unit:	1st Battalion, Auckland Infantry Regiment, NZEF
Date of act of bravery:	26 August 1918
Theatre of war:	Bapaume, France

For most conspicuous bravery and devotion to duty when, in an attack on enemy positions, he led a small bombing party under heavy fire and captured an enemy machine gun. He then proceeded up a sap alone, bombing three machine gun crews beforehand. Jumping out of the trench he ran ahead of the enemy. Then, standing on the parapet, he ordered the party, consisting of two officers and about ten men, to surrender. They instantly fired on him, but he threw a bomb and jumped down amongst them, killed two, put the rest to flight, and so captured two machine guns. This prompt and gallant action not only saved many lives, but also enabled the advance to be continued unopposed.

London Gazette, 29 October 1918

Rank and name: 10/2950 Sergeant John Gildroy Grant
Unit: 1st Battalion,
Wellington Infantry Regiment, NZEF
Date of act of bravery: 1 September 1918
Theatre of war: Bancourt, France

For most conspicuous bravery and devotion to duty near Bancourt on 1 September 1918, when Sergeant in charge of a platoon forming part of the leading waves of the battalion attacking the high ground to the east of Bancourt. On reaching the crest it was found that a line of five enemy machine gun posts offered a serious obstacle to further advance. Under point-blank fire, however, the company advanced against these posts. When about twenty yards from the posts Sergeant Grant, closely followed by a comrade, rushed forward ahead of his platoon, and with great dash and bravery entered the centre post, demoralising the garrison and enabling the men of his platoon to mop up the position. In the same manner he then rushed the post on the left and the remaining posts were quickly occupied and cleared by his company. Throughout the whole operation on this and two previous days Sergeant Grant

displayed coolness, determination, and valour
of the highest order, and set a splendid example
to all.

London Gazette, 26 November 1918

Rank and name:	No. 1153 Lance Corporal, Temporary Corporal Lawrence Carthage Weathers
Unit:	43rd Battalion, Australian Imperial Force
Date of act of bravery:	2 September 1918
Theatre of war:	North of Peronne, France

For most conspicuous bravery and devotion
to duty on the 2nd September, 1918, north of
Peronne, when with an advanced bombing
party.

The attack having been held up by a strongly
held enemy trench, Corporal Weathers went
forward alone under heavy fire and attacked
the enemy with bombs. Then, returning to
our lines for a further supply of bombs, he
again went forward with three comrades, and
attacked under very heavy fire. Regardless of
personal danger, he mounted the enemy parapet
and bombed the trench, and, with the support
of his comrades, captured 180 prisoners and
three machine guns.

His valour and determination resulted in the
successful capture of the final objective, and
saved the lives of many of his comrades.

London Gazette, 26 December 1918

Rank and name:	24/213 Sergeant Harry John Laurent
Unit:	2nd Battalion, New Zealand (Rifle) Brigade, NZEF
Date of act of bravery:	12 September 1918
Theatre of war:	Gouzeaucourt Wood, France

For conspicuous bravery, skill, and enterprise

when during an attack he was detailed to exploit an initial success and keep in touch with the enemy. With a party of twelve he located the enemy's support line very strongly held, at once charged the position, followed by his men, and completely disorganised the enemy by his sudden onslaught. In the subsequent hand-to-hand fighting which ensued he showed great resourcefulness in controlling and encouraging his men, and thirty of the enemy having been killed, the remainder surrendered, a total of one officer and one hundred and eleven other ranks in all. The success of this venture, which caused his party four casualties only, was due to his gallantry and enterprise.

London Gazette, 12 November 1918

Rank and name:	14/131 Private James Crichton
Unit:	2nd Battalion,
	Auckland Infantry Regiment, NZEF
Date of act of bravery:	30 September 1918
Theatre of war:	Crevecoeur, France

For most conspicuous bravery and devotion to duty, when although wounded in the foot, he continued with the advancing troops, despite difficult canal and river obstacles. When his platoon was subsequently forced back by a counterattack he succeeded in carrying a message which involved swimming a river and crossing an area swept by machine gun fire, subsequently rejoining his platoon. Later, he undertook on his own initiative to save a bridge which had been mined, and though under close fire of machine guns and snipers he succeeded in removing the charges, returning with the fuses and detonators. Though suffering from a painful wound he displayed the highest degree of valour and devotion to duty.

London Gazette, 12 November 1918

Rank and name:	7930 Sergeant John Daniel Hinton
Unit:	20th Battalion, 2nd NZEF
Date of act of bravery:	28–29 April 1941
Theatre of war:	Greece

On the night of 28–29 April 1941, during the fighting in Greece, a column of German armoured forces entered Kalamai; this column, which contained several armoured cars, 2 in. guns and 3 in. mortars and two 6 in. guns, rapidly converged on a large force of British and New Zealand troops awaiting embarkation on the beach. When the order to retreat to cover was given, Sergeant Hinton, shouting 'To hell with this, who'll come with me?' ran to within several yards of the nearest gun; the gun fired, missing him, and he hurled two grenades, which completely wiped out the crew. He then came on with the bayonet, followed by a crowd of New Zealanders. German troops abandoned the first 6 in. gun and retreated into two houses. Sergeant Hinton smashed the window and then the door of the first house, and dealt with the garrison with the bayonet. He repeated the performance in the second house, and as a result, until overwhelming German forces arrived, the New Zealanders held the guns. Sergeant Hinton then fell with a bullet wound through the lower abdomen and was taken prisoner.

London Gazette, 14 October 1941

Rank and name:	10725 Sergeant Alfred Clive Hulme
Unit:	23rd Battalion, 2nd NZEF
Date of acts of bravery:	20–28 May 1941
Theatre of war:	Crete

Sergeant Hulme exhibited most outstanding and inspiring qualities of leadership, initiative, skill, endurance, and most conspicuous gallantry and devotion to duty from the commencement of the heavy fighting in Crete on 20 May 1941, until he was wounded in action 28 May 1941. On ground overlooking Maleme Aerodrome on 20 and 21 May he personally led parties of his men from the area held by the forward position and destroyed enemy organised parties who had established themselves in front of our position, from which they brought heavy rifle, machine gun, and mortar fire to bear on our defensive posts. Numerous snipers in this area were dealt with by Sergeant Hulme personally; one hundred and thirty dead were counted here. On 22, 23 and 24 May, Sergeant Hulme was continuously going out alone or with one or two men and destroying enemy snipers. On 25 May, when Sergeant Hulme had rejoined his battalion, this unit counterattacked Galatos Village. The attack was partially held up by a large party of the enemy holding the school, from which they were inflicting heavy casualties on our troops. Sergeant Hulme went forward alone, threw grenades into the school, and so disorganised the defence that the counterattack was able to proceed successfully.

On Tuesday, 27 May, when our troops were holding a defensive line in Suda Bay during the final retirement, five enemy snipers had worked into position on the hillside overlooking the flank of the battalion line. Sergeant Hulme volunteered to deal with the situation, and stalked and killed the snipers in turn. He continued similar work successfully through the day.

On 28 May at Stylos, when an enemy heavy mortar was bombing a very important ridge held by the battalion rearguard troops, inflicting severe casualties, Sergeant Hulme, on his own initiative, penetrated the enemy lines, killed the mortar crew of four, put the mortar out of action and thus very materially assisted the withdrawal of the main body through Stylos. From the enemy mortar position he then worked onto the left flank and killed three snipers who were causing concern to the rearguard. This made his score of enemy snipers thirty-three stalked and shot. Shortly afterwards Sergeant Hulme was severely wounded in the shoulder whilst stalking another sniper. When ordered to the rear, in spite of his wound, he directed traffic under fire and organised stragglers of various units into section groups.

London Gazette, 10 October 1941

Rank and name:	8077 Captain Charles Hazlitt Upham
Unit:	20th Battalion, 2nd NZEF
Date of acts of bravery:	(a) 22–30 May 1941
	(b) 14–15 July 1942
Theatres of war:	(a) Crete
	(b) Western Desert

(a) Citation for award of the Victoria Cross

During the operations in Crete this officer performed a series of remarkable exploits, showing outstanding leadership, tactical skill, and utter indifference to danger. He commanded a forward platoon in the attack on Maleme on 22 May and fought his way forward for over three thousand yards unsupported by any other arms and against a defence strongly organised in depth. During this operation his platoon destroyed numerous enemy posts, but on three occasions sections were temporarily held up.

In the first case, under heavy fire from a machine gun nest, he advanced to close quarters with pistol and grenades, so demoralising the occupants that his section was able to 'mop up' with ease.

Another of his sections was then held up by two machine guns in a house. He went in and placed a grenade through a window, destroying the crew of one machine gun and several others, the other machine gun being silenced by the fire of his sections.

In the third case he crawled to within fifteen yards of a machine gun post and killed the gunners with a grenade.

When his company withdrew from Maleme he helped to carry a wounded man out under fire, and together with another officer, rallied more men together to carry other wounded men out. He was then sent to bring in a company which had become isolated. With a corporal he went through enemy territory over six hundred yards, killing two Germans on the way, found the company, and brought it back to the Battalion's new position. But for this action it would have been completely cut off.

During the following two days his platoon occupied an exposed position on forward slopes and was continuously under fire. Second Lieutenant Upham was blown over by one mortar shell, and painfully wounded by a piece of shrapnel behind the left shoulder by another. He disregarded this wound and remained on duty. He also received a bullet in the foot. The bullet was later removed in Egypt.

At Galatos on 25 May his platoon was heavily engaged and came under severe mortar and machine gun fire. While his platoon stopped under cover of a ridge Second Lieutenant Upham went forward, observed the enemy, and brought the platoon forward when the Germans advanced. They killed over forty with fire and grenades and forced the remainder to fall back.

When his platoon was ordered to retire he sent it back under the platoon sergeant, and he went back to warn other troops that they were being cut off. When he came out himself he was fired on by two Germans. He fell and shammed dead, then crawled into a position and, having the use of only one arm, rested his rifle in the fork of a tree and as the Germans came forward he killed them both. The second to fall actually hit the muzzle of the rifle as he fell.

On 30 May at Spakhia [sic] his platoon was ordered to deal with a party of the enemy which had advanced down a ravine to near force headquarters. Though in an exhausted condition he climbed the steep hill to the west of the ravine, placed his men in positions on the slope overlooking the ravine, and himself went to the top with a Bren gun and two riflemen. By clever tactics he induced the enemy party to expose itself, and then at a range of five hundred yards shot twenty-two and caused the remainder to disperse in panic.

During the whole of the operations he suffered from dysentery and was able to eat very little, in addition to being wounded and bruised.

He showed superb coolness, great skill and dash, and complete disregard of danger. His conduct and leadership inspired his whole platoon to fight magnificently throughout, and in fact, was an inspiration to the battalion.

London Gazette, 10 October 1941

(b) Citation for the award of a bar to the Victoria Cross

Captain C.H. Upham, VC, was commanding a company of New Zealand troops in the Western Desert during the operations which culminated in the attack on Ruweisat Ridge on the night of 14–15 July 1942. In spite of being wounded twice, once when crossing open ground swept by enemy fire to inspect his forward sections guarding our minefields and again when he completely destroyed an entire truck-load of German soldiers with hand grenades, Captain

Upham insisted on remaining with his men to take part in the final assault. During the opening stages of the attack on the Ridge, Captain Upham's company formed part of the reserve battalion, but, when communications with the forward troops broke down and he was instructed to send up an officer to report on the progress of the attack, he went out himself armed with a Spandau gun and, after several sharp encounters with enemy machine gun posts, succeeded in bringing back the required information. Just before dawn the reserve battalion was ordered forward, but when it had almost reached its objective, very heavy fire was encountered from a strongly defended enemy locality consisting of four machine gun posts and a number of tanks. Captain Upham, without hesitation, at once led his company in a determined attack on the two nearest strongpoints on the left flank of the section. His voice could be heard above the din of battle cheering on his men, and with heavy casualties on both sides, the objective was captured. Captain Upham, during the engagement, himself destroyed a German tank and several guns and vehicles with grenades and, although he was shot through the elbow by a machine gun bullet and had his arm broken, he went on again to a forward position and brought back some of his men who had become isolated. He continued to dominate the situation until his men had beaten off a violent enemy counterattack and consolidated the vital position which they had won under his inspiring leadership. Exhausted by pain from his wound and weak from loss of blood, Captain Upham was then removed to the Regimental Aid Post, but immediately his wound had been dressed he returned to his men, remaining with them all day long under heavy enemy artillery and mortar fire until he was again severely wounded, and being now unable to move, fell into the hands of the enemy when, his gallant company having been reduced to only six survivors, his position was finally overrun by superior enemy forces, in spite of the outstanding gallantry and magnificent leadership shown by Captain Upham.

London Gazette, 26 September 1945

Rank and name:	NZ 401793 Sergeant James Edward Allen Ward
Unit:	RNZAF, attached 75 NZ Squadron. RAF
Date of act of bravery:	7 July 1941
Theatre of war:	On operations over Holland

On the night of 7 July 1941 Sergeant Ward was second pilot of a Wellington bomber returning from an attack on Munster. While flying over the Zuider Zee at 13000 feet his aircraft was attacked from beneath by a German ME 110 which secured hits with cannon-shell and incendiary bullets. The rear gunner was wounded in the foot but delivered a burst of fire, sending the enemy fighter down apparently out of control. Fire then broke out in the Wellington near-starboard engine and, fed by petrol from a split pipe, quickly gained an alarming hold and threatened to spread to the entire wing. The crew forced a hole in the fuselage and made strenuous efforts to reduce the fire with extinguishers, and even coffee in their vacuum flasks, without success. They were then warned to be ready to abandon the aircraft. As a last resort Sergeant Ward volunteered to make an attempt to smother the fire with an engine cover which happened to be in use as a cushion. At first he proposed discarding his parachute to reduce wind resistance but was finally persuaded to take it. A rope from the aircraft dinghy was tied to him, though this was of little help and might have become a danger had he been blown off the aircraft.

With the help of his navigator he then climbed through the narrow Astro-hatch and put on his parachute. The bomber was flying at reduced speed but the wind pressure must have been sufficient to render the operation one of extreme difficulty. Breaking the fabric to make hand and feet holes where necessary and also taking advantage of existing holes in the fabric, Sergeant Ward succeeded in descending three feet to the wing and proceeding another three feet to a position behind the engine, despite the slipstream from the airscrew which nearly blew him off the wing. Lying in this precarious position he smothered the fire in the wing fabric and tried to push the engine cover into the hole in the wing and on the leaking pipe from which the fire came. As soon as he had removed his hand, however, the terrific wind blew the cover out and when he tried again it was lost. Tired as he was, he was able with the navigator's assistance to make a successful but perilous journey back into the aircraft. There was now no danger of fire spreading from the petrol pipe as there was no fabric left near it and in due course it burnt itself out. When the aircraft was nearly home some petrol which had collected in the wing blazed up furiously but died down quite suddenly. A safe landing was then made despite the damage sustained by the aircraft. The flight home had been made possible by the gallantry of Sergeant Ward in extinguishing the fire on the wing in circumstances of the greatest difficulty and at the risk of his life.

London Gazette, 5 August 1941

Rank and name:	6751 Sergeant Keith Elliott
Unit:	22nd Battalion, 2nd NZEF
Date of act of bravery:	15 July 1942
Theatre of war:	Western Desert

At Ruweisat at dawn on 15 July 1942 the battalion to which Sergeant Elliott belonged was attacked on three flanks by tanks. Under heavy tank, machine gun, and shell fire Sergeant Elliot led the platoon he was commanding to the cover of a ridge three hundred yards away, during which he sustained a chest wound.

Here he re-formed his men and led them to a dominating ridge a further five hundred yards away, where they came under heavy enemy machine gun and mortar fire. He located enemy machine gun posts on his front and right flank, and while one section attacked on the right flank Sergeant Elliott led seven men in a bayonet charge across five hundred yards of open ground in the face of heavy fire and captured four enemy machine gun posts and an anti-tank gun, killing a number of the enemy and taking fifty prisoners.

His section then came under fire from a machine gun post on the left flank. He immediately charged this post single-handed and succeeded in capturing it, killing several of the enemy and taking fifteen prisoners. During these two assaults he sustained three more wounds in the back and legs.

Although badly wounded in four places, Sergeant Elliott refused to leave his men until he had reformed them, handed over his prisoners, which were now increased to one hundred and thirty, and had arranged for his men to rejoin their battalion.

Owing to Sergeant Elliot's quick grasp of the situation, great personal courage and leadership, nineteen men who were the only survivors of B Company of his battalion, captured and destroyed five machine guns, one anti-tank gun, killed a great number of the enemy, and captured one hundred and thirty prisoners. Sergeant Elliot sustained only one casualty amongst his men, and brought him back to the nearest advanced dressing station.

London Gazette, 24 September 1942

Rank and name:	39784 2nd Lieutenant Moana-nui-a-Kiwa Ngarimu
Unit:	28th Battalion, 2nd NZEF
Date of act of bravery:	26–27 March 1943
Theatre of war:	Tunisia

During the action at the Tebaga Gap on 26 March 1943, 2nd Lieutenant Ngarimu commanded a platoon in an attack upon the vital hill feature Point 209. He was given the task of attacking and capturing an underfeature forward of Point 209 itself and held in considerable strength by the enemy. He led his men with great determination straight up the face of the hill, undeterred by the intense mortar and machine gun fire, which caused considerable casualties. Displaying courage and leadership of the highest order, he was himself first on the hill crest, personally annihilating at least two enemy machine gun posts. In the face of such a determined attack the remainder of the enemy fled, but further advance was impossible as the reverse slope was swept by machine gun fire from Point 209 itself.

Under cover of a most intense mortar barrage the enemy counterattacked and 2nd Lieutenant Ngarimu ordered his men to stand up and engage the enemy man for man. This they did with such good effect that the attackers were literally mown down, 2nd Lieutenant Ngarimu personally killing several. He was twice wounded, once by rifle fire in the shoulder and later by shrapnel in the leg, and though urged by both his company and battalion commanders to go out he refused to do so, saying that he would stay a little while with his men. He stayed till he met his death the following morning.

Darkness found this officer and his depleted platoon lying on the rock face of the forward slope of the hill feature, with the enemy in a similar position on the reverse slope about twenty yards distant. Throughout the night the enemy repeatedly launched fierce attacks in an attempt to dislodge 2nd Lieutenant Ngarimu and his men, but each counterattack was beaten off entirely by 2nd Lieutenant Ngarimu's inspired leadership. During one of these counterattacks the enemy, by using hand grenades, succeeded in piercing a certain part of the line. Without hesitation this officer rushed to the threatened area, and those of the enemy he did not kill he drove back with stones and with his tommy-gun.

During another determined counterattack by the enemy, part of his line broke. Yelling orders and encouragement, he rallied his men and led them in a fierce onslaught back into their old positions. All through the night, between attacks, he and his men were heavily harassed by machine gun and mortar fire, but 2nd Lieutenant Ngarimu watched his line very carefully, cheering his men on and inspiring them by his gallant personal conduct. Morning found him still in possession of the hill feature, but only he and two unwounded other ranks remained. Reinforcements were sent up to him. In the morning the enemy again counterattacked, and it was during this attack that 2nd Lieutenant Ngarimu was killed. He was killed on his feet defiantly facing the enemy with his tommy-gun at his hip. As he fell he came to rest almost on the top of those of the enemy who had fallen, the number of whom testified to his outstanding courage and fortitude.

London Gazette, 4 June 1943

Rank and name:	2841 Squadron Leader Leonard Henry Trent, DFC
Unit:	RNZAF, attached 487 NZ Squadron, RAF
Date of act of bravery:	3 May 1943
Theatre of war:	On operations over Holland

On 3 May 1943, Squadron Leader Trent was detailed to lead a formation of Ventura aircraft in a daylight attack on the power station at Amsterdam. This operation was intended to encourage the Dutch workmen in their resistance to enemy pressure and the target was known to be heavily defended. The importance of bombing it, regardless of enemy fighters or anti-aircraft fire, was strongly impressed on the aircrews taking part in the operation. Before taking off Squadron Leader Trent told the deputy leader that he was going over the target whatever happened.

All went well until the eleven Venturas and their fighter escort were nearing the Dutch coast. Then one bomber was hit and had to turn back. Suddenly large numbers of enemy fighters appeared. Our escorting fighters were hotly engaged and lost touch with the bombing force. The Venturas closed up for mutual protection and commenced their run up to the target. Unfortunately, the fighters detailed to support them over the target had reached the area too early and had been recalled. Soon the bombers were attacked. They were at the mercy of 15 to 20 Messerschmitts which dived on them incessantly. Within four minutes six Venturas were destroyed. Squadron Leader Trent continued on his course with the three remaining aircraft and in a short time two more Venturas went down in flames. Heedless of the murderous attacks and of the heavy anti-aircraft fire which was now encountered Squadron Leader Trent completed an accurate bombing run and even shot down a Messerschmitt at point-blank range. Dropping his bombs in the target area he turned away.

The aircraft following him was shot down on reaching the target.

Immediately afterwards his own aircraft was hit and went into a spin and broke up. Squadron Leader Trent and his navigator were thrown clear and became prisoners of war. The other two members of the crew perished. On this, his 24th sortie, Squadron Leader Trent showed outstanding leadership. Such was the trust placed in this gallant officer that the other pilots followed him unwaveringly. His cool, unflinching courage and devotion to duty in the face of overwhelming odds rank with the fine examples of these virtues.

London Gazette, 1 March 1946

Rank and name:	NZ 413515 Flying Officer Lloyd Allen Trigg, DFC
Unit:	RNZAF, attached 200 Squadron, RAF
Date of act of bravery:	11 August 1943
Theatre of war:	On operations over the Atlantic

Flying Officer Trigg of 200 Squadron, RAF, rendered outstanding service on convoy, escort and anti-submarine duties. He completed 46 operational sorties and invariably displayed skill and courage of a very high order.

On 11 August 1943, Flying Officer Trigg undertook, as Captain and pilot, a patrol in a Liberator bomber, although he had not made any previous operational sorties in this type of aircraft. After searching for eight hours, the Liberator sighted a surfaced U-boat. Flying Officer Trigg immediately prepared to attack.

During the approach the aircraft received many hits from the submarine's anti-aircraft guns and burst into flames which quickly enveloped the tail. The moment was critical. Flying Officer Trigg could have broken off the engagement and made a forced landing in the sea, but if he continued the attack the aircraft would present a no-deflection target to deadly anti-aircraft fire and every second spent in the air would increase the extent and intensity of the flames and diminish his chances of survival.

There could have been no hesitation or doubt in his mind. He maintained his course in spite of the already precarious condition of his aircraft and executed a masterly attack. Skimming over the U-boat at less than 50 feet, with anti-aircraft fire entering his opened bomb doors, Flying Officer Trigg dropped his bombs on and around the U-boat, where they exploded with devastating effect. A short distance further on the Liberator dived into the sea with her gallant captain and crew. The U-boat sank within 20 minutes and some of her crew were picked up later in a rubber dinghy that had broken loose from the Liberator.

The Battle of the Atlantic has yielded many fine stories of air attacks on underwater craft, but Flying Officer Trigg's exploit stands out as an epic of grim determination and high courage.

London Gazette, 2 November 1943

Endnotes

Introduction
Some signal act of valour

1 C.E. Lucas Phillips, *Victoria Cross Battles of the Second World War*, Heinemann, London, 1973, p. 1.
2 ibid., p. 2.
3 Phillip O'Shea in Ian McGibbon (ed.), *The Oxford Companion to New Zealand Military History*, Oxford University Press, Auckland, 2000, pp. 558–59.
4 Sgt E.G. Pilling, quoted in Robert Rhodes James, *Gallipoli*, Papermac, London, 1989, p. 253.
5 G.A. Bryant, *Where the Prize is Highest: The Stories of the New Zealanders who Won the Victoria Cross*, Collins, Auckland, 1972.

Chapter 1
A history of the Victoria Cross

1 The Order of the Bath was not available to officers below the rank of captain in the navy or major in the army. Michael J. Crook, *The Evolution of the Victoria Cross*, Midas Books, Tunbridge Wells, 1975, p. 11.
2 ibid., p. 6.
3 ibid., pp. 10–11.
4 ibid., p. 13.
5 ibid., p. 276.
6 ibid., p. 15.
7 ibid., p. 18.
8 ibid., pp. 23–24.
9 ibid., pp. 30–31. Crook believes the probable designer was H.H. Armstead, one of Hancocks' two designers, whose style is consistent with the VC.
10 Colonel M.P. Hancock, grandson of the founder of Hancocks, had donated the medal to the Royal United Services Institute Museum

in 1922. When this was dissolved in 1963 the medal was allocated to the Royal Fusiliers Museum at the Tower of London, this having been Col Hancock's regiment.
11 John Winton, *The Victoria Cross at Sea*, Michael Joseph, London, 1978, p. 12. Cascabels are the round knobs at the back of muzzle-loading guns. Ian Hogg, *The Illustrated Encyclopedia of Artillery*, Stanley Paul, London, 1987, p. 114.
12 P.P. O'Shea in Ian McGibbon (ed.), *The Oxford Companion to New Zealand Military History*, OUP, Auckland, 2000, p. 559. See also *Medal Yearbook 2005*, Token Publishing Ltd, Honiton, 2005, p. 87.
13 Russell Vallance 10 Mar 2003 at www.victoriacross.net.forum.asp-topicasp?topics=1000tid=817
14 Crook, op. cit. p. 267.
15 *The Register of the Victoria Cross*, 3rd edn, This England, Bath, 1997, p. 261. Lucas later became a rear admiral.
16 Lieutenant Colonel Bell, 23rd Foot; Lieutenant Knox, Scots Fusilier Guards; Brevet Major Lindsay, Scots Fusilier Guards; Sergeant McKechnie, Scots Fusilier Guards; Lieutenant O'Connor, 23rd Foot; and Private Reynolds, Scots Fusilier Guards.
17 Warrant Extending Eligibility for the Victoria Cross to Military Forces of the Honourable East India Company, dated 29 October 1857, and Warrant Extending Eligibility for the Victoria Cross to Cases of Conspicuous Courage and Bravery Displayed under Circumstances of Danger but not before the Enemy, dated 10 August 1858.
18 Warrant Extending Eligibility for

the Victoria Cross to Cases of
Conspicuous Courage and Bravery
Displayed under Circumstances of
Danger but not before the Enemy,
dated 10 August 1858.

19 Warrant Extending the Victoria Cross
to the Local Forces in New Zealand
and in the Colonies and
their Dependencies Generally,
dated 1 January 1867.

20 All four were members of the
Australian Army Training Team
Viet Nam: Warrant Officers Keith
Payne, Rayene Simpson and Kevin
Wheatley, and Major Peter Badcoe.

21 Crook, op. cit. p. 68.

22 Roberts' own son was awarded a VC
for acts of bravery during the Battle
of Colenso in the Boer War, despite
being killed in the same battle very
shortly afterwards.

23 McGibbon, op. cit. p. 316.

24 Third son of Sir Robert Peel.

25 Winton, op. cit. p. 30.

26 Lord Stamfordham 26 July 1920,
quoted in Crook, op. cit. p. 64.

27 Crook, op. cit. pp. 238–39.

28 ibid., pp. 239–40.

29 As at 18 March 2005 when the
award to Pte Johnson Beharry of the
Princess of Wales' Regiment was
announced for his conduct in Iraq.

30 Thomas Cooke, Alfred Shout, Percy
Storkey, and Lawrence Weathers.

31 Henry D'Arcy, William Rhodes-
Moorhouse, Bernard Freyberg, and
William Sanders.

Chapter 2
The New Zealand wars

1 Michael King, *New Zealanders at
War*, Heinemann, Auckland, 1981,
p. 27.

2 Tim Ryan and Bill Parnham,
The Colonial New Zealand Wars,
Grantham House, Wellington, 1986,
p. 1.

3 James Belich in Ian McGibbon
(ed.), *The Oxford Companion to
New Zealand Military History*, OUP,

Auckland, 2000, p. 373.

4 *London Gazette* 3 August 1860.
Subsequent scholarship has shed
some doubt on this picture of events,
however. For political reasons the
colonists needed to emphasise the
Maori threat. Some versions have it
that the *Niger*'s party stormed nothing
more than a nearly unoccupied camp.
James Belich, *The New Zealand
Wars*, Auckland, AUP, 1986, pp. 85–
87. If true, this would mean that New
Zealand's first association with the
VC had a spurious basis for award.

5 *London Gazette* 17 July 1861.

6 *London Gazette* 22 September 1864.
Drummer Stagpoole had already
won the Medal for Distinguished
Conduct on 25 September 1863 at
Kaipakopako.

7 *London Gazette* 16 January 1864.

8 Ryan and Parnham, op. cit. p. 211.

9 *London Gazette* 22 September 1864.

10 A simpler version of these events is
that Heaphy went to tend to one of
the wounded men from the 40th, and
that he rendered first aid under fire,
receiving three wounds in doing so.

11 *London Gazette* 16 August 1864.

12 Ryan and Parnham, op. cit. p. 87.

13 *London Gazette* 23 July 1864.

14 *London Gazette* 22 September 1864.

15 Ryan and Parnham, op. cit. p. 102.

16 *London Gazette* 4 November 1864.

17 *London Gazette* 28 November 1865.

18 The Heaphy Track, which runs from
the West Coast at Karamea to the
Nelson Bays, is named after him.

19 Later as Secretary of State for War,
Edward Cardwell was the driving
force behind the major reforms of
the British Army in the nineteenth
century. These included the end of
the purchase of commissions and the
reformation of the regimental system.
John Keegan and Andrew Wheatcroft,
Who's Who In Military History,
Leicester, Hutchinson, 1987, p. 59.

20 Crook, op. cit. p. 149.

21 ibid., p. 151.

22 ibid., p. 155.

23 ibid., p. 276. This was Prince Albert's fifth numbered point in his memorandum of 22 January 1855.

24 T.W. Gudgeon, *The Defenders of New Zealand*, H. Brett, Auckland, 1887, p. 126.

25 Ryan and Parnham, op. cit. p. 213.

26 *The Medal Yearbook 2005*, Token Publishing, Honiton, 2004, p. 89.

27 Jeffrey Hopkins-Weise, 'A Brief History of the New Zealand Cross', *The Volunteers*, Volume 28 Number 2, November 2002, p. 98.

28 Jeffrey Hopkins-Weise, op. cit. p. 97.

29 The Armed Constabulary companies were well trained and mostly veteran. It was the newly recruited Patea Rangers and Wellington Volunteers that proved a problem.

30 Ryan and Parnham, op. cit. p. 214.

31 These were short barrels of bronze mounted on a solid wooden base. They lofted a small explosive shell a short distance. These weapons were ideal in bush warfare as they were much less difficult to move than conventional artillery.

32 James Belich, *The New Zealand Wars*, Auckland, AUP, 1986, pp. 272–73. This woman may also have been his half-sister and there were issues of breaching 'mana tapu' in having a sexual relationship during war, when a warrior was meant to abstain from sex.

33 A similar analysis of the New Zealand Cross reveals a reversed ratio. Five NZCs were awarded for the rescue of a comrade, while the remaining 18 were for fighting or dangerous operations around the enemy.

34 www.dpmc.govt.nz/honours/overviews/gallantry-bravery-html

Chapter 3
In Africa

1 R.E. and T.N. Dupuy, *The Harper Encyclopedia of Military History* (4th edn), HarperCollins, New York, 1993, p. 657.

2 John Percival, *For Valour: The Victoria Cross in Action,* Thames Methuen, London, 1985, p. 39.

3 As Midshipman Wood, the later Field Marshal Sir Evelyn Wood had been Captain Peel's other aide, along with Edward Daniel, at the Battle of the Inkerman — where both Peel and Daniel won VCs. Daniel was subsequently to be the only officer to forfeit the VC for bad conduct and later served with the Armed Constabulary in New Zealand, where he died.

4 Patricia D'Arcy, *What Happened to a VC*, Dunalgan Press, Dundalk, 1975, pp. 47–49.

5 Donald R. Morris, *The Washing of the Spears,* Sphere Books, London, 1968, p. 490.

6 Crook, op. cit. p. 155.

7 D'Arcy, op. cit. pp. 56–57.

8 Morris, op. cit. pp. 563–64; *London Gazette* 9 Oct 1879.

9 Morris, op. cit. p. 588; D'Arcy, op. cit. p. 74.

10 D'Arcy, op. cit. pp. 81–82.

11 ibid., p. 8.

12 *The Dominion*, Wellington, New Zealand, 14/9/1992.

13 D'Arcy, op. cit. erratum. The sale was reported as far as New Zealand in *The Dominion*, 14/9/1992.

14 Mark Wheeler, *The Role of Mounted Infantry During the Anglo-Boer War, 1899–1902: Lessons for New Zealand Mounted Infantry of the Future,* Military Studies Institute, Upper Hutt, 2003, p. 7.

15 R.E. and T.N. Dupuy, op. cit. pp. 933–34.

16 John Crawford and Ellen Ellis, *To Fight for the Empire,* Reed, Auckland, 1999, p. 32.

17 Ian McGibbon (ed.), *The Oxford Companion to New Zealand Military History,* OUP, Auckland, 2000, p. 59.

18 T.N. Dupuy et al., *The Harper Encyclopedia of Military Biography,* Castle Books, New York, 1992, p. 634.

19 Crawford and Ellis, op. cit. p. 77.

20 R.E. and T.N. Dupuy, op. cit. p. 935.

21 McGibbon, op. cit. p. 59.

22 D.O.W. Hall, *The New Zealanders in South Africa, 1899–1902,* Department of Internal Affairs, War History Branch, Wellington, 1949, p. 40.

23 Crawford and Ellis, op. cit. p. 21.

24 ibid., p. 34

25 Hall, op. cit. p. 60.

26 ibid., p. 68.

27 Thomas Pakenham, *The Boer War,* Weidenfeld & Nicholson, London, 1979, pp. 390–95.

28 NZDF Base Records, Coutts H.D., Personal File: SA 96; 1 NZEF 33022, Medical Board NZ/M6 dated 6 Feb 1918. Coutts was considered in good health but over-age and suffering from myalgia. The proceedings of his provisional medical board noted 'should not have been sent'.

29 Coutts' Personal File, W.J. Massey, Minister of Lands, letter dated 10 April 1913.

30 Coutts' Personal File, British Army Magazine SL/7764 dated 7 July 1964.

31 Coutts' Personal File, War Office 7355/8504 M.S.I. (A.L.) dated 29 May 1902. Directed 'Queen's Scarf' was not to be included under 'Orders' with the VC. An entry was included in the *NZ Yearbook*, however. Government Statistician D253/C.C dated 3 July 1913. See also http://www.awm.gov.au/encyclopedia/scarf/doc.htm which encloses an extract from a note made in the Royal Archives 26 May, 1956:

> In a certain sense the scarves may be regarded as a greater honour* stitched as they were by the hands of The Queen herself, and strictly limited in number. But whatever their relative status, they can hardly be treated as the precise equivalent of the V.C. In the first place, they were not (so the Stationery Office informs us) gazetted. Secondly, they were awarded on a different basis from the V.C. One was to go to the bravest soldier in each of the four Colonial contingents fighting in South Africa. To be the bravest soldier in a particular contingent is not, in itself, sufficient qualification for the award of the V.C. Clearly, then, they must be treated as a separate honour.

32 Coutts' Personal File, letter dated 25 March 1913. 'I would like it to be placed among the New Zealand Records of Military matters and in some fitting place, and so I think that it should be handed to the Defence Minister of New Zealand to retain for New Zealand.'

33 Pte Dufrayer, NSW Mounted Rifles: scarf on display at Australian War Memorial, Canberra. Pte R.R. Thompson, Royal Canadian Regiment: scarf on display at Canadian War Museum, Ottawa. Henry Coutts' scarf was on display from 1913 in the General Assembly Library at Parliament until it was loaned to the Queen Elizabeth II Army Memorial Museum, Waiouru, in 1980. The scarf presented to the South African, Trooper L. Chadwick, of Robert's Horse, cannot be located at present. Chadwick was in fact an American, who had also won the Medal of Honour during the Spanish-American War. M.J. Moorehead, "Where is the South African Queen's Scarf?", *The Volunteers*, Volume 5 Number 9, December 1978.

34 Crook, op. cit. p. 259. One of the other cases he was deciding on at the

same time was Lieutenant Bell, an Australian.

35 NZ Archives, File 1251, Personal File of William James Hardham, VC.

36 It is pleasing to note that the officer notified of Hardham's death arranged the conduct of a military funeral at public expense, even though this was not strictly within the regulations of the time, and then notified his superiors that he had done so. Army Command accepted the officer's actions as ensuring a completely appropriate mark of respect. Personal File of William James Hardham.

Chapter 4
**The First World War:
problems and issues**

1 Chris Pugsley, 'Manahi: Was He Cheated?', *New Zealand Defence Quarterly* No. 22, Spring 1998, p. 30.

2 Figures for the number of soldiers who 'took to the field' are from C.E.W. Bean, *Anzac to Amiens* (rev. edn), Penguin Books, Melbourne, 1993, p. 532. The British ratio of one VC per 13,365 soldiers who took to the field is not a good comparison with those of the dominions. In the main the dominions provided front-line infantry soldiers and gunners; the British Army provided these plus the massive logistical support necessary to maintain the BEF in the field.

3 Godley to Allen, letter, 14 August 1915, WA 252/2 Letters of Colonel Hon. Sir James Allen and Sir Alexander Godley April–Dec 1915, Archives of New Zealand (ANZ).

4 Godley to Allen, letter, 20 October 1915, WA 252/2, ANZ.

5 Godley to Allen, letter, 10 November 1915, WA 252/2 ANZ.

6 General Sir Alexander Godley, *Life of an Irish Soldier*, London, John Murray, 1939.

7 Allen to Godley, letter, 10 April 1917, M1/15 Correspondence with Godley Part 2, Allen, J., Personal Papers, ANZ.

8 Godley to Allen, letter, 11 June 1917, WA 252/4 Letters of Col. Hon Sir James Allen to Sir Alexander Godley, 1917, ANZ.

9 Allen to Godley, letter, 7 August 1917, WA 252/4, ANZ.

10 Mr Parr, 17 August 1917, recorded in *New Zealand Parliamentary Debates*, Third Session, Nineteenth Parliament, Vol. 179, August 7 to September 7, 1917, Wellington, Government Printer, 1917, p. 367.

11 The Hon. Sir J. Allen, recorded in *New Zealand Parliamentary Debates*, Third Session, Nineteenth Parliament, Vol. 179, August 7 to September 7, 1917, Wellington, Government Printer, 1917, pp. 451-53.

12 The Hon. Sir J. Allen, recorded in *New Zealand Parliamentary Debates*, Third Session, Nineteenth Parliament, Vol. 179, August 7 to September 7, 1917, Wellington, Government Printer, 1917, p. 453.

13 The Hon. Mr David Buddo, recorded in *New Zealand Parliamentary Debates*, Third Session, Nineteenth Parliament, Vol. 179, August 7 to September 7, 1917, Wellington, Government Printer, 1917, p. 670.

14 The Hon. Mr V.H. Reed, recorded in *New Zealand Parliamentary Debates*, Third Session, Nineteenth Parliament, Vol. 180, September 11 to October 10, 1917, Wellington, Government Printer, 1917, pp. 9–10.

15 *Appendix to the Journals of the House of Representatives of New Zealand 1917.* Vol II, Wellington, 1917, Appendix H-19x.

16 Godley to Allen, letter, 27 October 1917, M1/15, Correspondence with Godley Part 3, Allen, J., ANZ.

17 Godley to Allen, letter, 2 November 1917, WA 252/4, ANZ.

18 Allen to Godley, letter, 28 January 1918, M1/15, Allen, J., ANZ.

19 Godley to Allen, letter, 1 March

1918, WA 252/5 Letters of Allen and Godley 1918–1920, ANZ.

20 Allen to Godley, letter, 16 March 1918, WA 252/5, ANZ.

21 Diary of J.L. Braithwaite, 28 August 1916, quoted in Terry Kinloch, *Echoes of Gallipoli: In the Words of New Zealand's Mounted Riflemen*, Exisle Publishing, Auckland, 2005, p. 250.

22 ibid.

23 Russell to My Dear Father, letter, 17 November 1915, QMS 0822 The Russell Saga Vol III, Alexander Turnbull Library (ATL).

24 Russell to Allen, letter, 7 November 1917, Series 9a Correspondence with Birdwood and Russell, Allen, J., ANZ.

25 Allen to Russell, letter, 29 January 1918, Series 9a, Allen, J., ANZ.

26 Russell to Allen, letter, 3 April 1918, Series 9a, Allen, J., ANZ.

27 Pugsley, op. cit. p. 29. See also Phillip O'Shea, 'Victoria Cross', in Ian McGibbon (ed.), *The Oxford Companion to New Zealand Military History*, Oxford University Press, Auckland, 2000, pp. 558–61.

28 Ormond Burton, 'A Rich Old Man', p. 138, unpublished manuscript, MS 0144 ATL.

Chapter 5
The Gallipoli Victoria Cross

1 Correlli Barnett, *The Great War*, London, BBC Worldwide Limited, 2003, pp. 70–71.

2 ibid., p. 73.

3 The figures are from Stephen Snelling, *VCs of the First World War: Gallipoli*, Sutton Publishing, Stroud (UK), 1995.

4 Quoted in John Crawford (ed.), *No Better Death: The Great War diaries and letters of William G. Malone*, Reed, Auckland, 2005, pp. 201–2.

5 Godley to Lord Liverpool, letter, 3 September 1915, WA 252/8, letters of H.E. Earl of Liverpool and General Godley 1914–18, NZA.

6 Christopher Pugsley, *Gallipoli: The New Zealand Story*, Sceptre, Auckland, 1990, p. 261.

7 C.E.W. Bean, *Official History of Australia in the War of 1914–1918: The Story of Anzac, from 4 May 1915 to the Evacuation of the Gallipoli Peninsula*, Vol 2, Angus and Robertson, Sydney, 1936, p. 576.

8 Pugsley, op. cit. p. 276.

9 Quoted in Pugsley, ibid., p. 279.

10 Sir Ian Hamilton, *Gallipoli Diary*, Vol II, Edward Arnold, London, 1920, pp. 57, 83.

11 Major Fred Waite, *The New Zealanders at Gallipoli*, Whitcombe and Tombes, Auckland, 1919, pp. 219, 221.

12 Pugsley, op. cit. p. 306.

13 Godley to Clive Wigram, 15 August 1915, WA 252/14 Micro Z5083, ANZ.

14 Pugsley, op. cit. p. 313

15 Cyril Bassett's Personal File, D2/6855, AD 36/26, ANZ.

16 Unsourced newspaper article, 12 August 1978, in MSZ 0933 Scrapbook relating to New Zealand Victoria Cross Winners, ATL.

17 Unsourced newspaper article, 12 August 1978, in MSZ 0933 Scrapbook relating to New Zealand Victoria Cross Winners, ATL.

18 Quoted in Snelling, op. cit. p. 186.

19 Unsourced newspaper article, 12 August 1978, in MSZ 0933 Scrapbook relating to New Zealand Victoria Cross Winners, ATL.

20 Undated newspaper article written a week after Bassett's death, Bassett File, New Zealand Defence Library.

21 George Skerrett, interview with Andrew Macdonald, recorded July 1991, text provided by Andrew Macdonald.

22 Taped interview with C.R.G. Bassett VC, Liddle Collection, Leeds University, quoted in Snelling, op. cit. p. 184.

23 Unsourced newspaper article,
12 August 1978, in MSZ 0933
Scrapbook relating to New Zealand
Victoria Cross Winners, ATL.

24 Waite, op. cit. p. 223.

25 NZEF Confidential Report,
19 January 1918, Cyril Bassett's
Personal File, D2/6855, AD 36/26,
ANZ.

26 Demobilisation Medical Form,
N.Z.E.F., 17 January 1919, Cyril
Bassett's Personal File, D2/6855, AD
36/26, ANZ.

27 Snelling, op. cit. p. 187.

28 Undated newspaper article (written a
week after Bassett's death), Bassett
File, New Zealand Defence Library.

29 Quoted in Snelling, op. cit. p. 187.

30 Quoted in Waite, op. cit. p. x.
Suprisingly, Hamilton's published
version of his diary makes no
mention of the VCs.

31 Les Carlyon, *Gallipoli*, Macmillian,
Sydney, 2001, p. 463.

32 Quoted in Waite, op. cit., xiii.

33 Godley to Allen, letter, 14 August
1915, WA 252/2, ANZ.

34 K.M. Stevens, quoted in Pugsley, op.
cit. p. 297.

35 Cecil Allison, quoted in Ted Andrews,
*Kiwi Trooper: The Story of Queen
Alexandra's Own,* Wanganui
Chronicle, Wanganui, 1967, p. 127.

36 Pugsley, op. cit. p. 310.

37 Ormond Burton, 'A Rich Old Man',
unpublished autobiography, MS 0144
Micro, ATL.

38 Snelling, op. cit. p. 161.

39 http://wikipedia.org/wiki, search for
'Alfred John Shout'.

40 Carlyon, op. cit. p. 367.

41 Barnett, op. cit. p. 74.

42 Mr T.K. Sidey, Addendum for
Questions and Replies, *New Zealand
Parliamentary Debates*, Fifth
Session, Nineteenth Parliament,
October 24 to December 10, 1918,
p. 1077.

43 Sir James Allen, reply to Mr Sidey,
New Zealand Parliamentary Debates,
Fifth Session, Nineteenth Parliament,
October 24 to December 10, 1918,
p. 1077.

Chapter 6
The Western Front: 1916

1 One was Lieutenant A.D. Herrick,
whom General Chaytor recommended
for a posthumous VC. The
recommendation was not supported.
See WA 40/4/3 Unregistered Files.
See also Major A.H. Wilkie, *Official
War History of the Wellington
Mounted Rifles Regiment 1914–1919,*
Whitcombe and Tombes, Auckland,
1924, pp. 169, 242. Another was
Lance Corporal Leonard George
Greenslade of the Canterbury
Mounted Rifles. The recommendation
dated 7 November 1917 states:

> For most conspicuous bravery
> and devotion to duty during
> engagement Ras el Nagb on
> 5th November 1917. Whilst
> assisting Trp Aubrey to convey
> a wounded man to safety L/Cpl
> Greenslade and Trp Aubrey were
> both wounded. L/Cpl Greenslade
> however managed to help the
> wounded man to safety and
> immediately returned to carry
> in Aubrey. He was killed in the
> attempt.

Both Brigadier W. Meldrum and
Major General E. Chaytor signed
the recommendation. Its brevity
may have contributed to its lack of
success. The recommendation is in
WA 22/5 Box 5, Item 17 Honours and
Awards (Confidential), ANZ.

2 Recommendation Number 34, WA
22/5 Box 1, Item 1, Honours and
Awards Numbers 1–500, ANZ.

3 Recommendation Number 101, WA
22/5 Box 1, Item 1, Honours and
Awards Numbers 1–500, ANZ.

4 H. Stewart, *The New Zealand
Division 1916–19: A Popular*

History Based on Official Records, Whitcombe and Tombs, Auckland, 1921, p. 47.

5 Ian McGibbon (ed.), *The Oxford Companion to New Zealand Military History*, Oxford University Press, Auckland, 2000, p. 511.

6 Andrew Macdonald, 'Troublesome Hero', *Southland Times* 24 April, 1999.

7 Brown, letter to his father, 11 May 1916, 'The Waitakian', quoted in Sir O'Moore Creagh and E.M. Humphris, *The V.C. and D.S.O.*, Standard Art Book, London, 1924, p. 241.

8 Brown, letter to his father, 28 August 1916, 'The Waitakian', quoted in Creagh and Humphris, ibid.

9 Brown, letter to his father, 11 May 1916, 'The Waitakian', quoted in Creagh and Humphris, ibid.

10 Private J. Baxter, letter to Mr Brown, 16 November 1916, 'The Waitakian', quoted in Creagh and Humphris, ibid.

11 According to the semi-official history by Stewart (op. cit. p. 114), on 1 October 1916 Brown 'single-handed . . . rushed at the gun and bayoneted the crew'. However, eyewitness accounts state that he used a captured German pistol.

12 Capt W.G.A. Gibson-Bishop MC, 10th (NO) Company, nd, 'The Waitakian', quoted in Creagh and Humphris, op. cit. p. 242.

13 Lt Col G.S. Smith, letter, 3 November 1916, 'The Waitakian', quoted in Creagh and Humphris, ibid.

14 Recommendation Number 729, WA 22/5 Box 1, Item 2, Honours and Awards Numbers 501–1000, ANZ.

15 Captain David Ferguson, *The History of the Canterbury Regiment, N.Z.E.F. 1914–1919*, Whitcombe and Tombs, Auckland, 1921, p. 116.

16 Recommendation Number 101, WA 22/5 Box 1, Item 1, Honours and Awards Numbers 1–500, ANZ.

17 Ferguson, op. cit. p. 117.

18 Quoted in Gary Sheffield, *The Somme*, Cassell, London, 2003, p. 149.

Chapter 7
The Western Front: 1917

1 Christopher Pugsley, *On the Fringe of Hell: New Zealanders and Military Discipline in the First World War*, Hodder and Stoughton, Auckland, 1991, p. 190.

2 Medical Report and Proceedings of Medical Board, Napier, 10 November 1926, Personal File of Samuel Frickleton, 6/2133, AD 36/27, ANZ.

3 H. Stewart, *The New Zealand Division 1916–19: A Popular History Based on Official Records*, Whitcombe and Tombs, Auckland, 1921, p. 190.

4 Medical Report and Proceedings of Medical Board, Napier, 10 November 1926, Personal File of Samuel Frickleton, 6/2133, AD 36/27, ANZ.

5 Frickleton, letter, to the OC, 1st Battalion, Wellington Regiment, 23 May 1934, Personal File of Samuel Frickleton, 6/2133, AD 36/27, ANZ.

6 Assistant Director of Medical Services to Director of Mobilisation, Confidential Minute, 30 November 1939, Personal File of Samuel Frickleton, 6/2133, AD 36/27, ANZ.

7 Recommendation Number 1006, WA 22/5 Box 2, Item 3, Honours and Awards Numbers 1001–1500, ANZ.

8 Recommendation Number 994, WA 22/5 Box 1, Item 2, Honours and Awards Numbers 501–1000, ANZ.

9 Stewart, op. cit. p. 194.

10 Quoted in Sir O'Moore Creagh and E.M. Humphris, *The V.C. and D.S.O.*, Standard Art Book, London, 1924, p. 251.

11 Brigadier A.E. Stewart to NZ Military Forces, Wellington, letter, 2 September 1919, Personal File of Leslie Wilton Andrew, 1/1054, AD 36/26, ANZ.

12 Ian McGibbon (ed.), *The Oxford*

Companion to New Zealand Military History, Oxford University Press, Auckland, 2000, p. 17.

13 Stewart, op. cit. pp. 311–12.
14 Recommendation Number 1001, WA 22/5 Box 2, Item 3, Honours and Awards Numbers 1001–1500, ANZ.

Chapter 8
The Western Front: 1918

1   McGibbon, op. cit. p. 319; Garry Clayton, 'Miles, Reginald, 1892–1943', in *Dictionary of New Zealand Biography*, updated 16 December 2003, URL: http.//www.dnzb.govt.nz.
2· Brigadier R. Miles, CBE, DSO, MC, MID, RNZA, Army Headquarters 24 May 1965, in Reginald Miles Personal File, Z/1645 & 6191, Personnel Archives, Trentham.
3   Note re: Seniority of Officers already serving and those newly appointed in the R.N.Z.A., Lieut-Colonel M.M. Gardiner, January 1920, Reginald Miles Personal File, Z/1645 & 6191, Personnel Archives, Trentham.
4   Stewart, op. cit. pp. 374–75.
5   Recommendation No. 2090, WA 22/5 Box 3 Item 5, Honours and Awards 2001–2282, ANZ.
6   Glyn Harper, *Spring Offensive: New Zealand and the Second Battle of the Somme*, HarperCollins, Auckland, 2003, p. 90.
7   Recommendation No. 2090, WA 22/5 Box 3, Item 5, Honours and Awards 2001–2282, ANZ.
8   Jim Henderson, *Soldier Country*, GP Books, Wellington, 1990, p. 84.
9   Quoted in Henderson, ibid., p. 88.
10 Richard Travis, letter to his mother, 30 May 1909, AD 36/29 Personal File of Richard Charles Travis 9/523, ANZ.
11 Statement of Corporal William Patterson, AD 36/29 Personal File of Richard Charles Travis 9/523, ANZ.
12 James Gasson, *Travis V.C.: Man in No Man's Land*, A.H. & A.W. Reed, Wellington, 1966, p. 32.

13 AD 36/29 Personal File of Richard Charles Travis 9/523, ANZ.
14 Undated newspaper clipping, ABFK W4312, Box 2, Sgt R.Travis VC, ANZ.
15 A.D. Swainson, letter, The Editor, *NZRSA Review* February 1938, in MSZ 0933 Scrapbook Relating to NZ VC Winners, ATL.
16 Stewart, op. cit. p. 85.
17 A Padre's Sketch, AD 36/29 Personal File of Richard Charles Travis 9/523, ANZ.
18 Patrol Report, 8.05 p.m. 11 Oct 1917, WA 76/1 War Diary 2nd NZ Inf Bde, ANZ, quoted in Glyn Harper, *Massacre at Passchendaele: The New Zealand Story*, HarperCollins, Auckland, 2000, pp. 65–67.
19 Statement of Pte H. Ellis, Recommendation Number 2282, WA 22/5 Box 3, Item 5, Honours and Awards Numbers 1001–1500, ANZ.
20 Stewart, op. cit. p. 400.
21 War Diary 2nd Otago Battalion, 24 July 1918, WA 80/1, NZA.
22 War Diary 2nd Otago Battalion, 25 and 26 July 1918, WA 80/1, NZA.
23 A Padre's Sketch, AD 36/29 Personal File of Richard Charles Travis 9/523, ANZ.
24 'In Praise of a Soldier: In Memory of Dick Travis, VC, DCM, MM' by 'Otago', *Quick March* 10 February 1920, in MSZ 0933 Scrapbook Relating to NZ VC Winners, ATL.
25 The book is James Gasson's *Travis V.C.*
26 Jim Henderson, *Unofficial History: Yarns From Old Soldiers*, Whitcombe and Tombs, Christchurch, 1964, p. 44.
27 Quoted in the *Dunedin Star*, 20 March 1965, ABFK W4312, Box 2, Sgt R.Travis VC, ANZ.
28 Ormond Burton, 'A Rich Old Man' p. 198, unpublished manuscript, MS 0144 ATL.
29 Mary Forsyth to Ormond Burton, letter, 1918, MS Papers 0438-033 Reverend Ormond E. Burton

Correspondence, ATL.

30 'New Zealand Victoria Cross brings $20,000 plus', undated newspaper clipping, MSZ 0933 Scrapbook Relating to NZ VC Winners, ATL.

31 G.A. Bryant, *Where the Prize is Highest: The Stories of the New Zealanders who Won the Victoria Cross*, Collins, Auckland, 1972, p. 105.

32 New Zealand Army Information Sheet, ABFK W4312, Box 2, Victoria Cross — R.S. Judson, ANZ.

33 Annual Confidential Report, 29 July 1920, Personal File of Reginald Stanley Judson, 24/1699, AD 36/28, ANZ.

34 Medical Report of an Invalid, 15 June 1924, Personal File of Reginald Stanley Judson, 24/1699, AD 36/28, ANZ.

35 Judson, letter, to Staff Officer in Charge, No.1 Regimental District, 17 August 1934, Personal File of Reginald Stanley Judson, 24/1699, AD 36/28, ANZ.

36 Judson, letter, to HQ Northern Military Command, 26 March 1936, Personal File of Reginald Stanley Judson, 24/1699, AD 36/28, ANZ.

37 V.F. Maxwell, letter, to M.J. Savage, 4 November 1937, Personal File of Reginald Stanley Judson, 24/1699, AD 36/28, ANZ.

38 F. Jones, letter, to V.F. Maxwell, 23 November 1937, Personal File of Reginald Stanley Judson, 24/1699, AD 36/28, ANZ.

39 Stewart, op. cit. p. 456.

40 Personal File of 10/2950 John Gildroy Grant, AD 36/28, ANZ.

41 Colonel J.E. Duigan, letter to General Headquarters, 10 May 1935, Personal File of 10/2950 John Gildroy Grant, AD 36/28, ANZ.

42 Gabrielle McDonald, *Jack Hinton V.C.: A Man Amongst Men*, David Ling Publishing, Auckland, 1997, pp. 177–78.

43 Personal File of 24/213 Harry John

44 'Death of Mr Henry John (Harry) Laurent VC', newspaper clipping 1 February 1988, MSZ 0933 Scrapbook Relating to NZ VC Winners, ATL.

45 Statement by Captain James Evans, Statements of the conduct leading up to the award of the V.C. to Pte J. Crichton at Crevecoeur, 30-9-18, NZEF Miscellaneous Record, WA 10/3 Box 3, ANZ.

46 Discharge Certificate, Personal File of James Crichton, 14/131, AD 36/26, ANZ.

47 *New Zealand Honours and Awards: The Victoria Cross*, Army Headquarters, Wellington, 1969.

48 Statement by Lt Col W.W. Alderman, Recommendation No. 2984, WA 22/5 Box 3, Item 7, Honours and Awards Numbers 2501–3000, ANZ.

49 Bryant, op. cit. p. 92.

Chapter 9
The First World War:
air and naval VCs

1 Christopher Chant in Bernard Fitzsimons (ed.), *Warplanes and Air Battles of World War 1,* Phoebus, London, 1973, p. 142.

2 The Germans developed the term 'Flugzeug Abwehr Flieger-Kanone', which was shortened to Flak as a general description of anti-aircraft fire. Ian Hogg, *German Artillery of World War Two,* Arms and Armour Press, London, 1975, p. 14.

3 David Devine, *The Broken Wing,* Hutchinson, London, 1966, pp. 74–75.

4 D.B. Tubbs in Fitzsimons, op. cit. p. 26.

5 Devine, op. cit. pp. 71–72.

6 B.H. Liddell Hart, *History of the First World War,* Cassell, London, 1970, p. 463.

7 E. Angelucci and P. Matricardi, *World Aircraft: Origins — World War 1,* Sampson Low, Maidenhead, 1977, p. 169

8   Chaz Bowyer, *For Valour: The Air VCs*, William Kimber, London, 1978, p. 26.

9   P.G. Cooksey, *VCs of the First World War: The Air VCs*, Sutton Publishing, Stroud, 1996, p. 4.

10 G.A. Bryant, *Where the Prize is Highest: The Stories of the New Zealanders who Won the Victoria Cross*, Collins, Auckland, 1972, p. 32.

11 Some sources do contend that he visited the North Island briefly while returning to England from America, but there are no records of this and it seems unlikely given the circuitous route this would require.

12 G.A. Bryant, author of *Where the Prize is Highest*, undertook considerable research and correspondence with the Moorhouse family in order to find out about Mary Ann's mother. They could find nothing. His correspondence and research material are in the Alexander Turnbull Library, MS 5009, Folder 2.

13 William Rhodes-Moorhouse undoubtedly thought of himself only as English, but given his maternal grandmother, although we cannot trace her whakapapa, he technically qualifies to be deemed Maori.

14 Robert B. Asprey, *The German High Command at War*, Little Brown, London, 1991, p. 257.

15 B.H. Liddell Hart, *Strategy*, Meridian, New York, 1991, p. 188.

16 Cyril B. Falls, *The First World War*, Longmans, London, 1960, p. 70.

17 John Keegan, *The First World War*, Hutchinson, London, 1998, p. 287.

18 Asprey, op. cit. pp. 133, 232.

19 A.J.P. Taylor, *World War I*, Octopus Books, London, 1973, pp. 84–85.

20 Asprey, op. cit. p. 214.

21 http://www.naval-historynet/WW1NavyBritishQships.htm

22 Stephen Snelling, *VCs of the First World War: The Naval VCs*, Sutton Publishing, Stroud, 2002, p. 159.

23 John Winton, *The Victoria Cross at Sea*, Michael Joseph, London, 1978, p. 143.

24 Snelling, op. cit. pp. 162–64.

25 *The Dictionary of New Zealand Biography: Vol 3, 1901–1920*, Auckland University Press, Auckland 1996, pp. 458–59.

26 Grant Howard, 'Sanders VC', *Zealandia's War at Sea*, in *Navy Today*, No. 83, Supplement 1–11, November 2003, pp. 5–6.

27 Snelling, op. cit. pp. 165–66.

28 http://qships.freeservers.com/LossofPrize.htm

29 Henry Newbolt, *History of the Great War: Naval Operations, Vol V*, Longmans, London, 1931, p. 110.

30 The Sanders Cup, for racing javelin skiffs, is still awarded in Auckland, and there are several memorials to him and a street named after him in the city.

Chapter 10
The Second World War: problems and issues

1   John Crawford (ed.), *Kia Kaha: New Zealand in the Second World War*, Oxford University Press, Melbourne, 2000, p. 3.

2   Ian McGibbon (ed.), *The Oxford Companion to New Zealand Military History*, Oxford University Press, Auckland, 2000, p. 484.

3   Crawford, op. cit. p. 3; McGibbon, ibid.

4   Phillip O'Shea in McGibbon, op. cit. p. 558.

5   ibid., p. 559.

6   ibid., p. 561.

7   John Percival, *For Valour: The Victoria Cross Courage in Action*, Thames Methuen, London, 1985, p. 93.

8   Figures are from C.E. Lucas Phillips, *Victoria Cross Battles of the Second World War*, Heinemann, London, 1973, pp. 9–10.

9   Peter Dennerly, 'The Royal New Zealand Navy', in Crawford, op. cit.

p. 121. The figures for personnel and naval vessels are also from Dennerly.

10 McGibbon, op. cit. p. 498.

11 Christina Goulter, in McGibbon, op. cit. pp. 10, 15.

12 Lucas Phillips, op. cit. p. 4.

13 John Frayn Turner, *VCs of the Second World War*, Pen and Sword Military, Barnsley, 2004, p. 30.

14 Lucas Phillips, op. cit. p. xii.

15 ibid., p. 128.

16 Kippenberger, letter dated 17 December 1941, quoted in Glyn Harper, *Kippenberger: An Inspired New Zealand Commander*, HarperCollins Publishers, Auckland, 1997, p. 128.

17 Heinz Werner Schmidt, Rommel's PA, later wrote: 'the November battle [CRUSADER] was won largely by the New Zealanders.' *With Rommel in the Desert*, Hamilton & Co., London, 1960, p. 90.

18 McGibbon, op. cit. p. 253.

19 Leslie Hobbs, Laurie Barber and John Tonkin-Covell, quoted in Glyn Harper, op. cit. p. 11.

Chapter 11
Greece and Crete 1941

1 Kippenberger, quoted in Glyn Harper, *Kippenberger: An Inspired New Zealand Commander*, HarperCollins Publishers, Auckland, 1997, p. 82.

2 Freyberg, Reflections leaving Alexandria, 6 March 1941, WAII 8/10 General-Historical Papers 1940-41, ANZ.

3 John Frayn Turner, *VCs of the Second World War*, Pen and Sword Military, Barnsley, 2004, p. 43.

4 Gabrielle McDonald, *Jack Hinton V.C.: A Man Amongst Men*, David Ling Publishing, Auckland, 1997, p. 26.

5 ibid., p. 32.

6 ibid., p. 52.

7 C.E. Lucas Phillips, *Victoria Cross Battles of the Second World War*, Heinemann, London, 1973, p. 12.

8 D.J.C. Pringle and W.A. Glue, *Official History of New Zealand in the Second World War 1939–45: 20 Battalion and Armoured Regiment*, War History Branch, Department of Internal Affairs, Wellington, 1957, p. 19.

9 ibid., p. 87.

10 McDonald, op. cit. p. 78.

11 W.G. McClymont, *Official History of New Zealand in the Second World War 1939–45: To Greece*, War History Branch, Department of Internal Affairs, Wellington, 1959, p. 456.

12 Pringle and Glue, op. cit. p. 87.

13 McDonald, op. cit. p. 81.

14 ibid., pp. 84–85.

15 NZPA, 29/6/97.

16 McDonald, op. cit. p. 91.

17 Sjt John Daniel Hinton, WA II Series 1 DA 409.2/2 Volume 4, Gray to Howe, ANZ.

18 Kippenberger, quoted in Harper, op. cit. p. 80.

19 ibid.

20 J.T. Burrows, *Pathway Among Men*, Whitcombe and Tombs, Christchurch, 1974, pp. 132–33.

21 John Daniel Hinton, Personal File, AD36/28, ANZ.

22 Report on the Conduct of NZ POW Sgt J.D. Hinton VC, Statement made by WO II James, 8 May 1945, John Daniel Hinton, Personal File, AD36/28, ANZ.

23 McDonald, op. cit. p. 168.

24 NZPA release, 1/7/97.

25 NZPA release, 25/4/02.

26 J.A.B. Crawford, 'Stott, Donald John, 1914–45', in *New Zealand Dictionary of Biography*, updated 16 December 2003, URL: http//www.dnzb.govt.nz.

27 Quoted in Cedric Mentiplay, *A Fighting Quality: New Zealanders at War*, A.H. & A.W. Reed, Wellington, 1979, p. 66.

28 H.S. Wogan, Director Base Records to Mrs M.K. Stott, letter, 17 February 1950, in Personal File, Donald

John Stott, Base Records, File D2061.11844, Trentham.

29 Glyn Harper, in Ian McGibbon (ed.), *The Oxford Companion to New Zealand Military History*, Oxford University Press, Auckland, 2000, p. 123.

30 Michael King, *The Penguin History of New Zealand*, Penguin Books, Auckland, 2003, p. 397.

31 D.M. Davin, *Official History Of New Zealand in the Second World War 1939–45: Crete*, War History Branch, Department of Internal Affairs, Wellington, 1953, p. 340.

32 King, op. cit. p. 398.

33 Lucas Phillips, op. cit. p. 45.

34 Quoted in Davin, op. cit. p. 129.

35 Lucas Phillips, op. cit. p. 45.

36 Hulme, interview with Angus Ross, n.d., quoted in Lynn McConnell, *Galatas 1941*, unpublished manuscript, p. 111.

37 Angus Ross, *Official History of New Zealand in the Second World War 1939-45 23 Battalion*, War History Branch, Department of Internal Affairs, Wellington, 1953, p. 95.

38 Hulme, interview with Angus Ross, n.d., quoted in Lynn McConnell, 'Galatas 1941', unpublished manuscript, p. 188.

39 G.A. Bryant, *Where the Prize is Highest: The Stories of the New Zealanders who Won the Victoria Cross*, Collins, Auckland, 1972, p. 144.

40 Ross, op. cit. p. 89.

41 ibid.

42 ibid., p. 95.

43 10725 Recommendation for Sergeant Alfred Clive Hulme, WAII Series 1 DA 409.2/2 Vol. 5, Hua–Low, ANZ.

44 Ross, op. cit. p. 96.

45 Personal File Alfred Clive Hulme, AD 36/28, ANZ.

46 Hulme, interview with Angus Ross, n.d., quoted in Lynn McConnell, 'Galatas 1941', unpublished manuscript, p. 219.

47 NZPA release, 23/4/99.

48 Lucas Phillips, op. cit. p. xii. Only three soldier have won the VC and bar. Charles Upham is the only combatant soldier to do so.

49 Personal File of Charles Upham, AD 36/29, ANZ.

50 From Kenneth Sandford, *Mark of the Lion: The Story of Capt. Charles Upham, V.C. and Bar*, Hutchinson & Co., London, 1962, pp. 43, 45. Upham always disputed that he had graduated bottom of his class.

51 Lucas Phillips, op. cit. pp. 15–16.

52 ibid., p. 16.

53 Sandford, op. cit. p. 57.

54 Private Melville Hill-Rennie, quoted in Pringle and Glue, op. cit. p. 108.

55 ibid., p. 109.

56 Upham, quoted in Davin, op. cit. p. 216.

57 Report by Capt. Upham, in Davin, op. cit. p. 219.

58 Phillips, op. cit. p. 35.

59 Quoted in Pringle and Glue, op. cit. p. 124.

60 Sandford, op. cit. p. 89.

61 Cpl Vincent, quoted in Pringle and Glue, op. cit. p. 143.

62 Kippenberger, quoted in *The Dominion*, 27 September 1945.

63 Captain D.J. Fountaine, statement, WAII 1 DA 409.2/2 Citations for Awards Vol. 10 Tro–Z, ANZ.

64 Kippenberger, quoted in *The Dominion*, 27 September 1945.

65 Sandford, op. cit. p. 112.

66 ibid., p. 107.

67 ibid., p. 117.

68 King, op. cit. p. 398.

69 Murray Elliott, *Vasili: The Lion of Crete*, Century Hutchinson, Auckland, 1987, p. 157.

70 ibid., pp. 157–58.

71 Quoted in Murray Elliott, ibid., p. 163.

Chapter 12
North Africa 1941-43

1 Glyn Harper, in Ian McGibbon (ed.),

The Oxford Companion to New
Zealand Military History, Oxford
University Press, Auckland, 2000,
p. 391.

2 Harper, ibid., p. 395.

3 D.J.C. Pringle and W.A. Glue,
   Official History of New Zealand in
   the Second World War 1939–45: 20
   Battalion and Armoured Regiment,
   War History Branch, Department of
   Internal Affairs, Wellington, 1957,
   p. 235.

4 Quoted in Pringle and Glue, ibid.,
   p. 241.

5 Kenneth Sandford, Mark of the Lion:
   The Story of Capt. Charles Upham,
   V.C. and Bar, Hutchinson & Co.,
   London, 1962, p. 151.

6 ibid., p. 156.

7 J.L. Scoullar, Official History Of
   New Zealand in the Second World
   War 1939–45: Battle for Egypt: The
   Summer of 1942, War History Branch,
   Department of Internal Affairs,
   Wellington, 1955, pp. 110–11.

8 C.E. Lucas Phillips, Victoria Cross
   Battles of the Second World War,
   Heinemann, London, 1973, p. 158.

9 ibid., p. 160.

10 Scoullar, op. cit. p. 246.

11 Sandford, op. cit. p. 166.

12 Quoted in Pringle and Glue, op. cit.
   p. 264.

13 Sandford, op. cit. p. 172.

14 ibid., p. 245.

15 Recommendation for the bar to VC,
   WA II 1 DA 409.2/2 Citations for
   Awards Vol. 10 Tro–Z, ANZ.

16 Sandford, op. cit. p. 261.

17 Lucas Phillips, op. cit. pp. 168–69;
   also in Sandford, op. cit. p. 263.

18 Recommendation for the bar to VC,
   WA II 1 DA 409.2/2 Citations for
   Awards Vol. 10 Tro–Z, ANZ.

19 Article dated 23/4/84, Scrapbook of
   VC Winners, MSZ 0933, ATL.

20 F. Jones, Press release dated 26/9/45,
   in Personal File Charles Upham, AD
   36/29, ANZ.

21 Undated article, Scrapbook of VC

Winners, MSZ 0933, ATL.

22 Article 'A Visit to Charles Upham',
   MS Papers 5009, Folder 2, Bryant
   G.A., ATL.

23 ibid.

24 ibid.

25 Kippenberger, letter to K.L. Sandford,
   22 July 1955, IA 77/30 K.L. Sandford
   Publication of book on Capt C.H.
   Upham, VC and bar, ANZ.

26 NZPA release 10/12/97.

27 ibid.

28 NZPA release 17/12/97.

29 T.P. McLean, article dated 23/4/84,
   Scrapbook of VC Winners, MSZ
   0933, ATL.

30 Keith Elliott VC and Rona Adshead,
   From Cowshed to Dogcollar, A.H. &
   A.W. Reed, Wellington, 1967, p. 24.

31 ibid., p. 32.

32 Personal File Keith Elliott, AD 36/26,
   ANZ.

33 Elliott and Adshead, op. cit. p. 33.

34 Keith Elliott, quoted in John Percival,
   For Valour: The Victoria Cross in
   Action, Thames Methuen, London,
   1985, p. 118.

35 Quoted in Percival, ibid., p. 120.

36 Elliott and Adshead, op. cit. p. 67.

37 ibid., p. 73.

38 Keith Elliott, quoted in Percival,
   op. cit. pp. 121–22.

39 Elliott and Adshead, op. cit. p. 93.

40 Percival, op. cit. p. 123.

41 Elliott, letter to FAHS, 14 January
   1942, quoted in Feilding Agricultural
   High School, War Memorial Volume,
   1948, p. 98.

42 Jim Henderson, Official History of
   New Zealand in the Second World
   War 1939–45: 22 Battalion, War
   History Branch, Department of
   Internal Affairs, Wellington, 1958,
   p. 175.

43 Major General Howard Kippenberger,
   Infantry Brigadier, Oxford University
   Press, London, 1949, p. 167.

44 Henderson, op. cit. p. 176.

45 The Dominion 22 April 1989.

46 Elliott and Adshead, op. cit. p. 111.

47 Scoullar, op. cit. p. 256.

48 Elliott and Adshead, op. cit. p. 111.

49 *The Dominion* 22 April 1989.

50 Quoted in Henderson, op. cit. p. 176.

51 Percival, op. cit. p. 114.

52 Quoted in Percival, op. cit. p. 126.

53 Elliott and Adshead, op. cit. p. 113.

54 Statement by Captain R.R.T. Young, 18 August 1942, WA II 1 DA 409.2/2 Citations for Awards Vol. 3 Dob–Grav, ANZ.

55 Scoullar, op. cit. p. 275.

56 Elliott and Adshead, op. cit. p. 115.

57 ibid., p. 117.

58 Note for Confidential File of Sgt Elliott VC, 15 July 1943, Personal File Keith Elliott, AD 36/26, ANZ.

59 Elliott and Adshead, op. cit. p. 117.

60 ibid., p. 120.

61 Undated newspaper article, Scrapbook relating to New Zealand VC Winners, MSZ 0933, ATL.

62 *The Dominion* 22 April 1989.

63 Personal File Keith Elliott, AD 36/26, ANZ.

64 Elliott and Adshead, op. cit. p. 158.

65 ibid., p. 140.

66 Mr Ron Jones, quoted in undated newspaper article, Scrapbook relating to New Zealand VC Winners, MSZ 0933, ATL.

67 Keith Elliott, letter to the Military Secretary, 25 January 1961, Personal File Keith Elliott, AD 36/26, ANZ.

68 Confidential Minute, 'Rev K. Elliott – Chaplain 4th Class – R of O General List – Wearing of VC', Personal File Keith Elliott, AD 36/26, ANZ.

69 Percival, op. cit. p. 134.

70 NZPA release 24/6/96.

71 Undated newspaper article, Scrapbook relating to New Zealand VC Winners, MSZ 0933, ATL.

72 Keith Elliott, letter to FAHS, 3 December 1942, *Feilding Agricultural High School, War Memorial Volume*, 1948, p. 63.

73 Whai Ngata, Review article, *RSA Review*, April 1993, MSZ 0933 Scrapbook, ATL.

74 Sir Charles Bennett, quoted in *Ngarimu, V.C.:A Maori Hero*, documentary directed and produced by Pere Maitai, presented by Wira Gardiner, 1993.

75 W.G. Stevens, *Official History Of New Zealand in the Second World War 1939–45: Bardia to Enfidaville*, War History Branch, Department of Internal Affairs, Wellington, 1962, p. 229.

76 J.F. Cody, *Official History of New Zealand in the Second World War 1939–45: 28 (Maori) Battalion*, War History Branch, Department of Internal Affairs, Wellington, 1956, p. 272.

77 Wira Gardiner, *Te Mura O Te Ahi: The story of the Maori Battalion*, Reed, Auckland, 1992, p. 170.

78 Cody, op. cit. p. 273.

79 Stevens, op. cit. p. 220.

80 Cody, op. cit. p. 273.

81 Stevens, op. cit. p. 231.

82 ibid.

83 Corporal P. Tamepo, Eyewitness Statement 4/4/43, WA II DA 409.2/2 Citations for Awards Vol.7 MAS-PAD, ANZ.

84 Freyberg, Secret Special Telegram to PM, 2 June 1943, AD1 DA 409.2/6, ANZ.

85 Peter Fraser, PM, Urgent Telegram to Hamuera Ngarimu, 4 June 1943, AD 36/29 Personal File Ngarimu, Moana Nui-A-Kiwa, ANZ.

86 Mr Hamuera Ngarimu, quoted in *Ngarimu, V.C.: A Maori Hero*, documentary directed and produced by Pere Maitai, presented by Wira Gardiner, 1993.

87 Kippenberger, op. cit. p. 314.

88 McGibbon, op. cit. p. 531.

89 Recommendation for 9234 Walter Babington Thomas, WA II 1 DA 409.2/2 Vol 9 Rut–Tol, ANZ.

90 W.B. 'Sandy' Thomas, compiled by Denis McLean, *Pathways to Adventure: An Extraordinary Life*, Dryden Press, Hororata, 2004, p. 82.

91 Stevens, op. cit. p. 327.

92 Cody, op. cit. p. 300.

93 ibid., p. 304.

94 Ian Wards, *Official History of New Zealand in the Second World War 1939–45: Takrouna*, War History Branch, Department of Internal Affair, Wellington, 1951, p. 25.

95 Lt General Sir Brian Horrocks, *A Full Life*, Collins, London, 1960, p. 163.

96 Quoted in Glyn Harper, *Kippenberger: An Inspired New Zealand Commander*, HarperCollins Publishers, Auckland, 1997, p. 231.

97 Cody, op. cit. p. 308.

98 Figures are from Stevens, op. cit. p. 339.

99 Wards, op. cit. p. 27.

100 Statement of Lt Ian Henry Hirst, WA II 1 DA 409.2/2 Citations for Awards Vol. 6 Low–Mas, ANZ.

101 Original VC Recommendation for Haane Manahi, No.13500, copy in author's possession.

102 NZPA release 22/1/97.

103 Draft of 'The Case for the Posthumous Award of the Victoria Cross to Sergeant H. Manahi for actions at Takrouna 19/20 April 1943', 1993, copy in author's possession.

104 NZPA release 24/1/97.

105 Gardiner, op. cit. p. 124.

106 NZPA release 21/1/97.

107 Prime Minister the Rt Hon Jenny Shipley, letter to the Hon Tuariki Delamere, 26 August 1999, in Manahi Personal File, Personnel Archives, Wellington.

108 ibid.

Chapter 13
The air VCs of the Second World War

1 Gerhard L. Weinberg, *A World at Arms: A Global History of World War II,* Cambridge University Press, Cambridge, 1994, pp. 149–50.

2 Ian McGibbon (ed.), *The Oxford Companion to New Zealand Military History,* OUP, Auckland, 2000, pp. 114, 156–7, 176, 262, 411–12, 459. New Zealand provided fully trained pilots as well as sending partially trained personnel to complete their courses in Canada.

3 ibid., p. 176.

4 ibid., pp. 449–50.

5 Max Lambert, *Night After Night: The New Zealanders in Bomber Command*, HarperCollins, Auckland, 2005, pp. 176–78.

6 ibid., p. 460. The aircraft were awaiting delivery to New Zealand and the 20 personnel had been sent to ferry them there. The squadron became part of the RNZAF at the war's end, and was disbanded in 2001.

7 Bill Gunston, *Aircraft of World War Two*, Peerage Books, London, 1985, p. 202.

8 Chaz Bowyer, *For Valour: The Air VCs*, William Kimber, London, p. 258. In most accounts it is the rear gunner who was both wounded and shot down the attacking fighter, but the account held on Ward's personal file states it was the front gunner who was wounded in the foot.

9 ibid., p. 260.

10 5/1/491 CR dated 16 February 1939 and Report dated 18/1/41 in NZ Archives, File 40/1793, Personal File of J.A. Ward, VC.

11 John Frayn Turner, *VCs of the Air,* Harrap, London, 1960, p. 51.

12 RNZAF Liaison Office Message 202 dated 13 September 1941 in NZ Archives, File 40/1793, Personal File of J.A. Ward, VC.

13 McGibbon, op. cit. p. 595; also Bowyer, op. cit. p. 261.

14 5/1/491 DPR dated 3 December 1945 by Flight Lieutenant L.E. Peterson, RCAF, in NZ Archives, File 40/1793, Personal File of J.A. Ward, VC.

15 Chris Chant, *Aircraft of World War II,* Brown Books, London, 1999, p. 215.

16 J. Sanders, *Venturer Courageous,*

Hutchinson, Auckland, 1983, pp. 88–89.

17   ibid., pp. 85–86. R.L. Kippenberger was the brother of Major General Howard Kippenberger. Feltwell had previously been the base of 75 Squadron.

18   ibid., p. 102.

19   ibid., p. 105.

20   It appears that one other bomber in the squadron, flown by New Zealander Owen Foster, was in fact still making its final run as Trent's plane fell out of control, but was so badly damaged it came down in the sea off Holland shortly afterwards. Max Lambert, op. cit. p. 236.

21   Max Arthur, *Symbol of Courage,* Sidgwick and Jackson, London, 2004, pp. 450–51.

22   Biographical Sketch in File 5/2/1034, Personal File of Leonard Henry Trent VC held in NZ Archives.

23   *The Dictionary of New Zealand Biography: Vol 5 1941–1960,* Auckland University Press, Auckland, 2000, p. 526.

24   Course Report dated 3 December 1937 in File 5/2/1034, Personal File of Leonard Henry Trent VC held in NZ Archives.

25   Boywer, op. cit. p. 314.

26   Paul Brickhill, *The Great Escape,* Faber and Faber, London, 1951, pp. 194–95.

27   ibid., pp. 211–12.

28   Sanders, op. cit. pp. 198–99.

29   NZ Archives 5/2/7160, Personal File of Lloyd Allan Trigg VC.

30   *London Gazette,* 2 November 1943.

31   Turner, op. cit. p. 116; *London Gazette,* 2 November 1943.

32   Bowyer, op. cit. p. 332 and NZ Archives 5/2/7160, Personal File of Lloyd Allan Trigg VC.

33   Turner, op. cit. p. 114.

34   Bowyer, op. cit. p. 332.

35   RNZAF Official News Service, Enemy's Tribute to Heroic Airman, New Delhi 1 February 1945, in NZ Archives 5/2/7160, Personal File of Lloyd Allan Trigg VC.

36   Turner, op. cit. p. 113.

37   Bowyer, op. cit. p. 330.

38   NZ Archives 5/2/7160, Personal File of Lloyd Allan Trigg VC.

39   ibid.

40   Air Force Message 114/31 dated 1 November 1943 in NZ Archives 5/2/7160, Personal File of Lloyd Allan Trigg VC.

41   http://www2.prestel.co.uk/stewart/ bbtrigg.htm. The medal group, including both the VC and DFC, sold at auction in 1998 for £120,000.

Chapter 14
The George Cross and Albert Medal

1   The content of this chapter, unless otherwise footnoted, is entirely drawn from *An Unknown Few* by P.P. O'Shea, the New Zealand Herald at Arms Extraordinary (Government Printer, 1981). This book remains the definitive work on this subject in New Zealand.

2   Warrant Redefining the Qualifications for the Victoria Cross and Extending Eligibility to Auxiliary and Reserve Forces, dated 23 April 1881.

3   Magnusson J.W. Personal File 13/927, NZDF Base Records. The evidence at the court martial states that he told Lieutenant Ruddock that he was a bloody idiot and said he 'was not fit to be pissed up against and also that he was not a man's arse'.

4   Ridling R.G. Personal File 23927, NZDF Base Records.

5   Transcript of Court of Inquiry evidence in Ridling R.G. Personal File 23927, NZDF Base Records.

6   Later Major General Sir George Spafford Richardson, New Zealand Administrator of Western Samoa.

7   Dale W.D. Personal File NZ 4861, NZDF Base Records.

8   Ian McGibbon (ed.), *The Oxford Companion to New Zealand Military*

History, OUP, Auckland, 2000,
p. 471.
9   Russell G.C. Personal File 30169,
in DA 447/21 in National Archives,
Wellington, New Zealand.

Conclusion
Ordinary men, extraordinary deeds
1   W.E. Murphy, *Official History of
New Zealand in the Second World
War 1939–45: The Relief of Tobruk*,
War History Branch, Department of
Internal Affairs, Wellington, 1961,
p. 337.
2   ibid., p. 338.

3   James Hargest, *Farewell Campo 12*,
Michael Joseph Ltd, London, 1945,
p. 20.
4   Murphy, op. cit. p. 338.
5   From information supplied by the
NZDF.
6   The authors are grateful to John
Crawford, the NZDF historian, for
alerting us to Bombardier Niven's
story.
7   *Dominion Post* 19 March 2005.
8   *The Dominion* 22 April 1989.
9   Keith Elliott VC and Rona Adshead,
From Cowshed to Dogcollar, A.H. &
A.W. Reed, Wellington, 1967, p. 120.

Bibliography

PRIMARY SOURCES

Three centres of research provided the bulk of the primary source material. They were the Alexander Turnbull Library and Archives New Zealand, both located in Wellington, and Personnel Archives located in Trentham Military Camp. The following files were particularly useful.

Archives New Zealand

WAII 8/10 General — Historical Papers 1940–41.

WA 10/3 Box 3, Miscellaneous Record.

WA 22/5 Box 1, Item 1, Honours and Awards Numbers 1–500.

WA 22/5 Box 1, Item 2, Honours and Awards Numbers 501–1000.

WA 22/5 Box 2, Item 3, Honours and Awards Numbers 1001–1500.

WA 22/5 Box 2, Item 4, Honours and Awards Numbers 1501–2000.

WA 22/5 Box 3, Item 5, Honours and Awards Numbers 2001–2282.

WA 22/5 Box 3, Item 6, Honours and Awards Numbers 2283–2500.

WA 22/5 Box 3, Item 7, Honours and Awards Numbers 2501–3000.

WA 22/5 Box 5, Item 17, Honours and Awards (Confidential).

WA 40/4/3 Unregistered Files.

WA 80/1, War Diary 2nd Otago Battalion.

WA 252/2 Letters of Colonel Hon. Sir James Allen and Sir Alexander Godley, April–Dec 1915.

WA 252/4 Letters of Col. Hon Sir James Allen to Sir Alexander Godley, 1917.

WA 252/5 Letters of Allen and Godley 1918–20.

WA 252/8, Letters of H.E. Earl of Liverpool and General Godley 1914–18.

WA 252/14 Micro Z5083, Godley correspondence.

WA II 1 DA 409.2/2, Citations for Awards Volume 3, Dob–Grav, ANZ.

WA II Series 1 DA 409.2/2, Citations for Awards Volume 4, Gray to Howe.

WAII Series 1 DA 409.2/2, Citations for Awards Volume 5, Hua–Low.

WA II 1 DA 409.2/2, Citations for Awards Volume 6, Low–Mas.

WA II DA 409.2/2, Citations for Awards Volume 7, Mas–Pad.

WA II 1 DA 409.2/2, Citations for Awards Volume 9, Rut–Tol.

WAII 1 DA 409.2/2, Citations for Awards Volume 10, Tro–Z.

AD1 DA 409.2/6, Miscellaneous.

IA 77/30 K.L. Sandford Publication of book on Capt C.H. Upham, VC and Bar.

Allen, J., Personal Papers.

Leslie Andrew Personal File, 1/1054, AD 36/26.

Cyril Bassett Personal File, D2/6855, AD 36/26.

Donald Brown Personal File, AD 36/26.

James Crichton Personal File, 14/131, AD 36/26.

Keith Elliott Personal File, AD 36/26.

Samuel Forsyth Personal File, AD 36/26.

Bernard Freyberg Personal File, AD 36/27.

Samuel Frickleton Personal File, 6/2133, AD 36/27

John Grant Personal File, 10/2950, AD 36/28.

William Hardham Personal File, 1251, AD 36/28.

John Hinton Personal File, AD 36/28.

Alfred Hulme Personal File, AD 36/28.

Reginald Judson Personal File, 24/1699, AD 36/28.

David George Russell Personal File 30169, AD 36/29.

Henry Laurent Personal File, 24/213, AD 36/29.

Moananui-a-Kiwa Ngarimu Personal File, AD 36/29.

Richard Travis Personal File, 9/523, AD 36/29.

Charles Upham Personal File, AD 36/29.

Leonard Henry Trent, AIR 2, File 5/2/1034, Personal File.

Lloyd Allan Trigg, AIR 2, File 5/2/7160, Personal File.

J.A. Ward, AIR 2, File 40/1793, Personal File.

Lt W. Sanders VC, Personal File, ABFK W4312, Box 2, Defence — Public Relations.

Alexander Turnbull Library

The Russell Saga Vol III, QMS 0822.

Ormond Burton, 'A Rich Old Man', unpublished manuscript, MS 0144.

Reverend Ormond E. Burton Correspondence, MS Papers 0438-033.

Scrapbook relating to New Zealand Victoria Cross Winners, MSZ 0933.

Papers of G.A. Bryant, MS Papers 5009, Folder 2.

New Zealand Defence Force Personnel Archives (Base Records)

Coutts H.D., Personal File

Dale W.D., Personal File NZ 4861

Magnusson J.W., Personal File 13/927

Manahi, H. te R., Personal File

Miles R., Personal File Z/1645 & 6191

Ridling R.G., Personal File 23927

Stott, D.J., Personal File D2061.11844

Other primary sources consulted included:

'The Case for the Posthumous Award of the Victoria Cross to Sergeant H. Manahi for actions at Takrouna 19/20 April 1943.'

The *London Gazette*.

The Register of the Victoria Cross (3rd edn). Bath: HMSO, 1997.

The Medal Yearbook 2005. Honiton: Token Publishing, 2004.

New Zealand Honours and Awards: The Victoria Cross. Wellington: Army Headquarters, 1969.

New Zealand Parliamentary Debates, Third Session, Nineteenth Parliament, Vol. 179, August 7 to September 7, 1917, Wellington, Government Printer, 1917.

New Zealand Parliamentary Debates, Third Session, Nineteenth Parliament, Vol. 180, September 11 to October 10, 1917, Wellington, Government Printer, 1917.

Appendix to the Journals of the House of Representatives of New Zealand 1917. Vol. II, Wellington, 1917, Appendix H-19x.

New Zealand Parliamentary Debates, Fifth Session, Nineteenth Parliament, October 24 to December 10, 1918.

Bassett File, New Zealand Defence Library.

New Zealand Press Association (NZPA) Material on VC Winners.

Feilding Agricultural High School, War Memorial Volume, 1948.

Warrant Redefining the Qualifications for the Victoria Cross and Extending Eligibility to Auxiliary and Reserve Forces, dated 23 April 1881.

Harper, Glyn (ed.). *Letters from the Battlefield: New Zealand Soldiers Write Home 1914–18*. Auckland: HarperCollins, 2001.

McDonald, Wayne. *Honours and Awards to the New Zealand Expeditionary Force in the Great War, 1914–1918*. Napier: Helen McDonald, 2001.

Polaschek, Alan J. *The Complete New Zealand Distinguished Conduct Medal* (rev. edn). Christchurch: Medals Research, 1983.

SECONDARY SOURCES
Books

Andrews, Ted. *Kiwi Trooper: The Story of Queen Alexandra's Own*. Wanganui: Wanganui Chronicle, 1967.

Angelucci, Enzo, and Matricardi, Paulo. *World Aircraft (Vol 1): Origins — World War 1*. Maidenhead: Sampson Low, 1977.

Arthur, Max. *Symbol of Courage: A History of the Victoria Cross*. London: Sidgwick and Jackson, 2004.

Asprey, Robert B. *The German High Command at War: Hindenburg and Ludendorff Conduct World War I*. London: Little Brown, 1991.

Austin, Lt Col W.S. *The Official History of the New Zealand Rifle Brigade (the Earl of Liverpool's Own): Covering the Period of Service with the New Zealand Expeditionary Force in the Great War from 1915 to 1919*. Wellington: L.T. Watkins Ltd, 1924.

Barnett, Correlli. *The Great War*. London: BBC Worldwide Limited, 2003.

Bean, C.E.W. *Anzac to Amiens: A Shorter History of the Australian Fighting Services in the First World War* (rev. edn). Melbourne: Penguin Books, 1993.

———. *The Story of Anzac, from 4 May, 1915, to the Evacuation of the Gallipoli Peninsula*. Sydney: Angus & Robertson, 1924.

Belich, James. *The New Zealand Wars and the Victorian Interpretation of Racial Conflict*. Auckland: Auckland University Press, 1986.

Bowyer, Chaz. *For Valour: The Air VCs*. London: William Kimber, 1978.

Brickhill, Paul. *The Great Escape*. London: Faber and Faber, 1951.

Brown, Malcolm. *The Imperial War Museum Book of the First World War: A Great Conflict Recalled in Previously Unpublished Letters, Diaries, Documents and Memoirs*. London: Sidgwick & Jackson, in association with the Imperial War Museum, 1991.

Bryant, G.A. *Where the Prize is Highest: The Stories of the New Zealanders who Won the Victoria Cross*. Auckland: Collins, 1972.

Burrows, James Thomas. *Pathway Among Men*. Christchurch: Whitcombe and Tombs, 1974.

Burton, O.E. *The Auckland Regiment, N.Z.E.F., 1914–1918*. Auckland: Whitcombe & Tombs, 1922.

———. *The Silent Division: New Zealanders at the Front, 1914–1919*. Sydney: Angus & Robertson, 1935.

Byrne, A.E. *Official History of the Otago Regiment, N.Z.E.F. in the Great War, 1914–1918*. Dunedin: J. Wilkie, 1921.

Carlyon, Les. *Gallipoli*. Sydney: Macmillian, 2001.

Chant, Christopher. *Aircraft of World War II*. London: Brown Books, 1999.

Cody, J.F. *Official History of New Zealand in the Second World War 1939–45: 28 (Maori) Battalion*. Wellington: War History Branch, Department of Internal Affairs, 1956.

Cooksey, P.G. *VCs of the First World War: The Air VCs*. Stroud: Sutton Publishing, 1996.

Corbett, Sir Julian Stafford. *History of the Great War Vol. 5: Naval Operations*. London: Longmans, Green and Co., 1931.

Crawford, John (ed.). *No Better Death: The Great War diaries and letters of William G. Malone*, Auckland: Reed, 2005.

———. *Kia Kaha: New Zealand in the Second World War*. Melbourne: Oxford University Press, 2000.

Crawford, John, with Ellis, Ellen. *To Fight for the Empire: An Illustrated History of New Zealand and the South African War, 1899–1902*. Auckland: Reed, in association with the Historical Branch, Department of Internal Affairs, 1999.

Creagh, Sir O'Moore, and Humphris,

E.M. (eds). *The V.C. and D.S.O.: A Complete Record of All Those Officers, Non-commissioned Officers and Men of His Majesty's Naval, Military and Air Forces Who Have Been Awarded These Decorations*. London: Standard Art Book, 1924.

Crook, Michael J. *The Evolution of the Victoria Cross: A Study in Administrative History*. Tunbridge Wells: Midas Books, in association with the Ogilby Trusts, 1975.

D'Arcy, Patricia. *What Happened to a VC.* Dundalk: Dundalgan Press, 1975.

Davin, Dan. *Official History of New Zealand in the Second World War 1939–45: Crete*. Wellington: War History Branch, Department of Internal Affairs, 1953.

Dennis, Peter, et al. *The Oxford Companion to Australian Military History*. Melbourne: Oxford University Press, 1995.

Devine, David. *The Broken Wing: A Study in the British Exercise of Air Power*. London: Hutchinson, 1966.

The Dictionary of New Zealand Biography: Volume Three, 1901–1920. Auckland: Auckland University Press; and Wellington: Department of Internal Affairs, 1996.

The Dictionary of New Zealand Biography: Volume Five, 1941–1960. Auckland: Auckland University Press; and Wellington: Department of Internal Affairs, 2000.

Dupuy, R.E. and T.N. *The Harper Encyclopedia of Military History* (4th edn). New York: HarperCollins, 1993.

Dupuy, T.N. et al. *The Harper Encyclopedia of Military Biography*. New York: Castle Books, 1992.

Elliott, Keith, and Adshead, Rona. *From Cowshed to Dogcollar*. Wellington: A.H. & A.W. Reed, 1967.

Elliott, Murray. *Vasili: The Lion of Crete*. Auckland: Century Hutchinson, 1987.

Falls, Cyril Bentham. *The First World War*. London: Longmans, 1960.

Ferguson, David. *The History of the Canterbury Regiment, N.Z.E.F. 1914–1919*. Auckland: Whitcombe and Tombes, 1921.

Fitzsimons, Bernard (ed.). *Warplanes and Air Battles of World War I*. London: Phoebus, 1973.

French, Edward Gerald. *Lord Chelmsford and the Zulu War*. London: John Lane and Bodley Head, 1939.

Gardiner, Wira. *Te Mura O Te Ahi: The Story of the Maori Battalion*. Auckland: Reed, 1992.

Gasson, James. *Travis V.C.: Man in No Man's Land*. Wellington: A.H. & A.W. Reed, 1966.

Godley, General Sir Alexander. *Life of an Irish Soldier*. London: John Murray, 1939.

Gordon, Briar, and Strupples, Peter. *Charles Heaphy*. Petone: Pitman Publishing, 1987.

Gudgeon, T.W. *The Defenders of New Zealand: Being a Short Biography of Colonists Who Distinguished Themselves in Upholding Her Majesty's Supremacy in These Islands*. Auckland, H. Brett, 1887.

Gunston, Bill. *Aircraft of World War 2*. London: Peerage Books, 1985.

Hall, D.O.W. *The New Zealanders in South Africa, 1899–1902*. Wellington: Department of Internal Affairs, War History Branch, 1949.

Hamilton, Sir Ian. *Gallipoli Diary* (Volumes I & II). London: Edward Arnold, 1920.

Hargest, James. *Farewell Campo 12*. London: Michael Joseph Ltd, 1945.

Harper, Glyn. *Kippenberger: An Inspired New Zealand Commander*. Auckland: HarperCollins, 1997.

———. *Massacre at Passchendaele: The New Zealand Story*. Auckland: HarperCollins, 2000.

———. *Spring Offensive: New Zealand and the Second Battle of the Somme*. Auckland: HarperCollins, 2003.

Hart, Sir Basil Henry Liddell. *History of the First World War*. London: Cassell, 1970.

———. *Strategy* (2nd rev. edn). New York: Meridian, 1991.

Henderson, Jim. *Official History of New Zealand in the Second World War 1939–45: 22 Batallion*. Wellington: War History Branch, Department of Internal Affairs, 1958.

———. *Soldier Country*. Wellington: GP Books, 1990.

———. *Unofficial History: Yarns From Old Soldiers* (selected from the *N.Z.R.S.A. Review*). Christchurch: Whitcombe and Tombs, 1964.

Hogg, Ian V. *The Illustrated Encyclopedia of Artillery: An A–Z Guide to Artillery Techniques and Equipment Throughout The World*. London: Stanley Paul, 1987.

Horrocks, Lieut General Sir Brian. *A Full Life*. London: Collins, 1960.

Hyde, Robin. *Nor the Years Condemn*. London: Hurst & Blackett, 1938.

———. *Passport to Hell: the Story of James Douglas Stark, Bomber, Fifth Regiment, New Zealand Expeditionary Forces*. London: Hurst & Blackett, 1936.

James, Robert Rhodes. *Gallipoli*. London: Papermac, 1989.

Keegan, John. *The First World War*. London: Hutchinson, 1998.

——— and Wheatcroft, Andrew. *Who's Who In Military History: From 1453 to the Present Day*. Leicester: Hutchinson, 1987.

King, Michael. *New Zealanders at War*. Auckland: Heinemann, 1981.

———. *The Penguin History of New Zealand*. Auckland: Penguin Books, 2003.

Kinloch, Terry. *Echoes of Gallipoli: In the Words of New Zealand's Mounted Riflemen*. Auckland: Exisle Publishing, 2005.

Kippenberger, Sir Howard Karl. *Infantry Brigadier*. London: Oxford University Press, 1949.

Lambert, Max. *Night After Night: New Zealanders in Bomber Command*. Auckland: HarperCollins, 2005.

McClymont, W.G. *Official History of New Zealand in the Second World War 1939–45: To Greece*. Wellington: War History Branch, Department of Internal Affairs, 1959.

McDonald, Gabrielle. *Jack Hinton V.C.: A Man Amongst Men*. Auckland: David Ling Publishing Limited, 1997.

McGibbon, Ian. *New Zealand Battlefields and Memorials of the Western Front*. Auckland: Oxford University Press, in association with the History Group, Ministry for Culture and Heritage, 2001.

——— (ed.). *The Oxford Companion to New Zealand Military History*. Auckland: Oxford University Press, 2000.

McLean, Denis (comp.). *Pathways to Adventure: An Extraordinary Life*. Hororata: Dryden Press, 2004.

Mentiplay, Cedric. *A Fighting Quality: New Zealanders at War*. Wellington: A.H. & A.W. Reed, 1979.

Morris, Donald R. *The Washing of the Spears*. London: Sphere Books, 1968.

Murphy, W.E. *Official History of New Zealand in the Second World War 1939–45: The Relief of Tobruk*. Wellington: War History Branch, Department of Internal Affairs, 1961.

Newbolt, Henry. *History of the Great War: Naval Operations, Vol V*. London: Longmans, 1931.

O'Shea, Phillip P. *An Unknown Few: The Story of Those Holders of the George Cross, the Empire Gallantry Medal, and the Albert Medals Associated with New Zealand*. Wellington: P.D. Hasselberg, Government Printer, 1981.

Pakenham, Thomas. *The Boer War*. London: Weidenfeld & Nicholson, 1979.

Percival, John. *For Valour: The Victoria Cross in Action*. London: Thames Methuen, 1985.

Phillips, C.E. Lucas. *Victoria Cross Battles of the Second World War*. London: Heinemann, 1973.

Pringle, D.J.C., and Glue, W.A. *Official History of New Zealand in the Second World War 1939–45: 20 Battalion and Armoured Regiment*. Wellington: War History Branch, Department of Internal Affairs, 1957.

Pugsley, Christopher. *Gallipoli: The New Zealand Story*. Auckland, Sceptre, 1990.

———. *On the Fringe of Hell: New Zealanders and Military Discipline in the First World War*. Auckland: Hodder & Stoughton, 1991.

Ross, Angus. *Official History of New Zealand in the Second World War 1939–45: 23 Battalion*. Wellington: War History Branch, Department of Internal Affairs, 1953.

Ryan, Tim, and Parnham, Bill. *The Colonial New Zealand Wars*. Wellington: Grantham House, 1986.

Sanders, James. *Venturer Courageous: Group Captain Leonard Trent V.C., D.F.C.: A Biography*. Auckland: Hutchinson, 1983.

Sandford, Kenneth L. *Mark of the Lion: The Story of Capt. Charles Upham, V.C. and Bar*. London: Hutchinson, 1962.

Schmidt, Heinz Werner. *With Rommel in the Desert*. London: Hamilton & Co. (Panther Books no. 508), 1955.

Scoullar, J.L. *Official History of New Zealand in the Second World War 1939–45: Battle for Egypt: The Summer of 1942*. Wellington: War History Branch, Department of Internal Affairs, 1955.

Sheffield, Gary. *The Somme*. London: Cassell, 2003.

Smyth, Sir John George. *The Story of the Victoria Cross*. London: Frederick Muller, 1963.

Snelling, Stephen. *VCs of the First World War: Gallipoli*. Stroud: Sutton Publishing, 1995.

———. *VCs of the First World War: The Naval VCs*. Stroud: Sutton Publishing, 2002.

Stevens, W.G. *Official History of New Zealand in the Second World War 1939–45: Bardia to Enfidaville*. Wellington: War History Branch, Department of Internal Affairs, 1962.

Stewart, H. *The New Zealand Division 1916–19: A Popular History Based on Official Records*. Auckland: Whitcombe and Tombs Ltd, under the authority of the New Zealand Government, 1921.

Taylor, A.J.P. *World War I*. London: Octopus Books, 1973.

Turner, John Frayn. *VCs of the Air*. London: Harrap, 1960.

———. *VCs of the Second World War*. Barnsley: Pen and Sword Military, 2004.

Waite, Major Fred. *The New Zealanders at Gallipoli*. Auckland: Whitcombe and Tombes, under the authority of the New Zealand Government, 1919.

Wards, Ian. *Official History of New Zealand in the Second World War 1939–45: Takrouna*. Wellington: War History Branch, Department of Internal Affairs, 1951.

Weinberg, Gerhard L. *A World at Arms: A Global History of World War II*. Cambridge: Cambridge University Press, 1994.

Wheeler, Mark. *The Role of Mounted Infantry During the Anglo-Boer War, 1899–1902: Lessons for New Zealand Mounted Infantry of the Future*. Upper Hutt: Military Studies Institute, 2003.

Wigmore, Lionel, and Harding, Bruce (eds). *They Dared Mightily*. Canberra: Australian War Memorial, 1963.

Wilkie, A.H. *Official War History of the Wellington Mounted Rifles Regiment: 1914–1919*. Auckland: Whitcombe and Tombs, 1924.

Winton, John. *The Victoria Cross at Sea.* London: Michael Joseph, 1978.

Wright, Matthew. *Freyberg's War: The Man, the Legend and Reality.* Auckland: Penguin Books, 2005.

Articles

Howard, Grant. 'Sanders VC', *Zealandia's War at Sea*, in *Navy Today*, No. 83, Supplement 1–11, November 2003.

Hopkins-Weise, Jeffrey. 'A Brief History of the New Zealand Cross', *The Volunteers*, Volume 28 Number 2, November 2002.

Macdonald, Andrew. 'Troublesome Hero', *Otago Daily Times*, 24 April 1999.

Moorehead, M.J. 'Where is the South African Queen's Scarf', *The Volunteers*, Volume 5 Number 9, December 1978.

Pugsley, Christopher. 'Manahi: Was He Cheated?', *New Zealand Defence Quarterly* No. 22, Spring 1998, pp. 28–34.

———. 'Russell of the New Zealand Division', in *New Zealand Strategic Management*, Autumn 1995, pp. 47–50.

Unpublished manuscript

McConnell, Lynn. 'Galatas 1941'.

Internet sources

http://www.victoriacross.net.forum.asp-topic.asp?topics=1000tid=817 (Source of bronze for VC medals)

http://www.mdani.demon.co.uk/esjd/ (The details of Edward St John Daniel, VC)

http://www.awm.gov.au/encyclopedia/scarf/doc.htm (Status of the Queen's Scarf)

http://qships.freeservers.com/About%20William%20Sanders.htm (Commander William Sanders VC)

http://qships.freeservers.com/LossofPrize.htm (Q-ship HMS *Prize*)

http://www.naval-history.net/WW1NavyBritishQships.htm

http://wikipedia.org/wiki

http://www2.pretsel.co.uk/stewart/bbtrigg.htm (Sale of Lloyd Trigg's medal group)

http://www.dnzb.govt.nz (Garry Clayton, 'Miles, Reginald, 1892–1943', in *Dictionary of New Zealand Biography*, updated 16 December 2003, J.A.B. Crawford, 'Stott, Donald John, 1914–45', updated 16 December 2003.)

http://www.dpmc.govt.nz/honours/overviews/gallantry-bravery-html

Documentary

Ngarimu V.C.: A Maori Hero, directed and produced by Pere Maitai, presented by Wira Gardiner, 1993.

Index

B

Bad Sulza 211
Baden-Powell, Robert 77
Baigent, Ivanhoe 80
Balaklava 21
Balikpapan 214, 215
Bancourt Ridge 91, 169
Bapaume 90, 164, 166, 167, 168, 169, 171
barbed wire 126
Barcelona 155
Bardia 251, 310, 311
Barnett, Corelli 105
Bassett, Cherry 118
Bassett, Cyril Royston Guyton 90, 92, 93, 113–19, 121, 312
Bassett Memorial Trophy 118
Bastard's Drift 80
Basutoland 65, 66
Bathurst 223
Bauchop, Arthur 82, 119–20
Bay of Bengal 199
Bay of Islands 41
Bay of Plenty 52, 59, 60
bayonet 68, 80, 115, 141, 150, 160, 166, 175, 216, 219, 226, 241–42, 255, 256, 265, 272
Bean, C.E.W. 109–10
Beaton, Lieutenant 191
Beaucourt 137, 138
Beharry, Johnson 313
Belgium 65, 139
Belhamed Ridge 155, 237
Bennett, Charles 201, 263, 266, 274, 275
Beresford, Lord 71, 72
Biddle, Benjamin 59
bilharzia 73
Birdwood, William 108
Black, Solomon 59
Black Sea 21
Blackball coal mine 140
Bledisloe, Lord 249

Bloemfontein 83
Blood River, Battle of the 71, 72
Bluff 261
Blundell, Denis 273–74, 275, 308
Boers 65, 66
Boer Wars 33, 37, 74–88, 122, 205, 312
Bofors gun 226, 311
Bolger, Jim 213
Bonaparte, Emperor III 70
Bonaparte, Louis Napoleon 70
Bonaparte, Napoleon 22, 70, 94, 186
Borneo 214, 307
Botha, Louis 81
Boulcott's Farm 42
Bowen, Governor 56
Box, Sergeant 284, 286
Bradford, George 79
Braithwaite, William 128, 136
Branton 296
Bren gun 225, 252
Bridge of Remembrance 247
Brisbane 55
Britain 21
Britain, Battle of 185, 198, 280, 282
British Empire 281
British military formations and units
British Expeditionary Force 139
British Military Mission (Greece) 214
Cape Frontier Light Horse 66, 69, 71, 73
Cape Mounted Rifles 72, 73
Mediterranean Expeditionary Force 105, 106
Middle East Headquarters 274

Officer Cadet Training Unit 142
Royal Army Pay Corps 74
Royal Engineers 151
Royal Marines 107
Special Operations Executive (SOE) 214, 231
Armies
Second 139
Third 102, 153
Fifth 152
Eighth 196, 199, 234, 235, 236, 237
Corps
Imperial Camel Corps 126
Wireless Corps 126
IV Corps 99
XXII Corps 99
XXX Corps 239
Battalions
1st Bn, Princess of Wales Royal Regt 313
Lancaster Fusiliers 101
5th Wiltshires 112, 116
6th Loyal North Lancastershires 112
7th Gloucesters 111
Royal Fusiliers 27
9th Lancers 71
Brigades
Highland Bde 45
5th Indian Bde 240
29th Indian Bde 109
8th Armoured Bde 263
Companies
42nd Field Coy, RE 216
Divisions
1st Armoured Division 240, 263
14th Division 132
29th Division 106
37th Division 153
40th Division 133
41st Division 132
Royal Naval (63rd) Division 107, 136, 137